KING ALFRED'S COLLEGE
WINCHESTER

———

To be returned on or before the day marked
below :—

PLEASE ENTER ON ISSUE SLIP:

AUTHOR WELLS

TITLE The Jesus of the early christians

ACCESSION No. 52844

The Jesus of the
Early Christians

The Jesus of

A Study in Christian Origins

the Early Christians

G A WELLS

Pemberton Books

First published 1971 by Pemberton Books
(Pemberton Publishing Co Ltd) 88 Islington High Street,
London N1

SBN 301 71014 7

Set in Monotype Garamond
Printed in Great Britain by
Richard Clay (The Chaucer Press) Ltd, Bungay, Suffolk

Contents

INTRODUCTION

Christianity is believed to have sprung from the career of Jesus which is depicted in the gospels. These documents have acquired such authority that one naturally assumes, in the first instance, that their contents are, at least in their essentials, true. However, this involves treating them in a very special and privileged way, not accorded to secular documents, nor even to the early documents of any other religion; for no Christian historian would be willing to accept as completely true any non-Christian document which abounded in miracles. Furthermore, miracles apart, there are contradictions which show that the events as narrated cannot all be true. The narratives are also uncorroborated by external evidence, and even when they do not contradict each other they often completely fail to bear each other out. For instance, critical common sense has long asked how miracles, even prodigies of raising from the dead, came to be separately recorded only in single gospels, each knowing nothing of the others. During the nineteenth century German Protestant theology set aside more and more gospel matter as unhistorical. Strauss and others argued that the followers of Jesus conflicted with rivals who followed other prophets, that to prove the authority of their dead leader they claimed he was a kind of Messiah, and substantiated the claim by inventing sayings and deeds which fulfilled, or appeared to fulfil, the Messianic prophecies. Contradictions between gospels or between different parts of a single gospel were explained by supposing that once written records existed, they were interpreted, corrected, distorted and embellished.

Recent apologetic literature has obscured the seriousness of the case presented by Strauss and his school. For instance, Vidler (276, pp. 69–72) writes on historical objections to Christianity, but the only ones he mentions are (1) 'striking inconsistencies' between the books of the NT; (2) 'uncertainty about when exactly most of them should be dated'; (3) 'legendary embellishments of the story even in the canonical gospels'. No examples are given, the difficulties are simply stated in these general terms, and remarks are appended suggesting that they are not serious obstacles. Thus the inconsistencies are due to 'a process of development or evolution' going on when the NT books were composed; and in spite of the embellishments 'the authentic personality of Jesus still does make its impact' (p. 76). No one could possibly infer from this writing how serious are the historical objections to be made against the view that Christianity began in the way suggested by the gospels and the Acts of the Apostles. One of the aims of Part One of the present volume (Chapters One to Eight) is to give the general reader more information on this subject.

Even the most radical criticism of the gospels (including that of Strauss) has usually contrived to leave a small core of historical truth in them. But can the existence of the documents be explained without our making the assumption that Jesus really lived? It is admittedly much harder to conceive how Christianity could have arisen if we deny his historicity, yet there are many legends and myths with no historical basis. Hercules, for example, is now not believed to have existed, although he was once extensively worshipped, and was described by ancient historians as a historical personage who went about doing good. Somehow such stories came to be believed as history. Part Two of my book (Chapters Nine to Ten) tries to show how this happens and that it could have happened in the time of the Roman Empire in Palestine.

If there was a historical Jesus who preached in Galilee and was crucified under Pilate about AD 30, we should expect the authors who at that time wrote about the state of Palestine to say something of him. In fact, however, the extensive rabbinical literature of the time does not mention him, nor does Philo of Alexandria; of the two passages in Josephus about Jesus the Christ, one is admitted to be a Christian interpolation and the authenticity of the other is disputed; and there are no pagan references which can be construed as relevant to Jesus' historicity until Tacitus, about AD 120, explained to his Roman audience that Christians are disreputable people who worship someone who was executed under Pilate. By this time the Christians were themselves alleging that their religion originated in this way, and Tacitus was simply uncritically repeating their view (see Chapter Seven below). But this is not what they were alleging in their earliest extant documents. The writer of the epistles of John admits that many people at the time of these early Christian records denied that Jesus had 'come in the flesh', and he is himself quite unable to produce any realistic proof that he had (see below, pp. 156, 171 ff.). Other very early Christian documents are Paul's epistles addressed to the Romans, Corinthians, Galatians, Ephesians, Philippians, Colossians and Thessalonians. All these are unanimously agreed to have been written well before the gospels, yet they exhibit such complete ignorance of the events which were later recorded in the gospels as to suggest that these events were not known to Paul. He has no allusion to the parents of Jesus, the virgin birth, John the Baptist or Judas; he mentions no Jesuine miracles or gospel teachings. He tells only of a cult, Jewish in origin, in which a crucified Jesus, called the Messiah, figures as an atoning sacrifice. Even to the crucifixion he gives no historical setting, no indication of place or time. Biographical details which place Jesus in a definite historical situation only begin to appear in later epistles and, on the whole, the later the document the fuller the details.

It is today usual to regard Jesus in one of three ways: as a divine personage; as such a remarkable reformer that he was certainly exceptional if not divine; or as an ordinary man who behaved nobly in difficult circumstances. Those who take the first of these standpoints appeal to the gospel miracles as support. The second view is usually based on Jesus' ethical discourses, while the adherents of the third believe that there was at least a historical crucifixion as an irrefragable residual fact after criticism has done its worst with the remaining traditions. It is particularly important to my purpose to show that even this third position is not tenable, and my evidence on this matter forms the substance of Chapters Six to Eight. Readers who regard Jesus neither as divine nor as an ethical genius may think my first two chapters superfluous. I am well aware that many Christians do not believe in miracles such as the virgin birth and the resurrection, but I have chosen to discuss them at some length in Chapter One, not only to controvert those who do accept them but also because the relevant narratives illustrate so well the type of difficulty and problem present in all parts of the gospels, including those sections which are normally accepted (and not only by Christians) as an authentic record of historical events. Again, my discussion of the ethical and eschatological discourses (the substance of Chapter Two) aims not only at showing that they do not justify the claims still commonly made for them, but also at indicating how such speeches could have been put into the mouth of someone who never existed. I think I can justly claim that Part One of this book discusses all the evidence on which any view of Jesus must be based, and may therefore be of interest to many who are quite out of sympathy with the theory of Christian origins suggested in Part Two.

In Part Two I show how Christianity could have originated without a historical Jesus. The theory I offer is consistent with the available evidence, but as this evidence is regrettably scanty, I cannot claim to demonstrate what actually did happen, only what might well have happened. I have indeed been able to make use of the Qumran documents as a vital element in my argument —an advantage not available to previous defenders of the theory that Jesus is an entirely legendary figure.[1] But even so, the paucity of the evidence is such that no one theory can be established to the exclusion of all others, and if the hostile reader objects that my hypotheses are speculative I can reply that in this field nothing else is possible. Further evidence may well show my theory to be wrong in important details, although it would astonish me if it transpired that Christianity originated in the way suggested by the gospels and Acts of the Apostles. At the moment the only alternative theories to mine are that it originated (1) from a god–man, frankly supernatural or (2) from a human being who somehow came to be regarded as a god within a generation of his death. I do not find these hypotheses more intelligible, nor more in accordance with the evidence than my own.

In the earliest Christian documents (e.g. the Pauline letters) Jesus (though not a historical Jesus) is mentioned at every turn. On what, then, was Paul's idea of Jesus based? The answer given in Part Two below can be summarized as follows. The idea of the god who died that we might live was common among the pagans of Paul's day. Attis, Tammuz, Adonis and Osiris were then widely worshipped as victims of an untimely death, resurrected for the salvation of the mourning world. The very name Jesus means, in

---

[1] The evidence of the scrolls was not available to Alfaric (11) and Cutner (75) who are the two most recent defenders of the theory.

Hebrew, 'salvation' (Ieshouah). Furthermore, the Jews of the time were expecting their Messiah,[1] and some thought he would suffer when he came. In consequence it was perfectly feasible for these two separate strands to become tied together, for a new sect to emerge which combined the pagan dying god with the Jewish suffering Messiah. This linkage would have been facilitated if some teacher of Messianic pretensions had actually been put to death, after which his followers carried on his teaching in the hope that he would come again. The Dead Sea Scrolls have, according to many authorities, shown that this was in fact the case, that the pre-Christian Essenes had a Messiah who was killed shortly before 63 BC.

The Essenes typify the religious developments which occurred in the last centuries of the pre-Christian era. The old gods were developing into saviours who died for mankind: their worship was becoming secret and was carried on in special brotherhoods where rites were performed which assured the initiates of resurrection in another kind of life. In the pagan world these new rites all derived from ideas associated with other older gods, Dionysus, Osiris, etc. The Essene brotherhood differed from these Greek mystery religions by being based on Jewish rather than on Greek or Egyptian theology. The connection between all these mystery religions and Paul's religious views is striking, and he is by no means the only early Christian writer who shows such affinities.

The catechumen of the mysteries did not ask where or when his god died. He was seeking ecstasy and an assurance of salvation rather than enlightenment. But the organizers of any particular sect had to defend its tenets and procedure from the counter-attractions of rivals, and here argument was called for. The early Christians' ideas had in part a Jewish basis, so one method of defending them was to search the scriptures for proof that they fulfilled the prophecies. Another technique was for writers to authenticate their views by claiming to have received special revelations, as Paul does. Another method of arguing the case for the death and resurrection of a particular god would be to place his death in a historical setting where it would seem plausible. I shall give evidence that this is the origin of the story that Jesus

---

[1] In Greek the one word 'Ιησοῦς designates both Jesus and Joshua, and I give evidence (p. 195 below) that it was believed that Joshua would be reincarnated as the Messiah. Paul's reference to 'another Jesus' (II Cor., xi, 4) is thus presumably to another Messiah.

suffered under Pontius Pilate.[1] Once a historical nucleus had thus been given to his career, further details were bound to be added. The emphasis of the early Christian societies on purity of living would lead the devotees to ascribe to their man–god all manner of ethical teachings. All the different strands—the Messianic redeemer, the man who saved the world with his blood, the teaching god—became fused in a composite biography.

Most men who write on Christian origins are trained theologians, committed to certain conclusions before they begin. Readers of my book must decide for themselves whether, once we have abandoned the habit of brushing aside any thesis more radical than is compatible with the tenure of a theological chair, we find ourselves led to admitting that Jesus is what Christians suppose other deities to have been—a figment of human brains. Educated people of today are apt to dismiss this suggestion with amused contempt[2] on the ground that it has already been discussed and found untenable.[3] To give it another hearing is the purpose of Part Two of this book.

I follow the usual terminology in calling the first three of the four canonical gospels 'the synoptics'. They are called synoptic because they frequently agree in the subjects treated, and in the order and language of the treatment. And while they thus take, to some extent at any rate, a common view of the facts, they all diverge markedly from the fourth gospel. I designate the four with the customary abbreviations, Mt., Mk., Lk., Jn.

The biblical quotations in this book are usually given from the RV published in 1881 as a revision of the AV or King James

---

[1] A. D. Howell Smith pertinently asked in 1942 (143, p. 14): if Jesus began as a myth, why did his worshippers ever take their god out of mythology into history? I agree that failure to give adequate explanation of this transition has characterized many statements of the myth theory, and it is one of the aims of the present volume to remedy this defect.

[2] 'Folly beneath discussion' is the phrase recently used in this connection by Althaus (14, p. 5).

[3] H. G. Wood, *Did Christ Really Live* (1938) is often regarded as a conclusive refutation of the hypothesis that Jesus never existed. In fact this work is no more than an examination 'in detail' of 'two propositions advanced by . . . J. M. Robertson', namely: (1) that the gospel passion story is 'not originally a narrative but a mystery drama which has been transcribed with a minimum of modification'; and (2) that this drama was 'inferrably an evolution from a Palestinian rite of human sacrifice in which the annual victim was "Jesus the Son of the Father"' (292, pp. 8, 32). These propositions, interesting as they are, are no part of my theory, although I recognize the possibility that the gospel passion story may ultimately derive from a dramatic ritual (see below, pp. 240–241).

Bible of 1611. The AV was made at a time when the important manuscripts were either unknown or incorrectly estimated, and I quote it in only a few cases where the RV has not substantially altered it. The RV is based on the oldest extant manuscripts, namely the Codex Vaticanus, which has been in the Vatican library for centuries, and the Codex Sinaiticus, discovered in 1859 in a monastery on Mount Sinai and now in the British Museum. Both date from the fourth century. Recent discoveries of third- and second-century material consist only of fragments, so the fourth-century codices are still our main sources.

At times I have quoted the *New English Bible* or NEB of 1961. In the Times Literary Supplement of March 24, 1961, the writer of an article entitled 'Language in the New Bible' complained of the clarity of this new translation. He compared it unfavourably with the AV, saying that 'what . . . is lost is dimension in depth and time, and with dimension, beauty and mystery. Undoubtedly, in many passages there is a gain of clarity, but there are others where clarity is not a proper gain to seek, and what is lost is the numinous' (p. 184). The quality of straightforward intelligibility which makes the new translation so unsuitable for this writer's purposes, renders it very suited to mine.

Brief notes on some of the writers mentioned or quoted will be found in the numbered list of references at the end.

I am glad to record my thanks to Professor Trevor-Roper for helpful suggestions concerning both my arguments and the presentation of my material. I am also grateful to my friends Dr D. V. Banthorpe, Mr C. Lofmark and Dr D. Oppenheimer for their constructive criticism. My deepest debt is to Mr F. R. H. Englefield, whose constant encouragement, advice and criticism has been invaluable.

Notes on quotations

To ease the reading of my text I have referred to the works of other authors by the numbers which these works are given in my bibliography below (pp. 333 ff).

PART ONE

THE HISTORICAL JESUS

CHAPTER ONE

The Gospel Miracles

(i) The virgin birth

(a) *The accounts of Mt. and Lk.*

The virgin birth of Jesus is not mentioned in the second gospel,
nor in the fourth, nor in any of the Pauline epistles. The only
evidence derives from Mt. and Lk., whose accounts are 'irre-
concilable and mutually exclusive' (274, § 4). Joseph's home in
Mt. is Bethlehem, in Lk., Nazareth.[1] In Mt. the angel visits
Joseph, not Mary, while in Lk. he visits Mary and not Joseph.
The divinity of Christ is attested in Lk. by the angel's words to the
shepherds and the song of the heavenly host (not mentioned in
Mt.), in Mt. by the appearance of the star in the east (not mentioned
in Lk.). The new-born Messiah receives his first adoration in
Lk. from shepherds (not mentioned in Mt.), in Mt. from the
Magi (not mentioned in Lk.). In Mt. the family of Jesus lived in
Bethlehem; they flee from the wrath of Herod by going into
Egypt immediately after the birth at Bethlehem; and afterwards
they avoid Archelaus, Herod's son, by settling at Nazareth. In
Lk., however, they lived in Nazareth from the first, only went to
Bethlehem for a census of the people (not mentioned by Mt.), and
after the birth they went first to Jerusalem, where the child was
presented in the temple, and then straight back to Nazareth

[1] Mt. does not explicitly say that Joseph and Mary lived originally in
Bethlehem, but certainly implies it. For he begins his second chapter by
recording the birth 'in Bethlehem of Judaea'; and at the end of this chapter
we are told that on leaving Egypt, they proposed returning to Judaea, and that
it was not until Joseph had been warned in a dream that they passed on 'into
parts of Galilee'. Lk., on the contrary, expressly says that they 'lived in a city
of Galilee named Nazareth' (I, 26).

(ii, 39), where, by the grace of God, the youth of the saviour was passed in uninterrupted growth (ii, 40): while in Mt., as we have seen, his earliest years were said to be disturbed by perils and changes of abode. In sum, 'Mt. looks on Bethlehem (ii, 1) as the . . . home of Joseph and Mary, and mentions their going to Nazareth as a thing unexpected and (ii, 23) a fulfilment of prophecy.[1] He also mentions (as fulfilments of prophecy) a flight into and a return from Egypt, and a massacre (Herod's slaughter of the Innocents) in Bethlehem. Neither of these is mentioned by Lk., and the massacre not by any historian', e.g. not by Josephus, who, in the first century AD, recorded the history of Herod and his family and stressed its seamy side 'in order to show the retribution of Providence' (see 5, § 22).

Both evangelists give genealogical tables which purport to show that Jesus is descended from David. The prophecies contend that the expected Messiah will come from the line of David, and so any man claiming to be the Messiah would have to be shown to belong to it. Now Jesus can only be descended from David through Joseph; for Mary, we are told, is kindred to Elisabeth, who is 'of the daughters of Aaron' (Lk. i, 5), i.e. of the tribe of Levi, not of Judah, as was David. These were regarded as two separate lines (e.g. by the author of the epistle to the Hebrews,

---

[1] Joseph 'came and dwelt in a city called Nazareth: that it might be fulfilled which was spoken by the prophets, that he should be called a Nazarene'. No such prophecy is extant, and Nazarene designates not a town but a sect, which, according to Epiphanius (87, § 19, 20, 29), acknowledged Jesus as the Son of God, but otherwise lived completely according to the Jewish law. If they were the same as the 'Nassarenes' he mentions earlier, then they existed in pre-Christian times. Drews (82, p. 26) surmises that they were called Nazarenes because they venerated the mediator-God or Messiah as the Guardian (Syrian, nasarya, Hebrew, Ha-nosri). According to Acts xxiv, 5 the first adherents of Jesus were called Nazarenes, and the term may have designated him not as the man from Nazareth but as the 'Guardian', the Saviour. 'Jesus the Nazarene' would thus have been a name comparable with Zeus xenios (the befriender) or Hermes psychopompos (the guider of souls), and his connection with Nazareth invented later to provide an acceptable explanation for the expression. He is never called 'of Nazareth' in the earliest documents (the Pauline letters). Weiss scorns these etymological observations, and affirms that Nazareth, an insignificant locality in the half-heathen Galilee, could never have been chosen without historical basis as the home of the Davidic Messiah, who was expected to hail from Bethlehem of Judaea (278, pp. 20–2; cf. Jn. vii, 41–2). But both Mt. and Lk. regarded the place not as insignificant, but as a 'city'. Whether it existed before Christian times is doubtful (it is not mentioned in the OT, in Josephus and in the Talmud, see 59a, § 3), and 'the present town of that name can be traced back with certainty only to the fourth century AD, when pilgrim traffic began' (218a, p. 34).

see below, p. 158). As Stauffer has noted (see below, p. 23), some Jews even expected the Messiah to come from Aaron's line, not David's, so the two must have been regarded as distinct. Moreover, if Lk. had wished to represent Mary as being of Davidic descent he would hardly have said, as he does (ii, 4), that on the occasion of the taxing, Joseph went with Mary to be registered because *he* was of the family of David, but rather 'because *they both* were of this family'. Furthermore, it is Joseph's ancestry that is traced in the tables, not Mary's. Lk.'s table (iii, 23 ff.) does not even mention her, and Mt. names her only as the wife of Joseph, the descendant of David. But according to the very same evangelists, Jesus is not born of Joseph at all, but of the Holy Ghost. So the whole genealogical apparatus which aims at showing his descent from David fails to do this because the virgin birth story has been grafted on it. In other words, the genealogies are, as Strauss observed, memorials of a time when Jesus was regarded as naturally begotten (262, ii, 14). That there was such a time is clear from a very old manuscript of Mt. (the Sinaitic palimpsest, on which see below, p. 113), which has for i, 16: 'Jacob begat Joseph; Joseph to whom was espoused Mary the virgin, begat Jesus, who is called the Christ.'

That Mary appeared in the story originally as Joseph's wife is strongly suggested by the text of Mt. Thus i, 18 tells that when 'Mary had been betrothed to Joseph, before they came together, she was found with child of the Holy Ghost'. Yet it continues 'And Joseph her *husband* . . .'. There follows the story of the angel's visit to him in a dream. Then 'Joseph arose from his sleep and took unto him *his wife* and knew her not till she had brought forth a son'. Some orthodox critics hold that 'betrothed' means 'married'; that although the wedding ceremony had therefore taken place, Joseph—for some reason—had not begun to live with Mary in the matrimonial home when the angel visited him; that he then 'took unto him his wife', i.e. set up home with her, but did not consummate the marriage until after the birth of Jesus. A recent commentator explains that 'betrothed' or 'espoused' 'means that she was already bound to Joseph although they were not yet married. Unfaithfulness after espousal was regarded as adultery' (NBC, p. 774).

If, then, the virgin birth story can be regarded as a late accretion, this will explain the otherwise puzzling silence of the other NT writers, and also the paucity of the references to it even in Mt. and

Lk. In Lk., for instance, it is stated in two verses only (i, 34 f.), and these in themselves raise difficulties. They occur after the angel has told Mary 'thou shalt conceive in thy womb'. She takes this as implying a natural conception, for she replies: 'How shall this be, seeing I know not a man?'—a question which can only mean: 'I have no such acquaintance with any man as might lead to the fulfilment of this prophecy'. But the exact opposite of this is involved in the actual situation. She is betrothed to Joseph (i, 27) and must necessarily have looked to the fulfilment of the prophecy through her marriage with him. Haag, a contemporary Catholic authority (119), can only explain her question by assuming that she has taken a vow to remain a virgin for ever. The fact that she has nevertheless become engaged and intends to marry is indeed perplexing, he says, but nevertheless we must assume that she intended to combine marriage with the preservation of her virginity. Otherwise, he says:

> This annunciation of conception to a woman who is engaged and about to be married would involve no miracle, the more so as Gabriel says nothing about the time when Mary will conceive . . . The difficulty that the ideal of virginity was unknown to the Jews and that Mary's intention would have been difficult to reconcile with her engagement and marriage, must be waived in the face of the clear sense the words of the text bear.

Thus he explains Mary's words by ascribing to her an intention which would be extraordinary in any woman in her position, and is admittedly quite out of tune with the ideals of the society in which she is supposed to have lived. Furthermore, the evangelist does not expressly say here that she had had this intention, and certainly never alludes to it subsequently. From Mt. i, 25, we learn that Joseph 'knew her not till she had brought forth a son'; from which we can only infer that he did, after that event, consummate the marriage, so that Mary's vow, if it was ever made, was not kept. Haag, of course, cannot solve the perplexity as many Protestant scholars have done, by regarding the two verses as an interpolation. For, as a Catholic, he regards the Bible as infallible, and expressly commits himself to the doctrine that it is 'completely free from error' (120).[1] It is therefore surprising that he

---

[1] The latest Catholic scholarship is not so rigid, especially in its interpretation of the OT. 'We know,' says Lohfink (175, pp. 18–19), that 'certain

admits that the only passage in the NT which says that the three persons of the Trinity are one is an interpolation, even though it is in the Vulgate and was, as he himself notes, declared genuine by the Vatican in 1897. He regards the passage as a marginal gloss, interpolated into the text during the fourth century, this being why it is absent from all the oldest manuscripts (113). However, any attempt to treat the two verses from Lk. in a similar way, he condemns as 'doing violence to the text' (119). But why is it out of the question that the two verses were present only in the form of marginal additions in the manuscripts of the third century, which have now perished, and then interpolated into the texts of the oldest surviving manuscripts? In the case of the Trinitarian passage, we can prove interpolation, because it occurred at a date later than the composition of the oldest extant manuscripts. But other interpolations may very well have occurred early enough to have become assimilated into these. Altogether, interpolations are frequent in the NT. A striking example is Jn. viii, 1–11 (the story of the woman taken in adultery). This is not only without synoptic parallel, but also absent from the best manuscripts of Jn.; and both Catholic and Protestant commentators admit that it breaks the sequence of the narrative in which it occurs. It was presumably inserted from some apocryphal source by a late editor who thought it too good to miss.

But let us return to the birth stories of Mt. and Lk. Mt. mentions Joseph only in his first two chapters, Lk. mentions him only in his first four, after which he disappears from the narratives. Mk. never mentions him at all. In addition, it is puzzling that Lk. in his second chapter repeatedly refers to Joseph as 'the father' of Jesus, or to Joseph and Mary as his 'parents' (ii, 27, 33, 41–3). Many Christians maintain that these are loose figures of speech employed to save some circumlocution. But this theory will not explain why Jn., who does not mention the virgin birth, should make not only the Jews (vi, 42), but also one of Jesus' disciples refer to him as the son of Joseph (i, 45)—these being the only occasions Joseph is mentioned in Jn. Jn. also makes it clear that the Jews expected the Messiah to be naturally born, 'of the seed of David' (vii, 41 f.). Our suspicions are increased when we find that some manuscripts have actually altered Lk. ii, 43, which, in the oldest MSS., reads 'and his parents knew it not' (so the RV) to

---

texts about Abraham are legends', although they 'of course contain a kernel of historical truth'.

'Joseph and his mother knew not of it' (so the AV). Thus it is at least possible that Lk.'s words 'father of Jesus' and 'parents of Jesus' were originally used to mean what they might normally be expected to mean, and that the virgin birth story is a later accretion.

Next, Lk., in his second chapter, represents the twelve-year-old Jesus as amazing the learned doctors in the temple by his wisdom —a story found only in Lk. When his parents discovered him they chided him, but he defended himself, saying 'how is it that ye sought me? Wist ye not that I must be in my Father's house' (ii, 50). The text continues: 'And they understood not the saying which he spake unto them.' The episode is introduced to show the first manifestation of the consciousness of his divine sonship in Jesus. But his parents do not understand the expression of it, and this blank failure to understand that their child was abnormal is certainly not what one would expect from a mother and foster-father who had been visited by an angel and told that he would be born of 'the Holy Ghost . . . and called holy, the Son of God' and would 'reign over the house of Jacob for ever, and of his kingdom there shall be no end' (i, 33, 35). In fact the behaviour of Joseph and Mary in the temple seems to imply entire oblivion of the annunciation, the conception, the massacre, the herald angels, the Magi—of all the stupendous circumstances of the nativity.

This episode appears all the stranger when we notice that Mt. and Lk. usually take some trouble to avoid implying that Jesus was misunderstood by the mother who, if anybody, must have known of his supernatural origin; for they omit or adapt stories in their sources which carry this implication. We shall see that there is wide agreement that Mk. formed one of their sources, and in Mk. iii, 20–3, Jesus' friends are represented as regarding him as 'beside himself' and needing to be forcibly restrained. According to verse 31 these friends seem to have included his mother and brothers. Mt. and Lk. omit this story altogether. Again, Mk. vi, 4 reads: 'A prophet is not without honour, save in his own country, and among his own kin, and in his own house.' Mt. cuts out the words 'and among his own kin', and Lk. does so too, saying simply 'no prophet is acceptable in his own country'. So once again the only two evangelists who mention the virgin birth have obliterated Mk.'s suggestion that Jesus was misunderstood by his own family.

Furthermore, if the whole nativity story is in fact a late addition, this will explain why in the first three gospels the mother of Jesus is not mentioned as being present at the crucifixion, namely because she had not been invented at the time when that part of the narrative was written. Mt. (xxvii, 56) and Mk. (xv, 40) represent 'many women' as being present and they name two Marys (Magdalene and the mother of James and Joses). But they do not mention Mary the mother of Jesus, and would surely not have mentioned the others instead of her had they wished to imply that she was there. Only Jn. represents her as present. In this gospel the dying Jesus commits her to the care of 'the disciple whom he loved' (xix, 25–7) in a saying from the cross which is, of course, unknown to the synoptics. Such discrepancies become intelligible if we can assume that the figure of Mary is altogether a late invention. This would also explain why Mk. only once names her as Jesus' mother (vi, 3); why she appears in Acts in a single verse only (i, 14) and then disappears from the narrative, and why she is never mentioned by Paul, nor by any Christian writer before Ignatius.

(b) *The critical defence*

It is of interest to see how the virgin birth is defended today. According to Haag, it is 'one of the best attested events in the NT'. One point in his defence is that Mt. and Lk.'s birth stories seem very modest and restrained compared with those found in later non-canonical Christian writings, 'apocryphal fables' as he calls them. Mt. and Lk., then, were writing sober facts, which were soon embellished and expanded by the later writers, and the sobriety and restraint of the evangelists suggests that they wrote the truth, whereas the authors of the later traditions were romancing (117). He sums up (119): 'Lk.'s narrative is impressive because of its calm objectivity and chaste simplicity.' The *Protevangelium Jacobi* or *Book of James* may be noted as an example of the apocryphal works Haag has in mind. It tells how Joseph and Mary, brought before the high-priestly council, both purged themselves of the charge of immoral intercourse by drinking unharmed of the water of jealousy (Num. v, 11–31); how Mary gave birth to Jesus in a cave which was miraculously illuminated; how a woman, Salome by name, satisfied herself by tactual examination that Mary was still a virgin after the birth, and how Salome's hand was burned, but was healed when it touched the child. The work is obviously later than the gospels because it combines their material, making an angel visit Mary in the words of Lk. i, 35 and then allay Joseph's misgivings with the words of Mt. i, 20. Joseph is made an aged widower with sons from a former marriage when Mary was handed over to his protection at the age of twelve, after a white dove had flown out of his staff and thereby indicated him as her proper guardian. By this detail, the author is able to imply that the 'brethren' of Jesus mentioned in the gospels are his step-brothers, not other children of Mary. The 'mother of God' can thus be regarded as never having indulged in the degrading business of sexual intercourse.

As Haag himself admits, the 'sober' evangelists relate the following miracles apropos of the nativity: 'appearances by angels, communications through angels, capacity to prophesy, supernatural loss and regaining of speech in the case of Zacharias, Elisabeth's conception in spite of advanced age, Mary's conception without intercourse, star of the Magi, and finally birth of the Messiah sent by God' (117). All this appears to him 'sober and modest'. But it is absurd to suggest that these stories are certificated as true simply because the Christian imagination of the first few centuries was capable of inventing more fantastic episodes. When a historian or biographer narrates miracles, this is usually held to detract from his authority, and Haag himself applies this principle when dealing with what he calls apocryphal fables. Although he refuses to apply it to the canonical gospels, their miracles are not better attested, those of Lk. being different from and uncorroborated by those of Mt. And Haag himself notes: 'Lk. tells us about Jesus' childhood exclusively things that are absent from Mt.' Furthermore, he is very ill-advised to dismiss non-canonical miracles as fables, for what then is to become of Catholic dogmas like the Immaculate Conception or Mary's bodily ascent into heaven for which there is no biblical warrant, but only the testimony of non-canonical tradition?

Haag's appeal to modesty and sobriety also endangers matter in the canonical gospels. For instance, all three synoptics tell that at Jesus' arrest one of his party 'drew his sword and smote the servant of the high priest, and struck off his ear' (Mk. xiv, 47 and parallels). All three go on to represent Jesus as asking those who arrest him: 'Are ye come out as against a robber with swords and staves to seize me?' Only Lk. records (between these two episodes) that Jesus touched the ear and restored it to its position.

Thus Lk. here alleges a miracle where Mk. and Mt. do not, even though they give a precise account of the very occurrences in the midst of which, according to Lk., the miracle was wrought.

Mt.'s version gives a clue as to how Lk.'s allegation of miracle may have arisen. It tells how Jesus said to the swordsman who had struck off the ear: 'Put up again thy sword into its place; for all they that take the sword shall perish with the sword.' Abbott notes (5, § 42) that these words are absent from Mk., and he comments: 'There was probably some tradition—ambiguous or obscure, and omitted by Mk.—that Jesus said (*a*) "let it (i.e. the sword) be restored to its place". This was misunderstood by Lk. as meaning (*b*) "let it (i.e. the ear) be restored". He therefore substituted (*b*) for (*a*) and amplified his narrative in such words as to leave no ambiguity.' Whether Lk.'s miracle is due to his thus misunderstanding a previous document or not, its omission by all other evangelists makes it, on Haag's principle that the most sober and modest account is the true one, strongly suspect.

Other points in Haag's defence of the virgin birth may be noted. First, he explains the silence of other NT writers by saying: 'Knowledge of this mysterious birth was in the beginning naturally restricted to a very small circle, and was . . . without immediate significance for the purpose of demonstrating his divine origin.' Catholic scholars take the resurrection as the decisive datum establishing his divine origin. But they are hardly justified in alleging that his being born of the Holy Ghost is not equally relevant to it. Second, Haag denies that the genealogies only make sense if Joseph and not the Holy Ghost is the father of Jesus. He says that 'to the Jewish way of thinking . . . legal paternity completely took the place of natural paternity, and Jesus would have been regarded as the son of David even if it were only his legal father who was descended from David'. Now there is no doubt that among the Jews and early Christians the Messiah was expected to be physically descended from David. Thus Jn. represents some Jews as saying that 'the scripture said that Christ cometh of the seed of David' (vii, 42). Admittedly they might have been persuaded to accept mere legal connection with David's family in the case of a candidate whose claim appeared strong on other grounds. But if Jesus was accepted as Messiah on this basis, why does Paul, who never mentions the virgin birth, say that he was 'born of the seed of David according to the flesh' (Rom. i, 3)? Catholic writers answer that Paul (who mentions neither Mary nor Joseph) is thinking of Jesus as the child of Mary, and that she was a descendant of David. But we have already seen that Lk. represents her as of the family of Aaron.

Haag does not admit any contradiction at all between Mt. and Lk., and he can only maintain such a position by evading some of the difficulties. For instance, according to Lk. the parents leave Bethlehem with the child 'when the days of their purification according to the law of Moses were fulfilled', i.e. a few weeks after the birth (see Lev. xii, 1–8), and go to Jerusalem 'to present him to the Lord' at the temple (ii, 22), after which they went straight home to Nazareth (ii, 39). According to Mt., however, after the wise men had left, the family fled from Bethlehem into Egypt, where they stayed until the death of Herod. Haag does not face this contradiction, but merely says that Mt. gives us gloomy episodes from the early life of Jesus, while Lk. narrates, on the whole, cheerful ones.[1] Gresham Machen deals with it by supposing that, after the presentation at Jerusalem, the family returned to Bethlehem, received there the visit of the Magi, and then fled into Egypt. He admits that this chronology is difficult to reconcile with Lk. ii, 39 where, after we have been told that Joseph and Mary went to Jerusalem to keep the law, we read: 'When they had accomplished all things that were according to the law of the Lord, they returned into Galilee to their own city Nazareth.' Nevertheless, he supposes that these words do not require an immediate return to Nazareth and so do not exclude a prior return to Bethlehem and a sojourn in Egypt. He argues that Lk. wishes only to establish that 'the well-known residence in Nazareth did not begin until after the requirements of the law had been satisfied in Bethlehem and Jerusalem. He is not interested . . . in . . . how many events took place between the presentation in the temple and the return to Nazareth' (110, pp. 196–7). Even if we accept this, it still fails to show how Mt.'s narrative is reconcilable with the verses following Lk. ii, 39. Mt. has it that the family flee into Egypt until the death of Herod, and even afterwards still avoid Judaea because they fear Archelaus his son; for this reason they settled in the distant Galilee. Lk., however, says that they went to Jerusalem for the passover every year from the birth.

[1] Käsemann (159, p. 133) has noted that Mt.'s more sombre account is obviously informed by the desire to model Jesus, the second deliverer, on Moses, the first. In both cases the birth of the child gives rise to uneasiness in the powers that be, followed by a massacre of children and a miraculous rescue, with Egypt as the land of refuge.

The virgin birth is also defended by Hastings (133) who states that 'the accounts in Mt. and Lk. appear to be independent of each other, while they yet correspond as to the main fact'. He says nothing about contradictions and obviously wishes to create the impression that the accounts are different but not discrepant. And the differences he explains by supposing that Mt.'s narrative is based on information supplied by Joseph, while Lk. had Mary as his source. The following table shows how completely the first two chapters of Mt. and Lk. diverge, and that agreement is not found until the third.

Stauffer has urged that Jn. is only apparently silent about the virgin birth, for Mary anticipated that Jesus would work a miracle at the wedding feast of Cana (Jn. ii, 5), and she could only have known of her son's powers if she had conceived him of the Holy Ghost (257, p. 22). Stauffer may be invited to explain whether he supposes that John the Baptist, who in the fourth gospel recognizes who Jesus is as soon as he meets him, was enabled to do so because he too was privy to the secret. We shall see that Jn. emphasizes the divinity of Jesus more than do the synoptics, and does so by making his great powers and divine status recognized by his followers from the first. Thus, in Jn.'s first chapter, Simon Peter's brother says 'we have found the Messiah (which is, being interpreted, Christ)'. And Nathanael, who has never seen Jesus before, says to him: 'Rabbi, thou art the Son of God, thou art the King of Israel.' Mary's early awareness of Jesus' power may be interpreted as simply another example of this technique.

Stauffer tries to show that the silence of Mk. is also only apparent. He refers to Mk. vi, 3, where the people call Jesus 'the carpenter, the son of Mary', and notes that 'a Jew is only named after his mother if the father is unknown . . . Therefore the Jews are saying: Jesus is . . . only the son of Mary, not of Joseph. This is naturally intended as a defamation' (p. 23). Apart from the fact that Stauffer's conclusion (Mk.'s knowledge of the virgin birth) does not follow from the premise (his making the Jews say something that implies Jesus' illegitimacy), the truth of the premise is unlikely. If Mk.'s statement really implied that the Jews thought Jesus illegitimate, then it is strange that in the parallel passages (Mt. xiii, 55 and Lk. iv, 22) they refer to him as 'the carpenter's son', 'the son of Joseph'; and that in Jn. 'the Jews murmured concerning him . . . And they said, Is not this Jesus,

Mt.	*Lk.*
I. Genealogy of Jesus.	I. Gabriel visits Zacharias and foretells John's birth.
Joseph finds Mary with child.	
	Gabriel visits Mary and foretells Jesus' birth.
An angel visits Joseph and reassures him that the child is 'of the Holy Ghost'.	
	Mary visits Elisabeth.
	Birth of John.
	II. Joseph and Mary go from Nazareth to Bethlehem for census.
Birth of Jesus. =	Birth of Jesus.
II. Visit of the Magi. Flight into Egypt.	Shepherds visit the babe. Joseph and Mary take the child to the temple at Jerusalem.
Massacre of the Innocents Return to Israel and residence at Nazareth.	Simeon's thanksgiving. Anna's thanksgiving.
	The twelve-year-old Jesus in the temple.
III. John's appearance and message. =	John's call and message.
His preaching of repentance. =	His preaching of repentance. His message to special groups.
Foretells the coming of the = Messiah.	Foretells the coming of the Messiah. Is imprisoned by Herod Antipas.
Baptizes Jesus =	Baptizes Jesus Genealogy of Jesus
IV. Temptation of Jesus = IV. Temptation of Jesus	

the son of Joseph, whose father and mother we know?' (vi, 41–2). References in Jewish literature (e.g. the Talmud) to the illegitimacy of Jesus are late, and establish nothing as to how he was regarded by his contemporaries.

As for the Christians, if they thought that Jesus was not the son of Joseph, how came the genealogies which trace his descent from David through Joseph to be written? On the one hand, in order to safeguard the virgin birth, Stauffer insists that Jesus is Mary's son, not Joseph's. On the other hand, however, he affirms that 'the Davidic descent of Jesus is historically firm' (p. 22), and bases his case for this, as do the gospel writers, on the Davidic descent of Joseph! He dismisses the argument that the descent from David has been concocted in order to fulfil Messianic prophecies, saying that some pre-Christian Jews were expecting a Messiah from Aaron—as if the argument depended on Messianic ideas being uniform! All that is necessary is that a Messiah ben David was widely expected, and this Stauffer admits to have been the case.

(c) *The genealogies*

Let us now consider the genealogical tables of Lk. and Mt. more closely. From Abraham to David they agree quite well, as one would expect, for the ancestry of David was available from the OT (I Chron. i and ii, and Ruth iv, 18–22). But from David down to Joseph different ancestors appear in each table, and this section of Lk.'s table, apart from containing different names, has about twice as many as the corresponding section in Mt. In 1835 Strauss inferred from this that the genealogies are unhistorical. He accounted for them by supposing that Jesus' lineage was utterly unknown, and that during the course of his life he acquired the reputation of being the Messiah. What, then, could be more natural than that tradition should, under various forms, have ascribed to him a Davidic descent, and that genealogical tables, corresponding with this tradition, should have been formed? These, however, as they were constructed upon no certain data, would necessarily exhibit such differences and contradictions as we find existing between the genealogies in Mt. and Lk.

Strauss was also able to show that other features of the tables make them suspect. For instance, the only two names common to both lists between David and Joseph are Shealtiel and Zerubbabel his son, both well known from traditions concerning the captivity. Again, Mt. makes the pedigree run from David through Solomon and the line of kings and yet omits four of these from the list given in the OT.[1] These omissions are quite intelligible if the genealogy is mythical. For Mt. gives three series, each of twice times seven names, seven being the most sacred number of the Hebrews; and he omits exactly the number required to bring out his second group of fourteen. Here are his series:

Abraham	Solomon	Jechoniah
Isaac	Rehoboam	Shealtiel
Jacob	Abijah	Zerubbabel
Judah	Asa	Abiud
Perez	Jehoshaphat	Eliakim
Hezron	Joram	Azor
Ram	Uzziah	Sadoc
Amminadab	Jotham	Achim
Nahshon	Ahaz	Eliud
Salmon	Hezekiah	Eleazar
Boaz	Manasseh	Matthan
Obed	Amon	Jacob
Jesse	Josiah	Joseph
David	Jechoniah	Jesus

Thus he is able to conclude his list with the words: 'So all the generations from Abraham unto David are fourteen generations; and from David unto the carrying away to Babylon fourteen generations; and from the carrying away to Babylon unto the Christ fourteen generations.' It is thus clear that Mt. makes the end of each series coincide with an important historical event, and to do this he has to count Jechoniah twice—at the beginning of the third series as well as at the end of the second. By these tricks, then, the pedigree of the Messiah 'is not merely derived in a general way from Abraham and David, but runs down to him in three uniform cascades of fourteen steps each, a sign, in the mind of the writer, that it was not blind chance that was at work here, but a higher power, ordering the destiny of man' (262, ii, 12).

---

[1] Mt. says there are only two generations between Joram and Jotham (i, 8–9), while according to I Chron. iii, 11–12 there are five. Mt. also omits Jehoiakim, whom Chron. interposes between Josiah and Jechoniah.

In Lk. numerical features are not so much emphasized although the sum total is still a multiple of seven (eleven times seven). Lk.'s table goes right back to Adam 'the son of God'. Some trouble was required to extend it this far, and whenever it leaves the guidance of the OT it is distinguished, as Strauss says, by 'numerous repetitions of the same names' which 'thus accumulated, point to the exhausted imagination of the writer' (p. 13). Again, while Mt. makes his table run from David to Solomon and then through the line of kings, Lk. selects Nathan from among the sons of David, and so traces Jesus' descent through a line not royal. Strauss is able to show that Lk. may well have avoided the royal line because he did not want to introduce Jechoniah into his genealogy—the king who was carried away into Babylon, and who is given a prominent place in Mt.'s table. Jeremiah (xxii, 30) had passed judgement upon this wretched king, saying that 'no man of his seed shall prosper sitting upon the throne of David, and ruling any more in Judah'. Now Lk. (but not Mt.) expressly says that God will give Jesus 'the throne of his father David, and he shall reign over the house of Jacob for ever' (i, 32–3), and so he had good reason to avoid making Jesus a descendant of the king whose seed had been rejected.[1]

(d) *The census*

Another example corroborates the suggestion that some details of Jesus' biography were constructed in order to endow him with the qualifications expected of the Messiah. Because of the prophecy of Micah (v, 2), the Jews believed that the Messiah would come from Bethlehem, David's city. 'But thou, Bethlehem . . . which art little to be among the thousands of Judah, out of thee shall come forth unto me that is to be ruler in Israel.' The birth of Jesus in Bethlehem is thus required for dogmatic reasons. Mt. copes with this requirement by making Bethlehem the home of Jesus' parents, and solves the problem of the family's later departure from the city with his stories of persecutions and angelic warnings (which are unknown to Lk.). Lk. however makes the parents resident in Nazareth, so his problem is to get them to Bethlehem for the birth. His solution is to make Joseph and Mary go there because Augustus had ordered a census of the

[1] For further attempts to reconcile the genealogies, see note I on p. 34 below.

whole Roman Empire. 'Now it came to pass in those days (i.e. "in the days of Herod, king of Judaea" i, 5), there went out a decree from Caesar Augustus, that all the world should be enrolled' (ii, 1). By enrolment is meant the registration of names and property as a basis for taxation. Lk. adds that 'this was the first enrolment made when Quirinius was governor of Syria'. There are a number of points to note:

(1) Herod reigned from 37 BC until his death in 4 BC, and Quirinius was never governor of Syria during this time. The governors of Syria during the last years of Herod's life were Titius (10 BC), Sentius Saturninus (9-6 BC) and Varus (6-4 BC). It is known that Varus had to suppress a revolt which broke out in Palestine after Herod's death and was therefore in office from 6 BC until at least some months after the king died. Quirinius governed Syria in AD 6, and according to Mommsen and other authorities, he may also have been governor during the earlier period of 3-2 BC; but even then Herod was already dead. The date of his death is too closely connected with known events in secular history to be in dispute,[1] and even early Christian scholars did not attempt to improve Lk.'s narrative by postponing it. Thus Tertullian (267, ii, 206-7) says that Jesus was born during a census held in Judaea by Sentius Saturninus in 8 BC. He has not changed the date of Herod's death, but has replaced Quirinius with the name of a man who governed Syria in Herod's lifetime.[2]

(2) Apart from Lk.'s testimony, there is no evidence for a census of the whole Roman Empire in the time of Augustus. The census posited by Lk. is not mentioned by the *Monumentum Ancyranum*, nor by Dio Cassius, nor Suetonius. The only authorities who speak of a general imperial census under Augustus are Christians, from the sixth century onwards, 'which is calculated to produce an exceedingly strong suspicion that they simply drew their information from Lk' (244, i, ii, 116).

(3) A Roman census in Palestine in Herod's time was in Mommsen's view out of the question (188, p. 176). Although then under Roman influence, it was not made part of the Empire

---

[1] Herod divided his kingdom between three sons who are known to have reigned, with Augustus' consent, from 4 BC.

[2] For discussion of recent attempts to make Quirinius governor in Herod's lifetime, see Note II on p. 36 below.

until AD 6, when Augustus deposed Herod's son Archelaus and incorporated his territory into the province of Syria. Herod was a client king, holding his title and authority from Caesar and the Senate; he had to defend the imperial frontier and was not allowed to make treaties or wage war at pleasure, but was permitted freedom in his management of Palestine's internal affairs. If the Romans had in fact done what Mommsen declared out of the question and had carried out a valuation census on his territory, this would have been extremely unpopular, calculated, as Schürer puts it, to cut into the very marrow of the people; in which case we should expect it to be recorded by Josephus, who narrates the events of the final years of Herod's life in considerable detail. He, however, makes no mention of it.

(4) Josephus mentions a census under Quirinius in the year AD 6. This was quite in order, for Judaea had just been converted into a Roman province, and the imperial legate proceeded to make a census, i.e. a list of the inhabitants and a reckoning of their landed property for the purpose of apportioning the taxation. Josephus says that this census was the first and that it was altogether novel for the Romans to raise a tax in Judaea (see the passages cited by Schürer, 244 i, ii, 313). He also says that it caused the Jews to revolt, under the leadership of Judas, the Gaulonite of Gamala. If we follow the majority of theologians and regard Acts as written by Lk., then we have definite evidence that this census of AD 6 was known to him; for he speaks in Acts v, 37 of 'Judas of Galilee in the days of *the* enrolment'—using, by the way, exactly the same word ἀπογραφή as occurs in Lk. ii, 2 to designate the numbering of the people in the time of Herod— evidence that both references are to the same incident. He would not have referred to this census of AD 6 as '*the* enrolment' if he had known of an earlier one under Herod; hence we must infer that in the gospel he had in mind the census of AD 6, but antedated it and supposed it to have occurred in Herod's lifetime.[1] If this is so, what then becomes of Mt.'s story that the holy family had to flee into Egypt to avoid the persecution of Herod? And how could Herod, then dead, proceed to slaughter the male children of Bethlehem (Mt. ii, 16)? Even Catholic authorities are at a loss here, and Haag admits (121): 'A satisfactory solution of these difficulties is still wanting.'

[1] For Stauffer's attempt to vindicate Lk.'s account of the census see Note III on p. 37 below.

B

There are more difficulties besides. According to Lk. every one, in obedience to the imperial decree, travelled 'to his own city' (ii, 3), that is, to the place from which his family originally descended. Joseph therefore went to Bethlehem because a thousand years earlier his ancestor David had been born there. But the object of this Roman census was entirely statistical and financial, and, as Strauss observes, it is most unlikely that the Romans would have 'moved a man for the purpose of entering his own name and that of his family, together with an account of his property, from the distant Galilee to Bethlehem, where they could have very little power of checking the entries he made' (262, ii, 27).[1]

From all these considerations we can hardly avoid the inference that Lk. has invented the journey of Joseph and Mary across eighty miles of difficult country in order to make Jesus be born in the place which, he stresses, is 'David's city' (ii, 11), as was expected of the Messiah.

(e) *The prophecy of Isaiah*

While the prophecy of Micah concerning Bethlehem has influenced, with different effects, the narratives of both Mt. and Lk., Mt. alone makes use of a passage from Isaiah in order to show that his birth narrative fulfils it. When the angel has told Joseph that Mary will bring forth Jesus of the Holy Ghost, the evangelist adds: 'All this is come to pass that it be fulfilled which was spoken by the Lord through the prophet, saying, Behold the virgin shall be with child, and shall bring forth a son, and they shall call his name Immanuel' (i, 22). The reference is to Isa. vii, 14, where the prophet is addressing king Ahaz. The Hebrew text tells that 'The Lord himself shall give you a sign; a young woman shall conceive and bear a son, and shall call his name Immanuel.' The original sense of the passages seems to be this: the prophet wishes to assure Ahaz that he has nothing to fear from his much-dreaded enemies, Syria and Ephraim, then trying to invade Judah. He therefore says to him: a certain young woman, is, or is about to be with child; and before this child is born the political situation will be so much improved that a name of good omen, Immanuel (meaning 'God with us') shall be given him. There is no mention of a virgin. The Hebrew word is 'almah' and means 'young wo-

[1] For further discussion of this matter see Note IV on p. 39 below.

man'. Driver gives 'the facts establishing the meaning of the Hebrew and Greek words commonly mistranslated "virgin" in theological works'. He says that 'the Hebrew *almah* . . . neither denotes nor connotes "virgin": a young woman so described may be such . . . or may not be such' (83, p. 309). It is the Septuagint (the Greek version of the OT) that uses a word meaning virgin (παρθένος, or νεᾶνις in later versions).[1] There the passage runs: 'the virgin shall be with child and thou [i.e. the husband] shall call his name Immanuel.' But even if we make Isaiah talk of a virgin, he is still not asserting anything supernatural. He is simply saying to Ahaz that a lady who is now a virgin will shortly fall pregnant and bear a son, and that by the time this has happened the political dangers will have been averted. To make his point quite clear he adds (verses 15–16) that before the tender palate of the child can distinguish between foods, the land now threatening Judah will have been laid waste.[2] Mt., however, has regarded the prophecy as pertaining to the birth of the Messiah. He obviously did not find it easy to use it in this way, and some manipulation was necessary. The Hebrew text contains the statement that the new-born child should be called Immanuel by its mother; the Septuagint says the appellation will come from the father. Jesus was not in fact called by this name at all, and so Mt., though he makes Joseph receive the Annunciation, represents *people in general* as destined to give Jesus this name, and alters the prophecy accordingly, making the angle say to Joseph: 'Thou shalt call his name Jesus . . . that it might be fulfilled which was spoken by . . .

[1] The substitution of νεᾶνις for παρθένος is explained by Driver (loc. cit.): 'παρθέους has in origin nothing to do with virginity. The basic element is θεν—denoting fulness or the like, so that παρθένος is a young man or woman "having full body and limbs, fully developed"' . . . Since, however, the ideal παρθένος was a virgin, the word came commonly and indeed most often to connote a virgin; but it always remained an equivocal term. Consequently νεᾶνις 'young woman' was substituted for it by post-Christian translators or revisers of the Greek Bible as unambiguous and therefore not likely to be misunderstood or misused.

[2] That Isaiah makes no reference to a virgin, and is concerned with the immediate political situation, is now admitted even by Catholic scholarship (e.g. by Lohfink, 176, p. 14). Lohfink, however, regards Isaiah's words as one of many OT references to a Davidic Messiah, whose true nature, as a supernatural saviour of all mankind, was not apparent until NT times. He is aware that this reasoning entails measuring the OT by the NT, and he does not shrink from this, as he is certain that 'the proclamation of Christ in the NT is for us the ultimate standard' (p. 15). This is, at any rate, a clear abandonment of the position that the gospel narratives are proved true by the predictions of inspired prophets.

the prophet,' namely, as Mt. goes on to say: 'Behold the virgin shall . . . bring forth a son and *they* shall call his name Immanuel.'

(f) *The origin of the virgin birth story*

It may well be asked where the idea of the virgin birth came from if it did not actually happen. There is certainly nothing in the Jewish sacred books to suggest that the Messiah or anyone else was, or was to be, born of a virgin. Even the passage in Isaiah just quoted does not suggest this, for, apart from anything else, the context says nothing about an expected Messiah. In the Graeco-Roman world, however, in the religions surrounding the Jews, the idea that important personages are virgin-born was widespread and derived from much older cults. Budge shows that the idea of a mystical birth was made familiar to the Mediterranean peoples centuries before the birth of Christ by the scroll of the virgin mother goddess Neith of Sais in Egypt; her fruit was the sun and her robe no male had raised. He also mentions that 'the belief in the conception of Horus by Isis through the power given her by Thoth, the Intelligence or Mind of the God of the universe, is . . . coeval with the beginnings of history in Egypt' (40, i, 454, 459 f.; ii, 220). Again, the mother of Attis, Nana, 'was a virgin who conceived by putting a ripe almond or a pomegranate in her bosom' (95, p. 347). Even Hera is described as going far away from Zeus and men to conceive and bear Typhon (220, p. 295 and refs.). Frazer indicates the origin of such stories when he says that they are 'relics of an age of childish ignorance when men had not yet recognized the intercourse of the sexes as the true cause of off-spring'. But a more important factor making for the survival of such tales in religious cults is stressed by Gilbert Murray. He notes that it is the saviour gods of paganism who are often reputed virgin-born. The father-god supplies the human race with a saviour, his son, by impregnating a goddess or a mortal. He must, however, not be regarded as actuated by lust. His purpose is the birth of a great saviour of mankind, and so the impregnation has to be effected without carnal intercourse. Hence Io was made pregnant by the laying on of the divine hand, Danae by the golden sunlight (199, p. 8).

There are also examples of gods or heroes born not of goddesses but of mortal virgins. The *Dictionary of non-classical mythology* mentions Poshaiynne (a hero of the Sia of New Mexico) born of a

virgin who had eaten two nuts; Fo Hi, the Chinese divinity born
of a maiden who ate a flower which clung to her garment while
bathing; and the Mexican deity Quetzacoatl, born of a pure
virgin who was called the 'queen of heaven'. An ambassador
from heaven announced to her that it was the will of God that she
should conceive a son without connection with man—an exact
parallel to Lk.'s story of the Annunciation, in a part of the globe
that was not discovered by Christians until the Middle Ages.
It is not surprising that to the Spanish conquerors of Mexico and
Peru many of the native rites appeared to be diabolical counter-
feits of Christian sacraments (95, p. 358, and 8a, pp. 208, 409–20).

Haag holds that these are no real parallels because 'in the
pagan myths there is no question of a *virgin* birth, which is what
Lk. stresses' (119). Some of the above examples show that this is
simply not true. Others concern goddesses who were not virgins
but were called so by way of adoring flattery, just as 'nearly all
male gods were at times termed beneficent, whatever might be the
cruelty of their supposed deeds' (220, p. 292). Hastings (133)
admits what Haag denies, yet he insists that the pagan tales of
virgin births 'have nothing whatever in common with the stories
of Mt. and Lk.' which 'move in a different atmosphere', in that
they are distinguished by their 'reticence' and sublime simplicity.
'The reticence is marked in comparison with the exuberant
language of the apocryphal gospels, and if the virgin birth
narratives are mythical, no myth was ever expressed in such bald
and restrained language.' So the historicity of the narratives is
established by reference to stylistic niceties; and for this purpose it
is presupposed that, in documents, simplicity of manner implies
truth of matter—a novel assumption in historical inquiry.

Another argument Haag uses to rebut the pagan parallels is
that 'the semitic designation for spirit is feminine,' so that the
Holy Ghost in Lk.'s story would not be thought of as a male
impregnator, as occurs in the pagan stories. In reply, Haag may
be invited to explain (1) whether Frenchmen are precluded from
thinking of *la sentinelle* as a male person because the gender of the
noun is feminine, (2) whether *die Kröte* denotes only the female of
the species, and (3) how the Hebrews and Christians conceived
the 'Holy Spirit' or Pneuma, whether on the male or female view
of its personality. It is noteworthy that in Jn. Jesus is repeatedly
referred to as God's 'only begotten son', implying divine father-
hood by impregnation.

There is clear evidence that this idea of virgin births, which was continually obtruded upon the Jews by their pagan neighbours, began to affect their own outlook, and although the OT does not supply any basis for the notion, we find that later Jews began to suggest that many OT worthies were virgin-born. Thus Philo of Alexandria (born about 20 BC), tells us that 'the Lord begat Isaac . . . Isaac is to be thought not the result of generation, but the shaping of the unbegotten'. And again, he says, concerning the birth of Isaac: 'It is most fitting that God should converse, in a manner opposite to that of man, with a nature wonderful and unpolluted and pure.' He records similar views about Leah, whose real husband is 'the unnoticed'; Zipporah, who is found by Moses 'pregnant but by no mortal'; Samuel, who was 'born of a human mother' who 'became pregnant after receiving Divine seed' (refs. in 5, § 21). It is fairly clear that these ideas were due to the original obtruding of the pagan ones on the Jewish mind. If the Jews could regard Isaac, Samuel and others, who were merely inspired by God's word, as virgin born, they would naturally attribute a similarly exalted origin to one who was regarded as being filled with the word, or who was the word himself. Here is the basis of an answer to Haag's objection that the 'language and background' of Lk. i, 26–38 are 'unmistakably Hebraic in style and Jewish in outlook, even though Lk. himself is a Hellenist' (119). Haag's point is that the passage is full of OT idiom, phraseology and ideas (stressing that salvation is to come from the Jews) and that the author of such Jewish-Christian material would not have alleged a mythical virgin birth, since virgin births were foreign to Jewish ideas. My quotations from Philo show that, on the contrary, the Jews had gone far in assimilating the pagan view. In this connection it may be noted that the Dead Sea Scrolls have shown that many ideas formerly thought Hellenistic were firmly rooted in Palestine (see 12, p. 128).

The traditional date of Jesus' birth has certainly been borrowed from other religions, for it is entirely without scriptural warrant, and was fixed by what the *Biblica* calls 'mythological analogy'. While the ancient Church (as the Armenian Church still does) commemorated the nativity as the feast of Epiphany (January 6), the Roman Church from the middle of the fourth century set apart the *natalis solis invicti*—December 25—as the anniversary of the saviour's birth (274, § 10: cf. 275). December 25 has been the birthday of the sun god in half a dozen religions, Egyptian,

Persian, Phoenician, Grecian, Teutonic. Dionysus, Adonis and Horus are all born on this day, which, in the Julian calendar, was the day of the winter solstice and was regarded as the sun's birthday, since the days begin to lengthen and the power of the sun increases from this turning point in the year. The *pagans* in Syria and Egypt represented the new-born sun by the image of an infant which on the winter solstice was exhibited to his worshippers, who were told: 'Behold the virgin has brought forth' (95, p. 358).

These striking similarities between Christian and pre-Christian dogmas and ritual can hardly be fortuitous. The Christians seem to have taken over pagan ideas in order to make Christianity more attractive to pagans, and so persuade them to be converted. They were more likely to embrace the new religion if it could be shown that they need not entirely forego their old views and rituals. The early Christian Father, Justin Martyr, expressly argues (158, i, 21) that 'with their doctrine of the virgin birth of Jesus, of his passion and of his ascension, the Christians were affirming nothing new as compared with what was alleged of the so-called sons of Zeus'. He goes on to say that if Christians called Jesus the Logos, here too was another point in common with the gentiles, who called Hermes the word of Zeus. Of course, he did not admit that the Christian stories were copies. He explained the prior existence of the pagan ones with the theory that the devil had circulated them before the time of Jesus in order to try to rob the manifestation of the true Son of god of its importance. (237, § 17). Thus he says: 'When I hear that Perseus was begotten of a virgin, I understand that the deceiving serpent counterfeited also this.'

In sum, there is very strong evidence that the gospel story of the virgin birth is a late accretion. Those who assert its historicity must do so in the face not only of its absence from the second and fourth gospels, but also of the absolute silence of the epistles. Furthermore, the evidence of the first and third gospels has been found contradictory, and finally pagan sources have been indicated by which the story could have been inspired.

Notes to Chapter 1 (i). The virgin birth

Note I. The genealogies.

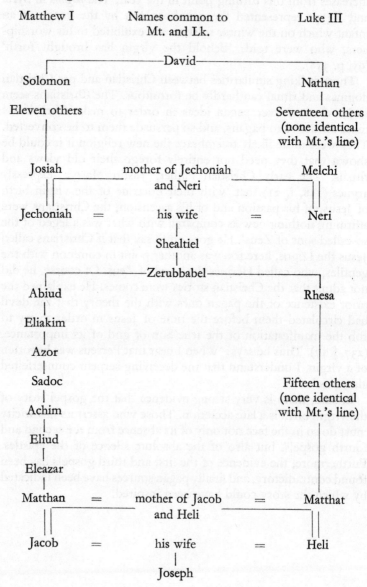

Matthew I	Names common to Mt. and Lk.	Luke III
	David	
Solomon		Nathan
Eleven others		Seventeen others (none identical with Mt.'s line)
Josiah	mother of Jechoniah and Neri	Melchi
Jechoniah =	his wife	= Neri
	Shealtiel	
	Zerubbabel	
Abiud		Rhesa
Eliakim		
Azor		
Sadoc		
Achim		Fifteen others (none identical with Mt.'s line)
Eliud		
Eleazar		
Matthan =	mother of Jacob and Heli	= Matthat
Jacob =	his wife	= Heli
	Joseph	

Haag (120) has alleged that Jacob is the natural, and Heli the legal father of Joseph. Now there is nothing in the text to suggest that Heli is merely the legal father. Lk. says: 'Jesus was the son (as was supposed) of Joseph, the son of Heli, the son of Matthat, the son of Levi', and so on (iii, 23). Haag would have us suppose that the word 'son' in the first, third and following places means a real son, and only in the second place, between Joseph and Heli, a legal or adoptive son. But waiving this point, let us see whether this theory really resolves the contradictions. Heli and Jacob must be related, otherwise the two tables could never converge upwards. And if it is to be intelligible that one of them was merely the legal father of Joseph, and yet that Joseph's descent might legitimately be traced through him and not through the natural father, then they must have been brothers. For it is provided in the law of Moses (Deut. xxv, 5 ff.), to prevent families dying out, that when a married man had died childless, his brother, if he had one, should marry the widow—this is known as a levirate marriage—and their firstborn son should be entered in the register of the family in the name of the deceased brother. Thus we may suppose that Joseph's mother had been first married to Heli, by whom she had no son, and that after his death his brother Jacob married her and had Joseph by her. Consequently Mt. will be correct in saying that Jacob begot Joseph, while Lk. will be right in calling Joseph the son of Heli, in whose name he was registered according to law. This theory was first set forth by Julius Africanus in the third century and is still advocated by the *Catholic Encyclopaedia* (51).

Strauss meets the theory by observing that if Jacob and Heli were brothers, then they would both have had the same father, and the two genealogies would have to coincide above them. But as we have seen, one table goes back to David through the royal line, while the other takes a completely different route. To overcome this difficulty it has been assumed that Jacob and Heli were only brothers on their mother's side and that their mother had two husbands in succession, one of whom belonged to the line of Solomon, the other to that of Nathan, in the family of David, and that of these two husbands one was the father of Jacob, the other of Heli (see the accompanying table, p. 34). This solution, however, does not meet all the difficulties, for higher up, the two tables come together, both naming Zerubbabel and his father Shealtiel, after which they again diverge. In Mt. Shealtiel's father is Jechoniah of the royal line, in Lk. Neri of the other line. So that 'again the same double hypothesis becomes necessary, first, that Jechoniah and Neri were brothers, and the one the natural, the other, according to the Levitical law, the lawful father of Shealtiel, and then that the two were only half-brothers on the mother's side, consequently that these two fathers married successively the same woman, and that moreover, exactly as before, the one generation took the legal, the other, in opposition to Mosaic ordinance, the natural father' (262, ii, 17). In addition we must suppose that the ancestors on Lk.'s side regularly married at half the age of those in Mt.'s table, since there are twice as many of them.

The *Catholic Encyclopaedia* makes light of the complications over Shealtiel and Zerubbabel, saying 'two levirate marriages will explain the difficulty' (art. cit.). It goes on, however, to suggest that the trouble can be resolved more simply 'if we do not admit that the Shealtiel and Zerubbabel occurring in Mt. are identical with those in Lk'. Admittedly, 'they must have lived about the same time, and the names are so rare that it would be strange to find them occurring at the same time in the same order in two different genealogical series'. Nevertheless 'these proofs for their identity are not cogent'. It is clear that from this writer's point of view any assumption, however improbable, is preferable to surrendering orthodox dogma.

Note II. Herod and Quirinius

In 1915 Ramsay tried to show that Quirinius did govern Syria before Herod died. He was able to prove from an inscription that Quirinius was elected 'duumvir' of the Pisidian Antioch, a Roman colony in Galatia, and that a plausible explanation as to why such an honour was conferred on him is that he played a prominent part in a certain war against the Homonadenses, who were a constant source of trouble to the Romans in Galatia. Ramsay showed that this war occurred in Herod's lifetime, and he argued that Quirinius must have been governor of Syria when he fought it, since there were no Roman legions stationed near the area of conflict except in Syria. Dessau, whom Ramsay himself designated the foremost authority on Roman history since Mommsen, replied that Augustus could quite well have entrusted one of the Syrian legions to someone who was not the governor of that province, e.g. to the governor of Pamphylia. The territory of the Homonadenses lay north of Syria but south of the provinces of Galatia and Pamphylia; and Ramsay had admitted that the war was waged on both fronts. Dessau further remarked that, in any case, whole legions were not wanted for this mountain war, but rather picked legionaries and, above all, light infantry (77, p. 612).

In view of the misuse some writers have made of Ramsay's inscription, it will be as well to quote it. It formed the base of a statue, and reads (in Ramsay's translation, 212, p. 285)

To Gaius Caristanius (son of Gaius of Sergian tribe) Fronto Caesianus Julius, chief of engineers, pontifex, priest, prefect of P. Sulpicius Quirinius duumvir, prefect of M. Servilius. To him first of all men at state expense by decree of the decuriones, a statue was erected.

The inscription proves only that Quirinius was elected chief magistrate (duumvir) of the colony and nominated Gaius Caristanius Fronto as his prefect to act for him. Nevertheless, some writers still assert that it removes the contradiction in Lk.'s narrative. As an example, I mention Keller, who asks whether it is possible that Lk. made a mistake in asserting that Jesus was born both at the time of the census under Quirinius and also in the reign of Herod. He answers:

> For a long time it seemed as if he had. It was only when a fragment of a Roman inscription was discovered at Antioch that the surprising fact emerged that Quirinius had been the Emperor's legate in Syria on a previous occasion, in the days of Saturninus the pro-consul. At that time his assignment had been purely military. He led a campaign against the Homonadenses (160, p. 327).

Dr Keller's readers will naturally suppose that the inscription actually says that Quirinius had been legate in Syria at this time; whereas this is neither stated, nor does it follow from what is.

Ramsay's theory is not mentioned by Wright who admits that Lk.'s references to Quirinius 'presents a chronological problem which has not been solved'. He mentions another attempted solution, namely that Lk. ii, 2 'should not be translated, as is usually done, "This census was the first during Quirinius' prefectureship of Syria"', but 'should be rendered "This census was the first before that under the prefectureship of Quirinius in Syria"'. He admits (in diplomatic language) that this is merely an arbitrary emendation, saying that 'the Greek text does not lend itself readily to such a translation' (295, p. 236).

Note III. The Census

Stauffer (257, p. 29) has tried to vindicate Lk. by distinguishing the written returns made by the population (the ἀπογραφή) from the final valuation of the sum due, which, he alleges, the authorities could only fix years later, after they had checked the returns by long and laborious measurements of the land. He holds that while Lk. clearly refers to the ἀπογραφή, which took place in Herod's day, Josephus' reference must be to the final valuation. But in fact Josephus is also referring to the ἀπογραφή, for he says that when Quirinius came, the Jews at first 'took the report of a taxation heinously' but were nevertheless persuaded to 'give an account of their estates without any dispute about it', until Judas raised a revolt (154, xviii, 1, 1).

A more common method of vindicating Lk. has been to try to show that kingdoms which were as independent as Herod's were nevertheless made subject to census. An example sometimes adduced is Tacitus' mention of a census forced on the Clitae in AD 34. But Schürer (244, I II, 123) showed that Tacitus does not say a Roman census was made, only that the king of the Clitae wished to make one according to the Roman custom (nostrum in modum). Stauffer has alleged that the city of Apamea in Syria shows that even independent towns could be made subject to census. An inscription proves that a census was conducted there by Quirinius, and Mommsen and others hold that this occurred in AD 6 (188, as cited), when the whole of Syria had to make returns. Apamea had been made autonomous by Antony, and historians have hitherto assumed that the census of Quirinius, in which it was treated as an ordinary provincial town, shows that it must have lost its autonomy some time after the battle of Actium. This is the view of Gardthausen (99, i, 461). Stauffer's case is that it was still autonomous when the census was held, and he refers to recent discoveries of coins minted by the town 'with the proud inscription "autonomos"' (257, p. 30). He gives no dates, but none of the coins to which he refers is later than AD 5 (see Bellinger, 26, p. 86). Another example mentioned by Stauffer is Mommsen's reference to an imperial tax-commissioner at the Red Sea port of Leuce Coma, in the client kingdom of Nabat. The Romans imposed an import duty on goods landed there destined for the caravan route which led into the heart of the kingdom, and Mommsen comments that, 'the bringing of a client state within the sphere of imperial taxation occurs elsewhere, e.g. in the regions of the Alps' (189, ii, 151 and note). An import duty is very different from a valuation census. The client kingdom may well have had some financial commitments, (Josephus mentions a man named Fabatus who was the finance official (διοικητής) of Augustus at the court of Herod). But Mommsen does not find this inconsistent with his statement that a census could not have occurred in Palestine before AD 6.

I have given some prominence to Stauffer because of the confidence with which he claims that recent discoveries have made the objections to Lk.'s narrative obsolete. He is particularly scornful towards Strauss whose ideas of the Roman Empire he calls 'primitive'. But some of his own arguments are much more worthy of this epithet. For instance, he refers to Josephus' comment on the narrative in Joshua (xviii, 9) that certain men 'passed through the land and described it by cities into seven portions in a book'. Josephus says that they measured the ground, and Stauffer comments that he is clearly interpreting the Biblical text from his knowledge of what the Romans did 'in his own time', and that this 'proves indirectly that Roman officials measured the ground *in Palestine in the early days of the Empire*' (257, p. 151). Josephus was not born until AD 37, and so the practice of the Romans in Palestine in his day establishes nothing as to what happened under

Augustus (who died in AD 14), let alone under Herod. To defend Lk. with an argument of this kind reveals a strong bias.

Note IV. *The journey to Bethlehem*

Schürer (244, i, ii, p. 20) notes: 'In a Roman census, the landed property had to be registered for taxation in the commune in whose territory it lay . . . For the rest, the person to be taxed had to enrol his name in the census at his dwelling-place, or at the chief town of the taxation district within which he resided. When, on the other hand, Lk. tells that Joseph travelled to Bethlehem, because he was of the house of David, it is assumed that the preparation of the taxation lists had been made according to tribes, generations and families, which was by no means the Roman custom.' If it be objected that the Romans may nevertheless have done this as a concession to the Jews, then this would have been a 'very remarkable' concession, 'since this method of conducting the census would be much more troublesome, and would lead to much greater inconvenience than the Roman plan. It is also extremely questionable whether a registration according to families and generations was any longer possible, since in regard to many it could not now be proved whether they belonged to this family or that.'

An Egyptian papyrus discovered since Schürer's death has been held to vindicate Lk. Wright (295, p. 235) states that it 'indicates that, in AD 103–4 at least, there was a census in Egypt which was apparently made on the basis of kinship, and proclamation was then made for all who were residing elsewhere to return to their family homes. This may illuminate the otherwise difficult problem as to why Joseph had to go from Galilee to Bethlehem.' The proclamation mentioned is the edict of Vibius Maximus of AD 104 that 'all who for any reason whatever are away from their own *Nomos* should return home to enrol themselves.' The word used for 'home' is 'ἴδια (see 186, pp. 193–4), and can mean either a man's private property or his 'peculiar district'. The former meaning seems required by the context, since, as Mitteis and Wilcken note, 'the census returns that have been preserved show . . . that the owners of houses had to give their names and the names of those living with them . . . and the address of the house as well', and 'the correctness of the entries was everywhere assured by official inspection by the local authorities'. Such inspection would have been difficult unless the returns were made where the property was situated. A recent biographer of Jesus (266, p. 43 n.) concedes that the edict seems to order people to return to their places of residence, and so does not help to solve the difficulties in Lk.

(ii) **The resurrection**

No stories could be more discrepant than the gospel resurrection narratives. In the different gospels the persons who come to the sepulchre on the morning of the resurrection are different; the purpose of their visit is different;[1] what they saw on arrival is different. For instance, according to Mk., Lk. and Jn., the visitors found that the stone at the opening had already been rolled away; according to Mt. (xxviii, 2), it was rolled back in the presence of the women by an angel, who in a great earthquake came down from heaven. According to Jn. the women saw two angels. Again, what the visitors were instructed to tell the disciples, and also what they actually did tell them, is different in the different gospels. Mk. has it that they said nothing to anyone, while Lk. reports that they told the eleven everything. Furthermore, according to Lk., the apostles remained in Jerusalem after the death of Jesus, and there beheld their risen Lord, whereas Mk. and Mt. require them to repair to Galilee before they could receive a manifestation of Jesus. The behaviour of Jesus and of the apostles at these manifestations is different in each gospel. To take just one detail: only in the fourth gospel does Jesus show the wound in his side to the disciples. And, of course, it is only in this gospel that he is wounded in the side while on the cross. In the synoptics the body hung unmolested until it was given to Joseph in the evening.

Apart from contradictions there are implausibilities.[2] Mt., the one evangelist who represents the sepulchre as guarded, makes the frightened soldiers run into the town to tell the priests and elders that Jesus is risen. The elders believe this story and bribe them to pretend that the body had been stolen while they were asleep. That the elders believed what they were told is unlikely; but if they were in fact convinced that Jesus had the power to rise from the dead, would they then try to hush the whole thing up with a bribe? And would the soldiers be likely to risk punishment from their officers by alleging that they had fallen asleep on

---

[1] Mt. represents the women as coming to look at the tomb; Mk. and Lk. say that they had looked at it before and came now to bring spices for the purpose of embalming the body. Jn. says in effect, that they brought no spices, and that the body had already been embalmed by Nicodemus.

[2] Some of the following discussion is copyright 1969 by the *Journal of the History of Ideas*, Inc. (see 282), and I am grateful to the editors for permission to reprint.

guard—an offence for which (according to Acts xii, 19), the penalty was death? It was perhaps because of these implausibilities that the other evangelists dropped the soldiers' testimony of the resurrection.[1]

The radical nature of the contradictions is admitted by the Archbishop of Canterbury, Dr Ramsey, who declares that, as the gospels are in conflict on everything else, we should be surprised, and even suspicious, if they were in agreement on the resurrection (213, p. 67). The worst discrepancy, he finds, is that Mt. makes the risen Jesus appear to his disciples in Galilee, while Lk. places the appearances in Jerusalem—a discrepancy due, he says, to Lk.'s 'editing', i.e. deliberate alteration, of the narrative in a previous gospel. He holds that Lk. derived his information, at any rate in part, from Mk. who makes the young man dressed in white, whom the women find in the empty sepulchre, say to them:

> Go, tell his disciples and Peter, *He goeth before you into Galilee*; there shall ye see him, as he said unto you (xvi, 7).

Lk. however, makes the occupant of the sepulchre say to them:

> Remember how he spake unto you, *when he was yet in Galilee*, saying that the Son of man must be delivered up into the hands of sinful men, and be crucified, and the third day rise again.

Ramsey admits that Lk. has here deliberately changed the wording so that he can place the appearances of the risen Jesus in Jerusalem (p. 64), but fails to explain why we should feel any confidence in a writer who thus twists his sources to mean the opposite of what they say. He also thinks that Lk. does not actually exclude appearances in Galilee (p. 71). Lk. has it that the women told their story to the apostles, who did not believe them; that *on the same day* two apostles went to Emmaus, a village about seven miles from Jerusalem, where Jesus appeared to them; that *without a moment's delay* they returned to Jerusalem, to be told by the others that he had in the meantime appeared to Peter; and that *during this conversation* he suddenly appeared in their midst, ate with them, told them that his death and resurrection were in accordance with scriptures, and led them as far as Bethany,

[1] On the implausibilities introduced into the narratives by their selection of the day of the Lord (Sunday) as the day of the resurrection see below, p. 176 n.

where he finally left them, having instructed them to stay in Jerusalem until blessed with the power from above. The gospel concludes with the statement that they returned to the city and spent their time in the temple, praising God. The appearances are clearly said to follow each other rapidly, and anybody reading Lk. without trying to harmonize him with other writers would naturally conclude that he assigns the final parting or ascension to the same day as the resurrection. That such a tradition existed is clear not only from Jn., but also from the epistle of Barnabas, where we read (chapter 19); 'We keep holy the eighth day [i.e. Sunday, see below, p. 176], in which also Jesus rose from the dead, and, after appearing, went up to heaven.' Ramsey, however, contends that this rapidity is only apparent, that although 'event *seems* to follow event in rapid succession from the walk to Emmaus to the parting at Bethany, . . . vagueness in chronology is one of Lk.'s characteristics as a writer'—as if there were anything vague in the expressions 'on the same day', 'without a moment's delay', etc. If we suppose a 'break in the discourse' long enough to permit the disciples to visit Galilee and return to Jerusalem, we have to place it in the middle of one of the appearances. This is what Ramsey suggests: he thinks we might assume a break at the end of verse 43—after Jesus had eaten, and before he goes on to explain that what had happened to him fulfilled the scriptures. If there was no break, he says, if all these appearances took place in one day, then the final parting 'would take place late at night, which seems improbable' (p. 65)— why is not explained.[1] He also refers to the evidence of Acts, where 'Lk. seems to correct any impression he may have left that the events all happened on the one day, for he tells us that the period of the appearances lasted "during forty days" '. But Acts still excludes appearances in Galilee, stating that while the risen Jesus was still with the apostles, he told them not to leave Jerusalem (i, 4), and after the forty days ascended into heaven from Mount Olivet near the city (i, 12). Furthermore, even though Lk. and Acts are by the same author, we are not entitled to assume that they do not contradict each other. Acts is clearly the later work, and it may be that the author posited the sojourn with the apostles because he had by then come to think that they needed a period of instruction before being sent out to convert

---

[1] Perhaps because the ascension could then not have been witnessed without a further miracle of daylight, which would also have been mentioned.

people; for the text tells that during these forty days Jesus taught them 'concerning the kingdom of God' (i, 3). As Schmiedel has noted (239, § 16), this period may have been suggested because this is the length of time spent by Moses on Sinai when receiving the law. Ramsey himself has shown how free the author of Lk.-Acts is in 'editing' traditions that were already circulating. If he did not hesitate to change the ideas of other writers when it suited his purpose, he may have treated his own in the same way to meet some doctrinal need. Ramsey concedes that Jn. 'wishes his readers to understand that the Ascension took place on Easter Day'. The 'puzzling' contradiction with Acts is resolved by the suggestion that 'perhaps Lk. and Jn. have different happenings in mind' (p. 87)!

In the upshot, Ramsey suggests that Lk. and Mt. are not altogether reliable because of the freedom with which they edit Mk. He even concedes that Mk. is sometimes not clear enough to be interpreted unambiguously (p. 71). He sets little store on agreement between the narratives and thinks it more appropriate to ask whether they include primitive traditions (p. 67). He regards the Emmaus story (which occurs only in Lk.) and Mk.'s story of the visit of the women to the tomb as primitive. The former tells how two of the disciples set out for the village, and are joined on the way by the risen Jesus, whom they fail to recognize and tell of their grief at their master's death. They add that some of their women-folk had claimed to have found the tomb empty, and to have seen angels there who declared that he was alive; and that the emptiness of the tomb had been confirmed by some of the apostles. The two are nevertheless still sceptical, whereupon their companion rebukes them, and, beginning with Moses and the prophets, explains all the passages which referred to himself (without disclosing his identity). By this time they have reached Emmaus, and they at last recognize the stranger when he sits down and breaks bread with them. Ramsey's argument is that their doubt and hesitation stamp the story as a true reminiscence and show that it is not Church propaganda (213, p. 61): and that likewise the terror of the women has an air of authenticity. The women, Mk. tells us, fled 'and said nothing to anyone: for they were afraid'. Ramsey comments: 'Silence and fear have their own message. They tell, more than words can, of the overwhelming reality of the Resurrection' (p. 76). But criteria of this kind would also certificate Mt.'s story of the guard as true, for the guard is terrified by the earthquake which removes the stone. Yet Ramsey tells us that this story is rejected even by many conservative critics and has clearly been fabricated from an ascertainable motive, namely to meet the allegation that the disciples stole the body (p. 63). Again, are we to believe Mt.'s story that at Jesus' death an earthquake split open graves and that the 'saints' occupying them were resurrected (on this see below, p. 103) on the grounds that the centurion and the other Roman soldiers concerned in the crucifixion were grudgingly moved to admit (on seeing all these remarkable phenomena) that Jesus was truly the Son of God? It is really too naïve to suggest that fear or incredulity among the characters of a story stamps it as true.

Schmiedel (239, § 24e) has shown how such stories as the sepulchre guard and the empty tomb could have arisen in stages without any historical basis. He imagines a Christian confronted with the charge that the disciples had stolen the body. The obvious retort would be: 'The Jews, we may be quite certain, saw to the watching of the sepulchre; they could very well have known that Jesus had predicted his rising again on the third day.' Another Christian, hearing this, might take it not for conjecture, but for a statement of fact, and pass it on as such. But if Roman soldiers guarded the tomb they must have witnessed the resurrection. What, then, did they see of it? The attempt to answer this would give rise to the story of the angel coming down from heaven and rolling away the stone. This again might well have originated as conjecture, but have been passed on as fact. And in order to explain why the soldiers did not tell of their experiences, it would be said that the Jewish authorities bribed them to suppress the truth and circulate instead the rumour that the disciples had stolen the body. A similar series of processes could have led to the story of the empty tomb. If Jesus was risen, his grave must have been empty. 'Therefore no hesitation was felt in declaring that, according to all reasonable conjecture, the women who had witnessed Jesus' death had wished to anoint his body and thus had come to know of the emptiness of the grave.' But why should not the disciples have gone to the sepulchre? Schmiedel answers: 'the earlier narratives represent them as fleeing and deserting Jesus at Gethsemane (Mk. xiv, 50; Mt. xxvi, 56), and remaining in concealment while they were in Jerusalem.' Lk.'s narrative changes this by very significantly omitting Mk.'s and Mt.'s statement that they dispersed at Jesus' arrest, and by saying that 'certain disciples' (xxiv, 24) did in fact go to the sepulchre. Jn. expands this, naming the visitors as Peter and the beloved disciple, and reporting upon their rivalry.

It is clear that if, for some reason, the belief that Jesus was risen was once established, all these other traditions could have arisen in the way indicated. Ramsey is not entitled, from his standpoint, to reject these suggestions, since he admits that later writers elaborated and edited the stories of their predecessors, and also that distortion occurred before there was any documentation at all, while the traditions were still oral (213, p. 60).

Ramsey believes that the resurrection stories are reliable not only because they contain primitive matter, but also because they 'concur with each other in their testimony to the main event'. 'They are,' he says, 'at one in that which they affirm,' namely 'the appearances of Jesus and the discovery of the empty tomb' (p. 61). The appearances are not the same in the different narratives, which concur only in their allegation *that* Jesus appeared and was not in his tomb. This amount of agreement is frequently found in stories admittedly mythical. For instance, Agamemnon is said to have been delayed at Aulis, where the Greek fleet was becalmed on its journey to Troy, because he had offended Artemis. One version has it that he had killed a stag in her grove; another that he had boasted that the goddess herself could not hit better; another that he had broken the vow he made in the year of Iphigenia's birth to sacrifice the most beautiful production of that year. Nevertheless, the traditions agree in the main fact—that the becalming occurred and was due to an offence against the goddess —and so, on Dr Ramsey's principles, we must accept it as historical.

It is often alleged in defence of the gospel story that eyewitnesses of an event give discrepant accounts of it, as is well known to the police. But if those who purported to be witnesses of a street accident disagreed as to *all* the details: if one affirmed that it took place in London, while another sited it in Manchester (corresponding to one evangelist making the risen Jesus appear only in Galilee and another only in Jerusalem), then it would be impossible to reconstruct what actually happened without further independent testimony. In the case of a street accident there are damaged vehicles or injured people to convince us that, whatever the contradictions of the witnesses, something untoward did occur. If in such circumstances the witnesses contradicted each other to the extent supposed, we should find this surprising. If, however, we had nothing but their contradictions to go on, and if these were of the most radical kind, we could not be sure that an accident had occurred at all. And that is our position with regard to the resurrection. We believe that Hannibal crossed the Alps (even though Livy's account of his route is quite different from that of Polybius) only because there is evidence independent of the contradictions of chroniclers that he was at one date on the Gallic and at a later date on the Italian side. But the only evidence for Jesus' return to life is from the contradictory gospel narratives which are confirmed neither by Paul nor by archaeology.[1] Schmiedel observes:

> Livy and Polybius lived centuries after the occurrence which they relate and they were dependent for their facts upon written sources which were perhaps wanting in accuracy and were moreover themselves derived from inadequate sources. If any deficiency, even of only an approximately similar character has to be admitted in the acquaintance of the writers of the Gospels with circumstances of the Resurrection of Jesus, there is little prospect of anyone being induced to accept it as a fact on the strength of such testimony, *unless he has from the beginning been predisposed to do so without any testimony.* As a matter of fact, we cannot avoid the conclusion from the contradictions between the Gospels that *the writers of them were far removed from the event they describe.*

This conclusion—that the gospels were not written by eye-witnesses of the events reported, nor by those who had their information directly from eye-witnesses—is of crucial importance. Later we shall see how scholars have been led to it not merely from

---

[1] Paul did not regard the resurrection as a historical event that occurred at Jerusalem (see below, pp. 146–148) Schmiedel notes that he is silent about such gospel details as the empty tomb, even though he had visited Jerusalem and would naturally have been anxious to glean all available evidence for the actuality of the resurrection, on which for him the whole truth of Christianity depended (235, § 138). As for the archaeological evidence, 'there is not a single existing site in the Holy City that is mentioned in connection with Christian history before the year AD 326, when Constantine's mother adored the two footprints of Christ on Olivet' (61, p. 9). She saw nothing else (ibid., p. 10). Thus 'all trace of knowledge of the place of crucifixion and of the tomb had vanished from the Christian community which is alleged to have arisen immediately after Jesus' ascension' (221, p. 69).

the crass contradictions of some gospel passages but also from the literary similarities of others, indicating dependence on previous documents.

A number of writers (including Dr Ramsey, 213, p. 39), have found the plausibility of the resurrection strengthened by the fact that it does not accord with Jewish Messianic expectations, and so could not have been invented in order to conform to them. But this is also true of the virgin birth, the turning of the water into wine (on this see below, p. 128) and many other gospel incidents which have been shown to have no historical basis. Jewish ideas were certainly not the sole source for Christian ones. And Ramsey's point entails admitting that the gospel attempt to show that the resurrection occurred 'according to the scriptures' consists of citing passages 'some of which may seem to us to be used in ways remote from their original meaning'; and that the OT evidence that the resurrection would occur on the third day is 'very slight' (pp. 24, 25). As with the virgin birth story we find that in this case also the pagan parallels are striking. In antiquity, any number of saviour gods died that we might live, and rose again, some of them on the third day.[1] We must later consider whether the Christian story is an imitation of these, and if so, what the motive for the imitation was.

While Ramsey defends the resurrection, a number of Christian scholars deal with the perplexities of the narratives by admitting that it never happened. They nevertheless usually go on to claim that the gospel allegation that it did is of great religious importance. For Bultmann, for instance, the resurrection is 'definitely non-historical' but nevertheless a 'cosmic event', for the statement that Jesus is risen tells us the truth that death has been deprived of its powers, so that we need not fear it. Bultmann talks a great deal about 'authentic life', by which he means life dominated by religious faith. The importance of the resurrection is that it 'opens up for men the possibility of authentic life' (43, pp. 34, 38, 39). He concedes that, once belief in Jesus' resurrection became current, it led to the belief that he was the Messiah, and this in turn led to fables in which he figures as the Messiah, e.g. Mt.'s 'thou art Peter' story and the Transfiguration. The truly historical Jesus that can be extracted from the documents is, for Bultmann, merely a preacher who worked no miracles and made no Messianic

---

[1] Leipoldt (169, p. 201) quotes traditions which make Osiris and Attis rise on the third day. cf. below, p. 231.

claims. Nevertheless, we can still believe in his divine or quasi-divine status, for belief is not to be dependent on historical testimony, but must be 'pure', i.e. independent of it (42, p. 26). One cannot help suspecting that if the historical testimony were not a source of endless difficulties, theologians would not find it necessary to resort to such shifts.

Bultmann regards the resurrection, the virgin birth, ascension and second coming as myths derived from Greek and Jewish sources. By 'demythologizing' the NT he understands interpreting such unacceptable stories so that they acquire acceptable form, 'trying to recover the deeper meaning behind the mythological conceptions'. His confidence that there is a deeper meaning rests in part on the fact that this sort of exegesis has been practised from a very early stage. 'Demythologizing has its beginning in the NT itself, and therefore [sic] our task of demythologizing today is justified' (44, pp. 18, 34). The method adopted in the sacred book cannot conceivably be wrong.

Bultmann links his method with the philosophy of Heidegger and claims to be interpreting the NT mythology 'existentially'. This means that when the Christian interprets the Bible he must relate what it says to his own self, his aspirations, beliefs and fears. When, for instance, the Bible says that God created the world, this must not be taken to mean what it says. It must mean something about the personal relation between the believer and his God. 'Only such statements about God are legitimate as express the existential relation between God and man . . . The affirmation that God created the world can only be a personal confession that I understand myself to be a creature which owes its existence to God. It cannot be made as a neutral statement, but only as thanksgiving and surrender' (44, p. 69). A 'neutral statement' seems to mean a detached objective statement about some process in the world not primarily or exclusively connected with my own personal existence. Here, then, we have the key. To understand scripture aright we must give it the relevance to ourselves which it appears to lack. 'To hear the scriptures as the Word of God means to hear them as a word which is addressed to me, as *kerygma*, as a proclamation. Then my understanding is not a neutral one, but rather my response to a call' (44, p. 71). In one frank passage Bultmann admits that it is because the Bible does not stand up to historical criticism that he has to introduce this emotional approach to it in order to make it religiously useful: 'It is precisely the mythological description of Jesus Christ in the NT which makes it clear that the figure and the work of Jesus Christ must be understood in a manner which is beyond the categories by which the historian understands world-history, if the figure and the work of Jesus Christ are to be understood as the divine work of redemption.'[1]

Bultmann's method is common among defenders of a faith. Certain texts or stories are regarded as sacred, yet at a certain stage of sophistication, believers cannot accept them as meaning what they say and so their allegations of fact are interpreted as philosophical allegories. In Christian apologetics this method is at least as old as Origen who, for instance, denied (206, p. 289) that the gospel Temptation story is literally true. The Rabbis and Greeks had used the same method in interpreting their sacred narratives, and the basis of medieval Christian exegesis was to seek the *sensus spiritualis* of the text (see 251). Always, the motive was to make unacceptable stories acceptable. To reject them altogether was out of the question.

(iii) The Gadarene swine

The story of the Gadarene swine is narrated in all three synoptics, with the usual considerable discrepancies, but is absent from the fourth gospel, as are all the exorcistic miracles which occupy such a prominent place in the synoptics. According to a recent Christian commentator, Jn. excluded them because they were a source of 'embarrassment' to him (265, p. 171). With these discrepancies, however, I shall not be concerned, and shall merely consider Mk.'s version of the incident. He tells (chapter v) how Jesus came to a raving madman possessed by many demons, and proceeded to cure him by transferring them to a herd of pigs; whereupon the whole herd of about two thousand rushed into the

---

[1] (44, p. 80) Bishop Robinson's *Honest to God* is based on Bultmann's premises. Both writers protest against the mythological guise (of miracles and fantastic prophecies) in which the evangelists cloak Jesus' divinity. This mythology, says Robinson, is however 'an important form of religious truth' in that it does draw attention to Jesus' divinity, which in fact consists in his unselfish love (for God is love). Jesus' virgin birth, for instance, 'can only legitimately mean' that his whole life was 'born not of the will of the flesh . . . but of God', i.e. that he lived an unselfish life (226, pp. 32–3, 49–50, 77). J. M. Robinson's book is also an attempt, on Bultmann's lines, to combine the quest of the historical Jesus with that of 'meaningful existence' (227, p. 152).

lake near by and drowned. The reader may be inclined to think
this a trivial incident on which little depends. But Huxley has
pointed out that 'the belief in the reality of witchcraft, justly
based, alike by Catholics and Protestants, upon this and innumerable other passages in both the Old and New Testaments, gave
rise, through the special influence of Christian ecclesiastics, to the
most horrible persecutions and judicial murders of thousands upon
thousands of men, women and children' (145, pp. 215–16).
Furthermore, 'if physical and mental disorders are caused by
demons, Gregory of Tours rightly considered that relics and
exorcists were more useful than doctors'.

Today there are few educated people who regard demoniacal
possession as anything more than a superstitious delusion,
although Catholics are committed to the doctrine because it is so
clearly accepted in the Bible, which for them is free from error,
and also because the Fathers are equally unambiguous in their
acceptance of it. And so we find the *Catholic Encyclopaedia* (50)
telling us that the demon who enters into the sufferer is 'an evil
spirit, one of the fallen angels'. But even Catholics cannot help
noticing the infrequency of demoniacal possession in civilized
areas. Tylor had no difficulty in showing that it has always been
the dominant theory to explain disease and inspiration among
primitive peoples; that it is gradually superseded by higher
medical knowledge; that this development first limits the theory
of possession to certain peculiar and severe affections, especially
those connected with mental and nervous disorders, such as
epilepsy, hysteria, delirium, idiocy and madness; and then
abandons it altogether (273, p. 139).

Premising, then, that demoniacal possession is a delusion,
Huxley indicates a number of possible ways of regarding the story
in Mk. We may believe that:

(1) Jesus did actually believe in demoniacal possession. His
words 'come forth, thou unclean spirit, out of the man', suggest
that this is so. Furthermore, acceptance of the current belief is
clearly the basis of his argument with the Pharisees in Lk. xi, 16 ff.
Huxley observes that if Jesus really held this belief, this can only
lower our estimation of his authority.

(2) Jesus was a divine personage who did not believe in
possession, but pretended to do so from deference to a popular
belief that was to be at the root of untold suffering and persecu-

tion. Had he declared that belief in witchcraft and possession is wicked nonsense, he would have rendered the long agony of medieval humanity impossible, but he chose not to do so. This Huxley finds incredible.

(3) Jesus was not divine, but an ordinary individual who pretended to believe in possession. Huxley finds that this hypothesis makes it difficult to understand the behaviour of the swine. A recent writer, premising, as Christian commentators usually do, that in the whole story 'we have a tradition of something which actually happened', admits that 'the greatest difficulty is the account of the swine. If we reject mythical explanations . . . and if we accept a psychological explanation of possession, we must explain the panic of the swine, as Weiss explained it, as occasioned by the paroxysm of the man's cure' (265, p. 278).

(4) Jesus did not believe in possession, but the evangelists, whose beliefs were those of their day and age, did, and have attributed their own ideas to him in their report of the incident. According to this view, it is not Jesus, but the evangelists who are discredited, and, as Huxley points out, this is just as serious a blow to the Christian position. For 'if their report on a matter of such stupendous and far-reaching practical import as this is unworthy, how can we be sure of its trustworthiness in other cases?' (145, p. 219). Their whole record of the sayings and deeds of Jesus may be only a popular version, falsely coloured and distorted by superstitious imaginings.

Huxley finds this fourth alternative the most plausible, and notes that there is nothing to countervail this evidence of the evangelists' unreliability; for we know 'absolutely nothing' about them, and there is no proof that their gospels existed, in the state in which we now find them in the AV, before the second century, or, in other words, sixty or seventy years after the events recorded. Between that time and the date of the oldest extant manuscripts, there is no telling what additions and alterations and interpolations have been made (145, p. 222). He adds that the compilers of the RV have shown that such things have happened even since the date of the oldest known manuscripts; for these lack the ending of Mk. (xvi, 9 to the end, which is printed as an appendix in the RV) and Jn.'s story of the woman taken in adultery. His comment is: 'If, after an approximate settlement of the canon of the NT, and even later than the fourth and fifth centuries, literary fabricators had the skill and the audacity to make such additions and interpolations as these, what may they have done when no one had thought of a canon; when oral tradition, still confused, was regarded as more valuable than such written records as may have existed in the latter portion of the first century?' (145, p. 232).

Huxley was a biologist, not a theologian, and his essays date from the end of the last century; but his standpoint is still unanswered.

(iv) The gospel miracles in general

Haag (122) rightly says that miracles are prominent in the activities of Jesus recorded in the gospels, and that to dismiss them as unhistorical while accepting the rest of the texts is quite arbitrary. Indeed, if the miracles are deleted from Mk. practically nothing is left. Every incident in his first chapter contains a miracle, and up to Jesus' triumphal entry into Jerusalem the only non-miraculous incidents are a few conversations between him and his disciples, a number of disputes with the Pharisees, a few parables (particularly Chapter Four), the blessing of children (ix, 36) and the repudiation of the rich man (x, 21–2).

Haag stresses that even Jesus' enemies did not question his miracles, and refers to Mk. iii, 22 where the scribes admit that he cast out devils. But pagan and Jewish miracles could equally well be accredited by pointing to Christian acquiescence. The disciples of the Pharisees cast out devils (Mt. xii, 27; Lk. xi, 19), so did the man who 'followed not' with Jesus' disciples (Mk. ix, 38–40; Lk. ix, 49–50) and the same is said of those whom in Mt. vii, 22–3 Jesus says he will reject in his final judgement. Stauffer mentions statements in the Talmud which he dates about AD 95 and which say that Jesus was a successful magician. He argues that if Jesus had not worked miracles, the Rabbis would have said he lacked the power, not that he was a magician, for 'the ancient Jews were very realistic in the question of miracles and at any rate the opponents of Jesus were very critical' (257, p. 19). But in truth the Jewish view of miracles was far from 'realistic'. Josephus tells that he himself had seen a Jewish exorcist draw devils from the noses of persons possessed by them (154, viii, 2, 5), and the Talmud is full of naïve miracle stories. It tells, for instance, how in the second century AD a Christian pronounced a spell which fixed three Rabbis in an arch; how one of the Rabbis retaliated with a spell which caused the Christian to be struck in a door. After releasing each other they all went to the lake of Galilee where the Christian divided the water and walked in the divide, whereupon a Rabbi commanded the angel of the lake and the water swallowed him up (Jerusalem Talmud, Sanh. 25d). Miracles were ascribed by the Rabbis to magic, and they regarded Egypt, where in their opinion Jesus learned his magic, as the special home of sorcery (Qidd, 49b). Stauffer is expecting too much in supposing that they would deny all miracles except the orthodox Jewish ones. He also tries to authenticate Jesus' miracles by saying that they are not magic tricks but mainly cures of sickness. This is by no means uncommon in religious lore. Tacitus tells how, at the instigation of the god Serapis, Vespasian cured a blind man in Alexandria by means of his spittle and a lame man by the mere touch of his foot. Stauffer supposes that there is something very elevating about Jesus' cures. But what is impressive about the deity, who has made man subject to all manner of disease and infirmity, curing a few hundreds of cases of the suffering for which he is himself responsible, and which he leaves uncured in many millions?

Haag complains that many Protestant writers have a 'philosophic prejudice' against miracles, and he meets it by saying that, 'if a fact is vouched for by immediate and trustworthy witnesses, then we have no right to doubt it just because it is unusual'. The 'if' introduces an important qualification and the conditions it lays down are not fulfilled in the gospels. But even in cases where miracles are attested by immediate and trustworthy witnesses, they are often denied, even by modern Catholics. The best example is the modern attitude to witchcraft. Lecky observes that 'the historical evidence establishing the reality of witchcraft is so vast and so varied, that nothing but our overwhelming sense of its antecedent improbability and our modern experience of the manner in which it has faded away under the influence of civilization can justify us in despising it'. In law courts, on the evidence of sworn 'eye-witnesses', accusations were made which convinced 'acute judges whose lives were spent in sifting evidence'. Lecky explains this legal and other testimony by noting that 'men are always prepared to accept, on very slight evidence, what they believe to be exceedingly probable' (166, pp. 2, 13, 80–1). What people observe depends at least as much on their habits of thought as on what is actually there. A firm belief in the miraculous and in the ceaseless efforts of the devil was the presupposition of the observations and reasonings of witnesses and judges alike, and the number of witnesses counts for very little when all are affected by the same underlying beliefs.

Modern Catholics do not deny the possibility of witchcraft. It is too unambiguously affirmed in the Bible. But the *Catholic Encyclopaedia* (52) takes the view that it is relatively rare, and that most victims of witch-hunts were innocent. This authority also notes that the Reformers were more zealous witch-hunters than were Catholics, and that 'it was in virtue of the Biblical command (Ex. xxii, 18) that Luther advocated the extermination of witches' —an interesting illustration of the consequences of setting up the Bible as a guide to conduct. In the view of this Catholic authority, then, miracles which were sworn to in courts by eye-witnesses are bogus. Yet we are to believe the miracles alleged in the gospels whose authors did not submit their evidence to such scrutiny, and who were men about whom, in Huxley's words, we know 'absolutely nothing', writing a considerable time after the events they allege.

CHAPTER TWO

Jesus as Teacher and Prophet

(i) **Ethical discourses in the gospels**

It is sometimes asserted that, however weak the evidence for Jesus' miracles, he stands out as an inspired ethical teacher, a moral genius who must certainly have been a historical personage. In fact, however, all the ethically acceptable doctrines in the gospels can be found in previous pagan writers, as was admitted by Bishop Thirlwall (269, pp. 37–8). Farrer (91, Chapter IX) quotes inculcations of unselfishness from Seneca; of brotherly love for all mankind from both Seneca and Cicero; of charity from these two and others; and of forgiveness, toleration and leniency from many pagan writers. What the ancient Egyptian regarded as his duty to his neighbour is shown by a series of addresses known as the 'Negative Confession', quoted by Budge from a Papyrus of the fourteenth century BC. The list was recited, it was believed, by each departed soul at its judgement, and comprises, as Budge observes (41, pp. 128–35), a very extensive code of morality. It runs:

1. I have not done iniquity.
2. I have not robbed with violence.
3. I have not done violence to any man.
4. I have not committed theft.
5. I have slain neither man nor woman.
6. I have not made light the bushel.
7. I have not acted deceitfully.
8. I have not purloined the things which belong unto God.
9. I have not uttered falsehood.

10. I have not carried off goods by force.
11. I have not uttered vile (or evil) words.
12. I have not carried off food by force.
13. I have not acted deceitfully.
14. I have not eaten my heart (i.e. lost my temper and become angry).
15. I have invaded no man's land.
16. I have not slaughtered animals which are the possessions of God.
17. I have not laid waste the lands which have been ploughed.
18. I have not pried into matters to make mischief.
19. I have not set my mouth in motion against any man.
20. I have not given way to wrath without due cause.
21. I have not committed fornication nor sodomy.
22. I have not polluted myself.
23. I have not lain with the wife of a man.
24. I have not made any man to be afraid.
25. I have not made my speech to burn with anger.
26. I have not made myself deaf unto the words of right and truth.
27. I have not made another person to weep.
28. I have not uttered blasphemies.
29. I have not acted with violence.
30. I have not hastened my heart (i.e. acted without due consideration).
31. I have not pierced my skin and I have not taken vengeance on the god.
32. I have not multiplied my speech beyond what should be said.
33. I have not committed fraud and I have not looked upon evil.
34. I have never uttered curses against the king.
35. I have not fouled running water.
36. I have not exalted my speech.
37. I have not uttered curses against God.
38. I have not behaved with insolence.
39. I have not made distinctions (i.e. been guilty of favouritism).
40. I have not increased my wealth except by means of such things as are mine own possessions.
41. I have not uttered curses against that which belongeth to God and is with me.
42. I have not thought scorn of the god of the city.

Christian commentators commonly ascribe to Jesus doctrines which are absent from the gospels. Although it is one of the commonplaces of present-day moralists that his teaching has promoted happy family life, this view is hard to reconcile with the texts where he encourages people to break up their families for religious reasons (Lk. xiv, 26). Equally striking is the gospel disparagement of married life (Mt. xix, 10–12). Paul's views on this subject are well known (I. Cor. vii). And in Rev. xiv, 4 we are told that the men who will be saved are 'they which were not defiled with women, for they are virgins'.

Before inquiring further into what standard of goodness Jesus sets up in the gospels, we may note his statements concerning the fate of those who are not good. The 'goats' get no mercy at the final judgement, but are told to depart 'into the eternal fire which is prepared for the devil and his angels' (Mt. xxv, 31–46). This doctrine of eternal punishment had been utterly rejected by Epictetus, Seneca and others (see 91, pp. 115 ff.). The inferiority of Christianity here is admitted with characteristic candour in the *Biblica* (55, § 82 and note).

If we read the gospels in order to discover what standard of goodness they advocate, we find that they contain less ethical teaching than is commonly supposed. In Mk. there is practically none. He records one miracle after another in order to convince us that Jesus was the Messiah, but he is not interested in what Jesus preached and repeatedly alludes to 'the gospel' and to Jesus' teachings without telling us wherein they consist (i, 15, 21, 39; iii, 14, etc.). There is no Sermon on the Mount in this gospel. The teaching in chapter iv is not ethical, but consists of parables of the kingdom of God. The first sign of ethical teaching comes in chapter vii, where Jesus condemns 'fornications, thefts, murders, adulteries, covetings, wickedness, deceit, lasciviousness, an evil eye, railing, pride and foolishness'. In chapter viii he advocates self-denial, and in chapter ix advises us to cut off our hand and foot and cast out our eye if they cause us to stumble, it being better 'to enter into the kingdom of God with one eye, rather than having two eyes to be cast into hell'. The next chapter prohibits divorce, and recapitulates the familiar commandments 'do not kill, do not commit adultery, do not steal, do not bear false witness, do not defraud, honour thy father and thy mother'. Chapter xii also quotes OT commandments: 'thou shalt love the Lord thy God . . . Thou shalt love thy neighbour as thyself'. To these Jesus adds, on his own authority: 'Go, sell whatsoever thou hast and give to the poor, and thou shalt have treasure in heaven' (chapter x). In the same chapter he declares that 'there is no man that hath left house, or brethren, or sisters, or mother, or father, or children, or lands for my sake and for the gospel's sake, but he shall receive a hundredfold now in this time, houses and brethren, and sisters, and mothers, and children, and lands, with persecutions, and in the world to come eternal life'. Mt. xix, 29 gives the same statement in a more intelligible form by omitting 'with persecutions'. Poverty, renunciation, abandonment of friends and relatives, universal abnegation—these are the ideals, and for these the reward will be power, majesty, authority, in short everything that on this earth has been renounced, but multiplied a hundredfold. The most reasonable ethical pronouncements in the rather meagre assemblage of Mk. are clearly those taken from the OT.

Lk. records more discourses, but it is often difficult to discover any ethical principle in them. For instance, in chapter vi Jesus begins the Sermon on the Mount by blessing the poor, the hungry, the weeping, the hated and cursing the rich, the full, the laughers, the reputable. An ethical principle is not discernible until verse 27—'love your enemies . . . judge not'. He goes on to inculcate reciprocity and mercy. Later he praises faith (vii, 50), inculcates self-denial, and even urges martyrdom on his disciples (ix, 23–4). He also tells them that 'he that is least among you, the same is great' (verse 48). They say that they found a man who was casting out devils in his name and restrained him because he 'followeth not with us'. Jesus tells them not to restrain him, 'for he that is not against you is for you'—in contrast, by the way, to Mt. xii, 30, where he teaches that 'he that is not with me is against me; and he that gathereth not with me scattereth'. He then begins his journey to Jerusalem and is coldly received in a Samaritan village. The indignant disciples ask him: 'Lord, wilt thou that we bid fire to come from heaven and consume them?' But Jesus 'turned and rebuked them', and according to the AV he continued: 'For the Son of man is not come to destroy men's lives but to save them' (verse 56). These words, being absent from the four oldest codices, were deleted by the RV. They well illustrate the way in which all manner of utterances were put into the mouth of Jesus during the history of the documents.

In the next chapter he sends out seventy, instructing them to tell everyone that 'the kingdom of God is come nigh unto you', and threatening all who refuse to listen with eternal damnation. In the same chapter he tells the parable of the good Samaritan to illustrate the precept 'love thy neighbour as thyself'. Some of the later parables (e.g. that of the unjust steward, xvi, 1 ff.) are admitted to be 'most difficult of interpretation' (7, p. 307) and the story of the unjust judge (xviii, 1–8) is positively offensive. The idea is that if an unjust judge listens to the plea of a widow just in order to get rid of her, how much more will God avenge his elect, if they cry to him day and night. Thus God is compared with a bad judge; and it is a question not of justice but of vengeance for his 'elect'. Another parable (chapter xix) ends with the good man ordering the execution of his enemies.

The parable of the good Samaritan is the first of a series which occur only in Lk. The others include the story of Martha and Mary, the parable of the covetous rich man, the doctrine that those who suffer many afflictions in this life are not necessarily more sinful than other people, the insistence that it is right to heal on the sabbath, the inculcation of humility, the angel's joy over one saved sinner, and the prodigal son. Since Lk. professes to edit previous narratives (i, 1–3) we must either assume that these parables were deliberately ignored by the earlier gospels, or that they are additions made to his some time after its completion.

Lk. frequently offers comfort to the suffering and oppressed by assuring them of retribution and stressing the great reversal of fortune that is to come, when the wealthy will be humbled and the poor exalted. 'Behold there are last which shall be first, and there are first which shall be last' (xiii, 30). But even this doctrine is not consistently held, since xix, 26 stipulates that 'Unto everyone that hath shall be given, but from him that hath not, even that which he hath shall be taken away from him.'

From Mt. we can, if we ignore contradictions and simply select what precepts are clearly ethical, distinguish the following:

From chapter v:
    1. Be meek and humble.
    2. Be merciful.
    3. Be pure.
    4. Obey the Jewish law.
    5. Avoid anger.
    6. Be forgiving and conciliatory.
    7. Avoid adulterous thoughts.
C

    8. Do not divorce your wife except for fornication.
    9. Do not swear.
  10. Do not resist evil.
  11. Be charitable.
  12. Love your enemies.

From chapter vi:
  13. Do not be ostentatious in well-doing.

From chapter vii:
  14. Do not judge.
  15. Do not give what is holy to the dogs.
  16. Do to others what you would wish them to do to you.
  17. Do not speak idle words.

From chapter xix:
  18. Be ready to neglect everything and everybody for the
      sake of Jesus.

No. 9 seems to mean 'always tell the truth'. I give below (p. 70) an example from an ancient Jewish document which shows that, in the writer's opinion, swearing oaths is wrong because it implies that those who do so are not normally truthful, and even today some people refuse to swear oaths for this reason. Jesus tells his audience to give a straight 'yes' or 'no' with no oath (Mt. v, 37) and this may fairly be taken as an injunction to be truthful. Thus if we omit nos. 4, 8, 15 and 18 we may sum up his precepts as inculcating humility, mercy, purity, avoidance of anger, forgiveness, veracity, non-resistance to evil, charity and reciprocity. The stress is on meekness—the obvious virtue for the depressed peoples of the Roman Empire (from whom the early Christians were recruited) where the pressure of poverty was so great that life was hardly worth living (134, pp. 32–5 and refs.).

What is very striking is that the gospels represent Jesus himself as failing to implement most of these eighteen ethical prescriptions. Admittedly, he nowhere infringes nos. 7, 8, 17 and 18, and if he is a divine personage, he is perhaps entitled to do what no. 14 forbids to mere mortals. But his conduct is appalling as regards nos. 4 and 5. If avoiding anger is so important, why did he 'look around at them with anger' (Mk. iii, 5)? As for no. 1, although in one passage he says he is meek and lowly in heart, in the very next chapter he claims to be greater than Solomon (Mt. xi, 29 and xii, 42). He also tells the disciples to go through the cities of Israel crying that the kingdom of heaven is at hand. Any city that disbelieves them is, he says, to be most frightfully punished in the day of judgement; it will meet a worse fate than the most infamous cities of tradition (Mt. x, 5–15). Disbelief in his prophetic claims is thus stamped as an unpardonable crime. Again, in Mk. xvi, 16 the risen Jesus lays it down that all who are baptized and accept his teachings are to be saved, whereas 'he that disbelieveth shall be condemned'. Such an attitude can scarcely be described as tolerant. Again, on the one hand he vetoes invective ('Whosoever shall say, Thou fool, shall be in danger of hell fire', Mt. v, 22) and on the other he freely indulges in it ('Ye fools and blind', Mt. xxiii, 17; and 'Thou fool, this night shall thy soul be required of thee', Lk. xii, 20). Everyone knows that he taught us to love our neighbours and even our enemies (no. 12). Yet he himself denounces the scribes and Pharisees, calling them hypocrites, serpents and vipers (Mt. xxiii, 29, 33). His abuse of the Pharisees has given rise to the belief that they were utterly worthless individuals. It is as if we should judge the Catholics of the Reformation period by relying exclusively on what Protestants said of them. Students who consult the Jewish as well as the Christian traditions are apt to take a different view (see 271, pp. 101 n., 160).

Apart from Jesus' failure to keep the standard, he does not consistently advocate any uniform standard. First, there is a striking difference between the teachings of the synoptics and those of Jn. The former are mainly concerned with how the kingdom of God can be entered, but in Jn. the leading theme is Jesus himself, his person and his dignity. We are told, for instance, that 'before Abraham was I am', that 'I am the resurrection and the life'. In this gospel Jesus gives what Schmiedel has called constant repetition of metaphysical propositions concerning his own person, no parables at all, and only two mentions of the kingdom of heaven. Schmiedel believed—and his view has found wide acceptance[1]—that the discrepancies between the mystic utterances of the fourth gospel and the synoptic discourses is so great that they could not have both been delivered by the same person (236, § 25, 37). Even if we restrict ourselves to the synoptic discourses we find marked discrepancies. Thus, although we are to love our enemies, yet the disciples are told: 'if thy brother sin

[1] It is endorsed, for instance, by Althaus in his lecture of 1960 (14, p. 6).

against thee and he hear thee not . . . then let him be unto thee
as the Gentile and the publican' (Mt. xviii, 17)—two classes who
are apparently not to be loved. In one chapter we are told: 'Let
your light shine before men, that they may see your good works,
and glorify your Father which is in heaven' (Mt. v, 16). The next
begins with the precept to conceal one's well-doing:

> Take heed that ye do not your righteousness before men, to
> be seen of them: else ye have no reward with your Father which
> is in heaven . . . When thou doest alms, let not thy left hand
> know what thy right hand doeth; that thine alms may be
> secret; and thy Father which seeth in secret shall recompense
> thee.

He goes on to extend the same doctrine to prayer (vi, 5–6) and
fasting (vi, 16–18): all these activities are to be performed in
seclusion.

Although all teachers are in some measure inconsistent, such
a mosaic of incompatibilities could surely not have come from
one person, particularly as they are supposed to have been delivered in one (or at most three) seasons' preaching (255, § 44).
In the following examples I shall list some contradictions which
betray what tendencies the evangelist is following and so help to
show how this medley of narrative came to be compiled.

(1) According to Lk. Jesus says 'blessed are ye poor . . . blessed
are ye that hunger' (vi, 20–1). But Mt. has it that he said 'blessed
are the poor in spirit: blessed are they that hunger and thirst after
righteousness'. Who can accept both versions and how are we to
decide for either? Lk. adds 'woe unto you that are rich', and this
is lacking altogether in Mt. Lk. is here following a trend prominent
in his gospel. Thus in his parable of Lazarus and the rich man, the
former goes to heaven, apparently only because of his poverty,
and the latter to hell, and is 'in anguish in this flame' (xvi, 24).
Commentators are apt to allege that he does not go to hell just
because he has had a good time on earth, but because of his bad
character. Of this there is nothing in the parable. It looks as though
Lk's sympathies with the poor have led him to put such speeches
and stories into Jesus' mouth, and that they are absent from, or
even at variance with, the other gospels because these follow
different tendencies.

(2) Jesus' statements concerning who is to be saved are full of contradictions. In Mt. xi, 28 he is represented as saying to the people 'Come unto me all ye that labour . . . I will give you rest'. But in Mk. iv, 12 he says that he is deliberately unintelligible to the people so that they shall not understand him, and so shall not have the opportunity of repenting and being saved. 'Unto you,' he says to the disciples, 'is given the mystery of the kingdom of God; but unto them that are without all things are done in parables, that seeing they may see and not perceive: and hearing they may hear and not understand: lest haply they should turn again and it should be forgiven them.' What are we to think of a god who is deliberately unintelligible so that those who hear him shall not be saved? Taylor tells us in his learned commentary (265, p. 257) that this is certainly what Mk. represents Jesus as saying, and he quotes (with approval) Professor Black, who says: 'Nothing is more certain than that Mark wrote and intended ἵνα (in order that) μήποτε (not at any time).' Taylor adds that 'both these expressions are used with telic force', i.e. indicate that it was the purpose of the parables to conceal the truth from the people. The key to the whole passage is the distinction made between the elect and 'them that are without', salvation being reserved for the former. A similar predestinarian standpoint is found in the ending given by Mt. (and only by him) to the parable where the king sends his servants into the highways to force all the people they can find to come to the feast he has prepared. The king then 'came in to behold his guests' and 'saw there a man which had not on a wedding-garment: and he saith unto him, Friend, how camest thou hither not having a wedding-garment? It is difficult to understand his surprise, since these people have been brought in on the spur of the moment from the highways. It is still more difficult to justify the sentence he passes on this man: 'Bind him hand and foot, and cast him out into the outer darkness; there shall be weeping and gnashing of teeth. For many are called, but few chosen' (Mt. xxii, 11–14). The king represents the king of heaven, and the idea seems to be that he reserves salvation for a small elect.

(3) From some passages it is clear that one evangelist has attempted to improve the ethical teaching of another or of their common source, and this seems to be the case with Mt.'s version of the story where Jesus says he is deliberately unintelligible to prevent people from repenting and being saved. Mt. xiii, 13

makes him say: 'Therefore speak I to them in parables because seeing they see not, and hearing they hear not, neither do they understand.' Mt. thus emphasizes the defective understanding of the multitude rather than the desire of Jesus not to be understood by them. Again, Mt. vii, 11 represents Jesus as saying: 'If ye then, being evil, know how to give good gifts unto your children, how much more shall your Father which is in heaven give good things to them that ask him?' Lk. xi, 13 has avoided any implication of materialism by changing 'good things' to 'the Holy Spirit'.

(4) A number of passages promise salvation not merely to a small elect of initiates, but to those who keep the Jewish law. And, corresponding to this, the law is sometimes represented as being ultimate and imperishable. Thus in Lk. xvi, 16–17 Jesus says that 'it is easier for heaven and earth to pass away than for one tittle of the law to fall'. Other passages however represent it as something ephemeral. Just before the utterance last quoted Jesus is made to say that the law and the prophets were until John the Baptist, but that since that time 'the Kingdom of God is preached'. The contradiction is much more striking in Mt. In Mt. v, 17, Jesus says: 'Think not that I came to destroy the law or the prophets: I came not to destroy, but to fulfil. For verily I say unto you, till heaven and earth pass away, one jot or one tittle shall in no wise pass away from the law, till all things be accomplished.' The expression 'the law and the prophets' designates the whole religious constitution of the OT, for 'the law' was the common Jewish name for its first five books, and 'the prophets' meant the books from Joshua to II Kings and from Isaiah to Malachi (see NBC, p. 779). Thus Jesus is saying that the most trivial commandment and the smallest letter of the law are alike imperishable. This is also stressed by what follows: 'Whosoever therefore shall break one of these least commandments, and shall teach men so, shall be called least in the kingdom of heaven.' But immediately after this unequivocal acceptance of the law, he is represented as introducing some major changes in it. The Mosaic law allows divorce, but he forbids it, except on the grounds of adultery. The law permits swearing of oaths, but he forbids it; the law says an 'eye for an eye and a tooth for a tooth', but he forbids retribution; the law enjoins love of one's neighbour, and, he implies, hatred of one's enemies; but he orders his followers to love their enemies. The incompatibilities will be clear beyond doubt if I quote one of these examples in context (verses 38–9):

Ye have heard that it was said, An eye for an eye and a tooth for a tooth. But I say unto you, Resist not him that is evil: but whosoever smiteth thee on thy right cheek, turn to him the other also.

Karl Adam admits that in these four instances Jesus 'breaks through the strict letter of the Mosaic law' but claims that its spirit is kept intact. The two most important commands of the law are said by Jesus himself to be love of God and love of one's neighbour, all the other being subordinate to these (Mt. xxii, 40). Adam infers that Jesus' amendments are therefore not true modifications, but only attempts to reach through the letter to the spirit. He is 'illuminating the Mosaic law in its deepest sense' (6, p. 87). So the real meaning of 'an eye for an eye' is 'practise universal forgiveness', and Jesus is not changing the meaning by one 'jot or tittle' when he replaces the former phrase by the latter! Adam's whole argument assumes that the Mosaic law forms a coherent whole, and is not a medley formed at different times by different hands, and also that all its stipulations aim basicly at inculcating love of God and of one's neighbour. Jesus, he says, simply rewords stipulations that do not appear to fulfil this aim so that they do.

(5) One of the most striking and persistent contradictions in the documents is that between passages which reserve salvation for the Jews and those which exclude them in favour of Samaritans or gentiles. In a few passages Mt. adopts an anti-Jewish attitude, saying for instance (viii, , 10–12) that many, but not the Jews are to be saved, and that the kingdom of God shall be taken from them and given to another nation (xxi, 43). If Jesus had really delivered such anti-nationalist teachings it is difficult to believe that he was welcomed at his entry into Jerusalem by the whole population with Hosannahs. And in fact Mt. usually makes him adopt an exclusively pro-Jewish attitude. Thus in xv, 24, Jesus justifies his initial refusal to heal the daughter of the Canaanitish woman by saying 'I am not sent but unto the lost sheep of the house of Israel'.[1] When he sends out the twelve apostles to warn people that the kingdom of heaven is at hand, he instructs them to bring their tidings neither to heathen nor Samaritans, but only

---

[1] Brandon (38a, p. 172) observes that the 'shocking intolerance' of Jesus' words here is obscured by our 'long familiarity with this story, together with the traditional picture of the gentleness of Jesus'.

to Jews (x, 5). These pro-Jewish instructions are omitted by Mk.
and Lk. And while Mt. stipulates that the Jews are to be given
another chance to repent and the Samaritans not, Lk. makes Jesus
tell the parable of the good Samaritan, where the Samaritans are
put in a most favourable and the Jews in a most unfavourable
light. This parable is told for the express purpose of indicating
'who is my neighbour', so that we shall know who is meant when
we are commanded to love our neighbour as ourself (x, 27–9). If
the anti-Samaritan precept is the utterance of Jesus, then the
pro-Samaritan parable is not; and if one of these sayings has
been falsely put into Jesus mouth, then surely it is clear how easily
anything could be.

Mt. has no occasion on which Jesus comes into contact with
Samaritans, or even mentions them, save in the prohibition
mentioned. Mk. has not even this prohibition. Lk., apart from
the parable where Jesus presents a Samaritan as a model, tells that
he healed ten lepers, and that the only one who came back to
express his gratitude was a Samaritan (Lk., xvii, 16). This is
evidently also tendentious.

Schmiedel has shown (235, § 112) that at least some of the few
anti-Jewish passages in Mt. cannot be regarded as genuine Jesuine
utterances, but were interpolated into the originally pro-Jewish
gospel. One example is Mt.'s version of the parable of the vine-
yard and the servants. It is addressed to 'the chief priests and the
elders of the people' (xxi, 23), just after Jesus has told them (verse
31) that 'the publicans and the harlots go into the kingdom of
God before you. For John came unto you in the way of righteousness, and ye believed him not: but the publicans and the harlots
believed him.' He continues, still addressing them:

> Hear another parable. There was a man that was a house-
> holder, which planteth a vineyard . . . and let it out to husband-
> men, and went into another country. And when the season of
> the fruits drew near, he sent his servants to receive his fruits.
> And the husbandmen took his servants and beat one, and killed
> another . . . Afterwards he sent unto them his son . . . And
> they took him . . . and killed him. When therefore the lord
> of the vineyard shall come, what shall he do unto those hus-
> bandmen? They say unto him, He will miserably destroy those
> miserable men, and will let out the vineyard unto other hus-
> bandmen, which shall render him the fruits in their seasons.

Jesus saith unto them, Did ye never read in the scriptures, 'The stone which the builders rejected, the same was made the head of the corner: this was from the Lord, and it is marvellous in our eyes'? *Therefore I say unto you, the kingdom of God shall be taken away from you and shall be given to a nation bringing forth the fruits thereof.* And he that falleth on this stone shall be broken to pieces; but on whomsoever it shall fall, it will scatter him as dust. And when the chief priests and the Pharisees heard his parables, they perceived that he spake of them.

Schmiedel points out that, apart from the sentence in italics, the whole indicts not the Jews but only certain classes of them, namely the chief priests, elders and Pharisees. It is they who are addressed, and the final sentence shows that they understood Jesus' words as referring to them. The verse which says that the kingdom shall be given to the gentiles is thus a later addition, as is clear from the context: for both before and after, Jesus is talking about the stone, and the interpolation breaks the connection. That the parable originally meant only the rejection of certain classes of Jews is also clear from comparison with Mk. xii, 10–12 and Lk. xx, 17–19 who omit the interpolated verse.

Mt. goes on to tell another parable, in which (xxii, 2 ff.) 'the kingdom of heaven is likened unto a certain king, which made a marriage feast for his son, and sent forth his servants to call them that were bidden to the marriage feast: and they would not come'. The text continues:

Again he sent forth other servants, saying, tell them that are bidden, behold I have made ready my dinner: my oxen and my fatlings are killed, and all things are ready: come to the marriage feast. But they made light of it and went their ways, one to his own farm, another to his merchandise: *and the rest laid hold on his servants, and entreated them shamefully and killed them. But the king was wroth; and he sent his armies, and destroyed those murderers, and burned their city.* Then saith he to his servants, the wedding is ready, but they that were bidden were not worthy. Go ye therefore unto the partings of the highways and as many as ye shall find, bid to the marriage feast. And those servants went out into the highways, and gathered together all as many as they found, both good and bad: and the wedding was filled with guests.

The passage in italics seems to have been added as an after-thought. Schmiedel's evidence for this is as follows:

(1) 'The rest', with which it begins, does not connect properly with the preceding statement that 'they went their ways'.

(2) After the military expedition, the preparations for the supper remain just as they had been, so the passage can be deleted and the text runs on naturally.

(3) In this passage the king burns the city of the guests who refused the invitation. But the rest of the parable implies that they lived in his own city.

Furthermore, the king represents the kingdom of heaven, and although a worldly king might well not only destroy those who murdered his servants, but also burn their city, such behaviour is not what one would expect from the king of heaven. Schmiedel solves this ethical difficulty by arguing (doubtless justly) that the passage is an insertion which 'points unmistakably to the destruction of Jerusalem in AD 70 as a punishment for the slaying of Jesus and his apostles'. It is only this insertion which makes plausible the usual interpretation of the parable, namely that the original guests were the Jews, and that once they rejected the kingdom it was offered to a wider circle. Without the insertion this parable, like the previous one, distinguishes not different nations, but different classes, the esteemed and the despised. And this is exactly what we find in Lk.'s version, where there is no military expedition, no burning of a city. Lk. (xiv, 16 ff.) tells not of a king but of a 'certain man' who 'made a great supper'. When the invited guests refused to come, he sent his servants to 'bring in the poor, the maimed, the blind and the lame' in their stead. Lk. is clearly boosting the poor and the weak in his usual manner. There were still some empty places, and so the servant was again sent out to compel people to come in from the highways and hedges. Commentators say that the first two classes of invited guests symbolize the esteemed and despised classes among the Jews, and that this third one represents the gentiles.

To sum up; especially striking among the contradictions of the gospel discourses is the sharp contrast between purely Jewish and gentilizing standpoints. Baur points to the fact that from time to time the twelve disciples are jealous, selfish, stupid, unsympathetic or traitorous (e.g. Mk. ix, 34, 50; Lk. ix, 46 ff). He holds that such episodes are the work of gentile sectaries who wished to be completely independent of the Jews and to this end invented stories discrediting the Jewish apostles. But later in the development of Christianity, when the Jewish Church was not so formidable a rival, stupendous miracles were attributed to them so that the prestige of the old religion should pass on to the new, and the new Church seem founded on the old (see 23, pp. 80–2).

The view that the gospel ethics form a coherent and acceptable system nevertheless persists. Cardinal Newman, for instance, endorsed Milman's statement that Jewish and pagan writers give moral truths only as 'unconnected aphorisms', whereas Jesus provides 'the groundwork of a complete system' (201, p. 240). Recently Althaus has claimed (14, p. 16) that 'all layers of the records' are permeated by such 'obviously genuine Jesuine views' as sympathy with the poor and the fallen, the publicans and sinners. He seems to have overlooked such passages as Mt. xviii, 17 and Lk. xix, 26.

(ii) The origin of the ethical discourses

Crucial changes of phrase in the two versions of the Sermon on the Mount—Mt.'s and Lk.'s—have been noted above (p. 62). Mt.'s version is also very considerably longer than Lk.'s. With Lk. the Sermon is delivered on a plain (vi, 17), whereas in Mt. Jesus addresses his disciples from on high. And at the end of Mt.'s version he is represented as having addressed not only the disciples but a multitude of people (vii, 28). Neither Lk.'s plain nor Mt.'s mountain is named. Both evangelists begin the Sermon with a series of blessings, some of which are almost verbally identical; both end with a passage containing the statement that a tree is to be known by its fruit and the parable of the house built on the sand. These parallels are as significant as the differences, and we shall have to bear both in mind when we later discuss the origin of the synoptic gospels. None of the facts so far stated excludes the possibility that the basis of both narratives, or of some parts of them, is a speech delivered by a historical figure. But the probability that either Lk.'s or Mt.'s version was ever delivered as a discourse becomes much reduced when we note that all its items have been shown to be paralleled in Jewish literature, early and late, quite independently of any Christian tradition (see the parallels quoted by Robertson, 220, pp. 404 ff.)

and that writings stringing together such ethical maxims for didactic purposes existed in the Jewish community just before the development of Christianity. Both these points can be illustrated from *The Book of the Secrets of Enoch* recovered in the form of Slavonic manuscripts. According to Charles (54) it was originally written by a Hellenistic Jew in Egypt, partly in Greek and partly in Hebrew near the beginning of the Christian era. It is thus certainly non-Christian, and earlier than any written form of the gospels (from which a Jewish author would not have borrowed, even had they been available). Some passages in it are strikingly similar to parts of the Sermon on the Mount. For instance: 'blessed is he who establishes peace' (lii, 11: cf. Mt. v, 9) and 'I will not swear by a single oath, neither by heaven, nor by earth, nor by any other creature which god made . . . If there is no truth in men, let them swear by a word, yea yea or nay nay' (xlix, 1: cf Mt. v 34–7).[1] In chapter xlii there are the following beatitudes which resemble the gospel ones in being both nine in number and also largely compiled from the Psalms, the prophets, and other Jewish literature:

Blessed is he who fears the name of the Lord, and serves continually before his face and brings his gifts with fear continually in this life and lives all his life justly and dies.

Blessed is he who executes a just judgement, not for the sake of recompense, but for the sake of righteousness, expecting nothing in return: a sincere judgement shall afterwards come to him.

Blessed is he who clothes the naked with a garment and gives his bread to the hungry.

Blessed is he who gives a just judgement for the orphan and the widow, and assists every one who is wronged.

Blessed is he who turns from the unstable path of this vain world and walks by the righteous path which leads to eternal life.

Blessed is he who sows just seed, he shall reap sevenfold.

Blessed is he in whom is the truth, that he may speak the truth to his neighbour.

Blessed is he who has love upon his lips and tenderness in his heart.

[1] We know from Philo that the Essenes forbad oaths, their conversation being 'yea, yea and nay, nay'. It is thus clear that Mt. v, 34–7 was a Jewish commonplace.

> Blessed is he who understands every work of the Lord and glorifies the Lord God: for the works of the Lord are just, and of the works of man some are good and others evil, and by their works those who have wrought them are known.

In chapter lii there is a further series of seven beatitudes alternating with curses. Charles notes that they are 'in the main derived from Ecclesiasticus'. I will quote only the first two:

> Blessed is the man who opens his lips to praise the god of the Sabaoth, and who praises the Lord with his heart. Cursed is every man who opens his lips to abuse and calumniate his neighbour.
> Blessed is he who opens his lips to the blessing and praise of God. Cursed is he who opens his lips to swearing and blasphemy before the face of the Lord all his days.

All this evidence goes to show not only that the hortatory method of the Sermon on the Mount is pre-Christian, but also that stringing together ethical maxims culled from previous Jewish lore was by no means unknown at the beginning of the Christian era. Schürer mentions the work of the scribes in compiling the Haggadah or Agadah, that portion of the Midrash which consists of an elaboration of the historical and didactic portions of the OT. Ethical treatises were composed 'by formulating dogmatic propositions from isolated prophetic utterances, by bringing these in relation to each other and thus obtaining a kind of dogmatic system' (244, ii, 1, pp. 339, 353). Hatch (135, p. 203) says the Jews who were 'carrying on an active propaganda, would have, among other books, manuals of morals, of devotion, and of controversy'; and it may be supposed, when we remember 'the contemporary habit of making collections of *excerpta*, and the special authority which the Jews attached to their sacred books, that some of these manuals would consist of extracts from the OT.' And Strack and Billerbeck (261, p. 473) remark that it is very striking how nearly all the ethical maxims of the Rabbis of the later period (i.e. the beginning of our era) are based on sacred texts, or at any rate supported by being brought into conjunction with them.

It seems quite likely that the early Christians possessed collections of OT quotations pertaining to a number of topics, not merely ethical, and that these were used for teaching purposes. Allegro (12, p. 139) notes that this theory has some backing from the fact that the Church is known to have used collections of this kind in later times, which may well be based on much earlier documents; and that the theory would account for the composite quotations to be found in the NT—where unconnected OT passages are joined as if they belonged together—and also for the ascription of passages to the wrong biblical writers where a number of *testimonia* from various places had been placed together under the name of one prophet. Thus Mt. xxi, 4 introduces a quotation with the words 'this is come to pass that it might be fulfilled which was spoken by the prophet', and then proceeds to quote a mixture of Zech. ix, 9 and Isa, lxii, 11. Again, in ii, 5 he refers to what 'is written by the prophet', and it turns out to be a mixture of Micah v, 2–4 and II Sam. v, 2. Allegro adds that new evidence on this point has been provided by the Dead Sea Scrolls, among which is a *testimonia* document, a pre-Christian collection of eschatological *testimonia*. As in the gospels, composite quotation occurs. He gives, as an example, Deut. v, 28–9, fused with Deut. xxviii, 18 in such a way as to make both refer to the coming Messiah. The existence of such composite quotations, then, suggests that we have, in them, relics of manuals which consisted of extracts from the sacred books.

Finally, the contradictions of the gospel teachings become intelligible when we note the extent to which Palestine was divided into factions with different ideas about the Messiah, in the first decades of the first century AD. Graetz characterizes this period as one when the belief in the advent of the Messiah swayed all classes of the nation, excepting the aristocracy and those who clung to Rome:

> During the short space of thirty years a number of enthusi-
> astic mystics appeared who, without any intention to deceive
> and bent upon removing the load of care and sorrow that
> weighed so heavily upon the people, assumed the character of
> prophet or Messiah, and found disciples who followed their
> banner faithfully unto death. But though it appears that every
> Messiah attracted ready believers, no one was acknowledged
> as such by the whole nation. The incessant friction between the
> various communities and the deep study of the sacred books,
> had awakened a critical spirit difficult to satisfy. The nation was

split into many parties, each entertaining a different idea of the future saviour, and rendering it therefore impossible that any one aspirant should receive general recognition as the Messiah.

The factions included the republican Zealot party, the disciples of Judas of Galilee, who were opposed to any form of obedience to the Romans. They pictured the Messiah as delivering Israel from his enemies by the breath of his mouth (as was expected of Jesus, see II Thess. ii, 8), destroying the Roman Empire and restoring the golden era of David's kingdom. Then there was the school of Shammai, a Rabbi who had carried Pharisaic principles to an extreme. His followers expected of the Messiah ardent religious zeal and perfect moral purity, in addition to the expectations entertained by the Zealots. There were also the followers of Hillel, who were less fanatical, and expected a prince of peace, who would bring tranquillity to the country and harmonize its relations with all the neighbouring states. Also there were the ascetic Essenes who declared that they would follow one who led a pure and spotless life, who renounced the vanities of the world (108, pp. 143–5). We shall later see that the gospel passages which reserve salvation for the elect are in line with Essene teaching, while the pro-Jewish passages harmonize with the standpoint of the Zealots.[1] The gentilizing passages represent an attempt to make the new religion appeal to the Greek-speaking gentiles of Asia Minor, where Paul had preached with such effect.

Theologians today are apt to accept Conzelmann's cautious dictum (64, vol. III, column 623) that utterances of the gospel Jesus which reflect neither Jewish standpoints, nor the opinions of early Christian communities, may be taken as genuine. But as both Jews and Christians were divided into so many factions, the application of this criterion can leave but a meagre residue.

(iii) **Jesus as prophet**

(a) *The development of the Jewish Messianic hope*

The gospels contain a number of discourses about the end of the world and the phenomena connected with it, namely the appearance of the Messiah, the final judgement and the resurrection.

[1] On the significance of the fact that one of the twelve disciples of Jesus is named 'Simon the Zealot', see Brandon (38, pp. 104–5). Brandon does not believe that the twelve were chosen by Jesus (cf. below, p. 149)

These will be more intelligible if we first study the development of the Messianic hope among the Jews. In the following summary I have drawn extensively on Schürer's very lucid account (244, II, II, p. 128 ff.), and on the work of Charles.

The Jews believed that God had given them laws and had at the same time bound himself to bestow his benefits upon them provided they observed these laws. Since neither individuals nor the nation as a whole seemed to receive the benefits in the proportion expected, it was assumed that they would be forthcoming at some future time. Thus looking forward to a happier future formed the core of the Jews' religious ideas from very early times. The original idea was that the nation would have a better future. The older prophets hoped that it would be morally purified from all bad elements, that its enemies would be destroyed, that it would be governed by a just, wise and powerful king of the house of David. Later the future hope was extended from the nation to the world, and with this enlargement of it is combined a far more decided reference of it to the individual. This change was doubtless caused by the breaking down of the tribal barriers and the absorption of the nation in a large empire (first the Greek and then the Roman). In the older days religion could still be a national, not an individual matter. The tribe could expect its God to succour it in affairs which concerned the well-being of all, such as the growth of its crops or its fortunes in war. But when the nation ceased to exist as an independent unit the deity could no longer be a tribal appurtenance, and, as the God and ruler of all men, he would be regarded as favouring not a particular tribe but rather particular individuals. As individuals were dying all the time, and as the virtuous were no less mortal than the wicked, the hope of a blessed future could no longer remain in the form of an expectation of earthly bliss, from which the dead would have been excluded. It had to become a belief in individual resurrection after death. While the belief related only to Israel as a nation there was no need for it to be supramundane. The nation would always be there to benefit from its fulfilment. But once the expectation had been transferred from the nation to the individual, it was necessary to provide for the virtuous dead.

Another consequence of the absorption of the nation in a large empire was the birth of the ideas that the whole existing world would be destroyed by a miraculous act and that God would inaugurate his kingdom with a universal judgement of the living and dead. These ideas are expressed in the Jewish apocalypses which succeeded the prophetic literature. The latter had promised the nation a speedy delivery from political and moral ills, and had prophesied fighting and great affliction before this would occur, but nothing in the way of supernatural catastrophes. The apocalypses, however, foretell a deliverance accompanied by the stars falling from heaven and the whole natural order passing away. It is not difficult to see how this type of writing sprang from the changed world situation of the Jews. When the prophets wrote, the world they knew consisted of God's people, a number of small nations (Edom, Moab, Syria) and the two large powers of Egypt and Assyria at opposite ends of the geographical horizon. The Jews could measure their strength with the small kingdoms, and even the two large ones were so countered by one another that Israel could always turn to the one for protection against the other. But with the rise of Alexander the Great's Empire, which extended from Greece to Persia, and later with the even more extensive Roman dominion, the Jews found themselves facing a situation where political independence was out of the question. The old hope of national prosperity had to fade, and it was not surprising that they should begin to think that only a cosmic act of God would have the power to break the vast empires oppressing them. However, even at the beginning of our era, the old hope of a glorious future for the nation was still alive, so that the ideas of these later times were a mixture of conflicting expectations. Old ideas survived alongside newer ones, as always.

What part did the idea of the Messiah play in this development? The Hebrew word means 'anointed', and was originally used to designate kings and high priests, who were always anointed with oil. Saul, the first Israelite king, is called 'the Lord's anointed' (I Sam. xxiv, 6) and even Cyrus, the king of the Persians, is called this by Isaiah (xlv, 1). Thus the term did not, at this stage, signify a future redeemer, but denoted the reigning king, and is used frequently in the historical books of the OT to refer to Saul and David. The word 'Messiah' does not occur at all in the OT or Apocrypha in the sense of a redeemer who is to come. It is used in this sense for the first time in the book of Enoch.

The inadequacies of the reigning kings caused the Jews to look forward to a future which would bring them more worthy monarchs. Isaiah, for instance, spoke the well known prophecies which begin 'for unto us a child is born' (ix, 6) and 'there shall come forth a shoot out of the stock of Jesse' (xi, 1). Klausner thinks that they refer to Hezekiah, son of king Ahaz who was reigning at the time, and that Isaiah was expressing the hope that the son would be a better king than the father. He notes that the Jews in the time of Justin Martyr still interpreted the prophecies in this way (161, p. 56 and note; 157, Chapters 43, 67, 68, 71). Micah too, also about 700 BC, looked forward to a strong king who would soon come and deliver the nation from the Assyrians (v, 5).

In the Psalms the phrase 'thy anointed' is used to denote the reigning king or the Davidic king as such without reference to a particular person. Three psalms which Klausner (161, p. 140) classes among the earliest contain the assurance that the throne of David will be established for ever. But by the time the Psalter became a liturgical handbook, the historical kingship had been brought to an end by Nebuchadnezzar's destruction of Jerusalem in 586 BC, and the transportation of the nation into captivity at Babylon. The pious Jews could not, however, believe that the references in their sacred books were simply to a historical situation that was over and done with; and so they 'looked again for an anointed king to whom the words of the sacred hymns should apply with a force never realized in the imperfect kingship of the past. Thus the psalms, especially such psalms as the second, were necessarily viewed as prophetic; and meantime, in accordance with the common Hebrew representation of ideal things as existing in heaven, the true king remains hidden with God' (58, § 1).

The second Psalm represents the whole world as organized against the Lord in deliberate opposition to his rule:

> Why do the nations rage,
> And the peoples imagine a vain thing?
> The kings of the earth set themselves,
> And the rulers take counsel together
> Against the Lord and against his anointed.

The NBC (p. 415) states that 'this is generally regarded as a Messianic Psalm, but was almost certainly based upon a historical occasion, such as that recorded in II Sam. v, 17 or x, 6'—the attack of the Philistines and of the Syrians on David. So the reference to the Lord's anointed which at first meant the existing king, came in time to be understood as referring to the future

Messiah. According to the same authority (p. 905), this interpretation of the second Psalm first appears in the seventeenth *Psalm
of the Pharisees*, (also known as the *Psalms of Solomon*), i.e. about
45 BC (see 216 and below, pp. 83, 325). We have already seen
that the first occurrence of the word Messiah in the sense of an
expected redeemer occurs in Enoch—according to Klausner and
others, in that part of Enoch written in the time of Herod the
Great. Thus, by the first century BC, the development which we
have been tracing in the meaning of the word 'Messiah' had
occurred.

David, the son of Jesse and the second Israelite king, naturally
became the prototype of the Messiah. His political skill in unifying
the tribes of Israel, his heroism and his victories made him in the
eyes of the people the greatest political saviour of all those who
defended Israel at any time (161, pp. 19–20). Thus 'son of David'
became a standing title of the King-Messiah. But the way in which
Messianic ideas fluctuated and became adapted to the circumstances of different ages is well illustrated by the thrusting aside
of this idea when the victories of the Hasmonean dynasty reached
their peak in the first century BC. At this time, a number of works
(e.g. the *Book of Jubilees*) allege that the Messiah is of the house of
Levi; the house, that is, of the Hasmoneans John Hyrcanus and
Alexander Jannaeus. Later, after Pompey had conquered Jerusalem, the *Psalms of the Pharisees* revert to the old idea of the
Messiah as the son of David, and criticize the Hasmoneans
harshly.

With the rise of the apocalyptic literature it was possible to
regard the Messiah as a supernatural being. We have seen how the
Jews came to think that only a supernatural act, involving the
destruction of the whole natural order, could liberate them from
the empires oppressing them. Although they could continue to
think of their Messianic king as a mortal who would be aided by
God's destruction of the heathen, they might equally well begin
to imagine him as a purely supernatural figure who would descend
from heaven in the last days in order to judge mankind and bring
the world to an end. Maybe some Jewish visionary, seeing things
get worse instead of better, proclaimed that no human leader
could be strong enough to rectify them, and that the foretold
redeemer must therefore be one of the angels in whom, and in
whose powers, the Jews firmly believed. Or, more likely, one
visionary proclaimed a powerful redeemer he himself regarded

as human, but some of his audience misunderstood him, and thought that the person described as having such powers must be one of these angelic beings. We shall see that misunderstandings of this kind have played an important part in the development of religious ideas. Even at the latest stage older ideas survived, so that in NT times some people seem to have looked for a human Messianic leader to free the nation from Roman yoke while others awaited a divine personage who would descend from the skies.[1]

In sum, then, the term 'Messiah' originally meant any anointed person, but came in time to mean a particular individual who was expected. Among the early Christians a further development occurred. The Septuagint and the Greek NT both render the term as 'Christos', and this came to mean not only the title of a particular person, but also to stand for his name. Many of the early Christians were gentiles who read their OT in Greek. Psalm II talks of 'the Lord and his Christ'. When 'Christ' came to be understood as a proper name, such passages were naturally regarded as prophetic references to Jesus. In some NT passages 'Christ' is still a title (e.g. 'God made him both Lord and Christ', Acts, ii, 36), but in others it is a name. Bousset remarks that already in the Pauline letters it has practically lost the significance of a title. 'Some consciousness of this significance seems to be preserved when Paul says, as he usually does, "the Christ Jesus", and only very rarely "Jesus Christ"; and when he puts the name Jesus in the middle in using a second title: "Lord Jesus Christ" ' (36, p. 77).

(b) *Ezekiel, Daniel, Enoch and Baruch*

Let us supplement this sketch of the development of the future hope with a survey of the books in which it is expressed. Ezekiel said about 580 BC that Israel was about to experience its last trials, ushering in an era of unclouded prosperity. He describes the mustering of the forces of Gog, their attack on Israel and their overthrow which, we are told, will serve as a lesson to the nations who henceforth will no longer molest Israel (xxxviii–xxxix). The final chapters tell how the nation is to dwell for ever in peace in its own land under its kings. Another prophet of this

---

[1] The expectation that the Messiah would he human is betrayed by Justin Martyr when he makes Trypho the Jew say: 'we all expect that the Christ will come into being as a man from men' (157, Chapter 49).

period, Jeremiah, promised that after seventy years the people should be restored from Babylonian captivity to their own land and there enjoy the blessings of the Messianic kingdom under the Davidic king (xxiii, 5–6: xxix, 10). After the return to Jerusalem from the captivity, Zechariah sadly admits (i, 12) that the seventy years have passed and that there is still no sign of the kingdom, but he promised that when the temple was rebuilt the glories of the Messianic time would come.

The book of Daniel attempts to explain away these failures. The writer interprets (ix, 24) the seventy years of Jeremiah as seventy weeks of years, i.e. each seven years are to count as one week so that in all 490 years will be required. He represents sixty nine and a half as having already expired, so there was only half a week (three and a half years) before the advent of the kingdom and the destruction of the empire oppressing the Jews. There is general agreement that Daniel's reference here is to the Greek Empire of the Seleucids, and that the work was written about 165 BC. It treats the reign of the Syrian Seleucid ruler Antiochus IV (Ephiphanes) in great detail, and was written while his repressive reforms in Palestine were in full swing. He was determined to hellenize all his empire, and in 168 he even marched into Egypt, but was met by envoys from Rome who required him to withdraw at once. Enraged and embittered, he resolved to devote all his power to hellenizing Judaea. He forbade the observance of the sabbath and the practice of the rite of circumcision; he laid waste the temple and had a heathen altar set up on the site of the great altar of burnt offerings in honour of Zeus, whereupon the Jews began the famous Maccabean rebellion. Daniel refers to the way in which the Roman forces, 'the ships of Kittim', compelled him to leave Egypt, and also to the statue of Zeus which his agents set up (xi, 30–1).

In chapter vii we learn that Daniel dreamed he saw 'four great beasts come up from the sea, diverse from one another' and representing the four heathen empires under which he supposes the Jews to have successively suffered (vii, 1–3, 17). Howie (142, p. 90) notes that the 'underlying assumption of the book is that the chronological order of the empires was Chaldean, Median, Persian and Greek', although in fact 'there is no chronological place for a Median Empire between the Chaldean and Persian'. The sea from which the beasts emerge is here, as so often in Jewish literature, a symbol of evil. 'It was thought that, if it were not for the restraining power of God, evil would break forth from the great deep' (142, p. 118). The fourth beast, representing the Seleucid empire as created by Antiochus, is 'terrible and powerful and strong exceedingly: and it had great iron teeth: it devoured and brake in pieces and stamped the residue with its feet' (vii, 7). It is a monster with ten horns, each one standing for a monarch (the ten predecessors of Antiochus, beginning with Alexander the Great). In the midst of these ten is 'another horn, a little one' —Antiochus himself—which blasphemes against true religion. This monster triumphs until the saints against whom he contends finally overcome him. 'I beheld, and the same horn made war with the saints, and prevailed against them until the ancient of days came, and judgement was given to the saints of the Most High; and the time came that the saints possessed the kingdom' (vii, 21–2).

As the kingdoms of the world are represented by beasts from the sea, so is the kingdom of the saints represented in the vision by a human form which descends from clouds of heaven. The coming up of the former from the sea indicates their evil nature, while the human form and heavenly origin of the latter indicate that he is divine. The text reads: 'I saw in the night visions, and behold there came with clouds of heaven one like unto a son of man . . . And there were given him dominion and glory and a kingdom, that all the peoples, nations and languages should serve him; his dominion is everlasting' (vii, 13–14). The apparition in human form, then, is simply a symbolical way of representing the 'saints of the Most High'. It is they to whom the kingdom is given, as the writer goes on to note when he explains the symbols he has been using. The core of Daniel's Messianic hope is thus the universal and eternal dominion of the saints. He thinks that this will be set up not merely by a judicial sentence of God, but by actual fighting between the saints and the others (ii, 44), so that the last times are to be characterized by universal strife. Nevertheless, 'at that time thy people shall be delivered, every one that shall be found written in the book' (xii, 1). The next verse expresses the hope of the resurrection of the body—the first clear and unambiguous expression of it in Messianic literature. 'And many of them that sleep in the dust of the earth shall awake, some to everlasting life, and some to shame and everlasting contempt.' Hence here, as formerly, the Messianic hope is that of a glorious future for the nation, but with the double modification that the future kingdom is conceived as a universal one, and that all the saints who have died will share in it.

The next attempt at reinterpretation was the book of Enoch. Both Daniel and Enoch are pseudonymous works. The author of the former pretends to have lived in the sixth century BC so that what he says about Antiochus Epiphanes is represented as prophecy. The book of Enoch purports to come from the hand of the Patriarch Enoch, the seventh in descent from Adam, but is now regarded as a composite work written in the second and first centuries BC. Pseudonymous works were then quite common, for when the prophetic canon was closed (about 200 BC), new prophetic books had to be regarded as ancient works if they were to be admitted to the sacred writings. The book of Enoch greatly influenced the early Christians but later fell into discredit and then disappeared altogether until an Ethiopic version was found about 150 years ago. Its influence on the NT appears in the epistle of Jude, the author of which accepts it as the work of 'Enoch' and quotes it as a reliable authority. Burkitt thought that when such pseudonymous works were rejected in ancient times it was on grounds of doctrine rather than of historical scepticism, 'although we may gather from Tertullian that some people did wonder how the book of Enoch escaped the flood' (45, p. 18).

The work depicts the coming Messianic times in very sensuous terms:

And then shall all the righteous escape, and shall live till they beget thousands of children . . . And then shall the whole earth be tilled in righteousness, and shall all be planted with trees and be full of blessing. And all desirable trees shall be planted on it, and they shall plant vines on it; and the vine which they plant thereon shall yield wine in abundance, and as for all the seed which is sown thereon, each measure of it shall bear a thousand, and each measure of olives shall yield ten presses of oil (x, 17–19. See Charles' edn., 56).

In later chapters (lxxxv–xc) the author has a dream vision of the history of the world up to the founding of the Messianic kingdom. He reviews the calamities that befall Israel from the exile onwards, and asks why it is that the nation is overrun by one gentile power after another and suffers far more than it deserved. He explains that these undue severities are not the work of God but of the seventy shepherds or angels into whose care he committed Israel. They have proved faithless to their trust and have destroyed the good, but they will be duly punished. Moreover, when the outlook is darkest and the oppression at its worst, a righteous league will be established and will include a family from which will come forth the deliverer, i.e. Judas Maccabeus. All the gentile nations will assemble for their final struggle against Israel, but God will appear in person, and the earth open its mouth and swallow them up. The new Jerusalem will be set up by God himself, and the surviving gentiles will be converted and serve Israel. The Jews dispersed abroad will be gathered together, and the righteous dead raised to take part in the kingdom. All this section of the book was obviously written in support of a Maccabean movement. As in Daniel, the end of the world is believed to be at hand. And just as Daniel reinterpreted Jeremiah's prophecy of the coming of the kingdom in seventy years to mean 490 years, so Enoch's idea of the seventy shepherds seems to be another reinterpretation of this old prophecy: the seventy years of Jeremiah are taken to denote the successive reigns of the seventy angelic patrons to whom God had committed the care of the world, and whose sway was visibly coming to an end.

The second section of the book, called the parables or similitudes of Enoch, contains his vision of the coming judgement, at which 'the kings and the mighty rulers of the earth perish, and be given into the hands of the righteous and holy' (xxviii, 5). While in Daniel it is God who sits in judgement, Enoch speaks of it being effected by a supernatural being he calls 'the Son of man'. He sits on God's throne (li, 3), possesses universal dominion (lxii, 6) and all judgement is committed to him (lxix, 9). This idea seems to be based on a misunderstanding of Daniel's seventh chapter. Daniel had spoken of one coming down from heaven in the form of a man. This was, for him, an allegorical way of representing the kingdom of the saints, while the heathen empires that had successively oppressed Israel he represented as animals which rise up from the sea (see above, p. 80). Enoch has mistaken the term 'Son of man' for a title of the Messiah. In Daniel the title is indefinite, 'like a son of man', but in Enoch it is made to refer to one person, '*the* Son of man'. Thus Enoch takes the coming down from heaven quite literally, so that the Messiah is, for him, no mortal but a supernatural being who comes down from on high. The misunderstanding is the more striking, as the book of

Daniel contains no definite allusion to a Messiah, but only looks forward to the rule of the saints. And the NT has preserved Enoch's blunder; like him, it tells of a Messiah who will come down from heaven, and calls him the 'Son of man'. Thus Jn. iii, 13 tells us that the Son of man came down from heaven, Mt. ix, 6 that he can forgive sins, and Jn. v, 22, 27 that all judgement is committed unto him.

Enoch's picture of the final judgement is strikingly similar to that given by Mt. (xxv, 31–46). Enoch says that 'the Lord of Spirits seated the Elect one on the throne of his glory'; Mt. reads: 'When the Son of man shall come in his glory . . . then shall he sit on the throne of his glory.' Both writers go on to describe how the righteous are vindicated while the rest are banished to flame and torment. Burkitt recognizes 'a real literary connection' here and declares that 'the one picture is evidently an adaptation of the other' (45, p. 24). Thus in the view of this eminent scholar, the passage in Mt. represents not the report of a discourse delivered by Jesus, but a literary adaptation of a Jewish work, which is then put into his mouth.

Another work written in the second century BC is *Ecclesiasticus*, also known as *The Wisdom of Jesus the Son of Sirach*. The author was a Palestinian Jew, and he believed that in the last days Elijah would return to earth (xlviii, 10–11). This idea had been expressed as early as the fourth century by Malachi (iv, 5), the last of the minor prophets. Jewish apocalyptic ideas may be further followed through the OT Apocrypha, the Psalms of the Pharisees (composed in the time of Pompey, 63–48 BC), the Assumption of Moses, written by a Pharisee at the beginning of our era, the Book of the Jubilees, and finally the apocalypses of Baruch and Ezra (viz. II Baruch and IV Ezra) representing the later part of the first century AD. During this interval the Greek Empire had been replaced by the Roman. Accordingly, 'the fourth and last Empire which, according to Daniel vii, 19–25, was to be Greek, was now declared to be Roman by the writer of II Baruch (xxxvi–xl) and likewise by the author of IV Ezra (x–xii)' (57, p. 29).

In the apocalypse of Baruch we find once again the idea that the last days will be heralded by a time of general and terrible confusion and fighting, including 'slayings of the great ones, the fall of many by death, famine and the withholding of rain, earthquakes' and other horrors (Chapter xxvii). Those who escape these ills will be delivered into the hands of the Messiah (xxix, 3).

He will destroy the hosts of the last of the empires oppressing Israel, take their last surviving prince captive to Zion, and kill him. He will, however, grant life to those who have submitted to the seed of Jacob. Then will come a period of universal peace and contentment:

> The earth . . . will yield its fruit ten thousandfold, and on one vine there will be a thousand branches, and each branch will produce a thousand clusters, and each cluster will produce a thousand grapes, and each grape will produce a cor [75 gallons] of wine (xxix, 5).

This passage seems to be an elaboration of the description in the book of Enoch (see above, p. 81) and was in due course ascribed to Jesus, who was represented as delivering the doctrine in a discourse. Thus Irenaeus, in the second century AD, musing on the millennium, speaks of

> The times of the kingdom, when the just, rising from the dead, will reign, when the created order will be made new and set free, and will produce an abundance of all kinds of food, from the dew of heaven and of the fertility of the earth. So the elders remembered, who had seen John the disciple of the Lord, that they had heard from him *how the Lord taught about those days and said*: 'The days will come in which vine will be produced, each one having a thousand branches, and in each branch ten thousand twigs, and on each twig ten thousand shoots, and on each shoot ten thousand clusters, and in each cluster ten thousand grapes, and each grape when pressed will give twenty-five meters of wine' . . . Papias, who was a hearer of John and an associate of Polycarp, a fine old man, bore witness to these things in writing . . . (146, p. 394).

This has every appearance of being a well authenticated saying of Jesus, for Irenaeus quotes Papias, who claims to have heard it at second hand from John who heard it delivered by Jesus. Yet it is obvious that Jesus said nothing of the sort, that Papias drew his exposition from the apocalypse of Baruch, which in turn imitated the Book of Enoch.

To sum up, we may say that in the first century AD the Jews expected the final period before the appearance of the Messiah to be a time of special tribulation; they expected the return of Elijah (some texts hold that he will anoint the Messiah and raise the dead). The Messiah himself they designated by various titles (the Anointed, the Christ, the Elect, the Son of man, son of David). Some expected him to be a human being, others awaited a super-natural figure. Some thought he would appear suddenly as a victorious ruler, others that he would be known as a child in Bethle-hem. According to Schürer, the belief that he would authenticate himself by miracles was universal. And the heathen were expected to assemble against him for the last attack.

(c) *The apocalyptic discourses of the gospels*

Turning now to the gospels, we find that many of these ideas find expression in them. Jesus is repeatedly represented as grounding his Messianic claim on his miracles, and he strengthens it by designating John the Baptist as 'Elijah which is to come' (Mt. xi, 14). If Jesus was to be regarded as the Messiah, then it would have to be shown that Elijah had already returned to earth, and assign-ing this dignity to the Baptist was the method adopted of solving the difficulty.

The idea that the coming of the Messiah will be preceded by a time of tribulation illuminates a number of gospel discourses that seem obscure or even disturbing. Jesus says: 'I am come to set a man at variance against his father and the daughter against her mother, and the daughter-in-law against her mother-in-law; and a man's foes shall be of his own household' (Mt. x, 35–6). This is a quotation from Micah vii, 6, and is taken by Mt. to refer to the woe which must necessarily precede the advent of the Messiah. The Talmud too says: 'With the footprints of the Messiah in-solence will increase and dearth reach its height . . . The young will insult the elders', and the writer then quotes the passage from Micah for support (see 161, p. 443).

Many more of the current Messianic ideas are given in Mt. xxiv, where Jesus prophesies the destruction of the temple at Jerusalem. The disciples then ask him: 'When shall these things be? And what shall be the sign of thy coming and of the end of the world?' He replies that, before the end, false Christs will arise, 'nation shall rise against nation . . . and there shall be famines and earth-quakes'. Here we have the idea that the last times will be a period of universal tribulation. He goes on to say (verse 14) that the end will not come until the gospel has been preached to the whole world. This does not harmonize with the discourse as a whole, which, as we shall see, stresses that the end is at hand. In what follows he connects it with what he was originally talking about, namely the destruction of the temple:

> When therefore ye see the abomination of desolation which was spoken of by Daniel the prophet, standing in the holy place (let him that readeth understand), then let them that are in Judaea flee unto the mountains . . . for then shall be great tribulation, such as hath not been from the beginning of the world until now, no, nor ever shall be. And except those days had been shortened no flesh would have been saved; but for the elect's sake those days shall be shortened.

Mt. is clearly reinterpreting Daniel's 'prophecy', just as Daniel had those of Jeremiah. Daniel's abomination of desolation was the statue erected by Antiochus in the temple. Mt.'s reference may be to the 'expressed intention of the emperor Caligula—which in AD 40 threw the whole Jewish world into the greatest excitement —to cause a statue of himself to be erected in the temple' (235, § 124b); or it may mean the capture and destruction of Jerusalem by the Romans in AD 70. Josephus (154, x, 11, 7) regarded the prophecy as fulfilled in the Roman siege. In either case, Mt.'s prophecy was, just as clearly as Daniel's, made after the event, and, as we shall see, Lk. appears to have been writing at a still later date and reinterpreting the data he found before him. Mt. goes on to specify the signs which will herald the parousia or second advent, the appearance of the Messiah, called here the Son of man, coming on the clouds:

> But immediately, after the tribulation of those days, the sun shall be darkened and the moon shall not give her light, and the stars shall fall from heaven, and the powers of the heavens shall be shaken: and then shall appear the sign of the Son of man in heaven: and then shall all the tribes of the earth mourn, and they shall see the Son of man coming on the clouds of heaven with power and great glory. And he shall send forth his angels with a great sound of a trumpet, and they shall gather together his elect from the four winds, from one end of heaven to the other.

These signs, he adds, will herald the coming of the Son of man as unambiguously as the fresh foliage on the fig tree is a sign of summer (verses 32-3). Finally he gives warning that 'this generation shall not pass away till all these things be accomplished'.

It is clear that he is here identifying two distinct occurrences, the destruction of the temple and the end of the world. The latter event is to occur 'immediately' after the former (verse 29), and both within the lifetime of the existing generation. This has, of course, caused commentators embarrassment, and they usually allege that Mt. has fused together distinct discourses, in one of which was foretold the destruction of the city and in the other the end of the world. But even this analysis leaves us with a Jesus who regarded the end of the world as imminent. And that he did expect the second coming to occur within the lifetime of some of his auditors is alleged in a number of other passages, e.g. Mt. xvi, 27-8.

Recently Bultmann has admitted that Jesus held these views and was therefore deluded (42, pp. 4, 22). He adds, however, that Jesus' message is 'free from all the learned and fanciful speculation of apocalyptic writers. Jesus does not look back as they did upon the past periods, casting up calculations when the end is coming; he does not bid men peer after signs in nature and the affairs of nations by which they might recognize the nearness of the end'. Does he not? How else are we to interpret the references to the abomination of desolation, and his association of the end of the world with the destruction of the temple? Bultmann is admitting that the gospels constitute one more Jewish apocalypse. Yet he would also affirm that they are superior to their predecessors, and the result is special pleading.

Bornkamm argues that Jesus taught that 'the commencement of the reign of God is an unobtrusive occurrence within this time and world', and that 'no man is to delude himself by supposing that he can discover visible signs to foretell what is to come' (33, p. 67). He quotes Lk. xvii, 21 (without noticing that this passage contradicts others where Jesus specifies momentous signs that will attend the coming of the kingdom) and he misinterprets Lk. xii, 54-6, where Jesus is complaining that, although people can anticipate the weather from the look of the sky or the direction of the wind, they fail to read the obvious signs that the world is about to end. Jesus is here urging them to look out for signs presaging the end, but Bornkamm supposes that he is discouraging them from doing so. To support this interpretation he refers to Mk. xiii, 21, but ignores verse 24 where Jesus specifies the signs presaging the end. Bornkamm is anxious to represent the historical Jesus as a quiet, gentle person who refused to legitimate himself with signs of power. In the interest of this thesis, he declares that even Jesus' apocalyptic discourses are 'sober' compared with other apocalyptic literature, and also superior in that they 'forego painting the terrors and joys of the world to come', and simply stress that 'God will reign' (33, pp. 60–1). This is not altogether true. The 'goats' are ordered off to 'the eternal fire which is prepared for the devil and his angels' (Mt. xxv, 41). Admittedly there are more details in, e.g. the apocryphal *Apocalypse of Peter*, where we are told that women guilty of abortion will be submerged up to their necks in boiling excrement, that girls who lost their virginity before marriage will have their flesh torn to pieces, and so on (147, p. 517). Bornkamm seems to wish to imply that the relative restraint of the canonical evangelists means that Jesus did actually speak the words they ascribe to him. If so, is what he said true, is eternal punishment in fire a reality, or was he deluded?

Even the hypothesis that the discourse in Mt. xxiv was delivered by a deluded visionary, rather than by a divine or divinely inspired personage, does not meet all the difficulties. It is too full of contradictions to have been delivered as it stands. Thus, after having explained, in the passages quoted, that the parousia is to be heralded by unmistakable signs, Jesus goes on to allege that it will take the world by surprise. After having stated that it will be preceded by universal strife and confusion, he goes on to say that it will catch men eating, drinking and enjoying themselves (verses 36–42).

Comparison of this chapter with the corresponding one in Lk. shows that Lk. was writing at a later date. Mt. identifies the 'last times' with the erection of 'the abomination of desolation'; when this event occurs, the faithful will know that it is time to flee into the mountains, and 'immediately after the tribulation of those days' Jesus will come 'on the clouds of heaven with power and great glory'. Lk., however, places the last times later. He skilfully makes the prophecy of Daniel about the setting up of a foreign image in the temple refer to the destruction of Jerusalem, changing Mt.'s 'abomination of desolation standing in the holy place' into 'the desolation of Jerusalem', effected by the armies encompassing it. And after describing the fall of the city as the result of a siege, he makes Jesus declare—not that the end of the world will follow immediately, but that the gentiles will trample down the city 'until their times are fulfilled' (xxi, 24). Then will come a time of 'distress'—not, however, now for Israel but for the gentiles, and amidst convulsions of nature the Son of man will come. The 'immediately' of Mt. xxiv, 29 has disappeared in Lk. xxi, 25, and so has Mt.'s statement that the days preceding the end shall be shortened for the elect's sake. Here are the relevant parts of the two accounts side by side.

Mt.	*Lk.*
When therefore ye see the abomination . . . standing in the holy place . . . then let them that are in Judaea flee into the mountains . . . for then shall be great tribulation such as hath not been from the beginning of the world . . . And except those days had been shortened no flesh would have been saved; but for the elect's sake those days shall be shortened . . . But immediately after the tribulation of those days the sun shall be darkened and the moon shall not give forth her light and the stars shall fall from heaven, and the powers of the heavens shall be shaken . . . and they shall see the Son of man coming on the clouds of heaven with power and great glory . . .	But when ye see Jerusalem compassed with armies then know that her desolation is at hand. Then let them that are in Judaea flee unto the mountains . . . for there shall be great distress upon the land and wrath unto this people. And they shall be led captive into all the nations: and Jerusalem shall be trodden down of the gentiles until the times of the gentiles be fulfilled. And there shall be signs in sun, moon and stars and upon the earth distress of nations . . . for the powers of the heavens shall be shaken. And then shall they see the Son of man coming in a cloud with power and great glory. But when these things begin to come to pass, look up, and lift up your hands because your redemption draweth high . . .
Verily . . . this generation shall not pass away till all these things be accomplished.	Verily . . . this generation shall not pass away till all things be accomplished.

Lk. then, like Daniel, Enoch, Mt. and all the apocalyptic writers, expects the end of the world soon. But unlike Mt. he represents it as being separated by a longish interval from the destruction of Jerusalem. From these facts we may infer that, while Mt. wrote soon after the destruction of the city, Lk. wrote many years later, at a time when its destruction could no longer be regarded as a recent event (235, § 153).

We find that Mk. has adapted Mt.'s predictions in a similar way. Mt. xvi, 27–8 makes Jesus say: 'For the Son of man shall come in the glory of his Father with his angels, and then he shall render unto every man according to his deeds. Verily I say unto you; there be some standing here which shall in no wise taste of death till they see the Son of man coming in his kingdom.' In Mk. ix, 1 the first sentence of Mt's version has been deleted, and the rest has become: 'There be some here . . . which shall in no wise taste of death till they see the kingdom of God come with power.' Mt.'s version, in which Jesus predicts that his contemporaries will see him return in person, is clearly the earlier; Mk. gives a more guarded form of it—one that might be said to have been fulfilled in the spread of the Church. Most of the canonical Mk. is however earlier than Mt. and formed, as we shall see, one of his sources. In this context I wish only to show from their discrepancies that the apocalyptic discourses of the gospels are not reports of utterances of a historical Jesus but literary concoctions which put into his mouth the beliefs of the writers, following the method adopted from Daniel onwards. This is not to accuse the gospel writers of fraud. Like other historians of the period they did not shrink from making up speeches out of what seemed to them authentic materials. Instead of saying 'The general purport of Jesus' teaching was as follows' they expressed themselves more naïvely: 'Jesus said'.

Schweitzer has tried to prove that some of the gospel speeches about the end of the world, far from being mythical are decisive evidence for Jesus' historicity. He constructs a Jesus who believed —at any rate at the time when he sent out the apostles to preach the advent of the kingdom—that the world would end within months, not years. Mt. x, 23 represents him as saying as he sends them out: 'Ye shall not have gone through the cities of Israel till the Son of man be come.' But, says Schweitzer, this prophecy was not fulfilled; the disciples returned to him, and the Son of man had not come down from the skies to bring the world to an end (247, p. 356). Also, when he sent them out, he prophesied that they would suffer persecution, yet they returned unharmed. Schweitzer's point is that, since Mt. goes on to show that these prophecies were not fulfilled, the whole speech in which they are made must be historical. For no evangelist would invent a speech full of prophecies and then go on to provide the evidence that they were bogus.

This argument will not hold if Mt. is to be regarded as a composite document, as separate pieces connected by an editor unconscious of their contradictions. Furthermore, Schweitzer obviously envisages the disciples making a hasty tour of the cities, rushing from one to another with their brief proclamation that the kingdom was at hand. He thinks that Jesus himself urged haste upon them by telling them to take only a minimum of money and equipment: 'Get you no gold, nor silver nor brass in your purses; no wallet for your journey, neither two coats, nor shoes nor staff' (Mt. x, 9–10). The underlying idea is, Schweitzer says, that they will not need provisions and changes of clothing because the end of the world is so near. But in the text Jesus gives a quite different reason for his injunction: they are to travel light because 'the labourer is worthy of his food', i.e. because they have the right to claim financial support from those they convert. The conversion is obviously going to be a long business, for Jesus warns them that they will be delivered up to councils, scourged in synagogues and brought before governors. When they are thus persecuted in one city they are to flee into the next. The statement that the end will come before they have 'gone through' all the cities of Israel could quite well presuppose a lengthy missionary activity in each, so that nothing more would be implied than that the end will come in their lifetime (or perhaps in the lifetime of their pupils who continue their work). That it will come before all the existing generation has died is the doctrine of Jesus in other passages. Only from this one can Schweitzer infer that Jesus then believed it would come in a matter of months. The passage is absent from the other gospels, for this whole section of Mt.'s narrative represents the standpoint of a writer who wishes the missionary activity of the Church to be confined to Israel, and this Jewish exclusiveness has been dropped in the parallel passages in Mk. and Lk. If the passage simply means that the end will come before the new faith has gained a hold in all the Jewish cities, Jesus is not here being made to say anything that a Jewish-Christian writer or editor of about AD 100 would have felt inappropriate to put into his mouth.

It has been argued that Jesus' declarations that the world will

D

end before all his contemporaries have died are fatal to the theory
that he never existed. A. Robertson, for instance, says (218a,
pp. 90–1): 'Whatever may be the date of the gospels in their present shape, the natural inference from these texts is that they, at
any rate, were committed to writing at a time when men still
living could remember a real Jesus.' In fact, all that these texts
suggest is that their authors supposed Jesus to have lived sufficiently recently for some of his contemporaries to be still alive.
As we shall see, Christians believed by the end of the first century
that Jesus had been on earth recently, and the tradition of the
crucifixion under Pilate was certainly established by AD 110, when
some who were alive in AD 30 could still have survived. All the
earliest Christian writers were convinced that the end of the world
was imminent, and this view could be ascribed to Jesus without
gross implausibility by the earliest evangelists. It is highly significant that Lk., the latest of the synoptics, while retaining (xxi, 32)
the doctrine of Mk. xiii, 30 and Mt. xxiv, 34 that 'this generation
shall not pass away till all things be accomplished', shows signs of
embarrassment, in that he is (as we saw) nevertheless concerned to
represent Jesus as declaring that the end will come later than Mt.
envisaged; while Jn., the latest of the canonical gospels, has
dropped all reference to the end of the world.

CHAPTER THREE

Straightforward Gospel Narratives

(i) The trial of Jesus

Hoskyns and Davey (141, pp. 66–7) have pointed out that even some of the gospel narratives which have the appearance of straightforward historical reporting seem in fact to be of literary origin. One of their examples is the statement (suspect because present only in Mk.) that after Jesus' arrest in Gethsemane 'a certain young man followed with him, having a linen cloth cast about him, over his naked body: and they lay hold on him; but he left the linen cloth and fled naked' (Mk. xiv, 51–2). Loisy and Keim, they note, have suggested that this incident was invented to provide fulfilment of the words of Amos (ii, 16), understood as a Messianic prophecy: 'he that is courageous among the mighty shall flee away naked in that day, saith the Lord'. In this chapter I shall inquire whether some of what are believed to be the salient episodes of Jesus' biography survive careful scrutiny of the documents.

The narratives of Jesus' trial are very detailed. In all four gospels he is first examined by the Jewish authorities and then passed on to Pilate. Mt. has it that after his arrest he is taken to the house of 'Caiaphas the high priest, where the scribes and the elders were gathered together' (xxvi, 57). False witnesses appear, but nothing can be established against him until two men testify that he claimed the power to destroy the temple and rebuild it in three days—a charge he refuses to answer. The high priest then asks him if he really claims to be the Messiah: 'tell me whether thou be the

Christ, the Son of God'. Jesus replies with the words 'thou hast said', whereupon the high priest declares him guilty of blasphemy and worthy of death. They then maltreat him, spitting in his face and striking him. All this is represented as having occurred on the night of the passover, the execution following the next morning (but still on the day of the festival, by the Jewish reckoning of a day from evening to evening). Many scholars have objected that the Jewish law forbids a capital prosecution and execution at the time of a sabbath or festival. But Professor Jeremias has recently pointed out that in Deuteronomy it is stipulated that certain crimes must be punished by death, and 'all the people shall hear and fear'. Since all the people are gathered only at the three pilgrim festivals (Passover, Pentecost, Tabernacles), the Rabbis held that, in spite of the prohibition of executions on festivals, in the cases covered by the ruling in Deuteronomy, the death penalty must be carried out at the feast. The Talmud shows that they regarded false prophets and their false witnesses as covered by this ruling, for it says that such miscreants 'are not executed at once, but they shall be brought to Jerusalem to the sanhedrim and be kept in prison until the feast and their sentence shall be executed at the feast'. Jeremias alleges that Jesus was regarded as a false prophet, and was therefore tried at once after his arrest, so that the execution could take place, according to the rule of Deut. xvii, 13, 'before the people' (148, pp. 72-3).

This evidence does not explain the execution of the two thieves on the same day,[1] nor why the trial was held during the forbidden period. The rabbinical law forbids judging on feast days, and also trials of capital crimes on the eve of a sabbath or feast day, on the ground that, if the prisoner is found guilty, the verdict would have to be given the day after the trial, for he must not be condemned to death on the day of his trial.[2] The Talmudic evidence given by Jeremias presupposes that the prisoner has been tried and condemned *before* the feast, and that his execution is postponed so that it can occur before all the people.[3] In the case of Jesus,

[1] Jeremias' only reference to them is in his statement that the Romans might well have regarded the turbulent period of the festival as an appropriate occasion for all three warning executions (p. 71).

[2] Jeremias thinks it 'very questionable' (p. 72) whether this prohibition was valid when Jesus lived.

[3] Even in such cases the practice would surely be not to soil the actual feast day, but to carry out the execution on a day immediately preceding or

however, the trial does not start until the passover has already begun, and the sentence is given immediately, not the following day. However, these are relatively minor matters, and on the basis of Jeremias' work, which makes it clear that an execution at the time of a sacred festival was quite possible, we could argue that the priests, wishing to get rid of Jesus, had him tried and condemned quickly (Mt. tells of witnesses appearing in the middle of the night) in spite of the stipulations of the law; that they were able to stamp his claim to be the Messiah as blasphemy and so condemn him to death. For according to Levitical law (Lev. xxiv, 16) a blasphemer was to be stoned.

It was not in itself blasphemous to claim to be the Messiah. A century after the death of Jesus, Simeon bar Cochba openly made this claim, which was accepted by Rabbi Aqiba, the greatest of the Pharisaic leaders of the time (272, p. 217 f.). About AD 44 Theudas claimed he was the Messiah, and Schürer (244, II, II, 149) mentions him as a typical example of claimants who 'found believers for their promises by hundreds and thousands'. However, a false claim of this nature would surely have been regarded as blasphemous and for the priests Jesus' claim was a false one.

Mk.'s account agrees with Mt.'s, but Lk.'s is different. Accordint to the two former Jesus is taken to the high priest's residence and tried there immediately on arrival: the scribes and elders were already 'gathered together' when he was brought in, and the trial proceeds during the night. In Lk., however, he is, throughout the night, merely kept under guard in the high priest's house; at break of day the sanhedrim assemble and lead him away to their council chamber to try him there (xxii, 66). No witnesses appear, but the elders at once ask him the decisive question 'if thou art the Christ, tell us'. This version—that the trial was held in the official hall—seems the more plausible, and Winter (291, p. 21) has pointed out that Lk.'s account is preferable in respect of other

---

following, when, as Lietzmann has said (170, p. 213 n.) the people would still be gathered in Jerusalem. Thus the Talmudic Jesus ben Pandira was executed on the day before the passover, 14th Nisan (cf. below, p. 247). Since the Jesus of the synoptics is not arrested until the day of the festival (15th Nisan), we might expect him to have been executed on 16th (rather than on 15th, as the synoptics allege, see below, p. 275). But Jeremias objects (p. 73) that some pilgrims would begin to leave the city on 16th, and so an execution then would not occur before 'all the people'.

details. For instance according to Lk., Jesus was mocked and maltreated by his jailors before the sanhedrim's session, whereas in Mt. and Mk. the mockery takes place after the session and is carried out by the sanhedrim itself—as if the senators would indulge in undignified mockery of a man they have just condemned to death. Again, according to Mk. and Mt. the sanhedrim found Jesus guilty of blasphemy and worthy of death, and we saw that the penalty for blasphemy is death by stoning. Yet the members of the tribunal who have just condemned him take no action in consequence of their decision; the council meets again in the morning (Mt. xxvii, 1; Mk. xv, 1) and proceeds as if nothing had happened the night before. The result of the morning consultation is that Jesus is extradited to Pilate to be tried. It is impossible to understand—from this—why he should stand trial before Pilate if he had already been tried and sentence passed (291, p. 23). It is true that Jn. motivates the trial before Pilate by making the Jews say: 'it is not lawful for us to put any man to death' (Jn. xviii, 31). But Mt. and Mk. nowhere mention any such restriction of the sanhedrim's authority, and if they had possessed the information provided by Jn., they would have recorded it so as to explain their story. So we must presume that they did not know of any legal impediment to the sanhedrim's authority. Winter argues that there was in fact no such impediment, and that Jn.'s allegation is mythical: 'There is abundant evidence that even in the period after the death of Jesus the supreme council of the Jewish nation exercised the function of a judicial tribunal in trying Jews on charges which involved capital punishment and inflicting the death penalty. It has every appearance of special pleading if all these instances are represented as irregularities, tacitly tolerated by an indulgent Roman government' (291, p. 15). In sum, Mt. and Mk. make the sanhedrim condemn Jesus to death, but take no steps to carry out the sentence. Lk.'s account, however, is free from this defect, for nowhere does he mention a formal sentence passed by the council. Winter notes that this absence must have been deliberately intended, as is clear from Acts (written also by Lk.), where Paul says: 'They that dwell in Jerusalem, and their rulers . . . found no cause of death in Jesus, yet asked they of Pilate that he should be slain' (xiii, 27–8). And again, when Jesus prophesies his own death, he makes no mention, in Lk., of a Jewish condemnation, whereas in Mk.'s version he does. Here are the two passages:

Mk. x, 33-4	*Lk. xviii, 31-3*
Behold we go up to Jerusalem; and the Son of man shall be delivered unto the chief priests and the scribes; and they shall condemn him to death, and shall deliver him unto the Gentiles; and they shall mock him and shall spit upon him, and shall scourge him and shall kill him.	Behold we go up to Jerusalem, and all the things that are written by the prophets shall be accomplished unto the Son of man. For he shall be delivered up unto the Gentiles and shall be mocked and shamefully entreated and spit upon: and they shall scourge and kill him.

Winter infers that the difference of the Lucan wording can be accounted for only by presuming that Lk. did not know what Mk. alleged, or that he knew it and deliberately discounted it, and followed another tradition which he regarded as more reliable.

If Mt. and Mk's story is suspect on all these grounds, it then becomes of interest to inquire under what conditions and with what aim it was composed. Winter points out that their report of Jesus' trial is framed by their story of Peter's denial. They show Peter sitting at the entrance of the high priest's house, among the servants; then the trial and condemnation of Jesus taking place inside; then the scene switches back to Peter who denies his master. The moral lies in the contrast between Peter's behaviour and that of Jesus. 'We are called upon to understand that whilst Peter was importuned by domestics of an influential personage, and succumbed in face of hostile interrogation, Jesus himself kept his faith and maintained his composure before the highest authority of the land, irrespective of the consequences.' Winter supports this theory that the story of Peter's weakness is a myth which points a moral by showing that it is only in Mt. and Mk. that the story of Peter's weakness is put as a frame to the trial. Lk. has it that (1) Jesus is brought to the residence of the high priest; (2) Peter denies him in the courtyard of this house; (3) inside, Jesus is mocked by the jailors; (4) at dawn he is led away to the council chamber and tried by the sanhedrim.

Winter distinguishes a further motive underlying Mt.'s and Mk.'s account that Jesus was sentenced by the sanhedrim—namely the desire to avoid offending the Romans. According to these two evangelists, 'Jesus was not arrested by Roman troops, not sentenced for political reasons by a Roman magistrate; . . . his condemnation and subsequent execution was due to some

obscure clause of the Jewish law which, of course, would be
devoid of relevance in the eye of a Roman reader after AD 70'.

All four gospels display, to some extent, this tendency. Thus
Lk. (and only he) even alleges a trial before Herod as well as
before Pilate in order to whitewash the Romans. And Mt. makes
Pilate say to the multitude: 'I am innocent of the blood of this
righteous man'; to which the reply is made: 'his blood be on us
and on our children' (xxvii, 24–5), thus fixing the guilt of the Jews.
Winter remarks that

> the stern Pilate grows more mellow from gospel to gospel. In
> Mk. he is greatly astonished and offers to release Jesus in whom
> he can find no guilt. In Mt. he renounces responsibility for the
> execution which he nevertheless orders. In Lk. he repeats three
> times his assertion of Jesus' innocence, yet he gives in to the
> will of the Jews. In Jn. he hands Jesus over for execution to
> the Jews themselves. Post-canonical traditions stress even more
> Pilate's benevolent disposition (p. 60).

In Jn. the trial of Jesus by the Jewish authorities is even more
attenuated than in Lk. We saw that Mt. and Mk. make the priests
find him guilty of claiming to be the Messiah and that they condemn him to death; that Lk.'s version makes him guilty of this
claim, but does not represent the priests as condemning him. In
Jn., however, he is not even charged with claiming to be the
Messiah. He is merely questioned concerning his disciples and his
doctrine (xviii, 19), and answers by saying he had delivered all his
teachings openly. For this reply he is maltreated by one of the
attendants, and is then sent to Pilate without the passing of any
sentence.

Let us now examine the accounts of the trial before Pilate,
beginning this time with Jn. When the Jews bring Jesus to Pilate
he asks them 'What accusation bring ye against this man?' They
prefer no specific charge, but merely describe Jesus as an 'evil
doer' (xviii, 29–30). Jn., then, neither makes the Jews accuse
Jesus of claiming to be the Messiah, nor does he represent them
as informing Pilate that this is what Jesus claimed. Pilate, nevertheless, having been told only that Jesus is an evil doer, opens his
interrogation of the prisoner with the question 'Art thou the King
of the Jews?' The interrogation takes place within doors, while
the priests remain outside from fear of levitical defilement (xviii,

28). There were thus no Jewish witnesses to report the trial. These are supplied by the synoptics who allege that the entire sanhedrim attended the trial before Pilate, although even the synoptics do not affirm that there were any Christian witnesses. In Mk., as in Jn., Pilate begins his interrogation before he has been informed what the indictment is. Only Lk. remedies this, by supplying an entirely novel indictment, making the whole sanhedrim tell him that Jesus was guilty of anti-Roman sedition, in that he stirred up the people and encouraged them to refuse tribute to Caesar, giving himself out to be 'Christ a king' (Lk. xxiii, 2). Pilate then asks him 'Art thou the King of the Jews?', and on receiving an affirmative answer declares: 'I find no fault in this man.' How commentators can shut their eyes to the incredibility of this is well illustrated by Wright, who tells us (294, p. 83) that the Romans felt insecure in Palestine, for in 40 BC the Parthian Empire had attempted to control it, and still constituted a threat to Rome's mastery during the lifetime of Jesus. Furthermore, there were rebellious spirits within the country, always plotting to throw off Roman control so that 'Rome was constantly on the alert against invasion or uprising. Hence a charge that Jesus was trying to make himself king (Lk. xxiii, 2) was something to be taken seriously.' The commentator's purpose is to show that the known political situation at the time helps to throw light on the gospel narrative. In actual fact, however, the reverse is the case: the narrative is incredible in the light of the known situation. For in the very passage to which reference is made, the Roman governor, whom we are to expect to be 'constantly on the alert against invasion or uprising' is represented as finding a man who allegedly stirred up anti-Roman sedition and claimed the title of king completely blameless. It is generally agreed that Jesus' words 'thou sayest' constitute an affirmative answer to Pilate; the same formula, used by Jesus in his trial before the scribes and elders, is taken by them to mean 'yes' (Lk. xxii, 70; Mt. xxvi, 64). Even if we take the words as an equivocation, it is still not plausible that Pilate should without further ado declare the prisoner blameless.

Although only Lk. makes the Jews accuse Jesus, before Pilate, of anti-Roman sedition, all the synoptics represent Pilate asking him whether he is the king of the Jews, receiving either an affirmative answer or none at all, and then immediately doing his best to have him set free. In Jn. however, Jesus does not admit that he is king of the Jews, but tells Pilate he is the king of truth and that his kingdom is not of this world; so that it is, from this version, intelligible that Pilate should turn to the priests and tell them that he can find no crime in him. It is also only in Jn. that Pilate's willingness to be bullied by the priests into nevertheless ordering the execution is made intelligible. Jn. represents them as countering the acquittal by pointing out that the claim to be any sort of king makes a man potentially dangerous to the Romans, and that the governor would be failing in his duty if he gave such a claimant the benefit of the doubt because his claim did not seem to be political (xix, 12). There is general agreement that Jn. is the latest of the four canonical gospels. It cannot but strike us as suspicious that only this relatively late document attributes Pilate's behaviour to motives that are in any way plausible.

Finally there is the behaviour of the multitude. How can we explain the contrast between the triumphal entry into Jerusalem a few days before and the absolute unanimity of the priest-led multitude in demanding the execution of Jesus against the wishes of Pilate? It is not that a complete volte-face on the part of a multitude is unbelievable, but that the narratives fail to give any indication of how it was motivated.[1] Wood deals with this difficulty by positing two distinct crowds (292, p. 44) and so asks us to believe that the multitude which hailed Jesus as the Messiah took no further interest in him, and raised no voice against his arrest and execution.

As history, the triumphal entry is as difficult to understand as the behaviour of Pilate. Winter notes that the gospel accounts of it give it 'the appearance of an unmistakable Messianic demonstration. As such it would have been open defiance of imperial authority—a proclamation of the will to national independence from Roman rule.' Jesus is greeted with such phrases as 'Hosanna to the son of David' (Mt. xxi, 9) and 'the king of Israel' (Jn. xii, 13). We know that under Vespasian, Titus and Domitian persons believed to be descendants of king David, and their adherents, were put to death in great numbers, the reason for this severity being 'the determination, on the emperor's part, to eradicate

---

[1] Brandon observes that the chief priests who persuaded the crowd to insist on Jesus' execution (Mt. xxvii, 20; Mk. xv, 11) are twice said by Mk. to have feared the people (xi, 32; xiv, 1–2). 'We can only wonder at the speed and efficiency with which these priestly aristocrats acted, on the spur of the moment, thus to influence the crowd to demand the death of Jesus, when that crowd had so enthusiastically supported him against themselves only a few days before' (38a, p. 261).

apocalyptic trends in Judaism and to nip in the bud any attempt to restore the Davidic dynasty and re-establish its rule over the Jewish people'. Again, while Mk. xi, 8 has it that the people cut branches from the fields and spread them upon the way, Jn. xii, 13 tells us that they 'took palm branches from the palm trees and went forth to meet him'. Winter comments:

> At the high altitude of Jerusalem no palms grow. If used in the welcome of Jesus, palm branches would have to be imported specially for that purpose. In modern times a symbol of peace, the branches of a palm tree were in ancient times employed as a symbol of triumph, and were presented to honour victorious conquerors. The branches thrown under the feet of Jesus, and particularly the palm branches, would signify the celebration of victory over the pagan oppressor (291, pp. 59, 141–2).

Another feature that makes the triumphant entry look like legend is that Mt. makes it take a certain form because he has misunderstood the prophecy of Zech. ix, 9, which tells that the king will come 'riding upon an ass, even upon a colt the foal of an ass'. Mt. supposes that two animals are implied and that the Messianic king sits astride both in order to fulfil the prophecy (xxi, 2–7). That Mt. has misunderstood his text is clear from comparison with Mk. xi, 2 ff. and Lk. xix, 30 ff., where Jesus rides but one animal into the city.

There is no difficulty in accounting for either the triumphal entry and the welcome of the crowd, or for the behaviour ascribed to Pilate in the synoptics once we can assume that both are legends. The first would be invented to prove that Jesus was recognized as the Messiah by the people, and the second to throw the guilt for his execution on the Jewish leaders, or (in Mt.'s version) on the whole nation—'his blood be on us and on our children'. The Roman authorities would naturally regard the early Christians as a Jewish sect. The gospel writers may well have put the blame for the execution on the Jews in order that in future the Christians might escape persecution as Jews.

Schweitzer has tried to make sense of the last days of Jesus' life by arguing that his consciousness that he was the Messiah was a closely guarded secret, shared only by his intimates. The triumphal entry was thus 'Messianic for Jesus but not the people', who looked upon him as a mere prophet, and greeted him as such. We have seen that the historicity of gospel stories has often been doubted on the ground that so many of their details seem to be made to agree with prophecy and Messianic expectations. Schweitzer holds that such details are historical and that Jesus, believing himself to be the Messiah, deliberately engineered them. Thus when he entered Jerusalem, 'he made a point of riding upon the ass, not because he was weary, but because he desired that the Messianic prophecy of Zech. ix, 9 should be secretly fulfilled' (247, p. 391). If this is to be treated as a serious suggestion we naturally ask for a more detailed account of the various ways in which Jesus arranges for so elaborate a stage management. As Schweitzer himself asks earlier: 'How does the Messianic entry occur? How was it possible, without causing the Roman authorities to intervene' (p. 331). He thinks his theory that the people welcomed Jesus not as the Messiah but as a prophet (Mt. xxi, 11) a sufficient answer. Their cries of 'Hosanna to the son of David' he rejects as an invention of the evangelist.

If, then, only Jesus and the twelve knew the secret, how did the high priest get to know that Jesus claimed to be the Messiah? Schweitzer's answer is: through the treachery of Judas. He can see the nullity of Mk.'s story that Judas identified Jesus to the mob sent by the priests—as if they would have paid solid cash to have a man identified who was well known to them as a public teacher. So he supposes that Judas must have betrayed, not Jesus' identity, but something not indicated by Mk., namely the Messianic secret. Once they know this the priests noise it abroad that Jesus claims to be the Messiah, whereupon the people at once regard him as a 'lunatic and blasphemer' (p. 394 f.). Schweitzer's theory is ingenious in that it supplies an explanation as to why the people are represented as wholeheartedly in favour of Jesus at the entry into Jerusalem, and wholeheartedly against him during his trial. However, the secret nature of Jesus' Messianic consciousness is impossible to reconcile with the texts: he is repeatedly greeted as the Messiah at various stages in his career and Schweitzer has to resort to elaborate special pleading to explain these references away (see below, p. 328 ff.).

(ii) **The Crucifixion**

All three synoptic gospels allege an unnatural darkening of the sun at the death of Jesus and declare that the veil of the temple was rent, but Mt. alone supplements these with further miracles which include an earthquake, the splitting of rocks, the opening of graves and the resurrection of the saints occupying them (xxvii, 45 ff.), who, however, did not emerge from their miraculously opened tombs until after Jesus' resurrection, when they are said to have entered the city and appeared to many (verse 53). This seems to be a clumsy attempt to harmonize this story of their resurrection at the time of Jesus' death with the tradition (preserved in Acts xxvi, 23) that he himself was 'the first that should rise from the dead'. The preternatural darkness for three hours (asserted by the gospels) and the earthquake (asserted by Mt. alone) are not mentioned by historians of the time. Gibbon notes (104, end of Chapter xv) that this prodigy of darkness 'happened during the lifetime of Seneca and the elder Pliny, who must have experienced the immediate effects or received the earliest intelligence of the prodigy' which is said to involve 'the whole earth, or at least a celebrated province of the Roman Empire'. 'Each of these philosophers', he continues, 'in a laborious work, has recorded all the great phenomena of nature, earthquakes, meteors, comets, eclipses, which his indefatigable curiosity could collect. Both the one and the other have omitted to mention the greatest phenomenon to which the mortal eye has been witness since the creation of the globe. A distinct chapter in Pliny is designated for eclipses of an extraordinary nature and unusual duration; but he contents himself with describing the singular defect of light which followed the murder of Caesar', which 'had already been celebrated by most of the poets and historians of that memorable age'. Strauss (262, II, 382) adduces this Roman legend as evidence of the motive underlying the gospel fiction: 'In proportion as the appearance of Jesus had been of importance, must nature have put on mourning for him. Such was the taste of the age.' Werner has recently suggested an alternative motive. The miraculous signs specified by Mt., he says, include, apart from the earthquake, clear motifs of an apocalyptic picture of the end of the world. The idea, then, was to suggest that the death of Jesus heralded the last days, when the world would come to a catastrophic end, in accordance with the expectations expressed in Jewish apocalypses (284, p. 33).

Unlike details in the stories of Jesus' ancestry and early life, the crucifixion and resurrection stories cannot have been invented in order to agree with prophecy and Messianic expectations.

Although it is true that Jesus himself, in the announcements of his sufferings, expressly appeals to the OT (Lk. xviii, 31; xxii, 37; xxiv, 25 ff.; Mt. xxvi, 54), nevertheless there is nothing in it to suggest that the Messiah would be crucified. Isa. liii, often quoted in this connection, will be discussed below (pp. 225 ff.). Ps. xxii is also often adduced. The writer appears to be an oppressed exile, who compares his tormentors to fierce animals (bulls and lions) and uses various similes to express his own weakness and helplessness. Then, in a new metaphor, he pictures his tormentors as a multitude of savage faces which enclose him like a ring of snarling dogs:

> For dogs have encompassed me;
> The assembly of evil-doers have enclosed me;
> They pierced my hands and my feet.

This clearly refers not to crucifixion, but to a man being hunted. The next verse compares the tormentors to brigands who strip the traveller of his clothing:

> They look and stare upon me:
> They part my garments among them,
> And upon my vesture do they cast lots.

The continuation runs:

> But be not thou far off, O Lord:
> O thou my succour, haste thee to help me.
> Deliver my soul from the sword:
> My darling from the power of the dog.
> Save me from the lion's mouth;
> Yea, from the horns of the wild-oxen thou hast
>   answered me.

Commentators say that 'my darling' is synonymous with 'my soul' in the parallel clause. Here, then, the writer returns to some of the metaphors he has used previously; and the Psalm finishes with praise and thanksgiving to God for his faithfulness. The piercing of the hands and feet and the stripping of the victim were probably usual at a Roman crucifixion,[1] and could well have suggested a

---

[1] See 49, § 4. Some scholars, however, maintain that hands and feet were secured by thongs at the period in question, not nails, and that Lk.'s reference to piercing (xxiv, 39–40) is probably influenced by Ps. xxii, 19.

crucifixion to those familiar (as the early Christians were) with such a form of punishment. But to take these things from their context and refer them to a crucifixion is quite arbitrary.

Paul makes no attempt to do this. He never says that the death of Jesus was according to the scriptures except in one passage which, we shall see, is an interpolation. He even argues, quoting Deut. xxi, 23, that the scriptures represent crucified persons as accursed, and that a crucified Messiah, so far from conforming to the Jewish expectations, was all but unacceptable to them: 'We preach Christ crucified, unto the Jews a stumbling-block, and unto the Gentiles foolishness' (I Cor. i, 23). And if the Jews were expecting their Messiah to be crucified, then the behaviour of the disciples is remarkable. Jesus tells them that they are going to Jerusalem, and that the prophecies are to be fulfilled: 'For he shall be delivered up unto the Gentiles and shall be mocked, and shamefully entreated and spit upon: and they shall scourge and kill him: and the third day he shall rise again' (Lk. xviii, 31-3). But they obviously did not know any such prophecies, and 'understood none of these things'. Consequently, when Jesus is executed, all the hopes which they had fixed on him as the Messiah were annihilated (Lk. xxiv, 20 f.). Nor were they expecting the resurrection, but regarded the report of the women as 'idle talk' (Lk. xxiv, 11; cp. Mk. xvi, 11, 13). The resurrection can only be extracted from the OT by an exegesis equally arbitrary as in the case of the crucifixion. Orthodox writers sometimes adduce Hosea vi, 1:

> Come let us return unto the Lord: for he hath torn and he will heal us: he hath smitten and he will bind us up. After two days he will revive us: on the third day he will raise us up, and we shall live before him.

The prophet is speaking of the people of Israel, not of the Messiah; he is saying that after a period of dejection, the nation will once again flourish; and the shortness of this period is indicated by the expression 'after two days he will revive us'. Nothing is said of any literal death and nothing of the Messiah.

However, although the crucifixion could not have been invented in order to conform to Messianic expectations, some of the incidents which the gospels allege happened during it, do seem to be so explicable. Let us compare the different narratives.

In Mt. and Mk., immediately after Pilate has delivered Jesus to be crucified, he is given a crown of thorns and mocked as king of the Jews. Lk. does not mention these incidents, and Jn. (xix, 2–5) places them before the crowd have persuaded Pilate to crucify Jesus. They are never mentioned in the Pauline letters. Mt. goes on to tell how Simon of Cyrene was made to carry the cross (xxvii, 32). With this Mk. and Lk. agree, but Jn. makes no mention of Simon and says that Jesus carried his cross himself (xix, 17–18). Jn. may very well have altered previous accounts quite deliberately on this point. Strauss noted that it would have seemed utterly perverse to him to introduce a substitute in the place of the Lamb of God who bore the sins of the world (262, II, 367).

In Mk. xv, 21 Simon is described as 'the father of Alexander and Rufus'. This detail, which is absent from the other gospels, is instanced by Wood as important evidence that Mk. 'is offering us early and genuine reminiscence of an actual historical event'. For 'such a reference to two living men could only have been made by a copyist who was writing for persons who knew them. It has no point otherwise. Moreover, it presupposes that Simon of Cyrene was known to the copyist and his readers as a historic person and that the events, real or supposed, took place when he could have taken part in them, i.e. within living memory.' Mt. and Lk., 'writing for other circles, not interested in Alexander and Rufus, naturally omit the reference' (292, pp. 118, 122). Wood's allegation that these two men were 'living' persons known to Mk. is gratuitous. Mk.'s reference to them may mean only that some tradition about them was known to the Christian community for which he was writing. They might, for instance, have been influential teachers of a previous generation, in which case his attempt to represent them as descended from someone acquainted with the historical Jesus would be a mere tendency-story to increase their prestige.

Lk. relates an incident between Simon's taking the cross and the arrival at Golgotha which none of the other gospels mention. Jesus urges the 'daughters of Jerusalem' to weep not for him but for themselves and their children (xxiii, 27–30). This is a good example of the way in which Lk. represents the destruction of Jerusalem in AD 70 as a punishment for the Jews' treatment of Jesus. The same tendency is visible in another passage which occurs only in Lk., where Jesus weeps over the city as he approaches it, because by its blindness it is bringing upon itself the misfortune of siege and destruction (xix, 41–4).

On arrival at the place of execution Mt. tells that 'they gave him wine [AV vinegar] to drink mingled with gall; and when he had tasted it he would not drink'. Mk. (xv, 23) tells us that it was 'wine mingled with myrrh' which was offered and refused. Some commentators regard this mixture as a refreshing drink, while others think it would have an opiate effect and that it was customary to offer such a pain-killer to those about to undergo crucifixion. Lk. and Jn. do not mention this incident, but all four evangelists tell of vinegar being offered to Jesus later, while he hung upon the cross. In Mt. (xxvii, 46–51) the drink is offered after he had cried 'My God, why hast thou forsaken me?'. Lk. does not record this saying but has others instead, which are unknown to Mt. and Mk.; and he represents the vinegar as being offered in a spirit of mockery (xxiii, 36–7). Jn. represents Jesus as actually asking for a drink in order to fulfil 'the scripture' (xix, 28–30). The reference appears to be Ps. lxix, 21: 'They gave me also gall for my meat; and in my thirst they gave me vinegar to drink.' Strauss thinks that the evangelists' desire to show that prophecies were fulfilled explains Mt.'s reference to a drink of gall and vinegar before the crucifixion. Mt. could not mention gall in connection with meat, which could have no place at the crucifixion, so he mixes it with the vinegar (262, II, 369).

The synoptics tell that when Jesus had been placed on the cross 'they parted his garments among them, casting lots' (Mt. xxvii, 35; Mk. xv, 24; Lk. xxiii, 34). We find that the sufferer mentioned in Ps. xxii complained (verse 18) that 'they parted my garments among them and cast lots upon my vesture'. Jn. expressly refers to this passage, and regards the behaviour of the soldiers as the fulfilment of this 'prophecy' which specifies not two acts but one. Parting the garments and casting lots upon them are two ways of describing the same thing, and this is how the synoptics understand the verse. But Jn. supposes that two acts are implied; first, he says, the soldiers (whom he represents as four in number) took Jesus' undergarments 'and made four parts, to every soldier a part'. This fulfils the first half of the prophecy. Then, he says, they took Jesus' coat which 'was without a seam, woven from the top throughout. They said therefore to one another, Let us not rend it, but cast lots for it, whose shall it be: that the scripture might be fulfilled . . .' (xix, 23–5). This striking difference between Jn. and the synoptics suggests that all alike have invented the incident in order to allege that another prophecy has been fulfilled.

The mockery of Jesus by the onlookers is suspect for the same reason. In Ps. xxii we read: 'All they that see me laugh me to scorn: they shoot out the lip . . . saying, Commit thyself unto the Lord; let him deliver him, seeing he delighteth in him.' Mt. makes the crowd reproduce the latter part of this exactly (xxvii, 43). Mk. and Lk. specify mockery, but without these words.

When we look at the accounts about the two thieves who were crucified with Jesus we find again discrepancies, contradictions and the desire to represent the incidents alleged as the fulfilments of prophecy. All four gospels represent Jesus as being crucified between two criminals. In the AV Mk. represents this as fulfilling Isa. liii, 12, 'And he was numbered with the transgressors'. This verse is, however, omitted in the RV on the ground that 'the documentary evidence in support of it is doubtful' (note on Mk. xv, 28 in CB). Lk. seems to regard this verse from Isaiah as finding its fulfilment at Jesus' arrest (xxii, 37). Again, Mt. and Mk. represent the two criminals as joining in the crowd's denunciation and mockery of Jesus (Mt. xxvii, 44; Mk. xv, 32). Lk. however tells that while one of the two mocked him, the other recognized him as the Messiah, and asked him to 'remember me when thou comest in thy kingdom' (xxiii, 42); Jesus replied 'Verily I say unto thee, Today shalt thou be with me in Paradise'. As history this is unintelligible. According to the gospels Jesus had on a number of occasions tried to inculcate into his disciples the doctrine of a dying Messiah, always without success (see above p. 105), yet this criminal, who had presumably never met him before, understands it without any instruction whatever.

We have already seen that Jesus' words from the cross differ in the different gospels. Mt. and Mk. each have only one saying, 'My God, my God, why hast thou forsaken me'. This is not recorded by Lk. or Jn., and turns out to be another quotation from Psalm xxii, which begins with these very words.[1] Lk. records three entirely different sayings, and Jn. another three, again different. Lk.'s three are (1) 'Father forgive them, for they know not what they do'; (2) the above-cited speech to the malefactor; (3) 'And when Jesus had cried with a loud voice, he said, Father into thy hands I commend my spirit'—a quotation from

---

[1] This is a sufficient answer to Wood's statements that 'the primitive Christian consciousness could never have imagined the idea of Jesus abandoned by God', and that 'only in a sincere and trustworthy tradition regarding a historic happening could such a trait be found' (292, p. 123).

Psalm xxxi, 5. The first of these three is absent from some of the ancient manuscripts, as the RV tells us in a note; thus even as late as the fourth century, some authorities did not know of this utterance, or did not believe it to have been made. It may be a late invention, constructed from Isa. liii, 12; 'He poured out his soul unto death . . . and made intercession for the transgressors'.

Jn. represents Jesus as addressing his mother and giving her into the care of the beloved disciple (xix, 25-7), while in the synoptic gospels she is not even present at the crucifixion. Nor, according to Mt. and Mk., were the disciples. The audience is said by Mt. to have consisted of (1) the Roman soldiers, (2) 'the chief priests, mocking him, with the scribes and elders' (3) the two criminals, and (4) 'many women'. Mt. has represented all the disciples as taking flight when Jesus was arrested (xxvi, 56). Only Peter follows him at a distance as far as the court of the high priest, where he sits outside while Jesus is being tried. The disciples are not again mentioned until they appear as witnesses of the resurrection. Mk.'s account is substantially the same. Lk., although he represents the disciples as witnesses of the crucifixion, places them too far away for Jesus to address them: 'All his acquaintance, and the women that followed with him from Galilee, stood afar off, seeing these things' (xxiii, 49).

Cheyne sums up by saying (59, § 5) that 'all that the evangelists seem to care for is (1) the opportunity which the Cross gave for Christ to make fresh disclosures, in speech, of his wonderful character, and (2) the proofs which the Passion gave, as it appeared to them, of a "pre-established harmony" between prophecy and the life of Jesus'. The extent to which Jesus' biography has been constructed from the OT is particularly apparent in the stories of his early life and last days. The evidence is put together in summary form by Couchoud (68, p. 179), and I reproduce his account here:

(1) Isa. vii, 14 (Septuagint). 'Behold the virgin shall bring forth.' Virgin birth of Jesus.

(2) Micah v, 2. 'But thou, Bethlehem, out of thee shall come forth unto me that is to be ruler in Israel.' Jesus born at Bethlehem.

(3) Num. xxiv, 17. 'There shall come forth a star out of Jacob.' The star in the east.

(4) Isa. lx, 6. 'They all shall come from Sheba; they shall bring

gold, and frankincense, and shall proclaim the praises of the Lord.'
The Magi.

(5) Hosea xi, 1. 'Out of Egypt I have called my son.' The flight
into Egypt.

(6) Jer. xxxi, 15. 'A voice is heard in Ramah; lamentation and
bitter weeping, Rachel weeping for her children; she refuseth to
be comforted for her children, because they are not.' Massacre of
the Innocents.

(7) Quoted from an unknown book of prophecy, Mt. II, 23.
'He shall be called a Nazarene.' The residence at Nazareth.

(8) Zech. ix, 9. 'Behold, thy king cometh unto thee; he is just
and having salvation; lowly and riding upon an ass, even upon a
colt the foal of an ass.' Triumphal entry of Jesus into Jerusalem.

(9) Ps. cxviii, 26. 'Blessed be he that cometh in the name of the
Lord.' The acclamation of the crowd as he enters the city.

(10) Zech. xiv, 21. 'And in that day there shall be no more a
trafficker in the house of the Lord of hosts.' The cleansing of the
temple.

(11) Ps. xli, 9. 'Mine own familiar friend, in whom I trusted,
which did eat of my bread, hath lifted up his heel against me.'
The betrayal by Judas.

(12) Zech. xi, 12–13. 'So they weighed for my hire thirty pieces
of silver . . . And I took the thirty pieces of silver and cast them
unto the potter.' Thirty pieces of silver are given to Judas, and
later used to buy a potter's field.

(13) Ps. xlii, 6. 'O my God, my soul is cast down within me.'
The agony in Gethsemane.

(14) Zech. xiii, 7. 'Smite the shepherd and the sheep shall be
scattered.' The flight of the disciples.

(15) Isa. liii, 5. 'He was wounded (or pierced) for our transgressions; he was bruised for our iniquities.' The passion.
verse 7: 'He was oppressed, yet he humbled himself, and opened
not his mouth.' Jesus keeps silence before his judges.
verse 12 (Septuagint): 'He was numbered among the transgressors.' Jesus between the two thieves.

(16) Isa. l, 6. 'I gave my back to the smiters and my cheeks to
them that plucked off the hair; I hid not my face from shame and
spitting.' The scourging.

(17) Ps. xxii, 1. 'My God, my God, why hast thou forsaken me.'
Jesus' last cry.
verse 17. 'They pierced my hands and my feet.' The crucifixion.

verse 18. 'They part my garments among them, and upon my
vesture do they cast lots.' The parting of Jesus' garments.
verse 7. 'All they that see me laugh me to scorn. They shoot out
the lip, they shake the head.' The scene at the cross.

(18) Isa. liii, 9. 'And they made his grave with the wicked and
with the rich in his death.' Jesus is buried in the tomb of a rich
man, Joseph of Arimathaea.

Sanday has observed that 'we know that types and prophecies
were eagerly sought out by the early Christians, and were soon
collected into a kind of common stock from which every one
drew at his pleasure' (232, p. 272). And we have already had
evidence that the early Christians possessed manuals of OT
quotations, on which they drew for teaching purposes (see above,
p. 71). Collections of Messianic passages from the OT would
stimulate believers to invent incidents in the life of Jesus which
fulfilled the supposed predictions.

All this evidence does not exclude the possibility that there was
a preacher who was tried and executed and that his career formed
the basis of the existing narratives. Although any detailed knowledge of his career is impossible because of the contradictions and
implausibilities in them, the muddle we find in the gospels does
not in itself point to the conclusion that he never existed. Sectarians meeting in the second century for some common purpose,
e.g. to advocate purer living, would cast about for traditions on
which to base their precepts. They would, perhaps, fasten on one
particular man of the past who had led a pure life, and, being
semi-literate, they would not check details, but father all sorts of
deeds on him, perhaps many of them performed by other men
with whom they had confused him. Stories would be told about
his conduct, and the sheer delight of telling and listening to stories
—felt at all times—would lead to their embellishment. In this
way, a great body of narrative of the kind we possess in the gospels
might grow up, and the hero could be a historical personage. But
although the evidence given so far does not exclude the possibility
that Christianity began with a historical Jesus, it does not point
to him as a necessary hypothesis to explain the origin of the new
religion. I shall perhaps be told that the growth of Christianity is
inexplicable except on the assumption of an initial 'great personality'. But if all religious movements that have been efficacious have
been so in virtue of their inception by a great personality, then

who gave Mithraism its long successes? Where are the great personalities who conduced to the rise of Dionysus and Osiris worship? To decide the question of Jesus' historicity we must see whether any gospel story is corroborated by evidence outside it. If so, we may plausibly set down such elements as historical. But before making this inquiry it will be as well to consider what further inferences we can draw concerning the origin of the gospels from the evidence already given.

CHAPTER FOUR

The Origin of the
Synoptic Gospels

Where does our NT come from? The four canonical gospels were
written originally in Greek for Greek-speaking communities. The
authorities for the text may be divided into three classes: Greek
manuscripts, 'versions' or translations into some other language,
and quotations by the Fathers of the Church. The quotations will
occupy us later, and, as already stated, the oldest extant Greek
manuscripts which are anything near complete date from the
fourth century.

The most important translations are in Latin, Syriac and Egyptian. One of the Egyptian versions (the 'Sahidic') dates from the
third century, and among the Syriac ones is the Sinai palimpsest,
discovered in 1892 in the same monastery which had yielded the
Codex Sinaiticus some years earlier. The palimpsest consists of
Syriac characters below Greek writing, and Herklots notes that
the date 200 has been suggested (138, p. 75). By the middle of the
fourth century many Latin versions existed. These were known to
be translations and so were amended and improved by various
hands, with the result that a confusing variety of texts was produced. About AD 383 Jerome undertook a major revision of these
Latin versions which he corrected with the aid of Greek codices
then reputed ancient and trustworthy. The Latin Bible thus
produced became the basis of the Vulgate, although many changes
were made between Jerome and the edition finally pronounced
authentic by the Council of Trent in 1546. Although the Vulgate
contains much that is unsupported by ancient authorities, Jerome's
Bible gives a Latin version of the gospels from Greek MSS.

probably as old as the second century, and is therefore as weighty an authority as the surviving Greek codices.

From all this we see that the oldest extant MSS. of the gospels are copies of earlier documents at the nature of which we can only guess. One problem is whether these lost sources are based on eye-witness reports. There is in fact little to support the conventional belief that the four gospels derive ultimately from information supplied by Matthew, Mark, Luke and John. Westcott notes that 'the titles of the books of the NT are no part of the text of the books themselves. Their ultimate authority is traditional, not documentary' (285, II, 321). Aland (9, p. 5) has recently reaffirmed this. Slater (250) remarks that the title 'The Gospel according to to St Matthew' is derived from church lectionaries, that is, from collections of gospels and epistles for reading in church. Furthermore, Mark and Luke are not named in the gospel lists of 'the twelve'. Mark is named in Acts and in four epistles as a companion of Peter and Paul. Luke figures in three epistles as a companion of Paul. Thus neither of these two gospels is assigned, even by tradition, to eye-witnesses of the events related.

The gospels were written by Christians for Christians, for believers trying to persuade others to believe. Christian scholars (e.g. Wood, 292, p. 12) express this by saying that they are not essays in historical portraiture, but in evangelism, or 'kerygmatic documents', inculcating a kerygma (message). This means, in plain language, that they are propaganda. The previous chapters have established that interpolations and contradictions occur in the synoptics: that in some cases one gospel writer appears to 'edit' or adapt the narrative of another, or of their common source; and that some passages are identical or nearly so, in two or even in all three of them. What can we say about their origin which will pay due regard to all these facts?

The identical passages are not confined to the discourses of Jesus, where they could be explained as an exact reproduction of his actual words,[1] but occur also in the narrative

---

[1] Although Jolley (153, p. 6) has remarked on the improbability of events, whose relative position is dictated by no internal necessity, being related in exactly the same order by three independent witnesses. In Jesus' parable of the sower, for instance, all the synoptics record first the seed that fell by the wayside, then that which fell upon stony ground, then that which fell among thorns, and finally that which fell upon good ground. How many auditors would accurately remember the order in which the first three kinds of ground are named?

parts.[1] Jolley remarks (153, pp. 8–11) that the improbability of the independence of the synoptics is enormously increased when we compare their miracle stories. The order of at least several of these is dictated by no internal necessity, nor did the evangelists profess to know their dates. Even in such cases the synoptics agree in the order of the events narrated.

If the synoptics are not independent, does one copy passages from another or does their agreement depend on their having drawn from a common source? Now it is impossible to believe that Mk. knew either Mt. or Lk., for he omits their account of the infancy, the Sermon on the Mount, and the Lord's prayer. These omissions cannot be explained as due to a wish to write a summary of Jesus' life, since he includes digressions such as his story of the beheading of the baptist (vi, 14–29). But although Mk., then, did not know either Mt. or Lk., there is general agreement that they knew him. They seem to have taken some of their material from his gospel (hence the passages that are verbally identical in all three) and some from another source (hence their inclusion of much that is absent from him). The question now arises whether Mt. and Lk. knew each other. This seems highly improbable, for each lacks much of the material present in the other, while no reason can be given for its exclusion. (Thus the cure of the demoniac at Capernaum, Lk. iv, 33 ff., is absent from Mt., while Mt.'s feeding of the four thousand, xv, 32–9 is absent from Lk.) Furthermore, their accounts of the same incident are often in violent contradiction (e.g. the infancy, the Sermon on the Mount, and the events after the crucifixion). Finally, there are a great number of verses absent from Mk. but present in Mt. and Lk., and showing general but not exact agreement. In such cases we cannot say that either evangelist gives what is obviously the more primitive form of the narrative and that one therefore revised the work of the other. What we find is that now one and now the other contains the more primitive version of an incident, and this can only be explained by positing a common source. The theory, then, is that Mt. and Lk. drew their information partly from Mk. (or from an early version of Mk.),[2] and partly from another source.

[1] An example is Mk. xi, 15, the first half of which coincides word for word with Lk. xix, 45; and the second half is closely paralleled in Mt. xxi, 12.

[2] This proviso must be made, since some (although not much) of the matter in the canonical Mk. appears to be later than the corresponding matter in Mt. and Lk. (we had an example above, p. 90), and was therefore not in the 'Mark' which served as the source material to them. But to simplify

This so-called theory of two sources 'ranks among those results of gospel criticism which have met with most general acceptance' (235, § 121; cf. 79, Chapter II).

That Mt. employed two sources can also be illustrated by the parable of the mustard seed. Mt.'s version shows him passing from one source to another. Mk. gives the parable in the form of a general statement, Lk. gives it as a narrative, while Mt.'s version consists of one half narrative and one half general statement. Here are the three versions:

Mk. iv, 30–3	*Lk. xiii, 18–19*	*Mt. xiii, 31–2*
And he said, how shall we liken the kingdom of God, or in what parable shall we set it forth? It is like a grain of mustard seed which, when it is sown upon the earth, though it be less than all the seeds that are upon the earth, yet when it is sown, groweth up, and becometh greater than all the herbs and putteth out great branches: so that the birds of the heaven can lodge near the shadow thereof.	He said therefore, unto what is the kingdom of God like, and whereunto shall I liken it? It is like a grain of mustard seed, which a man took, and cast into his own garden; and it grew and became a tree, and the birds of heaven lodged in the branches thereof.	Another parable set he before them, saying the kingdom of heaven is like unto a grain of mustard seed, which a man took, and sowed into his field; which indeed is less than all seeds; but when it is grown, it is greater than all the herbs and becometh a tree, so that the birds of the heaven come and lodge in the branches thereof.

Mt. and Lk., then, are not eye-witness reports but redactions of previous narratives, and other internal evidence also suggests that these gospels are considerably later in time than the events they describe. Mt. tells that the field bought with Judas' money is called the field of blood 'unto this day' (xxvii, 8). The phrase recurs in the statement that the saying that the disciples stole Jesus' body from the tomb 'was spread abroad among the Jews, and continueth until this day' (xxviii, 15). This verse is also remarkable for its mention of the Jews as an alien race—pointing to a time when the breach between Jews and Christians was wide.

Another indication of the date of Mt. comes in xxiii, 33–6, where Jesus tells the scribes and Pharisees that they will persecute wise men and prophets, but will pay for it with hell-fire; upon

---

my argument, I shall suppose that Mt. and Lk. drew on our canonical Mk., or at any rate on a document that strongly resembled it.

them 'shall come all the righteous blood shed on the earth, from the blood of Abel the righteous unto the blood of Zachariah son of Barachiah, whom ye slew between the sanctuary and the altar. Verily I say unto you, all these things shall come upon this generation.' Zechariah the son of Berechiah, the well-known prophet of the OT, did not suffer martyrdom. II Chron. xxiv, 20–1 tells of a Zechariah, the son of Jehoiada, who was murdered in the court of the temple. But this occurred 800 years before the Christian era, while the Zachariah of Mt. is plainly contrasted, as the last religious martyr, with Abel, the first. Now we know from Josephus that in the year AD 68 a Zachariah the son of Barneh or Berechiah was put to death 'in the forecourt of the temple'. As Schmiedel observes, the conjecture is a very obvious one that the author of Mt. had this event in mind. If it be correct, the date of composition will have to be placed some years later than AD 68, as the writer could not, very shortly after this event, easily have confounded this Zechariah with some other who had lived before, or in the time of Jesus (235, § 150). Slater admits (250, note on Mt. xxiii, 35) that 'the reference to Zachariah the son of Barachiah is one of the great historical difficulties of the gospel'.

Lk.'s gospel is decidedly later (cp. above, p. 90) and he himself affirms that he was redacting previous ones. He says (i, 1–4) the 'eye-witnesses and ministers of the word delivered' their testimony, by oral tradition; that 'many' then 'drew up a narrative' (they are not alleged to have been eye-witnesses), and that he proposes to improve on previous narratives. The NBC (p. 842) concedes that Lk. here professes to follow written records, and that he 'distinguishes himself from the eye-witnesses, but claims to have made a thorough investigation'. This points to a time when the supposed eye-witnesses had died, leaving the ground open to historians.

Brandon has noted (38, p. 185) that scholarly attempts to date the gospels earlier than the destruction of Jerusalem in AD 70 have now ceased except in the case of Mk. He himself finds evidence that Mk. too is of later date from this evangelist's deference to Rome in matters of taxation (Mk. xii, 13–17) and from his many references to the Jewish religious leaders as 'the bitter and determined enemies of Jesus, who constantly thwart and oppose him in his work, and finally plan and accomplish his death, being blind all the while to his divine character and mission and wilfully obdurate to the witness of his miracles' (p. 186). This tendency to represent Jesus as divorced from Jewish religious and national interests goes so far as to involve Mk. in designating the Davidic descent of the Messiah as the doctrine of the benighted Jewish scribes (Mk. xii, 35–7; cf. below, p. 311). The obvious motive for this repudiation of such an important piece of primitive Christian teaching was, says Brandon, to assure gentiles that Jesus and Christianity had no connection whatever with nationalist aspirations which had recently brought ruin to Jew and gentile alike in the ghastly war of AD 66–70.

Mk., like the other gospels, seems to be a redaction of previous documents. Schweitzer has drawn attention to what he calls the 'chaotic confusion of the narrative' in Mk. For instance, the successive contents of Mk. iv, 1–34 cannot have been set down in their present order by one man. The chapter begins with the parable of the sower: then the multitude departs and Jesus is left alone with his disciples. They ask him about the parables, and he explains that he uses them so as not to be understood except by the select few (see above, p. 63). He then explains the parable of the sower to them. He is still alone with them, nor is any hint given of his again addressing himself to the people. Yet after another parable, where the kingdom is likened to a grain of mustard seed, we are told that he had been addressing the people (verses 33–4).[1]

The story of the fig tree also suggests a redaction of an obscure tradition.[2] Mk. tells how Jesus, feeling hungry, came to a fig tree near Bethany, just before the passover, before the season for figs had come, and finding only leaves, cursed the tree, which was seen to be withered on the following morning. With this act he connected an exhortation to the disciples to have faith in God, since even mountains may be moved in prayer. Mk. expressly says that it was not the season for figs (xi, 13). That such unintelligible behaviour on the part of Jesus is traceable to an eye-witness report is hard to believe.

The extent to which some modern commentators admit serious

---

[1] Wrede pioneered sceptical assessments of Mk. when he argued that this gospel is concerned to represent Jesus as the Messiah with a life full of manifestations of this office (cf. above, p. 57), and yet also to suggest that Jesus contrived to conceal his true nature from mankind until his resurrection, and was recognized on earth only by 'unclean spirits', supernatural beings like himself (293, pp. 67, 125, 131). Weiss commented that to separate the oldest traditions from Mk.'s redaction of them was a formidable problem (278, p. 134).

[2] Jeremias (148, p. 85) gives evidence that 'redactional sutures' visibly link this story with its context.

inaccuracies in Mk. also suggests that his gospel is a late redaction rather than a first-hand report. Taylor, for instance, does not believe in the accuracy of his accounts of the Temptation, the Gadarene swine (265, p. 278), the raising of Jairus' daughter (p. 286), the Transfiguration (p. 388), and so on. Concerning the Temptation, he does not believe that Satan did the tempting, nor that Jesus remained unmolested in the company of wild beasts and was ministered to by angels; these features of the narrative he designates as 'an imaginative element'. Of the Gadarene swine he says that the story probably goes back to 'something which actually happened', although we cannot tell what. The raising of Jairus' daughter evokes from him the comment that 'it is hard to resist the conclusion that the evidence that the historical Jesus raised the dead is far from being decisive'. And as for the Transfiguration, 'it is impossible to say exactly what happened on the mount', but we may nevertheless believe that it was 'an incommunicable experience of prayer and insight'. To explain Mk. iv, 12, where Jesus says he is deliberately unintelligible to prevent repentance and forgiveness, Taylor supposes that Mk. has misunderstood what Jesus actually said. What the actual saying was he does not pretend to know (p. 257).

If, then, the existing gospels are not the original sources, we naturally ask what the earlier ones were, who were their authors and what was their authority. This is the so-called 'synoptic problem', which has engaged scholars, particularly in Germany, for more than a century. No solution seems possible. The evidence is insufficient, and Schmiedel, after discussing a number of theories, candidly acknowledges the fog which envelops the origin of the gospels (235, § 129(a)). 'Form-criticism', as it is called, has recently attempted to infer the primitive traditions underlying them. This is a reasonable (although necessarily speculative) endeavour, but less reasonable is the assumption of the form-critics (e.g. Dibelius) that the inferred primitive traditions possess greater historical trustworthiness.[1] Many admitted myths have primitive versions which are not on that account deemed reliable. Dibelius stresses that the evangelists are collectors and redactors, not original

---

[1] Dibelius seems aware that he is on insecure ground in alleging this (as he does, 80, p. 60); for he adds (pp. 61, 62) that traditions about the story of Jesus were first formulated in Christian preaching, and that 'just because they served the purpose of preaching, these stories could not have been told in a neutral fashion; they must meet the requirements of the hearer, support and prove the message'.

authors, and that the items they collected were the views of a sect or community, not the experiences of an individual (cf. Cullmann's summary, 71, p. 47). Cullmann concedes (72, p. 143) that in some cases the community 'created' these views, and in others 'remodelled' them from historical fact, so that it is now 'very difficult' to infer any reliable facts about the historical Jesus (cf. 71, p. 64). Grant has argued that the gospels are trustworthy because based on oral tradition that was a 'social' possession, the common property of the early Christian communities. He supposes that, whereas the recollections of individuals, directly recorded, might be untrustworthy, documents which reproduce n-th hand versions of them are bound to be reliable, since people do not believe what they are told, but inquire carefully into the evidence.[1] Would that this were so! The writings of the Fathers suffice to show how all manner of traditions found ready and uncritical acceptance.

Cullmann displays some anxiety lest those who deny the historicity of Jesus may profit from this 'new method' of form-criticism, and he argues against them as follows. He records with 'amazement' that Paul refers to Jesus almost exclusively in supernatural terms and says next to nothing about his life on earth—this at a time when Jesus' earthly life was so recent, and 'when the disciples and other eye-witnesses were still alive'. But, Cullmann adds, we never hear of any attack by Peter and his followers on Paul's christology; therefore even the eye-witnesses must have discerned the divinity in Jesus; there must therefore have been a 'mysterious element' in his life or death to evoke such veneration, and this element explains the 'dynamic force' with which traditions about him were invented by the early Christian community. The very fertility of early Christian invention is thus a witness to Jesus' historicity! (71, pp. 83–86). As I shall show below, the silence of Paul and other early Christian writers about a historical Jesus is one of the strongest arguments that no such person ever existed.

Attempts have also been made to establish that our Greek gospels are translations of Aramaic originals. By NT times Aramaic had long supplanted Hebrew as the current popular

---

[1] 'The memories of a few individuals might be mistaken . . . but the testimony of a group, even if anonymous, is more likely to have been verified, criticised, supported, culled and selected during the course of the first generation of early Church evangelism. The possibility of fabrication, by one or two individuals, is completely ruled out' (109, p. vii).

speech of the Jews in Palestine, and so if Jesus and the disciples existed at all, they probably spoke Aramaic, and an Aramaic gospel is more likely to have been written by people in direct contact with them than a Greek gospel.[1] One of the principal arguments for an underlying Aramaic original is that the language of the NT is peculiar, in that it is neither the literary Greek written by Plutarch, Philo and Josephus; nor the *koine* used by the ordinary unlettered people of the Greek-speaking world in the first century AD. It is full of apparent Semiticisms, suggesting strong Hebrew and Aramaic influence. C. C. Torrey, in a series of books and papers published between 1912 and 1941, argued that this strange Greek is really translated Aramaic, and in 1933 he 'retranslated' part of the NT, replacing what he considered to be the evangelists' misunderstandings of the supposed originals by his own interpretations of the Aramaic as reconstructed by himself. Albright, although polite to Torrey, points out the purely speculative nature of this attempt. The 'almost complete absence of contemporary Aramaic literature', he says, 'makes it impossible to know what the supposed original to our gospels could have been like' (10, pp. 179, 203).

The Hebraisms of the NT Greek can be readily understood without positing a Semitic original. In the Roman Empire Greek was widely spoken, and 'was a rival of Aramaic in Syria and Palestine'. Not only did most of the Jews of the Dispersion speak it but 'so did many who lived in Palestine, and from this group came some of the members of the very early Church' (294, pp. 80, 93). Thus, if the NT was written in Greek by Jews whose mother-tongue was Aramaic, it is quite intelligible that they should write a sort of Jewish Greek.

Many Catholic scholars maintain that Greek is the original language of Mk., Lk. and Jn., but that Mt. derives from an Aramaic original. This view is based ultimately on the statement by Papias (Bishop of Hierapolis about AD 140) that 'Matthew

---

[1] In order to reach behind the 'kerygma' of the early Christian communities, Jeremias has attempted to infer, from speeches in the gospels, not an underlying Aramaic gospel, but the actual Aramaic words Jesus used. He admits that this 'painstaking work over philological details' has as yet made little progress (149, p. 18). He describes as 'grossly exaggerated' the form-critics' view that the gospel biographies are coloured by the beliefs of the early Christian communities, and says that 'every verse' in them assures us that Christianity is based on a historical Jesus (p. 13). But I think it relevant to ask whether the assurance of the evangelists is reliable enough to settle the matter.

collected the oracles (τὰ λόγια) in the Hebrew language, and each interpreted them as best he could' (quoted by Eusebius, 89, III, 39). These 'logia' may be sayings of Jesus, as the writer has just stated that Peter made an arrangement of Jesus' 'logia', which was written down by Mark. Goodspeed, however, has urged (107, p. 2) that 'logia does not mean sayings, and what Matthew compiled probably consisted of OT oracles interpreted in relation to Jesus'.

A recent Catholic writer claims that the canonical Mt.'s 'use of the OT is also an indication of Semitic origin', for he frequently quotes the Hebrew and not the Septuagint, the Greek version of the OT (204, p. 852). An example is Mt. ii, 15, where Joseph and Mary are said to have fled with the child Jesus into Egypt 'that it might be fulfilled which was spoken by the Lord through the prophet, saying, Out of Egypt did I call my son'. The reference is to Hosea xi, 1, where the Hebrew reads 'I . . . called my son out of Egypt'. The Septuagint, however, has 'Out of Egypt I called his children'. The argument is that since our Greek Mt. quotes the Hebrew form, he must have been translating an Aramaic original, in which the OT quotations naturally appeared in Hebrew. But while it is true that the canonical Mt. follows the Hebrew OT more frequently than do the other evangelists (see 235, § 130), he nevertheless also sometimes follows the Septuagint, e.g. in passages which would not have been available had he used the Hebrew. As we have seen, it is only by quoting the Septuagint and not the Hebrew of Isa. vii, 14 that he was able to make the prophet foretell the virgin birth. Another striking example is Mt. iii, 3 which designates John the Baptist as 'he that was spoken of by Isaiah the prophet, saying, the voice of one crying in the wilderness, make ye ready the way of the Lord'. It is only the Septuagint version of Isa. xl, 3 that connects the 'voice' with 'in the desert', whereas the Hebrew has 'the voice of one that crieth, Prepare ye in the wilderness the way of the Lord'; here the crier is not in the wilderness at all, and so there can be no reference to John's preaching in the desert. Mt. seems to have had both the Hebrew and the Greek OT at his side as he wrote, and to have drawn on both. We cannot infer from this whether he wrote Semitic or Greek. What we can say is that our Mt. is in Greek and no Semitic original has been discovered.

CHAPTER FIVE

The Fourth and Some Apocryphal Gospels

That all manner of documents were written in order to plead certain dogmas, with no respect for historical truth, is well illustrated by the NT apocryphal writings, of which James remarks:

> As religious books they were meant to reinforce the existing stock of Christian beliefs: either by revealing new doctrines—usually differing from those which held the field; or by interpreting old ones—again, usually in a fresh sense; or by extolling some special virtue, as chastity or temperence; or by enforcing belief in certain doctrines or events, e.g. the Virgin birth, the resurrection of Christ, the second coming, the future state—by the production of evidence which, if true, should be irrefragable. For all these purposes the highest authority is claimed by the writings; they are the work, they tell us, of eye-witnesses of the events, or they report the utterances of the Lord himself (147, p. xii).

Some of them were long widely accepted. James admits that, in the formation of the canon, 'the processes of inclusion and exclusion were gradual'; that 'the best external test of the canonicity of a writing is, whether or not it was read in the public worship of Christian congregations which were in communion with the generality of other Christian congregations', and that this was in fact the case with some of the apocryphal writings (147, pp. xvi, xvii).

The early apocryphal gospels may be classified as Jewish-

E

Christian; Pauline or Gentile-Christian; and Gnostic. The Gospel of the Hebrews is an example from the first group. In one of the surviving fragments, Jesus urges a rich man to 'fulfil the law and the prophets' (147, p. 6). It is known that the work was in Aramaic and was, as Eusebius puts it, 'the especial delight of those of the Hebrews who have accepted Christ' (147, p. 2). This Aramaic work has often been claimed as one of the sources of our canonical Greek Mt. But if it had in fact been incorporated into our Mt., Jerome would not have needed to translate it separately, as he did into both Greek and Latin. It may well be nothing more than a translation of an original Greek gospel. Schoeps says that the surviving fragments suggest that the work was 'a targum-like version of the Greek Mt.—probably of a pre-canonical form of that gospel' (242, p. 26); that it was probably written about the same time as the canonical Mt. and survived into the fourth century in a solitary Jewish-Christian community, where Eusebius and Jerome discovered it, and supposed it to be the Aramaic original of Mt, of which Papias had spoken (see above, p. 121).

Another extant fragment of this gospel tells that James the brother of Jesus vowed at the Last Supper (where, according to our evangelists, he cannot even have been present) to eat nothing till he should have beheld Jesus after his resurrection. Jesus accordingly appeared to him first, brought bread, broke it and gave it to him (147, p. 3 and 235, § 155). From Eusebius we learn that this gospel also told the parable of the talents in what was for him a more acceptable form, in that it turned the threat not against the man who hid the talent but against him who had lived riotously.

Another Jewish-Christian gospel is that of the Twelve Apostles, also known as the Gospel of the Ebionites—the early Jewish Christians who denied the divinity of Jesus and the apostleship of Paul. The Jewish standpoint is betrayed by a fragment preserved by Epiphanius, which has it that the twelve were called 'for a testimony unto Israel' (147, p. 9).

The Gospel of Peter is an example from the Gentile-Christian group. It 'is known to have been used in the Church of Rhossus near Antioch. Serapion, Bishop of Antioch (190–203), at first permitted its use, but subsequently disallowed it on the ground of Docetic errors' (224, § 73). The Docetists held that Jesus was not born of Mary, but 'first appeared on the banks of the Jordan in the form of perfect manhood; but it was a form only, and not a substance; a human figure created by the hand of Omnipotence to imitate the faculties and actions of a man, and to impose a perpetual illusion on the senses of his friends and enemies' (104, v, 5, chapter 47). Such a phantom could not suffer, and so the Docetists denied that Jesus felt pain at his crucifixion. Accordingly, the Gospel of Peter says that 'they brought two malefactors and crucified the Lord betwixt them. But he kept silence, as one feeling no pain' (147, p. 91). The anti-Jewish character of the gospel is evident from its frequent condemnation of 'the Jews'. We shall see (p. 130) that the work nevertheless does not mention the treachery of Judas, and actually excludes it—strong evidence that the Judas story was not current at the time of its composition.

Another anti-Jewish gospel is that of Marcion, written about AD 125. In this work Jesus' saying 'I have not come to destroy the law but to fulfil', appears with 'fulfil' and 'destroy' transposed. Marcion's gospel is shown by extracts to agree largely with Lk. but to omit many passages peculiar to Lk. (5, § 98). Although his opponents described it as a mutilated form of Lk., 'it would be more correct to say that it took its place alongside of that gospel as an independent redaction of the common source' (179, § 7).

The third group of apocryphal gospels, the Gnostic, have nearly all perished. They were 'sacrificed to the destructive zeal of their ecclesiastic opponents' (85). It is, however, generally agreed that the fourth canonical gospel is in some degree representative of gnostic writing (179, § 7), and it is important to my purpose to show that it is just as much a 'tendency-writing' as the works we have just been considering.

Incompatibilities between the synoptic gospels and Jn. include the order of the principal events in Jesus' public life, the nature of his miracles as signs and the exorcistic miracles (see above, p. 49), the nature of his discourses (see above, p. 61), the details (including the date, see below, pp. 239, 275) of his trial and crucifixion. I do not propose to list discrepancies for their own sake, but to draw attention first to material in Jn. which suggests that his gospel was written later than the other three; and second to the way in which he manipulates the details of Jesus' life so as to stress his divinity rather than his humanity. I shall then try to show what bearing these matters have on our question of whether the gospels provide reliable information about a historical Jesus.

Jn. speaks of salvation coming to all who believe. This was still a matter of hot dispute when the Pauline letters were written, and also many passages from the synoptic gospels reserve salvation for the Jews. In Jn., however, the salvation of all believers is taken for granted, and the Mosaic law simply regarded as the law of the Jews, who are mentioned as though Jesus had no particular connection with them. He speaks to them of 'your law' and 'the feasts of the Jews' as if he were addressing aliens. That the Johannine Christ has risen so high above the difficulties which beset Paul and the Jesus of the synoptics suggests a later date. Furthermore, Jn. has dropped the expectation of the synoptic gospels that the world is coming to a speedy end. In Jn. Christ's second coming no longer means his appearance in the sky to end the world, but only the coming of the Holy Spirit into the hearts of believers (xiv, 16–18; xvi, 7, 13). Steinmann admits that 'the complete absence of any apocalyptic notes in Jesus' teaching in the fourth Gospel has not yet been adequately explained' (258, p. 114).

That Jn. is later than the synoptics is also suggested by the external evidence. Polycarp, who shows some knowledge of Mt. and Lk., shows none of Jn.—a fact which 'has never yet been satisfactorily accounted for by those who maintain with Irenaeus (*a*) that this gospel was written by John the son of Zebedee, and (*b*) that Polycarp was the disciple of this same John' (131, p. 257). Papias, who recognized Mk. and Mt., says nothing of Jn. And Justin, who quotes from the other gospels, does not quote Jn., even when to do so would have been to the point. For instance, 'it is generally recognized that the Synoptists do not teach, whereas Jn. and Justin do teach, Christ's pre-existence, the feeding on Christ's "flesh and blood" (as expressed in those precise words), the application of the term "only begotten" to Christ, and the Logos doctrine'. Justin puts these doctrines either without any appeal to authorities, or he appeals to 'pointless passages in the Synoptists instead of pointed passages in Jn.' (5, § 102). Abbott thinks that Justin knew Jn. and regarded it with suspicion, partly because it contradicted Lk., his favourite gospel (5, § 104). It seems reasonable to suppose that Jn. was in existence for some years before being accepted as authoritative, particularly since his gospel contradicts the others so flagrantly. Justin's pupil Tatian certainly knew it, ranked it with the other three, and composed his harmony of the gospels (dated about AD 170) from all four. He arranged the material into a single continuous narrative, trying to combine the texts and avoid overlap. His work shows both that these four gospels had acquired a certain authority at the time, and also that this authority 'was not so great that there was felt any impropriety in replacing the four individual texts by a single narrative' (70, p. 68).

From all this evidence, then, it seems likely that Jn. existed when Justin wrote (AD 150) and was accepted as authoritative within twenty or thirty years. The Muratorian fragment (part of a list of sacred books of about AD 180) also welcomes Jn. as making good the deficiencies of the other three, and Irenaeus accepts Jn. as authoritative.[1]

The following examples show how Jn. is prepared to contradict the synoptic narrative in order to emphasize the divinity of Jesus:

(1) In the fourth gospel the Baptist knows from the very first that Jesus is redeemer of the world. As soon as he sees Jesus he cries 'Behold the Lamb of God, which taketh away the sins of the world' (i, 29). He is even represented as knowing Jesus' pre-existence. 'This is he of whom I said, After me cometh a man which is become before me: for he was before me' (i. 30). In Mt. xi, 2 f. the Baptist sends his disciples to Jesus to ask whether he

---

[1] Albright has claimed (10, p. 240) that discoveries published in 1935 prove that Jn. existed earlier than previously supposed. He mentions a papyrus fragment of Jn. 'written in a hand attributed to the time of Trajan (d. 117) or more probably Hadrian (d. 135)'. This dating seems overconfident, for another Christian writer (97) thinks that a later date, up to AD 150, is arguable. Albright also mentions what he calls 'a fragment containing incidents drawn from all four gospels, dating from the first half of the second century'. But the scholars who published this fragment say that it is 'not a harmony of the canonical gospels, for it contains matter that is not in any of them' (25, p. 30). They consider that it is independent of the synoptics, contains one incident (an encounter with lawyers) which resembles Jn. v, 30, but is not derived from it, and 'may be, or derive from, a source used by that gospel' (pp. 34, 38). Dr Frend (97) also says cautiously that the encounter is 'on the lines' of that described by Jn.

Albright also adduces archaeological evidence in order to defend the general credibility of Jn. He mentions the excavation of the remains of a Roman pavement which can be correlated with the locality mentioned in Jn. xix, 13. He believes that the 'clear-cut tradition' preserved in Jn. 'must go back to the period before the pavement had been buried during the catastrophe of AD 70' (10, p. 245). Albright assumes that Jn. himself was completely ignorant of the nature of the architecture in Jerusalem before the revolt, and that if he makes Jesus do certain things in buildings which can be proved to have existed, this can only be because he possessed traditions which alleged these happenings in these places. But surely there might have been many traditions about this 'magnificent' pavement which acquainted Jn. with its existence and enabled him to give a real setting to imaginary episodes. The excavation of the pavement does not prove that Jn. is right in alleging that Pilate sat down on it in judgement of Jesus.

is really the Messiah. In the fourth gospel there is no question of such an inquiry: the Baptist recognizes him as the Messiah from the first; and this is his sole function in Jn. Of his preaching of repentance no mention is made.

(2) Jn. makes Jesus turn water into wine at Cana in the presence of all the disciples as the first of his signs, the first manifestation of his divinity. The synoptics do not mention this miracle, and according to Mk. he emphatically declined to work a sign before the eyes of his contemporaries (Mk. viii, 12).

(3) The miracles recorded by Jn. are enhanced as compared with those of the synoptics. 'None of the sick mentioned by the synoptists as having been healed by Jesus is recorded to have lain under his infirmity for thirty-eight years (Jn. v, 5). The blind man who is healed has been blind from birth (ix, 1). Jesus walks across the whole lake, not over a portion of it only (vi, 21). Lazarus is not raised on the day of his death, like the daughter of Jairus or the son of the widow of Nain (neither of whom is mentioned in Jn.) but after four days have elapsed' (236, § 20), that is, at a time when according to Jewish belief, the soul has irrevocably departed from the body. This prodigious miracle was, according to Jn., the chief cause of the applause that greeted Jesus' entry into Jerusalem, and of the priests' resolution to slay him (Jn. xi, 45–8; xii, 9–12). Yet the synoptic gospels do not mention it. In them the hatred of the authorities is brought to explosive point by the cleansing of the temple—an event which in Jn. is placed at the beginning of Jesus' ministry (ii, 13, 22) and has no outward consequences.

(4) Jn. represents the entire Roman cohort as falling to the ground at Jesus' arrest (xviii, 6). Then, 'of his own initiative he gives himself up. Judas has no need to betray him with a kiss and stands doing nothing . . . Jesus acknowledged to Pilate that he was king, not of the Jews but of something higher, of truth. There is no need for Simon of Cyrene to carry the cross; Jesus carries it himself. Immediately after his resurrection he will not allow Mary Magdalene to touch him (xx, 17) as she and the other Mary touch his feet in Mt. xxviii, 9. He does not taste food as in Lk. xxiv, 42; on the contrary, he enters by closed doors and imparts the Holy Spirit (xx, 22), which according to Acts ii, 1–13 was first poured out on the disciples at Pentecost' (236, § 26). All these changes tend to exalt him.

(5) Details which might be taken to depress his dignity are omitted by Jn. These include his baptism, his temptation in the

wilderness, his prayer in Gethsemane, and his forsaken cry on the cross. The failure to mention his baptism is particularly striking, and comparison of the gospel narratives is here instructive. Mk.'s account appears the most primitive. He has it that baptism is 'baptism of repentance for the remission of sins', and that Jesus simply submits to it. Mt., however, omits the phrase about repentance for sin, and represents the Baptist as hesitating to baptize him. Jn. tells how the Baptist saw the spirit descending upon Jesus 'as a dove out of heaven' (i, 32), and thus gives an account of what according to the synoptics were the circumstances in which Jesus' baptism took place. His own omission of it must therefore have been deliberate.

We see, then, that although Jn. gives many biographical details, he is nevertheless not interested in historical accuracy. 'A book which begins by declaring Jesus to be *logos* of God and ends by representing a cohort of Roman soldiers as falling to the ground at the majesty of his appearance, and by representing a hundred pounds of ointment as having been used at his embalming (xix, 39), ought by these facts alone to be spared such a misunderstanding of its true character as would be implied in supposing that it meant to be a historical work' (236, § 37). So even at a time when the synoptic narratives were established, it was possible to write an account of Jesus' life and conduct which, though incompatible with them, could nevertheless find general and lasting acceptance. If such a thing could happen at this relatively late stage in the development of the documents, we can feel little confidence in the accuracy of the gospels which were written earlier, at a time when they did not have to establish themselves against rival narratives, and when, in consequence, large-scale invention would be even less likely to be questioned.

Orthodox writers (e.g. Haag, 115, A: 116, A, 2C) frequently assert that the Church recognized four gospels as canonical from the first, and that these are older than the apocryphal gospels. Neither assertion will bear scrutiny. For instance, in Lk. Jesus is said to have been born in an inn-stable, Mt. simply specifies 'Bethlehem', and the other two canonical gospels have no birth story. However, early Christian writers, such as Justin and Origen, explicitly say he was born in a cave, and could not have done so had they known and accepted our four gospels as the only reliable authorities. As we have seen the apocryphal *Gospel of James* represents Jesus as cave-born (see above, p. 17)—as, by the way, was Mithra; Mithraic monuments show the new-born babe adored by shepherds, who offer first-fruits. Again, Justin relates that when Jesus came up out of the Jordan, fire appeared on the surface of the water (157, chapter 88). We know from Epiphanius (88, xxx, 13) that the *Gospel according to the Hebrews* asserted something similar, namely that, when Jesus came out of the water, 'forthwith a great light shone round about the place'. Marcion, who was in Rome soon after AD 140, was content with a single gospel in his canon, and it was in opposition to this, and as late as the second half of the second century, that the Church stood by its sacred four. Irenaeus, for instance, insists that 'the gospels could not possibly be more or less in number than they are'. There are four winds, he says, and so there must be four gospels to carry the glad tidings into the four zones of the earth (146, p. 382). But as we have seen (above p. 84), the way in which all manner of traditions outside our four gospels long found wide acceptance is well illustrated by Irenaeus himself.

Haag's other assertion—that the apocryphal gospels are all later than the canonical ones—is likewise untrue. The *Gospel of James* is obviously later than the canonical Mt. and Lk., since it tries to reconcile their contradictions. But in the fragment of the *Gospel of Peter* recovered in 1884, the narrator is made to tell how after the crucifixion 'we, the twelve disciples of the Lord, were weeping and were in sorrow', no hint being given of the defection of any one of the group (147, p. 94). This must have been written before the Judas story was current, i.e. either before the canonical gospels, or before the Judas story had been added to them.

Irenaeus' references show that by the end of the second century all four of our gospels existed, were regarded as the only reliable ones, and were also known by the names they now bear. They are also mentioned and named by the Muratorian fragment (about AD 180), by Clement of Alexandria (died 215) and Origen (died 254). From this time the references to them are legion. What we must next investigate is to what extent either they or the matter in them are quoted or alluded to by earlier writers.

CHAPTER SIX

Evidence of Early
Christian Writers

(i) The silence of Paul in his principal epistles

It is generally agreed that the NT epistles addressed to the Romans, Corinthians, Galatians, Ephesians, Philippians, Colossians and Thessalonians were written before the gospels and form 'the earliest Christian sources for the life of Jesus' (116, A2).[1] These early epistles exhibit such complete ignorance of the events which were later recorded in the gospels as to suggest that these events were not known to Paul or whoever it was who wrote the epistles. For instance, these Pauline letters have no single allusion to the parents of Jesus, let alone to the virgin birth; they never refer to the place of his birth, never call him 'of Nazareth'. They never use the title 'Son of man', so often used in the gospels to designate Jesus; and they mention none of the miracles he is supposed to have worked. They give no indication at all of the time or place of his public activities. They do not refer to his trial before a Roman official, nor do they say that his crucifixion took place at Jerusalem. They never mention John the Baptist, nor Judas, nor Peter's denial of Jesus. The latter is a particularly striking omission, since the author of Galatians opposes Peter very strongly (see below, p. 139) and would surely have alluded to his treachery had he known of it.

In II Cor. v, 16 Paul affirms that 'we henceforth know no man after the flesh; even though we have known Christ after the flesh,

[1] Recent scholarship has given the date of composition of Romans as AD 58 (184, p. 1) and that of I Cor. as about the same time (65, p. 16).

yet now we know him so no more'. The idea seems to be, not that he formerly knew a historical Jesus, but that he once had a 'carnal' conception of Jesus, that is, one dictated by worldly interests rather than by devotion to principle. The NEB brings this out: 'with us worldly standards have ceased to count in our estimate of any man: even if they once counted in our understanding of Christ, they do so now no longer'. Couchoud argues that the distinction made here corresponds to that made in Phil. i, 16–17 between those who preach Christ from ambition, and those who do so from love.

I Cor. ii, 8 gives what look like historical details saying that Jesus was crucified by 'the rulers of this world'. We who know the gospels immediately think of Pilate and Caiaphas the high priest. But some commentators have taken the reference to mean 'Satan and his angels'; and Satan is certainly frequently described as the prince or ruler of the world in early Christian literature. Thus in the epistle of Barnabas he is designated 'the ruler of the present era of lawlessness', and as 'the wicked ruler'. Ignatius frequently calls him 'the prince of this world', and so does the author of the canonical Jn. (xii, 31; xiv, 30; xvi, 11). Paul himself says (Eph. vi, 12) that we wrestle 'not against flesh and blood, but against the principalities, against the powers, against the world-rulers of this darkness, against the spiritual hosts of wickedness in the heavenly places'. Here, then, the powers and rulers of the world are expressly said not to be human beings. Furthermore, in the passage from Corinthians, Paul seems to imply that Jesus was crucified by *all* the rulers of this world. This again suggests Satan and his angels rather than Pilate and Caiaphas.[1] Here is the passage in context:

> We speak God's wisdom . . . which none of the rulers of this world knoweth; for had they known it, they would not have crucified the Lord of glory.

From Coloss. ii, 15 (NEB) we learn that on the cross 'he discarded the cosmic powers and authorities like a garment, he made a public spectacle of them and led them as captives in his triumphal procession'. This can hardly refer to Pilate.

I Thess. ii, 14–15 mentions 'the Jews, who both killed the Lord

[1] Brandon agrees (38a, pp. 11, 151) that Paul attributes the crucifixion to 'the daemonic powers that rule the lower universe', and that he says 'nothing of the location of the event in either time or space'. cf. below, pp. 288–297.

Jesus and the prophets'. This accords with the synoptics, although 'the bitterness of this reference to the Jews is unparalleled in Paul's writings and it has been suspected of being an interpolation' (NBC, p. 1055).[1] Even if it is not, and even if the passage in Corinthians does not refer to Satan, Paul tells us very little by way of historical details of the crucifixion.

These epistles also do not cite any of the gospel teachings of Jesus. The doctrine of Rom. xii, 14, 'Bless them that persecute you' is not represented as the teaching of Jesus. Nor is the command 'Let us not therefore judge one another any more' (Rom. xiv, 13). Yet according to Mt. vii, 1 Jesus himself said 'judge not'. Precisely where the author of Romans might be expected to invoke the authority of Jesus, he does not do so. Similarly the complaint (I Cor. vi, 7) that Christians go to law against each other—even before heathen judges—instead of suffering evil, is not supported by any citation from Jesus about turning the other cheek, even though according to Mt. Jesus put this doctrine precisely when he was speaking of litigation (Mt. v, 39–40). Again, Paul twice says that the law may be summed up in the one rule 'Thou shalt love thy neighbour as thyself' (Rom. xiii, 9. Gal. v, 14). A similar teaching is ascribed to Jesus in Mt. xxii, 40, Mk. xii, 31 and Lk. x, 27, where he says that the law can be reduced to love of God and love of neighbour. But Paul gives no indication that Jesus taught anything at all on this subject.

In I Cor. vii, 10, where Paul appears to allude to the teaching of Jesus, he contradicts what the gospels say: 'But unto the married I give charge, yea not I, but the Lord, That the wife depart not from her husband . . . and let not the husband put away his wife'. In Mt. v, 32 and xix, 9 Jesus allows adultery as an exception to this prohibition. Paul, however, makes no mention of this, yet goes on, on his own responsibility, to establish a new exception—saying that marriage with a non-Christian may be dissolved if there seems no prospect of its being continued in peace.

Again, he gives the Corinthian Christians detailed instructions such as:

Let the women keep silence in the churches: for it is not permitted unto them to speak; but let them be in subjection,

[1] Brandon (38, pp. 92–3) regards the passage as 'an interpolation made by some Gentile Christian with an anti-Semitic bias'.

as also saith the law. And if they would learn anything, let them ask their own husbands at home.

He adds: 'The things which I write unto you . . . are the commandment of the Lord' (I Cor. xiv, 34–7). The Lord gives no such commandments in our gospels, and if he gave them to Paul it must have been in a special revelation of the type Paul himself claimed to have experienced. For instance in Gal. i, 12 he declares that he has received his gospel 'through revelation of Jesus Christ', and this means a supernatural revelation, for no one supposes that he ever met Jesus. Even Acts (ix, 3–5) restricts his knowledge of Jesus to a supernatural revelation on the road to Damascus.

The one remaining passage where Paul claims to reproduce the words of the Lord is I Thess. iv, 15, which the NEB renders:

For this we tell you as the Lord's word: we who are left alive until the Lord comes shall not forestall those who have died; because at the word of command, at the sound of the archangel's voice and God's trumpet-call, the Lord himself will descend from heaven; first the Christian dead will rise, then we who are left alive shall join them, caught up in clouds to meet the Lord in the air.

Adeney has noted (8) that there is nothing in the gospels that corresponds to Paul's statements here, even though Jesus expatiates there on the subject of his second coming. Again it seems as though the reference is not to the teachings of a historical Jesus but to supernatural revelations made to Paul.

Some (e.g. Goguel, 105, p. 104) hold that Paul's claim for his right to financial support is based on a precept of the gospel Jesus. He says: 'Even so did the Lord ordain that they which proclaim the gospel should live of the gospel' (I Cor. ix, 14) and this is held to refer to Jesus' speech at the sending out of the twelve: 'And into whatsoever house ye shall enter . . . remain eating and drinking such things as they give: for the labourer is worthy of his hire' (Lk. x, 5–7). But a claim such as this is a natural one, made by priests at all times and represented as the will of God. Paul did not need to know anything of a historical Jesus so to represent it.

One striking example shows that if we take the gospels as history, Jesus gave the disciples instructions which both they and

Paul wilfully disregarded. In Mt. xxviii, 19 the risen Jesus bids the disciples 'go ye therefore and teach all nations, baptizing them in the name of the Father and of the Son and of the Holy Ghost'. From Acts (ii, 38; viii, 16; x, 48; xix, 5) and from the epistles (Rom. vi, 3; Gal. iii, 27; I Cor. i, 12 and vi, 11) it is clear that in the earliest times baptism was administered not with this Trinitarian formula but simply 'in the name of Jesus Christ' or of 'the Lord Jesus'.[1] Either Paul and the others deliberately defied Jesus, or the passage in Mt. could be a late interpolation written from a Trinitarian standpoint. This latter is the more likely hypothesis, especially since the passage has no parallel in Mk. or Lk. And if Jesus had enjoined the mission to all nations on his disciples as stated in Mt. it would be impossible to understand how they or their followers could have withstood Paul so hotly upon this very point (see 235, § 136).

Paul also appears to have no knowledge of the twelve apostles. Before we study his one reference to them it will be relevant to note that even in the gospels the accounts of the twelve are not free from difficulties. In Jn. the number is introduced with a suddenness that strongly suggests fabrication. From vi, 60, we learn that the disciples are 'many', yet a few verses later Jesus is suddenly made to address 'the twelve'. There has been no previous hint of the choosing of that number. In Mt. we are merely told: 'And he called unto him his twelve disciples', followed by the list (x, 1–4). Lk., however, does represent Jesus as selecting twelve from the more extensive circle of his adherents, although his list does not agree with Mt.'s. Lk. has two Judases, Mt. only one; while Mt. has a Thadaeus unknown to Lk. Mk.'s list (iii, 16–19) is different again.

There is an obvious basis for the belief that Jesus had twelve apostles. If, as Mt. holds, the disciples were sent to care for 'the lost sheep of the house of Israel', it would be appropriate that there should be twelve shepherds to tend the twelve tribes of the nation. That this is the basis of the story of the twelve is suggested by Lk.'s treatment of this topic. He does not agree with Mt. that Jesus was sent to redeem only the Jews. And so, after his account of the choosing of the twelve in chapter vi, he makes Jesus dispatch them to preach the kingdom in chapter ix, without any

[1] That even this was not universal is suggested by the mention of a prominent Christian teacher, Apollos, who 'knew only the baptism of John' (Acts xviii, 25)

nationalist restrictions about to whom they are to preach. Further-more, he adds in chapter x a story (unknown to all the other evangelists) of the choosing and sending out of a further seventy disciples (in some MSS. it is seventy-two). Jewish tradition divides mankind into seventy (or seventy-two) peoples and so Lk. is substituting a mission to the gentiles for a mission to the Jews. Whereas in Mt. twelve are sent out to proclaim exclusively for the benefit of Israel that the kingdom of heaven is at hand, Lk.'s tenth chapter has it that seventy are dispatched with this message 'into every city and place whither he himself would come'. Schmiedel observes that if we compare Lk.'s account of the two missions—(a) of the twelve (ix, 3–5) and (b) of the seventy (x, 1–12)—with Mt.'s account of the single mission (Mt. x, 7–15), then we find that (b) is almost entirely made up of that portion of Mt. which does not occur in (a).

In Acts Matthias is chosen by lot to fill the vacancy caused by the defection of Judas Iscariot, but is never mentioned again. 'Had there really been twelve apostles whose number was to be kept up, it ought to have been renewed after the first deaths in the circle (the first is recorded in Acts xii, 2); but it is not even pre-tended that this happened' (220, p. 346). Why, then, was the pretence made in the one case? Robertson thinks that the election of Matthias was an expedient to meet the difficulty that the Judas story subtracted one from the number of the twelve teachers, to whom twelve heavenly thrones had been promised in the gospel.[1] This suggestion has been endorsed by Johnson, who discusses the Matthias story apropos of the Dead Sea Scrolls, which show that the pre-Christian Essenes were ruled by a group of twelve laymen and three priests. The Essenes, like the Christians, ex-pected the immediate end of the world, and Johnson thinks that, among both, 'the twelve men are the community's council for the coming Messianic age, when they will sit on thrones judging the twelve tribes of Israel' (Lk. xxii, 29–30; Mt. xix, 28). (152, p. 134). Dupont-Sommer remarks (84, p. 90 n.) that the twelve laymen would represent the twelve tribes and the three priests the three levitical clans.

From Paul we hear of the 'chiefest apostles' (II Cor. xi, 5) and the 'pillars' (Gal. II, 9), and Cephas, James and John are named.

---

[1] Judas thus forfeited his throne because of his misconduct, not because of his death. Other apostles who died would be duly raised to their thrones, and did not have to be replaced.

But he only once mentions the twelve in a verse (I Cor. xv, 5) which contradicts the gospels, saying that the risen Jesus appeared to Peter and then to the twelve. This must be earlier than the Judas story of the gospels, for they allege an appearance to the surviving eleven. Mt. xxviii, 16 and Mk. xvi, 14 mention not 'the disciples' but expressly 'the eleven'. The whole passage in Corinthians runs:

> Now I make known unto you, brethren, the gospel which I preached unto you . . . For I delivered unto you first of all that which also I received, how that Christ died for our sins *according to the scriptures*; and that he was buried; and that he hath been raised *on the third day according to the scriptures*; and that he appeared to Cephas; *then to the twelve*: *then he appeared to above five hundred brethren at once, of whom the greater part remain until now, but some are fallen asleep; then he appeared to James*; then to all the apostles; and last of all, as unto one born out of due time, he appeared to me also.

Commenting: (i) this is the only passage where Paul, or any NT writer outside the gospels, speaks of the resurrection occurring 'on the third day'. And it is the only epistolary passage where the death and resurrection of Jesus is said to be 'according to the scriptures'. If the scriptures in question are the gospels, then the passage is at once proved an interpolation, for no scholar asserts that Paul had read the gospels. But the reference may not be to them. Admittedly they are the only scriptures according to which Christ died and rose on the third day. But this is not decisive, for in the gospels themselves Jesus foretells these events and says that they will happen in fulfilment of the ancient prophecies (see above, p. 104). Thus it may well be that both the gospel writers and the writer of this passage were trying to show that the death and resurrection of Jesus happened in fulfilment of OT prophecies. As we have seen, they did not find this easy.

(ii) The story of an appearance of the risen Jesus to 'above five hundred brethren at once' is not found in any of the gospels, nor is the appearance to James.[1] Assuming that they were written

---

[1] The clause which introduces the five hundred is the first of a series of main clauses, although consistent syntax would require here further subordinate clauses introduced with 'that' (ὅτι). This break in the syntax suggests that the passage has been manipulated.

after Corinthians one would expect to find the five hundred story in them; had it been current it would have been too welcome to be neglected. So it looks as though this story was interpolated into the epistle after the gospels had been written.

(iii) Paul is trying to convince doubters of the truth of the resurrection. This is why he gives the evidence of the appearances. He then continues (verse 12, NEB): 'Now if this is what we proclaim, that Christ was raised from the dead, how can some of you say that there is no resurrection of the dead?' If the previous passage about the appearances had already been written, one would have expected him to say not 'if this is what we proclaim' but something like: 'if, then, Christ appeared to many.'

(iv) If Paul had known and worked with the twelve we should expect some correlation between his various epistles and Acts, since the latter work sets forth the activities of both Paul and the original apostles. But we find it hopelessly at variance with the epistles. Let us look at the details:

(a) According to Acts, Paul, after his miraculous conversion, went to Jerusalem, where Barnabas introduced him to the apostles. He stayed with them, moving about freely there until the non-Christian Jews planned to murder him; whereupon the apostles saw him off to Tarsus (chapter ix). According to Galatians, nothing of the sort happened. Paul there tells that after his miraculous vision 'immediately I conferred not with flesh and blood; neither went I up to Jerusalem to them which were apostles before me; but I went away into Arabia' (i, 16–17). Only after three years does he meet Peter (verse 18), but even then, during this fortnight's sojourn in Jerusalem, he met none of the other apostles 'save James the Lord's brother', and he was 'still unknown by face to the churches of Judaea' (verse 22). The reason for the contradiction is that Acts is anxious to represent Paul and the others as working in complete harmony, hence the story of their common labour in Jerusalem. In Galatians, however, Paul is trying to show that he is independent of them, and so he says that he was for long a Christian without even meeting them, and hardly knows them even at the time of writing. Paul's statement that he was still unknown by sight to the churches of Judaea three years after his conversion is not intelligible as history. They must have known him very well from the days when, as he said (i, 13–14 and 23–4), he 'persecuted the church of God and made havoc of it'.[1] But it can be readily understood as a means of demonstrating his independence of the Jewish Christians. The original apostles are to convert Jews, Paul is to preach to gentiles (ii, 9), and he insists that he be given a free hand to preach what he wants. He was made an apostle not by them but by higher authority, 'not from men, neither through man, but through Jesus Christ' (i, 1). The allegation that he learned of the Lord's Supper by revelation and not from Peter (see below, p. 271) is likewise a device to put him on a level with the Jewish party. And so he maintains, or is made to maintain, that he is not behind the most apostolic of the apostles (II Cor. xi, 5); and that he had 'seen the Lord' in ecstatic vision (I Cor. ix, 1; xv, 8; II Cor. xii, 1 ff.).

(b) The writer of the epistles is not merely independent of the original apostles, but also in serious conflict with them. He refers to them sarcastically as 'those who were reputed to be somewhat' (Gal. ii, 2, 6). He appears to have Peter, James and John in mind, who, he says, 'were reputed to be pillars' (verse 9). Because the OT promises salvation only to the chosen race and to those received into it by circumcision, they maintained that Christians were obliged to keep the Mosaic law; while Paul held that all who believed in Jesus were to be saved, and that the Jewish law was not only useless, but pernicious (Gal. iii, 10, 13). James appears to be the chief culprit in demanding that the law be kept. Paul tells how Peter came to Antioch and at first ate with gentile Christians, thus breaking the law of Moses which forbids such defilement; but when 'certain from James' came, Peter withdrew from the gentiles, 'fearing them that were of the circumcision' (Gal. ii, 12); for which behaviour Paul calls him a hypocrite. Paul repeatedly complains of Judaizing plots to impose on the Galatians another gospel, that of circumcision (Gal. i, 8; vi, 12 f.); and of rivals who proclaim 'another Jesus' (II Cor. xi, 4). He detests this forcing of circumcision on the gentiles and says that obedience to one such detail of the law involves recognition of the whole of it as obligatory.

In Acts there is none of this conflict. There is no mention of Paul's dispute with Peter at Antioch and throughout the book

---

[1] Brandon (38, pp. 91–2) resolves the contradiction by supposing that Paul had persecuted Christians in Damascus, not Judaea. He rejects the testimony of Acts that the persecution took place in Jerusalem.

Paul is opposed only by the non-Christian Jews. On one of his visits to Jerusalem he is reproached by James and the elders because they have heard that 'thou teachest all the Jews which are among the Gentiles to forsake Moses, telling them not to circumcise their children, neither to walk after the customs' (Acts xxi, 21). They ask him to perform certain Jewish religious ceremonies in public in order to clear himself of this charge and he complies. Throughout Acts he is in no way hostile to the Jewish law, and even circumcises Timothy, a convert of mixed Jewish and Greek parentage, so as not to offend the Jews (xvi, 3). In sum, Acts shows a united Church, while the Paul of the epistles pours scorn on Peter and James in his fierce controversy with them. Moreover, in the epistles Paul acknowledges no human authority, and certainly not that of the original apostles. He goes to Jerusalem to see Peter and the others about the validity of the Jewish law because a revelation impels him (Gal. ii, 1–2); and he goes not with the intention of submitting to whatever decision they might reach, but in order to make clear to them that he had been entrusted with the gospel for gentiles as surely as Peter with that for Jews (verse 7): whereas Acts has it that he went as a mere delegate of the Church of Antioch and was prepared to submit to the decision of the apostles and elders; that Peter argued that gentiles need not observe the law and that it was agreed, following a motion of James, that they need not be circumcised, but must abstain from meat that has been offered to idols, from blood, from anything that has been strangled, and from fornication. (These are the main prescriptions of the Jewish law. For instance, in Lev. xvii, 10–16 the eating of blood is forbidden on the ground that the soul resides in the blood.) Paul and his companions are then represented as meekly carrying this decision back to Antioch (chapter xv). Altogether, the Paul of Acts is a docile creature who undertakes nothing except what others have initiated. In this work it is Peter who starts converting gentiles, and only after this example does Paul begin to preach to them. The passage in I Cor. about the appearance of Jesus to the twelve, to the five hundred, to James and 'last of all . . . to me also' shows a modesty quite unparalleled elsewhere in the epistles, for it continues: 'For I am the least of the apostles, that am not meet to be called an apostle, because I persecuted the church of God' (I Cor. xv, 9). This is further evidence of interpolation and of late interpolation at that, 'dating from a time when the rival claims of Paul and the "twelve" had to be somehow squared by second-century harmonists' (219, p. 117; 218, ii, 43–5).

To sum up: the mention of the twelve in a solitary verse of the Pauline epistles looks like an interpolation. If so, the twelve are absent from the earliest traditions and appear only in later documents, first in the gospels and then Acts.

Some (e.g. Jeremias, 148, pp. 95–7 and Conzelmann, 65, p. 296) have conceded that the language of I Cor. xv, 3–5 (which includes the reference to the twelve) is 'unpauline', but have argued that it represents 'kerygmatic' material (cf. above, p. 114) earlier, not later than Paul, who simply assimilated it into his text. The foundation for this view was laid by Dibelius, who held that the earliest Christians preached their recollections of Jesus in the form of standing phrases, and that I Cor, xv, 3–5 suggests that Paul is quoting the following such phrases that he has learned by heart: (1) Christ died for our sins according to the scriptures; (2) he was buried; (3) he rose on the third day according to the scriptures; (4) he appeared to Cephas and then to the twelve. But if such ideas formed the basis of the earliest Christian teaching, it is remarkable that they are so poorly represented in the earliest documents. Goguel argued (106, p. 33) that Paul's statement about a resurrection on the third day represents not an early tradition, but an idea later than some of the gospel material. It cannot, for instance, be reconciled with Mt. xii, 40, and this suggests that 'the tradition originally was not as precise as it has already become in I Cor. xv, 4.'

It is also very striking that Paul never alleges that the apostles, whether twelve or some unspecified number, had been in direct intercourse with Jesus. In Galatians the apostles whom Paul controverts (Peter, James and John) are Judaizing missionaries who preached circumcision—a practice not once enjoined by Jesus in the gospels. Nowhere is it suggested that they were 'taught by the Lord'; they are referred to simply as leaders of an existing sect. Gal. i, 19 does, however, refer to 'James the Lord's brother' (ἀδελφὸν τοῦ κυρίου) and I Cor. ix, 5 to 'the brethren of the Lord'. It is widely held that this title designated the actual kindred of Jesus, his brothers, cousins or more distant relatives, who had been his companions. But while, in the epistles, the brethren of the Lord are zealous believers, the gospels mention Jesus' kindred in order to illustrate how completely they repudiated him (e.g. above, p. 16. The only exception is Acts i, 14). So the gospel references may not be to the same people.[1] Now the title used in the epistles is perfectly intelligible as the group title of a fraternity of zealous Messianists. The phrase is 'brethren of the Lord' not 'brethren of Jesus' as in the gospels, and could have been used as a title by men who claimed no family kinship with the gospel Jesus. Paul repeatedly calls his fellow Christians 'brethren'. And in I Cor. i, 11–13 he complains of those factions among them which bear the group titles 'of Paul', 'of Apollos', 'of Cephas', and—most significant of all—'of Christ'. If there was a group called 'those of the Christ', there may well have been one called 'the brethren of the Lord' who would have had no more personal experience of Jesus than Paul himself. Brandon, who emphasizes the pre-eminence of James at Jerusalem, refers to evidence that the term 'brother' could in those days mean 'principal servant'. 'The vizier of the Nabataean kings regularly bore the title of ἀδελφὸς βασιλέως' (38, p. 20 n and refs).[2] This evidence accords well with my suggestion that the Lord's brothers were those most eminent and zealous in his service rather than his kinsmen (although Brandon regards them as his kinsmen).[3] Yet another possibility is that the brethren of the Lord are, like the Lord himself as Paul conceived him, members of the house of David. This would again not imply that they were personally acquainted with him.

To conclude my list of items of Jesus' biography apparently unknown to Paul there is the Last Supper. Only one passage can

---

[1] Some scholars deal with this difficulty by supposing that the brothers of Jesus named in the gospels were converted to the faith only after the crucifixion. Brandon has, more ingeniously, argued that e.g. Mk., writing after the Jewish war of AD 66–70, was anxious to suggest that Christianity had no sympathy with the nationalist tendencies which had inspired this uprising, and for this reason disparaged the brothers of Jesus because they included James who had led the nationalist Jerusalem church (38, p. 195). It is for the same reason, says Brandon (p. 191) that Mk. denies the Davidic descent of Jesus; such status 'would connect him with the nationalist aspirations of the Jews' (cf above, p. 118). Brandon also notes that none of the various James's mentioned in Lk. and Acts is called the brother of Jesus, nor even the brother of the Lord. Mt. and Mk. certainly mention a James who was the brother of Jesus, but Lk. says nothing of such an affiliation. Brandon holds that Lk's Pauline and gentile standpoint made him unwilling to admit that the Jewish-orientated James held such a position of unique authority in the primitive Church (p. 209).

[2] This is stated by Strabo, xvi, 4, 21 and L. Cerfaux (53, p. 141) mentions inscriptions which confirm that 'brother' was used as a title.

[3] The gospel Jesus refers to his followers as his 'brethren', ἀδελφοίς (Mt. xxviii, 10; Mk. iii, 33 ff.).

be construed as a reference to it, and there is reason to believe that this, too, is an interpolation. Even if it is not, I do not think that the passage can be justly interpreted as a reference to the historical occasion posited by the synoptic narratives. But I cannot intelligibly discuss this matter until I deal with the evolution of the Christian sacred meal (see below, p. 269).

It will doubtless be objected that my treatment of this passage, and also of Paul's sole mention of the twelve, is an arbitrary method of disposing of evidence inconvenient to a preconceived theory. The objection can be met by showing that the whole of I Cor. is full of contradictions which suggest that it was put together by an editor oblivious of them. They were first systematically set forth by Bauer (21), who observes that in his first chapter Paul praises the perfection of the Corinthians: they are rich in all things, lack no gifts, and are so perfect that they can but await the final revelation of the Lord. The testimony of Christ stands firm among them, and there can be no doubt that God will keep them upright until the day of the Lord (i, 4–8). Bauer asks how this can be reconciled with the stream of censure the author goes on to pour over them, saying for instance in iii, 3 that they are so carnal that he has hitherto been able to impart to them only the rudiments of Christian doctrine? Bauer argues that both passages are from the same hand—that of a writer who is trying both to stem the strife of warring Christian sects and also paint an idealized picture of the original Christians.[1] Again, chapter viii discusses whether Christians should eat meat that has been sacrificed to idols. We are told that we, the élite, have knowledge, we know that an idol is nothing at all, and that meat offered to it is not in any way different from any other meat:

'now concerning things sacrificed to idols; we know that we all have knowledge. *Knowledge puffeth up, but love edifieth. If any man thinketh that he knoweth anything he knoweth not yet as he ought to know, but if any man loveth God, the same is known of him.* Concerning therefore the eating of things sacrificed to idols, we know that no idol is anything in the world, and that there is no God but one' (viii, 1–4).

[1] The computer techniques recently tried on the epistles (see 192) have shown that I Corinthians is all from one hand, and that this writer also wrote Romans, II Corinthians, Galatians and Philemon. Whether Ephesians is from the same hand is disputed (see 69).

The words italicized run counter to the argument. Before and after them knowledge is something which enables us to see things in the right way, but in the italicized passage it is disparaged at the expense of love. The author goes on to say how the knowledge which the élite has is lacking to others; that if they see us eating meat sacrificed to idols, they will be tempted to do the same, thinking that the idol is a god and that they are performing a serious religious act (viii, 7–10). Two chapters after thus affirming that there is nothing intrinsically wrong in those who have knowledge sitting at meat in an idol's temple, that it is better to refrain from doing so only on grounds of expediency, for the sake of weaker brethren, Paul uncompromisingly affirms that such behaviour is downright idolatry, that those who eat meat sacrificed to idols have communion with devils, just as those who eat the body of Christ have communion with him:

> Wherefore my beloved, flee from idolatry . . . The bread which we break, is it not a communion of the body of Christ? . . . What say I then? *That a thing sacrificed to idols is anything, or that an idol is anything?* But I say that the things which the Gentiles sacrifice, they sacrifice to devils, and not to God: and I would not that ye should have communion with devils . . . Ye cannot partake of the table of the Lord and of the table of devils. Or do we provoke the Lord to jealousy? Are we stronger than he? (x, 14–22).

The words in italics represent the standpoint of chapter viii, that an idol is nothing, that meat sacrificed to it can be eaten like other meat. They do not fit in with the context which quite unambiguously affirms that to eat such meat is to commune with devils and provoke the Lord to jealousy.

One more example. The author of xi, 5 says that 'every woman praying or prophesying with her head unveiled dishonoureth her head'. Later, however, women are forbidden to speak in the churches (xiv, 34).

The inference from all this is that either the original epistle has been extensively interpolated, or a redactor has fused into one document writings representing opposed points of view; or both processes may have occurred, first interpolation then redaction, then perhaps more interpolation.[1] In any case, the epistle, even

---

[1] Bornkamm (34, p. 139) has recently conceded that both I and II Cor. raise compelling questions as to their literary integrity', and may well be 'a

as it now stands, is silent as to nine-tenths of the gospel data, and so we cannot but regard its one mention of the twelve and of the institution of the Supper as spurious.

All the principal epistles of Paul quote 'scripture', i.e. the OT, copiously. He will twist and torture the meaning he wants even from the most unpromising passages, which, he holds, are not just of historical interest, but were written to instruct us in order that, through the encouragement they give, we may maintain our hope with fortitude (Rom. xv, 4). An example of his method is his interpretation of Deut. xxv, 4, 'Thou shalt not muzzle the ox when he treadeth out the corn.' For him, this means that Christian teachers are to receive support from the communities they instruct (I Cor. ix, 9–12). This is, for him, the primary meaning of the passage, not just an accommodation of its meaning to the circumstances of the Christian community; for he says (verse 10 NEB): 'Do you suppose God's concern is with oxen? Or is the reference clearly to ourselves? Of course it refers to us, in the sense that the ploughman should plough and the thresher thresh in the hope of getting some of the produce.'

Apart from such exegesis of the OT, the principal theme common to these letters is the writer's conviction that the world is soon coming to an end and the second advent nigh (Rom. xiii, 12; I Cor. ii, 6; iv, 5; vii, 29–31; Philipp. iv, 6; II Thess. i, 6–10).

In addition to the facts about Jesus contained in the passages already discussed, Paul gives the following information about him:

Romans: Jesus is the Messiah and God's son (viii, 3) and on the human level, was born of David's stock (i, 3). God designated him to be the means of expiating our sins by his sacrificial death (iii, 25). He was delivered to death for our misdeeds, and raised to life to justify us (iv, 25). Our sin has been crucified with Christ. But just as he is risen from the dead, so we believe that we shall also come to life with him. Thus, in union with him, we are dead to sin and alive to God (vi, 6–11).

I Corinthians: Christ was crucified as a sacrifice, and raised from the dead to give us new life (i, 23; v, 7; xv, 12–25).

---

compilation of the correspondence of the apostle with the community, rather than documents complete in themselves'. Schmithals (241, pp. 13–17) regards I Cor. as a fusion of two letters by Paul.

II Corinthians: In Christ the old covenant is abrogated. He became poor by assuming human form. Sinless, he died on the cross for us all, and was raised. He who raised him will raise us too (iii, 14; iv, 10, 14; v, 21; viii, 9; xiii, 4).

Galatians: Christ was God's son, born of a woman, born under the law. He was crucified on a tree, for our sins, and was raised from the dead (i, 4; ii, 20; iii, 1, 13; iv, 4).

Ephesians: Our sins are forgiven through the shedding of his blood on the cross. He was raised from the dead (i, 7, 20; ii, 16). He gave himself up for the Church, that he might sanctify it, having cleansed it by the washing of the water with the word (v, 25–6).

Philippians: He died in human likeness on the cross and was resurrected (ii, 5–8; iii, 10).

Colossians: He is God's son, in whom our sins are forgiven. He died in his body of flesh and blood, and the shedding of his blood on the cross made God and the universe reconciled. He is the first to return from the dead (i, 13–22).

I Thessalonians: Jesus is God's son who died for us, and whom God raised from the dead (i, 10; iv, 14; v, 10).

II Thess. is the only one of these letters which fails to mention Jesus' death and resurrection. It is exclusively about the future, the second coming. My list shows that the other letters give few details about Jesus' career on earth, and that most details that are given are mentioned repeatedly in all the epistles (I have not given all the references to, e.g. crucifixion). It is hard to believe that the writer was acquainted with other biographical facts, that he deliberately made no mention of them but preferred to repeat again and again the sparse traditions he does record.

Even to the crucifixion he gives no historical setting. His letters tell only of a cult, Jewish in origin, in which a crucified Jesus, called the Messiah, figures as an atoning sacrifice, but counts for absolutely nothing as a teacher and wonder worker. Even if we identify the crucifixion mentioned in the epistles with the gospel affirmation of a crucifixion in Jerusalem under Pilate, we can hardly resist the conclusion that the teachings and miracles of Jesus are myths. Had a historical Jesus really said and done the things narrated of him in the gospels, it is inconceivable that a man so placed as Paul should pass them over in silence. Orthodox writers sometimes claim that he omitted references to Jesus' views

and behaviour because they were irrelevant to the matters discussed in his letters (see e.g. 230, p. 41). But this is hardly plausible. Romans advocates a negative attitude to the Mosaic law: the
new life 'under grace' stands in sharp antithesis to the old one
'under the law' (vi, 14). The various teachings of Jesus on the
subject can hardly have been omitted from the discussion because
regarded as not pertinent. Again, I Cor. xv is an attempt to convince doubters of the truth of the resurrection. Paul is emphatic
that the whole Christian faith depends upon this event (verse 14),
so he would hardly have omitted relevant testimony known to
him. Yet he mentions no appearances to women (which according
to the gospels, were the first the risen Jesus made) nor the empty
tomb. In II Cor. viii, 9, in order to induce the Corinthians to
contribute liberally to the collection for the poor in Palestine, he
mentions Jesus as an example of liberality—'though he was rich,
yet for your sakes he became poor, that ye through his poverty
might become rich'. The idea is that he became poor by becoming
human: the appeal is thus to the doctrine of the incarnation, not
to any biographical detail or ethical teaching. Paul does not, for
instance, cite Jesus' injunction to 'give to the poor' (Mk. x, 21).
The epistle to the Colossians opens with a portrayal of the dignity
of the Son 'in whom we have our redemption, the forgiveness of
our sins; who is the image of the invisible God, the firstborn of
all creation' (i, 14–15). None of the gospel details establishing his
transcendent glory—such as the virgin birth—are mentioned. As
we have seen, the doctrine of Rom. xii, 14 'Bless them which
persecute you', although found in the Sermon on the Mount, is
put without any suggestion that Jesus taught it.

It is often alleged that Paul would not specify details with which
his readers were already familiar. Yet he repeatedly specifies the
incarnation, death and resurrection with which they were, in the
terms of the case, fully familiar. In Philippians (ii, 1–10) for
instance, there is a christological digression containing nothing
which the readers would not know. In sum, we cannot avoid the
conclusion that the Jesus of Paul's epistles is a saviour god hardly
identifiable with the gospel Jesus. Paul, of course, believes that,
at some time in the past this deity appeared on earth, was born of
a woman, as a descendant of David and was crucified. But nothing
he says suggests that he knows or cares *when* this happened. He
says only that it occurred just at the right time (Rom. v, 6; Gal.
iv, 4) and does not imply that it happened recently enough for

any of the apostles to have known Jesus while he was on earth. Everyone agrees that Paul never met Jesus during his earthly life, that he saw him only in visions, and Paul himself suggests that his fellow-believers may also have seen Jesus only in this way; for he compares the way the other apostles had seen the Lord with the way he himself had seen him, saying: 'Am I not an apostle; have I not seen Jesus our Lord?' (I Cor. ix, 1).

Professor Brandon has recently conceded that Paul's insistence on the 'spirit-given origin of his own particular teaching' is tantamount to a denial on his part of the Jesus of history (38, pp. 55, 68). But Brandon argues that this is not ignorance, but deliberate denial, based on knowledge that Jesus had lived and died in the recent past. Only by such means, he says, was Paul, as a late-comer, able to assert his independence of the Jerusalem Christians led by James and Peter, who—so the argument goes—had emphasized the historical Jesus of Nazareth. Brandon is unable to support this latter allegation with direct evidence, as no document from these Jerusalem Christians has survived, and he is reduced to inferring their theology mainly from the synoptics. It is, of course, not difficult to impute knowledge of a historical Jesus to those whose ideas are inferred from such sources, but the justice of this procedure is questionable from Brandon's own avowal (p. 74) that all three synoptics were composed only after the destruction of Jerusalem in AD 70. However, he discerns some traces of the Jerusalem theology from Paul's polemic against it. He takes Paul's claim that he had 'seen the Lord' as evidence that the Jerusalem sect had accused him of not having been an eye-witness of the life of Jesus.[1] As I have just observed, it is equally possible to interpret Paul's statement to mean that he had received revelations as well as they. Brandon refers also to Paul's concession that he and his companions may seem to be 'beside ourselves' (II Cor. v, 13). He infers that Paul's enemies had charged him with being out of his mind because they based their faith on the historical Jesus, not on visions. But it could equally well be the case that they considered their own visions more reliable than Paul's, after the usual fashion of seers anxious to discredit rivals.

Brandon also claims that Paul himself makes occasional references to the historical Jesus which 'belie the integrity and independence of his own position' (p. 73). The principal passage

[1] p. 72. Howell-Smith (143, p. 78) also interprets Paul's words in this way.

(pp. 57–8) is I Cor. xv, 1 ff. where the risen Christ is said to have appeared to Cephas, to James, and to the twelve. I have given reasons for regarding this passage as an interpolation, and Brandon himself concedes (p. 49 and note) interpolation in respect of the reference to the twelve. For him it is 'extremely doubtful' that Jesus chose twelve disciples, since Paul names, as the leader of the Jerusalem Christians, James the brother of the Lord, who is not in the synoptic lists of the twelve.[1] Brandon of course believes that 'brother of the Lord' means brother of a historical Jesus, and this again prompts him to link the Jerusalem sect with the historical tradition.[2]

If Brandon were right in arguing that Paul suppressed mention of the historical Jesus in order to oppose Jewish Christians who stressed this personage, one would expect to find plentiful reference to the man Jesus in early Jewish Christian writers. In fact, however, as we shall shortly see, the epistle of James, which Brandon himself describes as 'a Jewish attempt . . . to stem the rising tide of Paulinism' (p. 239), has nothing at all to say of the man Jesus.

Paul's Jesus is a divine personage who has become credited with the work, commonly ascribed to the gods in pagan systems of the time, of dying for the redemption of the world; through him God chose 'to reconcile all things unto himself, having made peace through the blood of his cross' (Coloss. i, 20). What exactly this means will occupy us later.

(ii) The Pastoral epistles

The Pastoral epistles, namely the two to Timothy and the one to Titus, are ascribed to Paul and consist mainly of private directions to these men whom he had appointed to do pastoral work. Most critics agree that these three epistles are similar to each other in diction and doctrine, but differ in these respects from the other letters of Paul. In particular, faith which in the other letters is the root of everything, is simply one among other virtues in the

[1] These include only a James the son of Zebedee and a James the son of Alphaeus.
[2] In the very passage to which Brandon appeals (quoted above, p. 137), James is mentioned only as the recipient of the kind of supernatural vision that Paul himself claimed to have received. This in no way suggests that James staked his authority on a claim to have known Jesus while he was on earth.

Pastorals;[1] and these also contain evidence of a much more developed Church organization, mention being made of an episcopate. Furthermore, the difficulty of finding a place for the Pastorals in the life of Paul, as recorded in Acts and the other epistles, has led many scholars to deny that they are by him. But the most generally accepted hypothesis is that they consist of certain fragments of his letters, worked up into their present form by some disciple. Moffatt affirms as one of the 'best established conclusions in NT research' that the three are 'pseudonymous, composed by a Paulinist in Asia Minor not earlier than the close of the first century and not later than the second decade of the second century, based in part upon genuine fragments from the apostle's pen' (187, § 3). Harrison has endorsed this, and given reasons for regarding the Pastorals as 'the work of a Christian teacher at . . . the beginning of Hadrian's reign [117] who had before him (a) several authentic personal notes sent by Paul to Timothy and one to Titus, and (b) a collection of Pauline epistles consisting of our ten. The genuine notes are embodied in our II Timothy and Titus. I Timothy has no such material, but is otherwise composed, like the other two, largely of phrases taken from the ten Paulines. Apart from these genuinely Pauline elements, this author writes in a Greek which is strange to Paul but familiar in the first half of the second century' (131, p. 242, with ref. to 130). Harrison also notes that Polycarp's epistle to the Philippians is the first definite external witness to the existence of the Pastoral epistles, and we shall see that he gives reasons for dating Polycarp's letter at AD 135.[2]

The only suggestion of an acquaintance with Jesus' biography in the writer of the Pastorals is provided by one mention of Pontius Pilate: 'I charge thee in the sight of God, who quickeneth all things, and of Jesus Christ, who before Pontius Pilate witnessed the good confession' (I Tim. vi, 13).

[1] From Titus iii, 5 we learn that Jesus saved us 'through the washing of regeneration'. Hornton remarks (140) that 'regeneration' is a word not used by Paul and is found only in Mt. xix, 28: and that commentators agree in regarding the 'washing of regeneration' as baptism. He also notes that the teaching in 'the undoubted writings of Paul' is that we are saved by faith: so that it has been inferred that this passage 'did not come from the hand of Paul, but must be referred to that later Church doctrine which in the second century rapidly substituted baptism for faith as the means of salvation'.

[2] Hanson (127, pp. 1–3) summarizes recent discussion on the Pastorals. He agrees that they are not by Paul, and were written in the second century, before AD 135.

The following table sums up what else the Pastorals tell us about Jesus:

I Timothy: Jesus came into the world to save sinners. He is the mediator between God and men (ii, 5), who sacrificed himself to win freedom for all mankind.

II Timothy: Jesus Christ our Saviour appeared on earth. He was born of David's line, is risen from the dead and will appear again (i, 10; ii, 8; iv, 1).

Titus: Jesus sacrificed himself for us, to set us free from all wickedness (ii, 14). He saved us through baptism (iii, 5).

It is thus the one reference to Pilate that distinguishes the Pastorals sharply from the principal letters. It gives a definite historical setting to Jesus' career, and occurs in I Tim.—the letter which, in the opinion of Harrison, was written entirely by a Christian teacher of Hadrian's time and does not contain any fragment written earlier by Paul, the only Pauline matter being quotations from his principal epistles. This being so, we shall have to ask whether we are not entitled to infer that Paul knew nothing of the historical setting of the crucifixion and that it was only in the second century that Jesus came to be regarded as having suffered under Pilate.

(iii) **Other canonical epistles**

The non-Pauline epistles of the NT also display a remarkable ignorance of Jesus' life. Let us consider first the epistle of James. Its author (whom I shall call James) is unknown. Numerous men by the name of James are mentioned in the NT, Josephus, and early Church history, but the author might not be any one of these. The name James or John no more identifies a certain individual than Smith or Brown does today.

The author seems to have written later than Paul, whose doctrine he controverts. Paul had said a man is justified by faith in Christ apart from the works of the law (Rom. iii, 28, Gal. ii, 16), and he had given Abraham as an example (Rom. iv, 1: Gal. iii, 6). James seems to be attacking this when he says a man is justified by works and not by faith only (ii, 14) and when he goes on to cite Abraham as an illustration of the truth of his case (ii, 21–3). Another indication of late date is found in v, 13–15, where supernatural healing of the sick is effected through 'the elders', that is, the official body of presbyters: whereas in Paul's day the power to heal and work miracles pertained to believers indiscriminately (I Cor. xii, 9 f.). 'The embodiment of the function in an official class indicates a considerable development of ecclesiastical organization' (62, § 5). Furthermore, the epistle is not mentioned by Tertullian, who was writing at the end of the second century, perhaps because he, like Eusebius, classed it among the disputed books. It may have been written late in the first century.

James depicts the lamentable condition of the Churches and says there should be fewer teachers (since greater purity is demanded of them) and that tongues should be less unbridled. He complains too of worldliness, deference to the rich and scorn of the poor, an eagerness for trade and gain, jealousy and faction, wars and fightings and the absence of the wisdom that is from above. But he never refers to the gospels nor to Jesus as the source of the moral precepts in which his writing abounds. For instance, he urges his 'brethren' to 'swear not, neither by the heaven nor by the earth, nor by any other oath: but let your yea be yea, and your nay nay: that ye fall not under the judgement' (v. 12). This teaching is ascribed to Jesus in Mt. v, 34, 37, yet James gives it without any indication that Jesus taught it. Again, when James exhorts the brethren to 'be patient until the Lord comes', he mentions, as a shining example of patience in suffering, not Jesus but 'the prophets who spoke in the name of the Lord' (v, 7–11). When he does mention 'the Lord', there is no indication that the reference is to the man Jesus. And often the words 'the Lord' are a later addition to his text. Thus in i, 12, we are told that those who endure temptation will 'receive the crown of life which *the Lord* promised to them that love him'. The words italicized are not in the early manuscripts, and the NEB renders the passage without them as 'the gift promised to those who love God'.

James might never have heard of the man Jesus. He tells us even less than does Paul, and mentions neither Jesus' Davidic descent nor his crucifixion; in fact he gives no indication that Jesus had ever been on earth at all.[1] His epistle is comparable with II Thess. in that both are concerned only with the super-

---

[1] Sidebottom (249, pp. 14, 24) concedes that this lack of reference to 'basic Christian events' is 'remarkable', and that 'it really looks as though the author did not realize the importance of them'.

natural coming of Jesus, which, he assures his readers, is 'at hand' (v, 7, 8).

The next letter in the canonical collection is the first epistle general of Peter, which purports to come from 'Peter, an apostle of Jesus Christ'. He at least should have something to say about the life and works of the master. But, as Cone notes, the epistle contains 'no indication of the fresh and vivid recollections of an eye-witness of the life of Jesus' and does not mention the conspicuous ideas of his preaching (63, § 5). The author does, however, mention the 'sprinkling of the blood of Jesus Christ' (i, 2) and his 'resurrection from the dead'. He also seems to presuppose the truth of the legend of his descent to the underworld (iii, 19; iv, 6). He says too that the prophets foretold 'the sufferings of Christ and the glories that should follow them', and that they did so not for the benefit of their contemporaries but for that of the recipients of the epistle (i, 11–12). It is, of course, not true that the prophets suggest that the final reckoning will come at a time remote from their own day and age, and Christian commentators find it difficult to connect this allegation in the epistle with anything in the OT. For instance, Bennett comments weakly (27): 'Daniel indeed speaks of a day of judgement some time after, apparently soon after the fall of Antiochus Epiphanes; but this is not a very definite intimation that Christ would come about 160 years later.' All the prophets expected the final reckoning to come in the last times, that is, their own. Peter, however, places not only Jesus' second, but also his first coming in the last times. He says that Christ who redeemed us with his precious blood 'was foreknown indeed before the foundation of the world, but was manifested at the end of the times for your sake, who through him are believers in God, which raised him from the dead and gave him glory' (i, 20). This suggestion that his sufferings on earth belong to the relatively recent past is not present in the Pauline letters. So far we have met it only in the non-Pauline I Tim.

Unlike James, Peter does mention Jesus as an example when he is urging believers to endure undeserved suffering without flinching. But what he says in this context is drawn not from the gospels nor from traditions about Jesus' life on earth, but from the description of the sufferings of the 'servant of Yahweh' in Isa. liii. The Jews regarded this chapter as containing Messianic prophecies, so it is perfectly intelligible that a Christian writer should draw on it for details of Jesus' biography. Hoskyns and Davey (141, p. 57) have compared the relevant passages and have remarked that 'the language is so similar that the resemblance cannot be fortuitous'. They bring this fact out in the following table.

I Peter ii	*Isaiah liii (Septuagint)*
21 (Christ) also suffered for you leaving you an example that ye should follow his steps	4. he . . . is pained for us
22 who did no sin neither was guile found in his mouth.	9. he did no sin nor guile was in his mouth.
	(cf. 7 as a lamb before his shearers is dumb, so opens he not his mouth)
23 who, when he was reviled, reviled not again; when he suffered, threatened not; but committed himself to him that judgeth righteously;	(cf. 11 the Lord also is pleased to justify the just one)
24 who his own self bare our sins	11 and he shall bear their sins
in his body	(cf. 4–6 he bears our sins he was wounded on account of our sins and was bruised because of our iniquities
upon the tree, that we, having died unto sin, might live unto righteousness; by whose bruise ye were healed.	The Lord gave him up for our sins
	5 by his bruise we were healed
25 For ye were going astray like sheep; but are now returned unto the Shepherd and Bishop of your souls.	6 all we like sheep have gone astray.

This description of the passion in terms of Isaiah is not paralleled in the Pauline letters, but the one detail which Peter adds to Isaiah, namely the death of Jesus 'upon the tree', is present in Paul. Thus, in so far as Peter's account of Jesus' biography is fuller than Paul's, it is so because he has amplified Paul with Isaiah. Paul, urging the Ephesians to forgive one another, was not able to hold up Jesus as an example. He could not say that Jesus had forgiven his enemies, but only that God had forgiven us by sending Christ (iv, 32). Peter, however, is able—by drawing on Isaiah—to reinforce the ethical precept of forgiveness by citing Jesus' behaviour as an example.

At the end of the epistle the author appeals to the elders of the Christian community he is addressing, and describes himself as a 'fellow-elder and a witness of Christ's sufferings' (v, 1). 'Witness' (μάρτυς) does not imply eye-witness (ἐπόπτης, a word which occurs only in II Peter, discussed below). μάρτυρες means 'those who give testimony' (e.g. the two witnesses of Rev. xi, 3). Bennett comments on the claim in I Peter v, 1 to be a witness: 'The Greek connects this very closely with "fellow-elder", "one who is at the same time fellow-elder and witness". Hence it has been understood as "fellow-witness", i.e. both Peter and the elders bore witness by their preaching to the sufferings of Christ.'

Concerning the date of this work, Bennett has noted (27, pp. 4, 42) that it was certainly in circulation at the beginning of the second century and that its author was well acquainted with and dependent on Paul's letters. Both the late date and the dependence on Pauline ideas make it impossible to believe that the epistle was written by the Judaizing Peter who was Paul's opponent and rival.

The first epistle of John was also circulating at the beginning of the second century. It is anonymous. That the author was John is stated only in the title, and the titles of all these non-Pauline letters 'were not parts of the books themselves but were added later on by unknown hands some time before AD 300' (27, p. 4). The traditional assumption that I John was written by the author of the fourth gospel is not very plausible, since the second coming of Christ is still spoken of in I John ii, 28 as a visible occurrence in time, whereas in the fourth gospel all trace of this eschatology has disappeared and the second advent means the coming of the Holy Spirit into the hearts of believers (see above p. 126).

The author of I John claims to have heard a message from Jesus, namely that God is light and in him is no darkness (i, 5). Like the author of I Peter, he believes that Christ was sinless, that his blood 'cleanseth us from all sin', and that he is our 'Advocate with the Father' (ii, 1–2). Next he mentions a criterion for distinguishing the true believer: 'Whoever claims to be dwelling in him, binds himself to live as Christ himself lived' (ii, 6 NEB). As he immediately goes on to say that haters are not true Christians he seems to presuppose that Jesus' conduct while on earth was forgiving and conciliatory. This, we saw, is what I Peter had inferred from Isaiah.

Chapter v contains the statement that Jesus 'came by water and

F

blood'. Commentators usually interpret the water as a reference to his baptism.

The author of this epistle, and also the author of II John, complain of 'many deceivers' who deny that Jesus 'has come in the flesh'. How could anybody have denied this if his activities, as recorded in the gospels, had formed the basis of the cult? And if these canonical writers had known about his earthly life, why did they not meet the denial by giving some of the details, e.g. by alluding to his earthly parentage?[1] All that the author of I John can do to controvert these sceptics is to assure his readers that 'we have beheld and bear witness that the Father hath sent the Son to be the Saviour of the world' (iv, 14). Whether this means that the author had actually seen Jesus while he was on earth is not clear. There is certainly nothing else in this epistle which suggests that the writer saw Jesus in the flesh. The letter does indeed open with the words:

That which was from the beginning, that which we have heard, that which we have seen with our eyes, that which we beheld, and our hands handled, concerning the Word of life (and the life was manifested, and we have seen, and bear witness, and declare unto you the life, the eternal life, which was with the Father, and was manifested unto us); that which we have seen and heard we declare unto you also, that ye also may have fellowship with us: yea, and our fellowship is with the Father, and with his Son Jesus Christ: and these things we write that our joy may be fulfilled.

By 'that which' the author seems to mean not the Son but the truth concerning the nature and work of the Son. This interpretation seems required by 'concerning'. When Paul said that he had 'seen the Lord' this meant that he had had a vision, like the one that converted him. I John's claim to have 'beheld' that the Father sent the Son to be the saviour of the world may also refer to a vision.

Let us next consider the epistle to the Hebrews. In most Bibles it is ascribed to Paul, but in actual fact it does not even purport to

---

[1] It may be urged that the 'deceivers' complained of in these two epistles were Docetists, who did not deny that Jesus lived, but that his body was real (see above, p. 124). It remains, however, true that the author of the epistles is unable to confute the deceivers with concrete biographical evidence, whereas later writers who criticize Docetists do precisely this (see below, p. 171).

come from him. The oldest MSS. bear the title 'To the Hebrews', and the NEB follows them in calling the work simply 'A letter to the Hebrews'. The authorship has been in dispute since the end of the second century. Both Luther and Calvin pointed out that Paul, who lays such stress on the fact that his gospel was not taught to him by man but came by direct revelation, could not have written Hebrews ii, 3–4, where the author classes himself among those who received the message of salvation from the personal disciples of the Lord on the evidence of miracles which confirmed their word. The writer shows an acquaintance with both the ideas and some of the letters of Paul. And within the Christian community he recognizes no distinction between Jew and gentile. The whole problem as to these distinctions has for him disappeared. This, then, is a relatively late work, and the *Biblica* suggests the end of the first century as its probable date. It is also clear that the author believes, with the author of I Peter, that Jesus was on earth in the recent past. For he claims to have been convinced by the miracles performed by those who had heard the Lord. There is no suggestion that Jesus wrought miracles, only that those who heard him convinced others when they supported their reports with miracles. When the writer later quotes words allegedly spoken by the Son (ii, 11–14), these have nothing to do with anything said by the gospel Jesus, but are quoted from the Psalms and from Isaiah.

Other passages confirm that the author places Jesus' appearance on earth in the last days. He says that in former times God spoke to our forefathers through the prophets, but that 'in this the final age he has spoken to us in the Son' (i, 2 NEB). The point is reiterated when we are told that Christ 'has appeared once and for all at the climax of history to abolish sin by the sacrifice of himself' (ix, 26). Crucifixion is specified as the manner of his death (xii, 2), and it is stressed that he was an offering without blemish. This allegation of his sinlessness may well have been taken from Isaiah.

The purpose of the writer is to demonstrate that Jesus the Son of God is superior to the angels. Only for a short period (his time on earth) was he 'made lower than the angels' (ii, 9). Now he is raised far above them (i, 3–4). Such argumentation presupposes that some were disposed to think of him as a supernatural but not divine being.

The writer also contrives to show that Jesus is a 'high priest' (iv, 14). This was not easy to prove since priests were of the tribe of Levi, while Jesus was in the line of David. The author specifies this difficulty (vii, 13-14) and solves it, as Allegro (12, p. 154) says, by concluding that Jesus, the Davidic Messiah, has been given a special priesthood of a unique order, surpassing that of the old Aaronic line, and patterned after the ancient priest-king Melchizedek. Ps. cx, 4 says: 'Thou art a priest, for ever, after the order of Melchizedek.' This remark was apparently addressed to the first of the priest-kings, Judas Maccabeus. But for the writer of Hebrews such statements were prophecies referring to Jesus.

In v, 5 we are told that Christ was addressed with the words, 'Thou art my Son, this day have I begotten thee.' They do not occur in the gospels, but are quoted from Ps. ii, 7, and the author of Hebrews is again assuming that the person addressed in the psalm is Christ.

The author's knowledge of the man Jesus is slender enough. Jesus is not so much a human high priest with a human biography, as 'a high priest who hath passed through the heavens' (iv, 14). His time on earth is not what interests the writer, who stresses instead his present function as our advocate before God (ii, 16-18).

Chapter xi consists of an eulogy of faith, and many OT characters and their deeds are mentioned as signal examples, but none of the instances familiar to us from the gospels, e.g. not the centurion whose faith impressed Jesus (Lk. vii, 9); nor the faith of those who brought the sick man to him, confident that he had power to cure him (Mt. ix, 2); nor the woman of whom he said 'thy faith hath made thee whole' (Mt. ix, 22); nor the blind men of Mt. ix, 29. Can we really believe that the author of Hebrews was acquainted with traditions of this kind and yet preferred to them the OT traditions about Abel, Enoch, Noah, Abraham, Isaac, Jacob, Sarah, Joseph, Moses and his parents, Rahab, and others whom he mentions as examples of faith?

Chapter xiii, verse 12 brings an interesting and novel detail, namely that Jesus suffered 'outside the gate'. Lev. xvi, 27 stipulates that the carcases of the sacrificial victims shall be burned outside the camp and the writer of Hebrews alludes to this passage when he says (NEB): 'As you know, those animals whose blood is brought as a sin-offering by the high priest into the sanctuary, have their bodies burnt outside the camp, and therefore Jesus also suffered outside the gate, to consecrate the people by his own blood.' He also regards this as symbolical of Jesus' detachment

from the world, for he continues: 'Let us then go to him outside
the camp, bearing the stigma that he bore. For here we have no
permanent home, but are seekers after the city which is to come.'
Either he was acquainted with a tradition that Jesus was put to
death outside a city, or else he has invented this detail for his
doctrinal ends and it was later elaborated by the gospel writers.

In v, 7 we are told that 'in the days of his flesh' Jesus 'offered up
prayers and supplications with strong crying and tears unto him
that was able to save him from death'. This is usually taken to be
a reference to the agony in Gethsemane, but it may only be an
application of the words of Psalm xxii to Jesus. Earlier, Hebrews
gives (ii, 12) as words of Jesus a quotation from this Psalm—
words not ascribed to him in the gospels. And we saw in a previous chapter how many details of the passion were invented by
drawing on this Psalm. That the reference in Hebrews v, 7 is in
fact to the OT and not to the situation specified in the gospels is
suggested by the continuation, which says that because of Jesus'
humble submission his prayer was heard. His prayer in Gethsemane to be spared death was not granted. The statement in
Hebrews is however quite intelligible if it be regarded as a reference to Psalm xxii, 24, 'But when he cried unto him he heard'.

Finally we turn to the second epistle of Peter. This is very
different from the kind of writings we have hitherto been considering. The opening chapter contains a clear reference to the
gospel story of the Transfiguration by way of proving the writer's
claim to have been an eye-witness of Jesus' works:

> For we did not follow cunningly devised fables when we
> made known unto you the power and coming of our Lord
> Jesus Christ, but we were eye-witnesses of his majesty. For he
> received from God the Father honour and glory, when there
> came such a voice to him from the excellent glory, This is my
> beloved Son, in whom I am well pleased: and this his voice we
> ourselves heard come out of heaven when we were with him
> on the holy mount.

The writer also remarks that Jesus warned him that he must
soon die. This appears to be a reference to Jn. xxi, 18–19, where
the risen Jesus predicts a martyrdom for Peter. II Peter goes on
to refer to I Peter and to Paul's letters, which are even designated
as 'scriptures' on a level with the OT. We shall see that the writers

of the first century never use this word to designate the NT. The writer of II Peter also incorporates whole verses of the epistle of Jude into his work. And while I Peter had simply affirmed that 'the end of all things is at hand' (iv, 7), II Peter is at pains to explain why the expected end has yet to come: it is not that the Lord is slow in fulfilling his promise, but because he is patient and wants to give everyone a chance to repent (iii, 9). That II Peter is later than I Peter and the Pauline letters is confirmed by external evidence, for the first certain traces of the epistle do not occur until the third century, when its ascription to Peter is mentioned but not fully accepted (see 27, p. 63). Sidebottom (249, pp. 98–99) gives evidence for dating it as late as AD 130.

Summing up, we may say that all these non-Pauline epistles are agreed to be later than Paul's letters and (with the exception of James) give fuller details of Jesus' earthly life. I Peter and I John agree that Jesus, the sinless one, was crucified for our sins, that he showed patience in his sufferings and rose again from the dead. Novel to I John is the detail that he came 'by water' as well as by blood. Hebrews adds that he spoke words recorded in the Psalms and in Isaiah, and that he suffered crucifixion outside the gate. I Peter and Hebrews agree that he suffered in the last times. All these writings stress that he will soon return. II Peter, later than the others, refers to details that definitely belong to the gospel traditions.

This tendency for the later documents to give more details of Jesus' life than the earlier is continued in the gospels. Mk. devotes one third of his space to describing the last week of Jesus' life, while later evangelists give a more complete biography.

(iv) Acts of the Apostles

My allegation that Paul was silent about Jesus' biography because it was not known to him will be strengthened if it can be shown that Christian writers to whom it was known refer to it in some detail. The author of Acts expressly claims an acquaintance with it, and states that he has already, in a former treatise, recorded 'all that Jesus began both to do and to teach'. Most scholars have long held that he was in fact the author of Lk.: both works are dedicated to 'Theophilus'; and Acts follows Lk. in a number of details where Lk. differs from the other gospels.

We have already studied the contradictions between Acts and

Paul's epistles which suggest that Acts is the work of a second-century harmonist, trying to represent the early history of the Church as a period of concord.[1] The work is also an appeal to the Romans for toleration, for it repeatedly represents Roman officials as finding the disputes between Jews and Christians trivial internal matters, not necessitating Roman intervention. Haenchen argues (123) that this tendency to find a modus vivendi with Roman rule could be pursued only by a writer who had abandoned the early Christian expectation that the world would soon end. Schmiedel suggested AD 105-30 as the period when the work was written (234, § 16), Weiss argued for the date AD 100 (278, p. 96), and some recent writers favour an even earlier date, e.g. Bieder (30) proposes AD 80. But the author of Acts says that he wrote the work after his gospel, and I have given reasons for dating Lk. considerably later than AD 70 (see above, pp. 90, 117). Haenchen shows (124, pp. 1-6) that no Christian writer earlier than Justin (martyred about AD 167) can be proved to have known and used Lk.-Acts.

Some apologists have followed Ramsay (211, p. 74) in arguing that the work must have been written in the first century because it shows such accurate knowledge of the geographical and political conditions of the Roman empire of that time. Thus Williams (289, p. 30) notes that Lk. distinguishes correctly between senatorial and imperial provinces in that in Acts xiii, 7 and xviii, 12 he correctly designates as proconsuls the governors of the provinces of Cyprus and Achaia, which were then senatorial (and therefore governed by a proconsul), although they had not always been senatorial. In fact, however, Cyprus was senatorial continuously from 22 BC, and Achaia was also continuously governed by proconsuls except for a brief period under Tiberius (see 208). It is in any case gratuitous to suppose that a second-century writer could not have had accurate information about the earlier state of the empire.

That Acts is so crowded with miracles as to be suspect as a historical record has repeatedly struck critical writers. The opening chapters include such incidents as Jesus' ascent into heaven,

---

[1] See above, p. 140. In particular, the author represents Peter and Paul as ideal apostles, whose work proceeds on parallel lines. Each delivers eight speeches, opposes a magician, cures a lame person, raises one person from the dead, and is led by a divine revelation to convert gentiles (see Bieder, 30). This latter is obviously a tendency-story, written to persuade Christians that the mission to the gentiles has divine sanction.

while two angels announce to the apostles his future return; the descent of the Holy Spirit upon the disciples in the form of a 'mighty wind' which enables them to speak the language of every nation; many miraculous cures by Peter and John; and the release of the apostles from prison by an angel. Then Philip effects many cures in Samaria. An angel tells him to repair to the Gaza road, where he converts and baptizes a eunuch, and is then spirited away. Next, Saul is miraculously converted by the voice of Jesus from heaven, and Peter cures a man of the palsy, raises Tabitha from the dead, and has the vision which leads him to start converting the gentiles. Church history of this kind looks like second-century propaganda rather than first-century chronicle.

Acts, then, is later than the Pauline letters and is written by one who avows his familiarity with the gospel story. We should expect it to allude to a good many details in Jesus' life, and in fact the following events are mentioned:

(1) Jesus was of Nazareth, performed many miracles and signs (ii, 22) and went about doing good and healing all oppressed of the devil (x, 38).

(2) God anointed him 'with the Holy Ghost and with power', and Jesus himself said: 'John indeed baptized with water, but ye shall be baptized with the Holy Ghost' (xi, 16).

(3) His teaching included the words 'it is more blessed to give than to receive' (xx, 35).

(4) He prophesied the destruction of the temple (vi, 14), had twelve disciples and was betrayed by one of them, Judas, who acted as a guide to those who arrested him (i, 16).

(5) He was committed for trial by the Jews and repudiated by them in Pilate's court. Pilate wished to release him, but they insisted that he release a murderer instead (iii, 13–15). Jesus was also tried by Herod and the trial took place in Jerusalem (iv, 27).

(6) He was put to death on a gibbet and then laid in a tomb (xiii, 29). The execution was carried out by heathens (ii, 23).

(7) God raised him from the dead (xiii, 30) and after the resurrection he showed himself to the apostles in Jerusalem for more than forty days. He ate and drank with them and taught them about the kingdom of God, and after this he was taken up to heaven (i, 1–4; x, 41).

(v) The Apostolic Fathers

(a) *The documents and their dates*

Now that we have seen how Jesus' biography becomes more definite and detailed in the later documents of the NT, we must turn to early Christian writings outside the canon to see whether we find the same course of development. Our question is whether and in what degree either the gospels themselves or the traditions embodied in them were known to the so-called 'Apostolic Fathers' —Clement of Rome, Ignatius of Antioch and Polycarp of Smyrna. These writers are so named because they were thought of as the immediate successors and disciples of the apostles, to whom they assign great authority, although the only ones they mention by name are Peter and Paul. The following writings are ascribed to them:

(1) To Clement, an anonymous letter from the Church of Rome to the Church of the Corinthians, known as the first epistle of Clement (I Clement).

(2) To Ignatius, six letters to the Christian communities of Ephesus, Magnesia, Tralles, Rome, Philadelphia and Smyrna; and a letter to Polycarp. These are not anonymous but actually purport to be written by Ignatius.

(3) To Polycarp, an epistle to the Philippians, again not anonymous.

All these writings were known to Irenaeus and so must have been written before AD 180.[1] Clement's epistle must be considerably earlier, for Dionysius, bishop of Corinth, says it was read in the public worship there in AD 170. Ignatius' epistles were written later than Clement's for they combat second-century heresies unknown to him. On the other hand, Clement obviously wrote later than Paul, for he quotes I Cor. by name and paraphrases a passage from Romans. The opening words of his epistle tell that it was composed at a time of persecution. From these facts we can infer that it was written under Domitian, and AD 96 has been widely accepted as its date (e.g. by the Catholic commentator Kleist, 162, p. 4).

[1] For the most recent discussion of the dates of these documents, see Barnard (19) and Goodspeed (107).

Ignatius is said to have been taken to Rome and thrown to the lions about AD 110. One of the best clues as to the date of composition of his epistles is provided by his references to episcopacy, and to see the force of this evidence we must follow the gradual development of this institution.

In Paul's epistles to the Corinthians 'no mention is anywhere made of any heads of the community. For effecting the cures of the malpractices which have crept in, Paul addresses himself not to any such officers, but to the community as a whole. So also the community awards punishments and chooses delegates by decision of a majority' (238, § 9). By the time Clement wrote this state of affairs had changed. His epistle, written to the same Church of Corinth, rebukes the Corinthians for ejecting certain elders of the Church from their office. He makes no distinction between elders (or presbyters) and 'bishops' or 'overseers'. It is, he says, a sin to turn those men out of their ἐπισκοπή (office of oversight). Blessed, he goes on, are the elders who have gone before and are safe from such treatment (Chapter 44). In Chapter 47 he describes the offence as a revolt against the elders. Clement, then, recognizes a ruling class and a serving class within the Church. The apostles, he says, 'appointed men to be overseers and servants' (ἐπισκόπων καὶ διακόνων) of the Christian community (Chapter 42). But as yet there is no suggestion that the ruling class was itself ruled by one individual. The first indications of such a state of affairs come in the Pastoral epistles of the NT where the authority of the bishop is described in a way that suggests he is independent, and not merely a member of a governing board (see I Tim. iii). By the time the epistles of Ignatius were written, monarchical episcopacy had been established. He tells us that the bishop ought to be regarded as the Lord himself is regarded (Ephes. Chapter 6), and obedience given to him as to Christ (Trall. Chapter 2).

Nevertheless it seems that the monarchical episcopacy known to Ignatius is more primitive than that known to writers from Irenaeus onwards. Lightfoot remarked that, unlike Irenaeus, Ignatius does not regard the bishops as the successors of the apostles; nor does he mention a diocese. The bishop and presbyters are ministers of a city. Lightfoot also pointed out that the evidence suggests that, when Ignatius wrote, only the Asian churches had been driven by the spread of false doctrines and the activity of schismatics, to tighten their organization and centralize their authority; while in Rome this was not so; for in his epistle to the Roman Church 'not a word is said about the Roman bishop. Indeed there is not even the faintest hint that a bishop of Rome existed at this time . . .' Lightfoot showed that these facts help to prove that Ignatius' epistles are genuine and not late forgeries; for from the latter part of the second century, it was believed that, from the very beginning, a single monarchic bishop had ruled over every local Church in the Roman Empire. This idea was 'a second-century development, read back into the earlier history by Irenaeus and his contemporaries' (see Harrison, 131, pp. 48, 49, 284). Hence, if the epistles of Ignatius had been written even a generation later than AD 110, they would not have represented Rome as being without a governing bishop.

Polycarp wrote after Ignatius, for he refers to the latter's epistles. The evidence bearing on Polycarp's life is too complicated to give here, but has been fully stated by Harrison (131, pp. 269–83). There seems to be general agreement that he was martyred in AD 155. Harrison's theory is that his epistle to the Philippians is a fusion of two separate communications dispatched at different dates. The first is Chapter 13, which assumes that Ignatius was still on his way to Rome, or had only just arrived there, while the remaining chapters presuppose his death. Harrison dates the two original documents about AD 115 and 135 respectively, and he fixes the latter date from a close scrutiny of the heresy combated in the epistle (131, pp. 54, 205, 207). His suggestions have found wide acceptance. They are endorsed by Kleist (163, p. 70), although Barnard (19, p. 36) thinks that the second document may have been written soon after the first—about AD 120 rather than AD 135.

(b) *Their knowledge of gospel material*

(1) *Clement*: On the rare occasions when these Apostolic Fathers quote NT writings by name, the reference is always to one of the Pauline epistles, not to the gospels. Thus we saw that Clement names Paul's letter to the Corinthians, Ignatius names Paul's epistle to the Ephesians (Ephes., Chapter 12), and Polycarp, writing to the Philippians, calls attention (Chapter 3) to the instructions Paul had given them in his letter. These writers also use the word 'scripture' or the phrase 'it is written' exclusively

to designate the OT, which they quote copiously. They never so designate the writings of the NT.

Like the authors of the canonical epistles, Clement does not allude to gospel matters when it would have suited his argument very well; and the inference is that the gospel incidents in question were unknown to him. A few examples will help to show the justice of this:

(1) Chapters 3–6 are devoted to showing that jealousy and envy bring no good. He gives the following illustrations: jealousy and envy caused Cain to slay Abel; jealousy led Jacob to fly from his brother Esau; it caused Joseph to be persecuted; it compelled Moses to flee from Pharaoh; it caused Aaron and Miriam to lodge outside the camp; it sent Dathan and Abiram alive to Hades, and caused David to be persecuted by Saul. Clement also mentions some instances from his own time, and says that it was through jealousy and envy that Peter and Paul were persecuted unto death, and many other Christians tortured. What he does not mention is the example one would expect to come to mind of a Christian writer before any of these, namely the gospel tradition that the death of Jesus was caused by the envy of the multitude. Mt. xxvii, 18 and Mk. xv, 10 tell us that Pilate tried to persuade the people to let him release Jesus, 'for he knew that for envy they had delivered him up'.

(2) When Clement undertakes (Chapters 7 and 8) to prove that the Lord has given all men opportunity for conversion, he quotes Ezekiel and Isaiah to this effect, and says too that Noah and Jonah both urged repentance, and those who heeded them were saved. But he does not mention the repeated injunction of Jesus (and of the Baptist) 'repent ye'; nor Jesus' words 'except ye repent ye shall all likewise perish' (Lk. xiii, 3); and 'except ye be converted and become as little children, ye shall in no wise enter into the kingdom of heaven' (Mt. xviii, 3).

(3) Chapters 9–12 review those who hoped and trusted in the Lord. As examples Clement praises the faith of Enoch, Noah, Abraham, Lot and Rahab; but he does not mention any of the relevant gospel incidents (listed above, p. 158).

(4) In Chapter 13 he urges us to be humble and merciful, and here he does quote 'words of the Lord Jesus' to carry his point. How these are related to the gospels we shall see shortly. Next he inculcates kindness, quoting Proverbs and Psalms, and in Chapter

15 the injunction to 'associate with those who piously cultivate peace' is supported with quotation from Isaiah and Psalms, but with nothing from the gospels.

(5) In Chapter 16 we learn that 'the Lord Jesus Christ did not, for all his power, come clothed in boastful pomp and overweening pride, but in a humble frame of mind'. We might here expect some reference to Jesus' birth in a humble family, or to such of his dicta as 'I am meek and lowly in heart' (Mt. xi, 29); or to the passion narrative of the gospels. But instead Clement gives long quotations from Isaiah liii (about the suffering servant of Yahweh) and from the Psalms.

(6) Chapter 17 urges us to 'imitate the example of those also who wandered about dressed in sheepskins and goatskins, heralding the advent of Christ'. As he goes on to give examples of whom he has in mind, we should expect him to mention John the Baptist. But instead he says: 'We mean the Prophets Elias and Eliseus, as well as Ezechiel, and in addition to these the men of attested merit', viz. Abraham, Job, Moses and David.

This analysis of the first seventeen chapters of Clement's epistle gives evidence enough that he ignores gospel matter which would surely have sprung to his mind more readily than some of his examples had it been known to him. However, he was obviously acquainted with some traditions about Jesus, and implies that Jesus taught certain doctrines. He does not, however, claim to have his knowledge of this teaching from written gospels, but from the preaching of the apostles, who in turn had it direct from Jesus (Chapter 42). They 'went forth . . . to preach the good news that the kingdom of God was close at hand'.

In one passage Clement speaks as though not only the apostles but also he and his fellows had the authority to determine what Jesus said: 'Should any disobey what has been said by Him through us, let them understand that they will entangle themselves in no small danger' (Chapter 59). This might even imply that the doctrines of Jesus had been communicated to Clement and others in supernatural revelations.

In two passages he claims to reproduce actual words of the Lord. He urges his readers to

remember the words of the Lord Jesus which he spake inculcating gentleness and long-suffering. This is what he said: 'Show mercy, that you may be shown mercy; forgive that you may be forgiven; as you treat others, so you shall be treated; as you give, so you shall receive; as you judge, so you shall be judged; as you show kindness, so kindness shall be shown to you; the measure you use in measuring shall be used in measuring out your share' (Chapter 13).

These are not quotations from the gospels but strongly resemble certain sayings in them. It is possible that Clement knew the gospels and was quoting them loosely from memory, but this is unlikely since he does not allude to gospel stories when they would have suited his purpose very well. What the passage does prove is that certain traditions about what Jesus taught were current when Clement wrote, not that he drew his information from the gospels. It is quite possible that the gospels were written later and drew on the same traditions.

In Chapter 45 Clement again urges us to

... Remember the words of Jesus our Lord. He said: 'Woe to that man! It would have been good for him if he had not been born, rather than cause one of my elect to stumble; it would have been better for him to have a millstone hung round him and be sunk in the sea, than to have seduced one of my elect.'

The gospel parallels are:

(1) Mk. xiv, 21: 'Woe unto that man through whom the Son of man is betrayed! Good it were for that man if he had not been born.' This is said of Judas at the Last Supper.

(2) Mk. ix, 42: 'And whosoever shall cause one of these little ones that believe on me to stumble, it were better for him if a great millstone were hanged about his neck and he were cast into the sea.'

If it were at all likely that Clement knew our gospels, we could explain his quotation by assuming that, quoting Mk. from memory, he ran these two passages together. He certainly combines OT passages in a similar arbitrary way. Now we saw above (p. 72) that composite quotations from the OT seem to have been drawn from manuals where OT sayings were collected, rather than directly from the sacred books, and it has been suggested that Clement was quoting from some collection of Logia or sayings of Jesus. Such collections certainly existed. At the beginning of this century three papyri were discovered at Oxyrhynchus in the Nile valley, which contain a few sayings of Jesus written in Greek, and in 1945 the *Gospel according to Thomas* was found near Nag Hamadi in Upper Egypt. It consists of about 114 sayings of Jesus, (including those found on the Oxyrhynchus papyri), and Quispel holds that it was neither compiled from the NT nor constitutes one of its sources, but is an ancient independent tradition, dating to about AD 140 (cp. Frend, 96, p. 263). It begins:

These are the secret words which the Living Jesus spoke and Didymos Judas Thomas wrote.

There follow the sayings, each one introduced by 'Jesus said', with no indication of where or when. They include many which, in the gospels, appear in a definite situation, and scholars have inferred that such collections of Logia formed the earliest traditions about Jesus' teaching, and that the gospel writers have invented historical situations in which certain of these teachings were delivered. Thus when Clement records Jesus as saying that it were better for the man who caused one of the elect to stumble never to have been born, he may have been quoting a manual where this saying was given with no context; and later, the gospel writers fitted it into their story of Judas. This is substantially the conclusion reached by the committee of scholars of the Oxford Society of historical theology, investigating the references to the NT in the Apostolic Fathers. They 'are inclined to think' that Clement gives 'a citation from some written or unwritten form of "Catechesis" as to our Lord's teaching, current in the Roman Church, perhaps a local form which may go back to a time before our gospels existed' (60, p. 61).

Finally, Clement, like Paul, stresses Jesus' atoning sacrifice, saying that 'the blood of Christ . . . is precious to the Father, because, poured out for our salvation, it brought to the whole world the grace of conversion' (Chapter 7). Also like Paul, he regards the resurrection of Jesus as a promise of our own future resurrection (Chapter 24). These two elements remain constant in Christian writings from the first. What we shall have to investigate is the way in which a detailed biography of Jesus was gradually added to them.

(2) *Ignatius*: The seven epistles of Ignatius are together only about as long as the single one of Clement, but they contain more gospel matter. Furthermore, Ignatius mentions a 'gospel' which he contrasts with 'the prophets' in such a way as to suggest that what he had in mind may have been not simply 'good tidings' but a written document, and which he calls 'the flesh of Jesus', perhaps because it is the record of his earthly life (Phil., Chapter 5). In Chapter 9 he says:

> The gospel contains something special—the advent of the Saviour our Lord Jesus Christ, His passion and His resurrection. The beloved Prophets announced His coming, whereas the gospel is the imperishable fulfilment.

In the letter to the Smyrnaeans (Chapter 7), he urges us to 'study the prophets attentively and especially the gospel, in which the passion is revealed to us and the resurrection shown in its fulfilment'.

If Ignatius was acquainted with some of the canonical gospels, he did not rely on them exclusively for his information. For instance, he describes the 'star in the east', but not as Mt. does:

> A star shone in heaven, brighter than any other star, its light was unspeakable and its strangeness caused amazement: and all the other stars, with the sun and moon, became a chorus for that star, which outshone them all; and all were troubled to know whence came this strange appearance, so unlike them (Ephes., Chapter 19).

From this we may infer that Ignatius either embellished Mt.'s narrative from his own imagination, or from another source; or that some traditions about the star were known to Ignatius, and were drawn on independently by Mt.

Whether he knew any of our gospels or not, Ignatius mentions more facts from the life of Jesus than any previous writer. He is the first to mention the virgin birth and to name the mother of Jesus (Ephes., Chapter 17). These details are given in order to controvert the Docetists or 'seemers' whom he characterizes as 'mad dogs who bite in secret'. Against their view that Jesus was purely divine and only seemed to be a man, he declares that 'God became man, true life in death, sprung from both Mary and from God, first subject to suffering, then incapable of it' (Chapter 7).

It is again to confute the Docetists that he tells that 'Jesus Christ, David's scion and Mary's Son, was really born, and ate and drank, really persecuted by Pontius Pilate, really crucified and died while heaven and earth and the underworld looked on; and also really rose from the dead' (Trall., Chapter 9). In the letter to the Smyrnaeans (Chapter 1) we have a similarly detailed list of biographical particulars:

> He is really of the line of David . . . really born of a virgin and baptized by John that all righteousness might be fulfilled by him . . . Under Pontius Pilate and the tetrarch Herod he was really nailed to the cross in the flesh for our sake—of whose fruit we are, in virtue of his most blessed passion.

Kleist remarks that Ignatius here confutes Docetism by 'triumphantly pointing out fact after fact of Christ's life' (162, p. 139). The striking thing is that the writer of the canonical epistles of John, faced with a kindred heresy, had been unable to meet it in this way. He had warned against 'false prophets' and had said that only those who admitted that Jesus had 'come in the flesh' were to be accepted (I Jn. iv, 1–3). But he had not given a single biographical detail to confute these false teachers. So it looks as though the knowledge of Jesus' biography available to Ignatius was not available to him.

When Ignatius says that Jesus was baptized by John 'that all righteousness might be fulfilled by him', he may be following Mt. For Mt. alone makes Jesus say to John (after the latter has expressed reluctance to baptize him): 'Suffer it now: for thus it becometh us to fulfil all righteousness' (iii, 15). Streeter thinks that the absence of this phrase from the other gospels shows that it is the work of the editor who compiled Mt. from previous written sources, and is not drawn from them, and that Ignatius' knowledge of it therefore proves him to have known Mt., and not merely his sources, (263, pp. 16, 505).

Although Ignatius may have known Mt., he did not know (or did not trust) Lk; for in order to controvert the Docetists he tries to show that Jesus existed as a physical body not merely before his death but even after his resurrection:

> For I know and believe that even after his resurrection he was in a physical body: and when he came to Peter and his

companions he said, 'Take hold and feel me and see that I am not a bodiless phantom'. And immediately they touched him and believed, when they had had contact with his flesh and blood . . . And after his resurrection he ate and drank with them as being in a physical body, though in spirit he was united with the Father (Smyrn., Chapter 3).

Jerome alleged that the quotation 'Take hold and feel me', etc., is from the apocryphal *Gospel according to the Hebrews*. It certainly does not come from a canonical gospel. Now the details given in Lk. xxiv, 39–43 would have suited Ignatius' needs much better. He is alleging that the risen Jesus ate and drank, it being the established belief that an angel or spirit might live familiarly with men for a long period, but could not eat (see Tobit, xii, 9). However, the quotation he gives omits all mention of eating and drinking, whereas Lk. specifies not only the act of touching, which is mentioned in Ignatius' quotation, but also that of eating. Can we really believe that Ignatius knew and trusted Lk., yet preferred to quote from an unknown authority a passage which is not nearly so much to his point? Abbott has remarked that 'apologists usually depreciate what they call "a mere argument from silence"; but it has weight varying with circumstances. Here it is extremely weighty. The evidence is almost as strong as if Ignatius said expressly "I did not know Lk.", or else, "I knew Lk., but did not believe it to be so authoritative as the tradition from which I quoted" ' (5, § 30 and note).

One reason he may have had for distrusting the third gospel was that, being not one of the twelve but a mere companion of Paul, Luke could not report as an eye-witness. The disadvantage is stressed by the Muratorian fragment of about AD 180. The writer says that it was not until 'after the ascension' that Paul took Luke as a companion, that he had 'not seen the Lord in the flesh' and set down facts 'as far as he could ascertain them' (Quot. 5, § 78). Some of the Fathers (e.g. Irenaeus and Tertullian) tried to counteract Luke's disadvantage by alleging that he committed to writing the gospel preached by Paul. Origen, too, took the third gospel to be meant when Paul speaks of 'my gospel'—meaning, of course, not a book but tidings (Rom. ii, 16). Eusebius alludes to these patristic traditions when he tells us that Luke 'was long a companion of Paul', and that 'they say that Paul was actually accustomed to quote from Luke's gospel, since when writing of some gospel as his own he used to say "according to my Gospel" ' (89, iii, 4). Schmiedel notes that in this way, it was possible to 'assign a quasi-apostolic origin to the work of one who was not himself an apostle'. These expedients of the Fathers show clearly enough that 'it is vain to look to them for trustworthy information on the subject of the origin of the gospels' (235, § 147).

(3) *Polycarp*: Polycarp's epistle is short (eight pages in Kleist's edition, whereas Clement's fills forty), but he nevertheless shows some acquaintance with the doctrines of Jesus. Thus he says: 'Let us fervently implore the All-seeing God not to expose us to temptation, since the Lord has said: the spirit is willing but the flesh is weak' (Chapter 7). This strongly resembles Mt. xxvi, 41. Polycarp also gives sayings similar to those in the Sermon on the Mount. He tells us to

bear in mind what the Lord taught when he said: 'Do not judge, that you may not be judged: forgive, and you will be forgiven: show mercy that you may have mercy shown you; the measure you use in measuring will be used in measuring out your share': and 'Blessed are the humble souls and those that are persecuted for conscience sake, for theirs is the kingdom of God'.

Some of this had already been quoted by Clement, but here the quotations are fuller, and indicate that the writer may have known Mt. or Lk. or both, for, as Harrison notes:

Polycarp . . . substitutes again and again for Clement's loose wording the exact terms now of Mt., now of Lk., and now of a combination of these two, adding at the same time matter contained in them for which Clement has no equivalent, and omitting matter contained in Clement for which neither gospel has any equivalent. This fact is all the more significant because (*a*) he is himself so prone to be inexact in his borrowings from books which he certainly knew quite well, (*b*) he is generally . . . more influenced by the language of Clement than by any book of the NT, except perhaps I Peter (131, p. 286).

Polycarp shows no knowledge of Jn. If Harrison's dating of his epistle is correct, the inference is that at least two of our gospels were circulating by AD 135.

To sum up, we may say that more gospel material was known to Ignatius and to Polycarp than to Clement. Harrison quotes Bigg's finding that the total number of quotations from the NT is: in I Clement, 26; in Ignatius, 17; in Polycarp (although his work is the shortest), 46. Harrison adds that on Lightfoot's showing Clement and Ignatius quote from ten NT books, while Polycarp quotes from fifteen (131, p. 233).

(vi) Other early Christian writers

(a) *Barnabas*

The epistle of Barnabas unfortunately cannot be accurately dated. It is later than the destruction of the temple in AD 70, which it mentions. Altaner thinks it may have been written any time between AD 70 and 145 (13, p. 81).[1]

The writer of the epistle reproves Christians who lean towards Judaism and say 'their covenant is also ours' (Chapter 4). He tries to controvert them by showing that the Jewish law must be understood spiritually. Thus circumcision really means a circumcision of the heart, i.e. a contrite heart. And everywhere in the Jewish law and in the OT narratives he sees 'the glory of Jesus' prefigured. The 318 servants whom Abraham circumcised signify, to him, Jesus on the Cross; for the Greek T (=300) indicates the cross by its form, while IH (=18) means Jesus ($'IH\Sigma OY\Sigma$). Just as the Freudian critic of today assumes that the poetry he is interpreting is basically about sex, whatever the apparent subject-matter, so these early Christian writers assumed that everything in the OT somehow refers to Jesus. In some cases they even went so far as to invent the OT passages they claimed to be expounding. Justin, for instance, found the wood of the cross in Ps. xcvi, 10 by adding 'from the tree' to the words 'The Lord reigneth' (157, pp. 153-4).

In Chapter 4 Barnabas writes 'Let us give heed lest, as it is written, we be found "many called but few chosen" '. This may be a reference to Mt. If so, and if the epistle was written in the first century, then this instance of the application of the title

---

[1] Barnard (19, p. 74 and refs.) thinks it 'probably dates from the early years of the reign of Hadrian (AD 117-38)'. Goodspeed (107, p. 20) detects in the epistle a reference to 'the heathen rebuilding of the temple of Jupiter on the temple site in Jerusalem', and this would 'date the letter about AD 130, when Hadrian ordered the rebuilding of the new city'.

'scripture' to the NT is unique. However, it seems doubtful whether the author was in fact acquainted with any of our gospels. For in Chapter 4 he tells us that the last days are at hand:

> The last offence is at hand, concerning which it is written, as Enoch said, 'For to this end hath the Lord cut short the times . . .'

If he had known Mk. xiii, 20 or Mt. xxiv, 22, he might have quoted them about the 'cutting short of the times', instead of treating Enoch as 'scripture'. Also, when he says the temple was destroyed because the Jews went to war, he gives no indication that Jesus foretold this event. Again, in the same fourth chapter, he urges Christians not to 'court solitude' but to attend the common meetings and join in discussing what contributes to the common good. To carry this point he quotes Isaiah, but makes no reference to Jesus' words 'where two or three are gathered together in my name, there I am in the midst of them' (Mt. xviii, 20).

In the next chapter he quotes Isaiah liii as prefiguring the passion. Here he gives no details of Jesus' ordeal, but in chapter 7 he tells us that, when crucified he was given vinegar and gall (ὄξει καὶ Χολῇ) to drink. This may be an echo from Mt. (Mt. alone of our gospels refers to Χολή), or both Mt. and Barnabas may be independent traditions influenced by Psalm lxix, 21: 'They gave me also gall for my meat and in my thirst they gave me vinegar to drink.' The Oxford committee thinks that the latter alternative is the case, since Barnabas' wording is closer to that of the Psalm than it is to Mt. xxvii, 34, 48. The committee adds that 'in general, Barnabas' handling of the Passion in terms of OT types, especially from Psalms, seems parallel to, rather than dependent on, Mt.'s narrative' (60, p. 18). These scholars also regard Barnabas' quotation of the phrase 'many called but few chosen' as indicating that 'Barnabas and Mt. probably drew on a common source for the saying, whose proverbial character seems proved by its addition to Mt. xx, 16 in some copies'.

Barnabas also says that Jesus 'preached teaching Israel and performing so many wonders and miracles' (Chapter 5), and that 'he chose his own apostles from the worst type of sinners, since it was not his mission to call saints but sinners'. With this we may compare Lk. v, 29-32 and also the following synoptic passages.

Mt. ix, 10–13

And it came to pass, as he sat at meat in the house, behold many publicans and sinners came and sat down with Jesus and his disciples. And when the Pharisees saw it, they said unto his disciples, why eateth your master with the publicans and sinners? But when he heard it, he said, 'They that are whole have no need of a physician, but they that are sick. But go ye and learn what this meaneth, I desire mercy and not sacrifice; for I came not to call the righteous but sinners.'

Mk. ii, 16–17

And the scribes of the Pharisees, when they saw that he was eating with the sinners and publicans, said unto his disciples, He eateth and drinketh with publicans and sinners.

And when Jesus heard it, he saith unto them, They that are whole have no need of a physician, but they that are sick.

I came not to call the righteous but sinners.

The sinful character of the apostles (that Barnabas asserts) is excluded by all three narratives. It is not they but the publicans and sinners to whom Jesus' saying 'I came to call sinners' refers. The Oxford committee infers that 'this points to Barnabas' knowledge of a Logia tradition only partly parallel to the tradition common to our Synoptics' (60, p. 19).

Barnabas is also at variance with the gospels in holding that Jesus is 'not a son of man but a son of God; though revealed by a type in the flesh' (Chapter 12). To establish this, he does not, as one might expect, allude to the virgin birth. Instead he denies that Jesus is descended from David, and remarks that 'David himself, fearing and comprehending the error of the sinners [viz. that Christ was the son of David] calls him Lord and does not call him Son' (Chapter 12).

From Chapter 8 we learn that 'those whom he empowered to preach the gospel were twelve in number, to represent the tribes of Israel, which were twelve'. To argue against observance of the Jewish sabbath he says (Chapter 5) that on 'the eighth day [of the week, viz, the first day after the lapse of the preceding week] Jesus rose from the dead; after which he manifested himself and went up to heaven'.[1]

---

[1] It was clearly opposition to Jewish practice that made Sunday the day of the Christian Lord, just as Mohammed made Friday the day of Islam in opposition to both Jews and Christians. On the origin of the expression 'the eighth day', see Rordorf (229, pp. 271–80). Christian acceptance of Sunday as the Lord's day led in time to gospel narratives which (not without strain)

The way in which he 'handles the Passion in terms of OT types' is again made clear in Chapters 6 and 7. He quotes Psalm xxii, 'for my garment they have cast a lot', but gives none of the details mentioned in the gospels, even though all four record the casting of lots on Christ's garments. He also says that the scapegoat is 'the type of Jesus that was to suffer'. The scapegoat was set apart for the great Day of Atonement as a sin-offering. The high-priest confessed over it all the sins of the Israelites, laying them on its head and sending it out into the wilderness to Azazel, (Lev. xvi, 8–10, 21–2). Barnabas says that the scapegoat is wreathed with thorns and scarlet wool, and that this crown 'is a type of Jesus set forth for the Church, since whosoever should desire to take away the scarlet wool, it behoved him to suffer many things owing to the terrible nature of the thorn, and through affliction to win mastery over it. Thus he saith; they that desire to see me, and to attain unto my kingdom, must lay hold on me through tribulation and affliction.' This saying is not in the gospels.

(b) *Papias*

Papias, bishop of Hierapolis in Phrygia, is the first writer to mention written gospels (Mk. and Mt.) by name. His book, *The exegesis of the Lord's oracles*, is lost, and only fragments quoted by later writers survive. The work was known to Irenaeus, and was therefore written before AD 180. Furthermore, Philip Sidetes tells that Papias says in his book that those whom Christ raised from the dead survived until Hadrian's time. Hadrian reigned from 117 to 137, and Papias' reference to 'Hadrian's time' means that he could not have written earlier than about 120, and much more probably wrote after AD 137. Irenaeus alleges that Papias was 'a hearer of John and a companion of Polycarp'. He may well have accompanied Polycarp (whose epistle, we saw, is dated AD 135) but he could not have heard John; for Eusebius (89, III, 39), quoting the preface of Papias' book in support, shows that he did not know the original apostles personally, but received their teachings indirectly from their followers. It is obviously more

---

make his resurrection take place on that day. For instance, the women, who witnessed his burial before the Sabbath, went to anoint his body 'when the Sabbath was past' (Mk. xv, 47; xvi, 1). This, says Schwartz (246, p. 38), violates all ritual, and is inconceivable in a Palestinian climate. But they had to find the tomb empty on a Sunday because this is the day of the Lord.

probable that Irenaeus—influenced by the natural tendency of Christian controversialists to exaggerate the continuity of Christian tradition—hastily declared Papias to be a 'hearer of John', than that Eusebius, subsequently reviewing all the evidence, was mistaken in denying it (see 5, § 69). From all this evidence, the year 140 has been widely accepted as the date of Papias' book.

Even the few surviving fragments (given by Kleist, 163, pp. 114–24) allege a far greater wealth of detail about Jesus and the disciples than we have found in the whole works of earlier writers. The data include: Jesus' choosing of the apostles, who include Peter, John, Philip, Thomas and Matthew (whereas earlier writers name only Peter and Paul); a story about a woman who had been accused before the Lord of many transgressions; and another to the effect that Justus, surnamed Barsabas, was forced by unbelievers to drink snake poison, but was, in the name of Christ, preserved unharmed. We have seen already that Papias also knew of raisings from the dead. Papias' brief statement on Mt. has been discussed above (p. 121). He does not claim to have read the other gospel he names (Mk.), but merely repeats what the Presbyter John had told him, namely that:

> Mark, having become Peter's interpreter, wrote down accurately everything that he remembered, without however recording in order what was either said or done by the Lord. For he neither heard the Lord, nor followed him, but subsequently attached himself to Peter, who used to frame his teachings to the needs of his hearers, but had no design of giving a connected account of the Lord's discourses (λογίων). So Mark made no mistake, while he thus wrote down some things as he remembered them. For he made it his own care not to omit anything that he heard, or to set down any false statement therein (quoted by Eusebius, 89, III, 39).

The document to which Papias refers is thus a record of the fragmentary conversations or addresses of Peter. Now the canonical Mk. certainly does not read like a collection of discourses by Peter, and Papias may be referring to one of its sources rather than to the completed gospel. If, however, he was describing the canonical Mk., then the important statement in his testimony is that Peter supplied its contents orally. The truth of this is hard to reconcile with Mk.'s brevity, his neglect of much of Jesus' preaching, and his inclusion of such clearly unhistorical elements as the Judas story, not to mention his profusion of miracles. Did Peter have no knowledge of the Sermon on the Mount? Or did he prefer to withhold from Mark his reminiscences of the longest and most important discourses ascribed to the Lord? And had he also forgotten all about the Lord's prayer, and the authority conferred on him in the 'thou art Peter' passage, both of which are absent from Mk.?

Taylor affirms (265, pp. 26, 31) that Mk. 'was written in the decade AD 60–70', and that 'there can be no doubt that its author was Mark, the attendant of Peter. This is the unbroken testimony of earliest Christian opinion *from Papias onwards.*' Taylor himself dates Papias' book at AD 140 and admits that earlier writers such as Clement, Barnabas and Polycarp do not appear to have known Mk. (p. 1). But how can their silence be explained if Mk. existed by AD 70? And what is the value of testimony as to its authorship which is unknown until seventy years after its appearance?

Papias, on whose authority we are to believe that Mk. had his information from an eye-witness, is not a writer on whom we can place much reliance. We saw (above p. 84) that he held Jesus to have taught the famous millennium grape story. And he believed what a modern Catholic writer (163, p. 106) has designated as 'grotesque legendary matter' about Judas, Papias evidently regarded many traditions as authentic, apart from those recorded in Mt. and Mk. His statement that Mk. is based on Peter's discourses was embellished by the later Fathers (see 125, p. 11 n.). Catholic apologists urge that the Fathers were intelligent, impartial men who sifted evidence carefully and committed themselves to a doctrine only after profound and prolonged study. But we have seen how often they in fact romance. Apart from Papias and his grape story, Justin proved the Messiahship of Jesus by quoting non-existent passages from the OT, Tertullian alleged that Pilate and Tiberius believed in the divinity of Jesus (see p. 189 below), and Irenaeus proved that there can be only four gospels because there are four winds. Such are the authorities on whom we are to depend.

Papias makes no mention of Lk. or Jn. in any extant passage, and we can infer that he never mentioned them at all, for his evidence has been preserved by Eusebius, who made a point of gathering all he could from earlier writers on the question of the composition of the scriptures. Eusebius promises to record the quotations of ecclesiastical writers from 'disputed books', and what they have said about the canonical scriptures and the un-canonical as well (89, III, 3). But he gives no extracts from Papias about Lk. and Jn. Had Papias known Lk., or at any rate regarded this gospel as authoritative, he would surely have mentioned it while dwelling on the defect of 'order' or 'arrangement' in Mk.; for Lk. avowed it as one of his objects to write 'in (chronological) order'.

(c) *Aristides*

Another Christian writing dated about AD 140 (e.g. by Cross, 70 p. 47) is the *Apology for Christianity* written by Aristides, who describes himself as an Athenian philosopher, and addresses himself to the emperor Antoninus Pius (AD 138–161). Three-quarters of this brief work consists of criticism of non-Christian religions, but in the little he does say about the Christians, he refers both to a written gospel and to the principal biographical facts:

> The Christians reckon the beginning of their religion from Jesus Christ, who is named the Son of God most High; and it is said that God came down from heaven and from a Hebrew virgin took and clad himself with flesh . . . This is taught from that gospel which a little while ago was spoken among them as being preached; wherein if ye also will read, ye will comprehend the power that is upon it. This Jesus, then, was born of the tribe of the Hebrews, and he had twelve disciples, in order that a certain dispensation of his might be fulfilled. He was pierced by the Jews: and he died and was buried; and they say that after three days he arose and ascended to heaven; and then these twelve disciples went forth into the known parts of the world and taught concerning his greatness with all humility and sobriety. (Chapter 2, See 215, p. 36.)

(vii) Summary of the early non-canonical evidence

The following table sums up what we have learned of Jesus from all these early writers. The numbers represent dates.

Clement (96). Jesus taught mercy, forgiveness, reciprocity. He warned against causing the elect to stumble.

Barnabas (?110 or later). Jesus was not a descendant of David. He was a teacher and miracle-worker. He chose twelve apostles for the purpose of preaching his gospel. He drank vinegar and gall at the crucifixion. He rose from the dead on the eighth day of the week, manifested himself and went up to heaven.

Ignatius (?110). Possible references to a written gospel. Jesus born of the virgin Mary. At his birth a star shone brighter than any other star. Baptized by John. Crucified under Pontius Pilate and the tetrarch Herod. Appeared to his followers after his resurrection and ate and drank with them as a real body.

Polycarp (135). Parts of Sermon on the Mount. Jesus taught that the spirit is willing but the flesh weak.

Papias (140). Mentions Mt. and Mk. Jesus taught of the millennium. He chose as apostles Peter, John, Philip, Thomas and Matthew. He raised people from the dead. A woman was accused before him of many transgressions. Judas' body became bloated and he died a hideous death.

Aristides (140). Refers to a written gospel. Jesus born of a Hebrew virgin. He had twelve disciples. He was crucified by the Jews, buried, and rose again after three days.

It is clear that details of Jesus' biography only begin to appear about the beginning of the second century and that they consist of multifarious details derived from a variety of sources.[1]

(viii) Justin Martyr

The next writer of importance is Justin Martyr, who lived until about AD 167. His extant works show that not only the gospel matter but also written gospels were available in his day, and were regarded as equally sacred as the OT. In his first Apology (Chapter 66) he mentions the words of the institution of the Eucharist and then says: 'So the apostles handed down in the Memoirs made by them, which are called gospels.' He goes on to tell that these were read in the religious assemblies of the Christians together with the 'writings of the prophets'. His dialogue with the Jew Trypho contains many references to these memoirs in order to show that Jesus fulfilled OT prophecies. In some cases the quotations give exactly the words of our synoptics. It

[1] For correlation with the canonical evidence, see table on pp. 210–211 below.

is very striking, however, that even Justin never mentions how many gospels there are, nor the names of the evangelists. The only book in the NT which he assigns to an author is the Revelation, which, he says, was written by 'John, one of the apostles of Christ' (157, Chapter 81). We saw already that the names by which our gospels are now known were attached to them relatively late (see above, p. 114). In fact, no name was connected with any gospel for about a hundred years after the supposed date of the crucifixion; and we do not find all four gospels mentioned by name until Irenaeus.

In the *Dialogue with Trypho* Justin is doing what the author of the epistle of Barnabas had done, namely showing that the OT is full of prophecies about Jesus and his work. But he is able to allege many more details in Jesus' life as fulfilment of prophecy. To point the contrast I need only summarize what he states about Jesus' birth and early life. The numbers refer to the chapters of the *Dialogue*.

He was born of the virgin Mary, who was of the tribe of Judah and David (43). Joseph, who was espoused to her, first thought to cast her out, supposing that she was with child of human intercourse; but 'an angel appeared to him saying: "that which she has conceived is of the Holy Ghost"'. 'Moved therefore by fear he did not cast her out, but as the first enrolment under Quirinius was then taking place in Judaea, he came back from Nazareth where he was living to Bethlehem, to which he belonged, to enrol himself. For he was by descent of the tribe of Judah that inhabited that land. Then he is commanded, together with Mary, to go into Egypt and to be there together with the child until it should again be revealed to them that they should return into Judaea' (78). Joseph was a carpenter (88). Jesus was born 'in a cave nigh the village'. Wise men came from Arabia and worshipped him after they had first been to Herod (77) and told him that they knew 'by a star that had appeared in heaven that a king had been born in your land'. When they had worshipped the child and offered him gifts of gold, frankincense and myrrh, they were commanded by revelation not to return to Herod. Joseph, Mary and the child went into Egypt, and meanwhile Herod commanded that all boys in Bethlehem should be slain (78). The holy family stayed in Egypt until his death (103).

Justin gives an equally full account of Jesus' relations with John the Baptist, and of his teachings (which include the parable of the sower, woes upon the scribes and Pharisees, warnings about strife, false prophets and false Christs, and all sorts of ethical teachings). He also mentions the Temptation, Peter's recognition of Jesus as the Christ, Jesus' miracles, prophecies about his own death and resurrection, entry into Jerusalem, cleansing of the temple, agony, arrest, trial, crucifixion and words from the cross, burial and resurrection.

Justin wrote this *Dialogue* between AD 150 and his death in 167; for Chapter 120 contains a reference to his first Apology (Chapter 26), and in this work he gives (Chapter 46) his own date of writing as 150. It is clear that he writes as one would expect a Christian who knew the gospel story to write. There is a world of difference between his Jesus and the crucified phantom of Paul, and even the nascent teaching God of Clement. So far we have seen that the later the document the fuller the biographical details. They increase steadily from Paul through Clement to Barnabas, Ignatius and Papias. By Justin's time a fairly full biography had been constructed. Some of the details he alleges could not have been taken from the canonical gospels (e.g. the birth in a cave, the fire kindled at Jesus' baptism, the descent into hell). There were, then, many traditions available, and by the time he wrote, Christians had reached the stage where, instead of adding to them, they found it necessary to select and allow only a limited number as reliable. Thus, although Papias, writing well before Justin, had mentioned Judas, Justin is silent about him, even though he tells us of the Last Supper and Jesus' arrest. With Irenaeus, writing about 180, this tendency to select has become much stronger and has led to the formation of a canon.

(ix) Conclusion

It is the evidence given in this chapter that has led me to the conclusion that Christianity as we know it has not evolved from the activities of the Jesus whose career is given in the gospels. I said earlier that the lateness of the gospels, the muddle we find in them, and the obvious desire of their writers to make Jesus behave in such a way as to fulfil the Messianic expectations, do not in themselves exclude the possibility that in some of the narratives we have references to the behaviour of a historical personage who inaugurated the new religion. But in this chapter we found that the gospel traditions are unconfirmed by the earlier Christian records, that the Jesus of the earliest records is not the historical figure of the gospels at all. It is not that Paul and other early Christian writers are silent about this or that historical detail, but that nothing they say about Jesus suggests that they have in mind the specific historical situation portrayed in the gospels.

The decisive fact is not that the earliest Christian writers fail to refer to written gospels. Granted the orthodox assumption of a historical Jesus of Nazareth, it would be perfectly intelligible that written records of his career were made only at a relatively late stage, and so were not available to the earliest writers. What is decisive is the failure of the earliest writers to mention any concrete facts about him at all when these are supposed to have formed the historical facts later recorded in the gospels. We shall see shortly that pagan and Jewish testimony also strikingly fails to confirm the allegations of the gospels. So it looks as though we shall have to seek another basis as the starting point of Christianity.

CHAPTER SEVEN

Pagan and Jewish Testimony

There are three pagan texts which have been regarded as relevant to the historicity of Jesus—one in Suetonius, one in Tacitus and one in the younger Pliny.[1] The latter is in fact unimportant as regards Jesus' existence, and consists of a report to Trajan (AD 112) that Christians appear to be harmless people who meet at day-break and sing hymns to the honour of the Messiah as to a god ('Christo quasi deo'). Suetonius wrote in the second century of a movement of Jewish revolt at Rome in the reign of Claudius 'impulsore Chresto' (one Chrestus instigating). Claudius reigned from AD 41–54 and it is unlikely that Christianity not merely spread as far as Rome within fifteen years of Jesus' death, but also became powerful enough to have caused a revolt there. Suetonius does not, in fact, say the revolt was caused by Jewish Christians. He speaks not of Christians, but of Chrestus, and this was a common name among slaves and freemen and occurs more than eighty times in the Latin inscriptions of Rome (the list is given by Linck, 173, p. 106, n.2). Suetonius may be referring to some unknown agitator of this name, but more probably he wrote Chrestus in-stead of Christus, the Messiah, and meant to say that there was a disturbance caused by Jews thinking that the Messiah had come or was about to come. Gibbon has stressed the rebellious spirit of the Jews in the Roman Empire and said that it was stimulated by the 'flattering promises which they derived from their ancient oracles that a conquering Messiah would arise, destined to break their fetters' (104, II, 3, Chapter 16). So the 'Chrestus' of Suetonius

[1] Aufhauser (17) gives the pagan and Jewish texts, with a bibliography of the critical discussion of them.

is likely to have been an agitator who caused disturbances in the Roman ghetto by coming forward as the Messiah.

Tacitus (*annals*, xv, 44) does mention Christians, and says that Nero accused them of setting fire to Rome in AD 64. Gibbon (104, II, 15, Chapter 16) renders the passage as follows:

> He inflicted the most exquisite tortures on those men, who, under the vulgar appellation of Christians, were already branded with deserved infamy. They derived their name and origin from Christ, who, in the reign of Tiberius, had suffered death, by the sentence of the procurator Pontius Pilate. For a while this dire superstition was checked; but it again burst forth, and not only spread itself over Judaea, the first seat of this mischievous sect, but was even introduced into Rome, the common asylum which receives and protects whatever is atrocious. The confessions of those who were seized discovered a great multitude of their accomplices, and they were all convicted, not so much for the crime of setting fire to the city as for their hatred of the human race. They died in torments, and their torments were embittered by derision and insult. Some, smeared over with combustible materials, were used as torches to illuminate the darkness of the night. The gardens of Nero were destined for this melancholy spectacle.

The style of this passage is genuinely Tacitean, especially the cynical aside about Rome. And what Christian interpolator would refer needlessly to the temporary setback of Christianity or to the Christians' betrayal of their fellows and their hatred of the human race? Hochart, however, regards the passage as interpolated on the ground that Tacitus mentions Pilate only on this occasion, yet fails to tell us what province he governed and on what charge he condemned Jesus; and that this suggests that the passage was written by a Christian who had Christian readers in mind, to whom Pilate would be a familiar name needing no elucidation (139, p. 70). This argument can be met by a reminder that that part of Tacitus which deals with the reign of Gaius is lost, and that he might very well have made Pilate familiar to his readers there. In any case, Tacitus cannot be expected to give the life history of every incidental character he mentions. I therefore propose to regard the passage as authentic.[1] But does its reference to Christ's

[1] We may, however, note that other evidence adduced by Hochart in favour of his view is that neither Juvenal, nor the elder Pliny, nor Dio

execution under Pilate establish the historicity of this event? The *Annals* are commonly dated about AD 120 and by this time (see my summary of the evidence on pp. 151, 181, above) Christians had themselves come to believe that they were followers of a victim of Pilate. Tacitus, who is trying to give his readers some idea of what Christians believe, was presumably aware that this was their own view of their mode of origin, and there was surely nothing in this view that would have struck him as unlikely. On the contrary, this Christian admission that Christ was, in Roman eyes, a criminal, would agree very well with his belief that Christianity was altogether repugnant. Why, then, should he not have adopted this view without any historical investigation? The alternative supposition would be that he derived his information from a Roman record of the crucifixion. Even if records of executions in Palestine ninety years earlier were available, and even if it had been his practice to consult original documents (which, according to Fabia, 90, p. XIII, it was not), why should he have undertaken such an inquiry in this particular instance, when all he appears to have aimed at was to give his readers some idea of who these disreputable Christians are? A modern European writer who dislikes Buddhists and who is writing for an audience that knows little or nothing of them, might perhaps explain that they are followers of a man who preached in the forest near the city of Benares in the sixth century BC. This statement would not necessarily stand for any historical investigation. It could merely

Cassius in his *Roman History* say anything about Christians in Rome; nor does Josephus, even though he mentions some atrocities of Nero. I shall argue below that Nero's victims may have been Jews, not Christians, and that while Tacitus confused the two, other writers did not.

Suetonius does mention a Neronian persecution of Christians in the following passage which corroborates Tacitus:

> Numbers of abuses were severely censured and punished. Many regulations were also made for preventing them: limits were set to luxury; public feasts were reduced to simple distributions of food: it was forbidden to sell cooked foods in cabarets (with the exception of vegetables and garden produce), unless all sorts of dishes had already been served there previously. *The Christians were executed—a sect of men who had embraced a new and criminal superstition.* The excesses of chariot drivers were terminated. Profiting from a long-standing tolerance, they had amused themselves by continually robbing and deceiving people (Quoted by Hochart, 139, pp. 259–60)

Hochart justly says that this reference to the execution of Christians in the middle of enumeration of minor police reforms is a clear interpolation. But this does not establish that the passage in Tacitus was interpolated.

G

represent an uncritical acceptance of the Buddhist view or even an eager acceptance of this detail of Buddhist teaching, which could be used to indicate that Buddhism is very remote in time and place and is better ignored by modern Europeans.[1]

A. Robertson has declared that Tacitus was more likely to record the 'official Roman view' of the origin of Christianity, than to repeat what Christians themselves said about the origin of their sect (219, p. 93). But Robertson does not state what this official view was—nor does he give evidence that there was one. Commentators have pointed out that the charge of 'hatred of the human race' would have been much more plausible against apocalyptic Jewish fanatics. Whittaker (288, pp. 23–5) surmises that there were no Christians in Rome under Nero, and that Tacitus was confusing the Christians of his own day with Messianic Jews of Nero's time.[2] The basis of the confusion may well have been provided by Suetonius' phrase 'impulsore Chresto'. The hypothesis would explain why Tacitus speaks of a 'great multitude' of Christians at Rome in AD 64. If these were in fact Jews, he need not be accused of exaggerating; whereas it is difficult to envisage large numbers of Christians at Rome so early. From Whittaker's premises the early Christians say so little of the Neronian persecution because the victims were orthodox Jews, and so it was not part of their own tradition. This early Christian silence is otherwise difficult to explain, except on Hochart's hypothesis that the passage in Tacitus is interpolated. Acts, Justin and Origen say nothing of a Neronian persecution. Acts ends with the statement that Paul taught in Rome 'with all boldness, none forbidding him'. Only later traditions allege he was martyred there.[3]

[1] This criticism of the passage in Tacitus was made by Dupuis in the eighteenth century (See 282), and was endorsed by Weiss (278, p. 88). Windisch (290, pp. 284–5) arbitrarily alleges that AD 120 allows 'too short' a period for a fictitious tradition of an execution under Pilate to have arisen.

[2] This seems to be suggested by Gibbon, who says that Tacitus was writing under Hadrian, sixty years after the fire, and that 'it was natural for the philosopher to indulge in the description of the origin, the progress and the character of the new sect not so much according to the knowledge or prejudices of the age of Nero, as according to those of the time of Hadrian' (104, II, 18). Gibbon also notes that if Nero persecuted Christians, then this persecution was 'sudden and transient', and the only example of Roman intolerance up to the time of the Jewish war. He shows too that Trajan and his successors were the first to establish a legal mode of procedure against Christians (from AD 112), and that even then there were so few executions that 'the learned Origen . . . [could] declare in the most express terms that the number of martyrs was very inconsiderable' (Ibid., p. 28; cf. 205, III, 8).

[3] Tertullian does indeed make Nero a persecutor, but as Hochart has

It is clear that the only biographical fact even alleged in these three pagan references is Christ's execution under Pilate, and this in a document not earlier than the second century. All three texts refer to Christ, not to Jesus.

The silence of pagan writers was a source of embarrassment to Christians, and there were attempts to make it good, both by forging documents under pagan names and by simply alleging that pagan documents concerning Christianity did exist. Of the forgeries the best known is a Latin correspondence between Seneca and Paul, first attested by Jerome and held by him and Augustine to be authentic. It is now universally admitted to be a forgery, written in Rome in the later fourth century. The other method of overcoming the pagan silence is illustrated by Justin and Tertullian. Justin, addressing the emperor in his first Apology, summarizes the story of the crucifixion and then says (Chapter 35): 'That all these things were so you may learn from the Acts which were recorded under Pontius Pilate.' This suggestion was taken up and elaborated by Tertullian, who alleged (writing in Carthage in AD 197) that Pilate wrote a report to Tiberius telling him of all the miracles and prodigies at the crucifixion and resurrection, and that it can still be consulted in the Roman archives (*Apology*, Chapter 21). In Chapter 5 he tells us that Tiberius reacted by bringing the matter before the senate and proposing to set

---

shown, he seems to think that the emperor persecuted only Peter and Paul, not a 'great multitude'. Hochart refers (139, pp. 221, 230–2) to the various apocryphal *Acts of Peter and Paul* (ascribed to Marcellus, Abdias and Hegesippus) where we see Peter and Paul in Rome, competing with their rival Simon Magus. Nero has to decide which of them is truly inspired by God, and to this end he has a tower constructed. Simon Magus astonishes everybody by jumping from it and ascending towards heaven. Peter, however, invokes the aid of Christ, whereupon the magician falls to the ground and is killed. Nero accuses Peter and Paul of homicide, and condemns them to be drowned; then, on the advice of his prefect, he decides to have them crucified. The crowd try to save them and burn Nero, but Peter dissuades them in order that the will of God be accomplished. The death of the apostles causes Nero to be hated; he is forced to flee and dies of hunger in the woods. Tertullian, says Hochart, seems to have stories such as these in mind when he says in Chapter 21 of his *Apology*: 'The apostles, in obedience to their Master's command, went preaching through the world, persecuted by the Jews to the last degree ... at length, the infidels taking advantage of the barbarous Nero's reign, they were forced to sow the Christian religion in their own Christian blood.' And when he tells us in Chapter 5 that Nero was 'the first emperor who dyed his sword in Christian blood, when our religion was but just arising in Rome', he presumably has in mind this persecution of the two apostles, not a general persecution of a 'great multitude' of Christians.

Christ among the gods, which, however, the senate declined to do. This story was repeated and believed by later Christian writers (Eusebius and others). But no apologist before Tertullian mentions it, and 'no modern historian believes it' (28, p. 229 n). We are asked to believe, said Gibbon:

'that Pontius Pilate informed the emperor of the unjust sentence of death which he had pronounced against an innocent, and, as it appeared, a divine person; and that without acquiring the merit, he exposed himself to the danger of martyrdom; that Tiberius, who avowed his contempt for all religion, immediately conceived the design of placing the Jewish Messiah among the gods of Rome; that his servile senate ventured to disobey the commands of their master; that Tiberius, instead of resenting their refusal, contented himself with protecting the Christians from the severity of the laws, many years before such laws were enacted, or before the Church had assumed any distinct name or existence; and lastly, that the memory of this extraordinary transaction was preserved in the most public and authentic records, which escaped the knowledge of the historians of Greece and Rome, and were only visible to the eyes of an African Christian, who composed his apology one hundred and sixty years after the death of Tiberius (104, II, 39, Chapter 16).

We turn next to Jewish references to Jesus. Josephus is the obvious writer from whom we should expect some reference to Jesus. He wrote two major works on the history of Palestine: (1) *The Jewish War*, which covers the period from Antiochus Epiphanes to AD 73. He writes of some of the later of these events as an eye-witness, and Vespasian, Titus and King Agrippa II praised the accuracy of his work. It does not mention Jesus at all.

(2) *The Antiquities of the Jews*, written AD 93 and giving the history of the Jews from the creation of the world up to the outbreak of the war in AD 66. It contains two references to Jesus, the first of which reads:

And there appeared at this time Jesus, a wise man, if indeed he may be called a man. He was a doer of marvellous acts, a teacher of such men as receive the truth with delight. And many Jews and many too of the Hellenic race he brought over to himself. He was the Christ [ὁ χριστός]. And when, on the evidence of the most influential among us, Pilate had condemned him to the cross, his first adherents did not forsake him: for he appeared to them on the third day alive again, divinely-inspired prophets having foretold this and myriad other wondrous things about him. And even now the tribe of Christians, named from him, is not extinct. (154, XVIII, 3, 3.)

It is hard to believe that Josephus, who was a Pharisee, would have given such a glowing description of Jesus. Many Christian writers suggest that, although he did not write this passage, he said something about Jesus at this point in his narrative, and that what he said has been worked over by a Christian editor. This is what Haag implies when he says that the passage is '*for the most part* a Christian insertion'. Obviously, the total silence of Josephus about Jesus would, if true, constitute an embarrassing fact. Smith has, however, shown by his examination of the context that the whole passage is an interpolation, not a reworking of an original.[1] The two paragraphs preceding it may be summarized as follows: (1) Pilate removes the army from Caesarea to Jerusalem for winter quarters and, against all precedent, brings Caesar's effigies by night into the Holy City. The Jews flock to Caesarea protesting for five days, but in vain; the sixth day Pilate forms a plan to massacre them, but, struck with their heroic devotion in laying down their bared necks, he relents and orders back the images from Jerusalem to Caesarea. (2) Pilate undertakes to supply Jerusalem with water, using sacred money. The Jews protest, so he distributes soldiers in citizen's dress among the populace. When the Jews refuse to disperse, the soldiers draw their concealed daggers and a massacre takes place. There follows paragraph (3) about Jesus, already quoted. Then (4) 'And about the same time another terrible misfortune confounded the Jews ...' (5) More misfortunes: 4,000 Jews are banished from Rome for the wickedness of four. The passage about Jesus thus occurs in a context which deals exclusively with the misfortunes of the Jews, with which it clearly has no connection, except, as Drews (82, Tl.II) noted,

[1] Smith's arguments (252) were stated independently by Norden a year later. He too shows that removal of the passage leaves a text which runs on in proper sequence, and even brings words together which Josephus puts by side in a single sentence on other occasions (203, p. 649). For another view see Winter (230a).

from the standpoint of a Christian, who would naturally regard the condemnation of Jesus at the demand of the Jewish leaders as the very worst misfortune the Jews had ever incurred. Moreover, that (4) follows immediately upon (2) is obvious from the opening words of (4)—'*another* terrible misfortune'. The obvious reference is to the massacre mentioned in (2). There is no possible reference to (3).

This internal evidence is substantiated by the decisive fact that (3) was unknown to Origen. He alludes three times to a reference in Josephus to James the brother of Jesus, which we shall examine next. But (3) he never mentions, although it would have served his polemic against unbelievers far better. Nor, of course, is the passage mentioned by earlier writers (Irenaeus, Tertullian, Clement of Alexandria, etc.). It is first quoted by Eusebius in the fourth century (see 244, I, 1, 103 and 252, pp. 231–3). Origen could not have known it because in his polemic against Celsus he professes admiration for Josephus 'although he did not believe in Jesus as Christ' (I quote the passage below), whereas in the interpolated passage Josephus is made to say expressly of Jesus 'he was the Christ'. Proof that Christian writers have interpolated the works of Josephus was provided by the discovery, at the beginning of this century, of fifteenth century manuscripts of a Russian translation of his *The Jewish War* containing information about John the Baptist, Jesus and his disciples (for details see 245, pp. 262–6).

The other passage where Josephus mentions Jesus is said by Haag (116) to be the most important Jewish reference to him. The text states that the high priest

> assembled a sanhedrim of judges and having brought thither the brother of Jesus, him called Christ (James was his name), and some certain others, and having made accusations against them as lawbreakers, he delivered them to be stoned (154, XX, 9, 1).

Brandon notes (38, pp. 96–7) that the authenticity of this passage 'has been the subject of long and unceasing controversy'. The stoning of James is not recorded in Acts. Moreover, Hegesippus, a Jewish Christian who wrote a history of the Church about the year AD 170—fragments of it have been preserved by Eusebius—says that James the brother of Jesus was killed in a tumult, not by sentence of a court. (He was thrown down from

the wing of the temple, stoned, and finally dispatched with a
fuller's club.) Clement of Alexandria confirms this, and is quoted
by Eusebius accordingly (see 18, p. 8).

Schürer thought (244, I, II, 186–7) that Josephus' allusion to
Jesus in his account of James is a Christian interpolation, since
Origen's comments on Josephus' mention of James do not square
with the passage on James that I have quoted from the *Antiquities*.
Instead of quoting or alluding to this passage, Origen quotes
another, allegedly from the same work, which is not in any of the
extant manuscripts, and is obviously a Christian interpolation.[1]
He says (*Contra Celsum*, I, 47) that Josephus

> although he did not believe in Jesus as Christ, sought for the
> cause of the fall of Jerusalem and the destruction of the temple.
> He ought to have said that the plot against Jesus was the reason
> why these catastrophes came upon the people, because they
> had killed the prophesied Christ; however, although un-
> conscious of it, he is not far from the truth when he says that
> these disasters befell the Jews to avenge James the Just, who
> was a brother of Jesus, him called Christ.

Chadwick notes (205, p. 43) that Origen also quotes this as from
Josephus in his commentary on Mt. and that Eusebius (89, vol. I,
p. 177) gives Josephus' alleged words in direct (not reported)
speech. Chadwick concedes that 'the passage may be a Christian
interpolation in the text of Josephus'.

The passage about James that is in the extant manuscripts of
Josephus does not link his murder with the siege of Jerusalem.
On the other hand, Hegesippus concludes his account of James
with a sentence which implies such a link. It is quoted by
Eusebius (89, vol. I, p. 175) as follows:

> And so he suffered martyrdom . . . This man became a true
> witness both to Jews and Greeks that Jesus is the Christ, and
> at once Vespasian began to besiege them.

What seems to have happened is that a writer, who had acquired
the notion (preserved in Hegesippus) that God caused the Romans

[1] Schürer's translator (244, I, II, 186) makes him say that 'this passage is
in some of our manuscripts of Josephus'. But Schürer says clearly 'in none'
of them (See the 4th edn. of his *Geschichte*, Berlin, 1901, I, 581. MSS. of the
Antiquities are few and late. Of Bk. xviii, for instance, three are extant, the
earliest from the eleventh century (291a, p. 292).

to destroy Jerusalem in order to punish the Jews for the murder of James, interpolated a passage to this effect into some manuscripts of Josephus, none of which have survived.[1] The interpolation includes the phrase 'the brother of Jesus, him called Christ'. It is a reasonable inference that this same phrase in the passage which is present in the extant manuscripts, is also there an interpolation.[2]

Brandon discusses the disparity between Origen's comments and this latter Josephan passage (38, pp. 96-7, 111-14), which he regards as a Christian adaptation of a lost original in which Josephus wrote rather differently of James. This admission destroys the value of the mention of Jesus in the passage. We know from the Pauline letters that a James led a sect in Jerusalem, and Josephus may well have had occasion to say something of him. A Christian familiar with the epistles and gospels who adapted such a passage would take Paul's designation of this James as 'the brother of the Lord' to mean the brother of Jesus mentioned e.g. in Mt. xiii, 55 (I have argued above p. 142 that this identification is erroneous), and would in this way introduce Jesus into the passage. In sum I agree with Brandon (38, p. 52) that we may reasonably conclude that Josephus had made some allusion to James. But I do not agree that he identified this person as the brother of Jesus.

If Josephus really thought that Jesus had been 'called the Christ', i.e. was a leader of Messianic pretensions, it is surprising that he did not tell us something about his fortunes. Admittedly he does not dwell on Messianic movements; he wished to reconcile his countrymen to Roman rule, and so did not stress these frequent sources of futile political revolt. Yet he does not suppress mention of them and in fact specifies three Messianic agitators.

[1] Some scholars have argued the alternative that Origen made the mistake of ascribing to Josephus what he had read in Hegesippus. But, as Brandon notes (38, p. 111) such an explanation means convicting Origen of an 'incredible blunder', since 'the very *raison d'être* of his citation was the fact that Josephus acknowledged the righteousness of James . . . whereas, on the other hand, it would have been known that Hegesippus was a Christian writer, who had lived only about one generation before the time of Origen, and whose testimony in this connection would have had no force whatsoever'.

[2] Dunkerley (83a, p. 35) says that there is 'no evidence at all' that this phrase is a Christian addition. But he does not discuss Origen's references to James. Norden (203, p. 649 n.) argues that, as our manuscripts are free from the 'heavy-handed interpolation' that Origen read at this point, they give the genuine reading.

First, Judas of Galilee, who opposed the census ordered by
Quirinius in AD 6 and founded the Zealot party, which recognized
no master but God (154, XVIII, 1, 6; 155, II, 8, 1). Second, Theudas the magician, who (*c.* AD 44–6) led a multitude to the Jordan,
promising to conduct them over dryshod like Joshua before
Jericho; but the cavalry of Fadus captured and beheaded him
(154, XX, 5, 1). The story is of interest as showing the prevalence
of the belief that Joshua would reappear in the character of the
Messiah. Third, the Egyptian Jew who led a crowd as far as the
Mount of Olives (*c.* 52–8), promising that the walls of Jerusalem
would fall down at his word. The procurator Felix sent his troops;
four hundred fanatics were killed, and the Egyptian disappeared
(154, XX, 8, 6; 155, II, 13, 5). If Jesus was a Messianic agitator,
Josephus would surely have devoted as much attention to him as
to these three.

Josephus, then, is silent concerning the details of Jesus' life,
although he was reviewing the time and place of the occurrences
which are posited in the gospels (e.g. the reign of Herod, see p. 12
above, and the deeds of Pilate) and had the facts been what they
allege he would not have ignored them.

There are no other Jewish references to Jesus in the first
century. The Jewish philosopher Philo of Alexandria never
mentions him; he travelled in Palestine and speaks of the Essenes
he saw there, but he says nothing of Jesus or his followers. We
know too that the historian Justus of Tiberias, writing about
AD 80, was equally silent about Jesus and primitive Christianity,
for though his books have been lost, Photius, Christian patriarch
of Constantinople, who read them in the ninth century, remarks,
with surprise: 'This Jewish historian does not make the smallest
mention of the appearance of Christ, and says nothing whatever
of his deeds and miracles' (quoted in 18, pp. 10–11).

Baring-Gould explains what he calls 'the strange silence of
Philo, Josephus and Justus' as due not to 'ignorance of the acts
of Christ and of the existence of the Church', but to 'deliberate
purpose' (18, p. 42). He argues that the Christians of the first
century consisted of two factions—a Petrine, holding to the Jewish
law, and a Pauline, repudiating it—and that the two differed more
from each other than the Petrine party did from the orthodox
Jews. In fact, he says, the followers of Peter were in many
respects indistinguishable from the Jewish Essenes. Thus the
question why Josephus never mentions Christians must be

resolved into two parts: first, why does he not mention the Pauline Christians? The answer, says Baring-Gould, is that these people were almost exclusively gentiles. It was a religion accepted only by Greeks and Romans, and had no observable connection with Judaism. To Jewish historians 'it was but another of those many religions which rose as mushrooms, to fade away again on the soil of the Roman world', and therefore of no interest to them. Second, why does Josephus not mention the Petrine faction? Baring-Gould's reply is: Josephus belonged to the Pharisees, who believed in the resurrection of the dead, and who were at odds with the Sadducees, who did not. Now we learn from Acts that the Petrine faction enraged the Sadducees, by preaching that the resurrection of Jesus proved that there would be a general resurrection of the dead. The Pharisees, in their opposition to the Sadducees, would begin to feel some sympathy with the Christians and regret the part they had played in persecuting and executing Jesus. So they would not be anxious to allude to these events in their writings. Josephus describes the Essenes, and among them he reckoned the Petrine Christians who resembled them closely. To give any more details would entail mentioning Jesus and his conflict with the Pharisees, and 'it was not a time to rip up old wounds' (18, p. 41). Justus was also a Pharisee and so had the same motive for silence.

Baring-Gould draws attention to Acts xxiii, where the Pharisees are represented as defending Paul at his trial, against the Sadducees. This incident, however, does not prove any alliance between Pharisees and Christians; for Paul, before the court of justice, describes himself as a Pharisee, says nothing about his Christianity, alleges that he is accused only because he believes in the resurrection of the dead, and calls upon the Pharisees, as his 'brethren', to support him. They clearly defend him as one of themselves, not as a Christian. So there is no positive testimony for Baring-Gould's thesis that Pharisees and Christians supported each other. There is, however, evidence from Acts that the Jewish Christians of Jerusalem attracted many priests and Pharisees to themselves (Acts vi, 7; xv, 5). Baring-Gould's thesis becomes more plausible if we delete the underlying assumption of a historical Jesus who had in the recent past abused the Pharisees. It is not really likely that they would suppress all mention of Jesus in order not to alienate a party whose founder had repeatedly stigmatized them as 'hypocrites' and 'vipers', who 'made void the word of

God'. If, however, Jesus as portrayed in the gospels never existed, and the first Christians were an offshoot from the Essenes, then it is much more intelligible that they should have attracted some of the Pharisees, and also that Josephus, although he mentions Essenes, does not record anything about Christians.

The likelihood that Baring-Gould's hypothesis represents the truth would be increased if it could be shown that Jewish writers who were not Pharisees, and who thus lacked their alleged motive for silence, had something to say about Jesus. But the extensive rabbinical literature of the time does not mention him, even though, as Baring-Gould goes on to note, 'many of the Rabbis whose sayings are recorded in the Mishnah lived in the time of our Lord, or shortly after' (p. 51). He explains this silence by asserting that 'our Lord's teaching made no great impression on the Jews of his time'. But this is not to be reconciled with the gospel records. In Mt., for instance, there are repeated references to 'multitudes' who followed him (vii, 28: viii, 1, 28, 34: ix, 8, 33, etc.). From Mt. iv, 24–5 we learn that 'the report of him went forth into all Syria', and that he was followed by 'great multitudes from Galilee and Decapolis and Jerusalem and Judaea and from beyond Jordan' (cf. xix, 2: xx, 29).

The earliest references to Jesus in rabbinical literature occur not earlier than about the beginning of the second century. Before examining these it will be necessary to give a brief survey of this literature.

The Mishnah, or codification of the law, was completed about AD 220. It contains precepts to which the religious life of the Jew must conform, and also illustrative and explanatory notes, historical and personal reminiscences, designed to show the purpose of the precepts. Later,

the Mishnah in its turn became the subject of commentary, interpretation and expansion. The name given to this super-added commentary is Gemara, which means completion. But whereas there is only one Mishnah, there are two Gemaras. The Mishnah was studied not only in the schools of Palestine, but also in those of Babylonia. And by the labours of these two groups of teachers there was developed a Palestinian Gemara and a Babylonian Gemara . . . The Gemara of Palestine was ended . . . towards the close of the fourth century; while it was not until the sixth century that the Gemara of

Babylonia was reduced to the form in which we now have it. The name Talmud is given to the whole corpus of Mishnah plus Gemara; and thus it is usual to distinguish between the Palestinian Talmud (otherwise known as the Talmud of Jerusalem) and the Babylonian Talmud (270, p. 19).

Thus 'the Talmud consists of two parts, Mishnah and Gemara, related to each other as text and commentary'. And although both Gemaras are later, they nevertheless 'contain a great deal of material handed down from the period covered by the Mishnah. These two main periods, represented by the Mishnah and the Gemara, are known as the period of the Tannaim [teachers] and of the Amoraim respectively' (p. 350).

Another collection of precepts, independent of the Mishnah, is known as Tosephta, meaning 'addition' or 'supplement', and this, like the Mishnah, belongs to the early or Tannaite period. The same is true of the Baraithas, which are precepts and discussions in the Gemaras earlier than the bulk of the material, and are distinguished as such in the Talmud. Thus the earliest rabbinical literature in which we might expect to find mention of Jesus is the Mishnah, the Tosephta and the Baraithas. As already said, he is not mentioned at all in the Mishnah. A number of scholars, however, think there is a reference to him in the passage which tells that Rabbi Shim'on ben 'Azai said he had found a roll of pedigrees in Jerusalem, and that it told him that 'a certain person' was of illegitimate birth (quoted by Herford, 270, p. 43, from Jeb. IV, 13). Herford thinks it probable that the reference is to Jesus. The Christians said that he was virgin born, and the Jews would naturally retort that he was born out of wedlock. Rabbi Shim'on ben 'Azai was active about the beginning of the second century, and one would certainly expect to find Jews coming to terms with Christianity by this time.

In one of the Baraithas we read that Rabbi Eliezer was asked the opinions of 'a certain person as regards the world to come' (Quot. 270, p. 45). Eliezer was a well-known teacher at the end of the first century. Again, a reference to Jesus at this time is what one would expect. But why should he be mentioned in this oblique way? Laible thinks this may simply be due to the loathing the Jews felt for him. He compares these examples with the practice of Friedrich Jahn, who detested Napoleon so much that he never called him by name (165, p. 31). Alternatively, the round-about way of referring to Jesus may be due to extensive censorship of the original texts. Strack notes that 'the assertion that the Talmud is full of spiteful remarks about Jesus and his mother, about the Christians and their religion gave rise, from the thirteenth century, to a persecution of the Talmud, to destruction of many manuscripts (and later of early printed editions), and to censorship of the text by Christians and by the Jews themselves' from fear of the Christian authorities (260, p. 3; 259, pp. 74-5). Strack thinks that the censorship may have taken the form of both altering and deleting passages (259, p. 68), some of which have been restored in later editions, although the original state of the documents can no longer be ascertained with certainty. It is, of course, possible that the passages permanently lost may include some from the earliest parts of the Mishnah. But the absolute silence of these parts concerning Jesus is nevertheless striking: for it is reasonable to assume that censorship would have affected all parts equally, so that, had he been mentioned in the early parts to anything like the extent one would expect from the orthodox view of his career, some of these references would have survived.

The references in the Tosephta are also few, and also belong to the end of the first century. We are there told, for instance, that according to Rabbi Eliezer, 'ben Stada' was a magician who cut charms into his flesh (Shabb. XI, 15; quoted by Herford, p. 54). The Gemara tells that ben Stada is the same as ben Pandira, and the latter is sometimes referred to by his full name 'Jeshu ben Pandira' (270, pp. 36-7). It is therefore usually assumed that ben Stada and ben Pandira both mean Jesus. Herford cannot explain why he was given these names, but suggests that they may be 'relics of ancient Jewish mockery against him, the clue to whose meaning is now lost' (270, p. 40). Rabbi Eliezer, we saw, flourished at the end of the first century.

Elsewhere in the Tosephta (Hull II, 22, 23) we are told that Rabbi Eliezer ben Damah was bitten by a serpent; and a man came to cure him 'in the name of Jeshua ben Pandira'. Rabbi Ishmael, however, did not allow the cure to be performed. Ishmael lived in the first half of the second century, so this tradition may well be as old as the previous one. Hull II, 24, tells how Rabbi Eliezer was brought before a (Roman) tribunal and charged with being a Christian. Although acquitted, he was greatly distressed by the imputation, whereupon one of his disciples, Aqiba, suggested that he might perhaps have fallen under suspicion because he had been in contact with the Christian heresy. Eliezer, thus reminded, recalled an interview he had once had with a certain 'Jacob' who spoke to him 'in the name of Jeshu ben Pantiri' (Quot. 270, pp. 138, 143).

The final reference in the Tosephta concerns the legal procedure to be used in the case of a deceiver who has tempted others to apostasy; it is set forth in Sanh. X, 11, where we are told that the deceiver is encouraged to talk in the presence of two concealed witnesses, and that 'thus they did to Ben Stada in Lud: two disciples of the wise were chosen for him and they [brought him to the Beth Din] and stoned him' (Quot. 270, p. 79). It is remarkable that the compiler of the Tosephta makes Jesus die in Lud (viz. Lydda), not in Jerusalem, and by stoning. This does not suggest a reminiscence of the events alleged in the gospels. Incidentally, Jesus is nowhere in the Talmud said to have been executed by the Romans; his death is represented as solely the work of the Jews: and nowhere is his alleged Messiahship mentioned, not even as a reason for putting him to death.

The Baraithas supplement this information by telling that ben Stada learned his magic art in Egypt, and that he was tried and hung at Lud on the eve of the Passover. None of these references in the Tosephta or Baraithas are earlier than the end of the first century. By then Christian communities undoubtedly existed, and the Rabbis would naturally have to come to terms with them and their alleged founder. What is so striking is the absence of earlier references to Jesus. Stauffer says that the Talmud gives early polemic against Jesus which corroborates the gospels, and claims that 'some of the ancient rabbinical testimonies about Jesus go back into his lifetime and to the early apostolic age'. But when on a later page he lists the Jewish material, the only evidence he can give of polemic against Jesus prior to AD 100 is from the gospels! (257, pp. 15, 147).

In the Gemara, which, as we have seen, consists of later material, Pappos ben Jehudah is said to have been the husband of the mother of Jesus (Shabbath 104b). This man, says Herford, 'lived a century after Jesus . . . and was contemporary with, and a friend of Rabbi Aqiba' (270, p. 40). On the other hand, elsewhere in the Gemara, Jesus is said to have been persecuted by King Alexander Jannaeus who reigned from 103 to 76 BC (Sanh. 107b). On this confusion Herford comments that we must 'bear in mind that the Rabbis had extremely vague ideas of the chronology of past times' (270, pp. 52–3).

The Gemara sums up Jesus' activities by saying (Sanh. 43a) that he 'practised magic and deceived and led astray Israel'. This man who learned magic in Egypt and scratched charms on his flesh has little resemblance to the gospel Jesus. The two are so unlike that it has been argued that the Talmudic Jesus is not the Christian one at all, but a pre-Christian Jewish apostate. This view founds on the passage where Jesus is said to have been persecuted under King Alexander Jannaeus. It tells of 'Rabbi Joshua b. Perahiah who thrust one of his disciples away with both his hands'. MSS. and old editions read 'Jesus the Nazarene' instead of 'one of his disciples'. The passage goes on to explain the incident. 'When king Jannaeus put the Rabbis to death, Rabbi Joshua b. Perahiah fled to Alexandria but later . . . came back and found himself in a certain inn . . . He said "How beautiful is this *aksania*".' The word means both 'inn' and 'female innkeeper'. The Rabbi intended it in the first sense; but Jesus his disciple understood it in the second, and replied, 'Master, her eyes are narrow'; whereupon the Rabbi excommunicated him for his wicked thoughts. Jesus then turned apostate and persuaded others to do the same (Sotah, 47a and Sanh. 107b). The persecution of the Pharisees under Jannaeus is well attested. Löw thought that the Jesus of the Talmud fled into Egypt during this persecution, learned magic there, and later founded the Essene sect, which he says, is named after him (178, p. 352). We shall see that the evidence of the Dead Sea Scrolls will throw an interesting light on this hypothesis.

The reader will note that the Talmud passages I have quoted are usually in the form of 'Rabbi A. says in the name of Rabbi B', or 'Rabbi A says that Rabbi B says that Rabbi C says', etc. Herford explains that among the Jews no teacher could base his teaching merely on his own authority. The author of Mt. vii, 28-9 is clearly recording his disapproval of this rabbinical method when he states that Jesus 'taught the people as one having authority and not as their scribes'.

The Talmud contains many more references to 'Minim' than to Jesus. It is generally agreed that heretics are meant, and there is fairly wide agreement that the Minim are in fact Jewish Christians. Herford gives evidence to support this view, and finds confirmation of it in Jerome's statement that the Minim are a sect of Jews who profess to be both Jews and Christians, and are in fact neither (270, p. 378). The description could only apply to the 'Petrine' christians who still held by the Jewish law. In the

Talmud the first mention of these Minim occurs in connection with a formula condemning them which can be dated at approximately AD 80 from its mention of Rabbi Gamaliel II. It thus belongs to the time after the destruction of the temple in AD 70. Herford notes that only after this catastrophe was any real break between the Petrine type of Christians and the Jews necessary: 'As long as the temple yet stood, the Jewish Christians in Jerusalem appear to have taken part in the ritual observances equally with the non-Christian Jews . . . But when the temple was destroyed, and the ceremonial law thereby became a dead letter, there was ground for a divergence of opinion as to the real meaning of that event . . . The Jews maintained the validity *de jure* of the whole ceremonial law, though *de facto* its operation was suspended. But it was equally possible to maintain that *de jure* also the ceremonial law was abrogated, and that henceforth its meaning was to be regarded as symbolic instead of literal' (p. 383). He thinks that many Jewish Christians may well have taken this view, and we know for certain that disputes among the early Christians about the validity of the law were prolonged and bitter. Jewish Christians who broke away from Judaism to the extent of reducing the law to a symbol would naturally evoke Jewish opposition; hence the condemnatory formula of the Talmud.

The relations between Jews and Minim were probably most hostile at about this time (the end of the first century), for it was not, then, evident to the Jews that 'the development of the Christian Church would proceed on gentile lines and would leave the Minim behind'. The Jews did not fear gentile Christianity, which was completely alien to them. Their rabbinical literature 'takes scarcely any notice of it at all'. Herford supports these suggestions by showing that 'the strongest denunciations of the books of the Minim are those of Rabbi Ishmael and Rabbi Tarphon, in the early part of the second century' (270, pp. 391–4).

In sum, if the early Christians were not followers of the gospel Jesus but Jews who believed that the Messiah, named Jesus, had come and would return, and who were otherwise orthodox, keeping the law and attending the temple, then the silence of the rabbinical literature about Jesus and about Christians up to the end of the first century, when the decisive break occurred, is quite intelligible; whereas if there was a historical Jesus who had the career ascribed to him in the gospels, it is not.

The sparse pagan and Jewish notices of Jesus are repeatedly

quoted (e.g. by Conzelmann, 64, vol. III, column 622) as evidence
that no ancient writer doubted his historicity. The argument is
that, if Jesus were a legendary figure, critics would have said so
when the legend of his life in Galilee and Judaea arose. But it is
surely unrealistic to expect such critical scrutiny of the past from
Rabbis who are so vague in their chronology that they differ by
as much as two hundred years in the dates they assign to Jesus
(see above, p. 200). The only witness apart from the Talmud is
Tacitus, and he, I have argued, had no motive for inquiring into
the accuracy of the story that Jesus suffered under Pilate. Johannes
Weiss, who treated with derision the theory that Jesus never
existed, nevertheless conceded that Tacitus' account can impress
only those who believe, on independent evidence, that there was
a historical Jesus (see above p. 188 n.). The only writers sufficiently familiar with and interested in the Christian antecedents
to challenge allegations about Jesus' biography would have been
Christians; and if Jesus is a legendary personage, one might expect some protest over biographical particulars from Christians
who preferred to continue to think of him in purely supernatural
terms. As I have shown, this expectation is fulfilled, even in the
NT, where the authors of I and II John complain of 'many
deceivers' who deny that Jesus has 'come in the flesh' (see above,
p. 156).

CHAPTER EIGHT

Criteria of Historicity

We assume the historicity of Caesar and Mohammed because we possess so much and so varied testimony that the existence of these individuals is the simplest hypothesis that will explain it all and account for its high degree of consistency. I have tried to show that, with Jesus, this is not so clearly the case. Yet Frazer holds that the testimony of the gospels, confirmed by the hostile evidence of Tacitus and the younger Pliny, establishes that Jesus was a great religious and moral teacher who was crucified at Jerusalem under Pilate, and that the doubts which have been cast on his historical reality are 'unworthy of serious attention' (94, p. 412). I have examined the gospels, Tacitus and Pliny already, and am here concerned only with Frazer's further assertion that the historicity of Jesus is on a par with that of Mohammed, Luther and Calvin. I propose to consider first the case of Mohammed and then that of the Athenian statesman Solon in order to discover the type of evidence that has led historians to agree that they were historical personages. I shall then discuss a clear case of myth (Peter as bishop of Rome), and in a final section try to specify criteria of historicity.

(i) Mohammed

It is believed that Mohammed was born at Mecca about AD 570 and was in the habit of spending periods in meditation on Mount Hira nearby, where he received his first divine communication in his fortieth year. At first the Meccans seem to have laughed at him, but finally they rose in fierce opposition, driving him and his few adherents to Yathrib, now called Medina. From the year of his migration or Hegira the Moslem era is dated, so that AD 622 is AH 1. He soon came into serious conflict with the many Jews in Medina, and when the breach became past healing he ordered his supporters to turn in the direction of Mecca while praying, and no longer towards Jerusalem as formerly. From this time he assumes a more authoritative tone and demands obedience not only to Allah but also to himself.

The next years are marked by battles between the Koreish tribe at Mecca and Mohammed's supporters at Medina. The details are: the battle at Bedder, twenty miles from Mecca; that on Mount Ohud, six miles from Medina; the unsuccessful siege of Medina under Abu Sophian; then the capture of the town of Kheibar, the seat of the Jewish power in Arabia. While fighting the Meccans Mohammed was careful to protect himself from attacks from other quarters. As lord of Medina he concluded alliances with a number of Bedouin tribes in which the parties pledged mutual assistance. In AH 6 (AD 627) he signed a ten-year truce with the Meccans. But two years later his native city surrendered, and he was publicly recognized as chief and prophet.

With what justification do we believe all this? First, the swift rise of Mohammed's religion to power—overrunning the whole of Arabia in his lifetime and defeating Christian armies in Palestine within two years of his death—is a relevant factor, for it meant that the evidence for his existence would be critically examined at an early stage, far earlier than could have occurred in the case of Christianity, which long remained an insignificant sect and took 300 years to attain state recognition. Second, although there are many legendary and traditional sources for Mohammed's biography, there are also contemporary records. Foremost among these is the Koran, the first compilation of which was made within two or three years of his death at the direction of the caliph Abu Bekr. According to the *Britannica*, 'when Mohammed died separate pieces of the Koran appear to have been already written down . . . But many portions had been committed to memory. The first complete written version is attributed to Zayd ibn Thabit, who had been Mohammed's secretary, and was instructed in the reign of Abu Bekr to collect the scattered portions into one volume.' This was done during the years AH 11–14. Deviations from this original text soon crept into the copies made from it. In the reign of Uthman, the caliph was warned to interpose and 'stop the people before they should differ regarding their

Scripture as did the Jews and Christians' (Quoted by Muir, 195, p. XXII). The caliph heeded the warning and Zayd was again appointed in AH 30—this time with three others—to prepare an authoritative version. Copies of this were sent to the chief cities of the empire, and earlier codices burned. This recension has been handed down to us unaltered. 'There is probably in the world no other work which has remained twelve centuries with so pure a text. The various readings are wonderfully few in number' (195, p. XXIII). The significance of this fact is enormous. Contending and embittered factions, originating in the murder of the caliph Uthman within a quarter of a century after Mohammed's death, have ever since rent the Moslem world. 'Yet but one Koran has been current among them, and the consentaneous use of it by all proves that we have now before us the self-same text prepared by the commands of that unfortunate caliph who was a Moslem martyr' (editor's note to 104, V, 240, Chapter 50). The contrast with the early Christians, where the written records are so late that rival sects could possess entirely different gospels, could hardly be more striking. Furthermore, the Koran has every appearance of being what it purports to be, namely a collection of isolated sayings of the master. Hence the 'interminable repetition the wearisome reiteration of the same ideas, truths and doctrines' (195, p. XXVI). The success of modern scholars in arranging these sayings chronologically depends partly on the fact that some of them can be related to his precarious situation in Mecca; thus the numerous passages urging toleration were revealed at Mecca, while the eighth and ninth chapters, which are the loudest and most vehement, point to Medina. As Gibbon notes: 'The prophet of Medina assumed, in his revelations, a fiercer and more sanguinary tone, which proved that his former moderation was the effect of weakness.' There is, then, evidence of his teaching before his period of success and notoriety. And finally, in the whole of the Koran, the master himself works no miracles, and makes no claim to divinity; only in the traditions of the following centuries do his features become magnified into supernatural proportions. In all these respects the book differs markedly from the gospels.

Further contemporary testimony to the existence of Mohammed is provided by a collection of treaties. An example is the one signed in AD 628 during the wars between Medina and Mecca, and providing for a cessation of hostilities for ten years. The text has been preserved by Wakidi, the biographer of Mohammed, who died in 803. Wakidi's biography contains 'a section expressly devoted to the transcription of such treaties, and it contains two or three scores of them. Over and over again, the author (at the end of the second or the beginning of the third century) states that he had copied these from the *original* documents' (195, p. lxxii). Muir records Sprenger's assertion that some of these treaties were still in force in the time of Haroun al-Rashid (AH 170–93; AD 791–814) and were then collected. 'This,' he says, 'is quite conceivable, for they were often recorded upon leather and would invariably be preserved with care as charters of privilege by those in whose favour they were concluded.' He adds the following evidence that Wakidi's transcriptions are genuine:

Some of the most interesting of the treaties [e.g. those which specify] the terms allowed to the Jews of Kheibar and to the Christians of Nejran, formed the basis of political events in the Caliphates of Abu Bekr and 'Omar; the concessions made in others to Christian and Jewish tribes are satisfactory proof that they were not fabricated by Muslims; while it is equally clear that they would never have been acknowledged if counterfeited by a Jewish or a Christian hand.

Many of the treaties in which Mohammed allied himself with bedouin tribes while he was fighting the Meccans from Medina are given by Sperber, who has transcribed a number of the earliest of these from Mohammed's biographer Ibn Sa'd. He remarks that they are neither dated nor preserved by other historians; nevertheless, he is able both to date them and prove them genuine on internal evidence. This is in part linguistic: the archaic language stamps them as very old (256, p. 8). He also shows that some of the treaties are purely political, and thereby distinguished from later ones, in which Mohammed demands that the other party accept his religion. This points to an early stage of his career at Medina, when he was still not powerful enough to demand religious allegiance. His motive in signing these treaties was to isolate his enemies, the Koreish at Mecca, and so he is glad to ally himself with bedouin tribes, even though they remain heathens. Only after the unsuccessful siege of Medina by the Meccans does he feel strong enough to demand religious conversion as a token of political allegiance, and Sperber gives a number of treaties where this demand is made.

Mohammed is also mentioned by contemporary poets whose works are extant.[1] Muir remarks that 'there can be no doubt as to the great antiquity of these remains, though we may not always be able to fix with exactness the period of their composition'. Their approximate age is fixed by their 'ancient style and language'. And 'their poetical form is a material safeguard against change and interpolation' (195, p. lxxiii). These early references do not paint Mohammed as a divine figure, but as a human individual with a biography. Several old poems, for instance, say that he belonged to the family of Hashim, one of the better-class families of Mecca. And 'that he was recognized by them as one of themselves is evident from the fact that only the protection of a fairly powerful family could have made it possible for him to stay in Mecca as long as he did in face of the hostility of his fellow-citizens' (86). The poet Hassan ben Thabit tells how, when the prophet's position in Mecca was becoming more and more difficult, Mutil b. Adi took him under his protection; and how later, during the skirmishes between Medina and Mecca, Mohammed's supporters continually harassed the Meccan caravans (ibid.). Hassan's odes on 'The Battle of the Ditch' and on 'The taking of Mecca' give more biographical details.

In the treaties in which Mohammed, as Lord of Medina, allies himself with bedouin tribes, he appears as a political strategist, not as a divine or semi-divine figure. Once again we must note the great contrast with Jesus. While Mohammed is mentioned by his contemporaries, Jesus is not, and the oldest Christian references to him are to a mystic sacrifice, not to a human individual who lived at a definite time and place.

The biographies of the prophet are admittedly later, but refer to early poetic and other material. I have taken my information from Rodwell (228, p. XV) and Bury (47), and the following table is an attempt to make the rather complicated statements of Bury clear. Biographers whose works are extant are underlined, those whose works survive as quotations in later writers have a dotted line beneath them. Arrows indicate sources, and dates the death of the writer (AH).

The table shows the importance of Al Tabari's work from which we can check the lost sources of the extant works of Ibn Hisham and Ibn Sa'd. Bury remarks that Tabari 'had no historical faculty,

---

[1] For details see C. Brockelmann, *Geschichte der arabischen Literatur*, Weimar, 1898, I, 36–9.

no idea of criticizing or sifting his sources; he merely puts side
by side the statements of earlier writers without reconciling their
discrepancies or attempting to educe the truth'. His method thus
reveals the nature of the now lost materials which he used. It was
largely to his work that the loss of that material in its original
form is due. 'His work was so convenient and popular that the
public ceased to want the older books, and consequently they
ceased to be multiplied.'

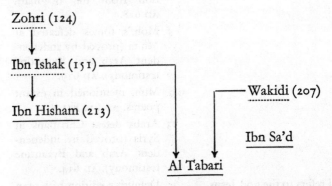

Zohri (124)

Ibn Ishak (151)

Ibn Hisham (213)

Wakidi (207)

Ibn Sa'd

Al Tabari

Tabari and other Arabic writers can be compared with the Greek
authorities for the Moslem conquests, namely the patriarch Nicephorus and the monk Theophanes who both lived at the end of the
eighth century. Theophanes' *Chronicle* covers the period AD
284–813 and Nicephorus' *History* the period 602–769. They both
used a common source of which we have no record. In sum,
then, early Arabic evidence has been preserved by Tabari, and
although the two Greek writers were not contemporaries of the
Moslem expansion, their evidence agrees in the main with his.
For instance, Mohammed's forces suffered a serious defeat in the
first considerable attempt to extend his authority over the Arabs
on Byzantine soil, at Mu'ta in Transjordan in AH 8. Al Tabari,
Ibn Hisham and Wakidi tell us what happened, and their narra-
tion is confirmed by the independent testimony of Theophanes
(268, p. 335). And both Tabari and Nicephorus date the Arab
conquest of Syria as beginning in AD 634.

The following table sums up what has been established in the
above pages; the figures indicate the number of years that have
elapsed since the alleged beginning of Jesus' public ministry, taken
as *c.* AD 30; and since the beginning of Mohammed's move to
Medina, AD 622 or AH 1.

Jesus	Mohammed
	5 Moh. allies himself with bedouin tribes against Meccans (letters extant). AD 626.
	7 Treaty with Meccans (survives in Wakidi's transcription from the original). AD 628.
	8 Moh.'s forces defeated at Mu'ta (proved by independent Arab and Byzantine testimony). AD 629.
	9 ff. Moh. mentioned in extant poems. AD 630 ff.
	13 Arabs defeat Christians in Syria (proved by independent Arab and Byzantine testimony). AD 634.
30 Paul refers to the god Jesus, but gives no indication of where or when he lived on earth. AD 60?	30 Definitive edition of Koran available (proof of this date is that all later Moslem factions have the same edition). AD 651.
63 Bare mention of Jesus as the brother of James in Josephus' *Antiquities*, with no biographical details. AD 93. Probably a later, Christian insertion.	
66 Clement refers to Jesus as a teacher who was either recently on earth, or who recently promulgated his teachings by means of supernatural revelations. AD 96. At about this same time, I Peter and Hebrews both allege that Jesus was recently on earth.	
c. 70 First rabbinical allusions to Jesus. (*c.* AD 100)	

Jesus	Mohammed
80 Ignatius alleges that Jesus was crucified under Pilate. AD 110.	c. 80 Christian formula for abjuration of Moslem religion extant. AD 701.
82 Pliny mentions Christians. AD 112.	
87 I Tim. alleges that Jesus was crucified under Pilate. AD 117.	
90 Tacitus mentions execution under Pilate. AD 120.	93 Death of Zohri, Moh.'s biographer, whose work survives in quotations of later writers. AD 714.
	120 Death of Ibn Ishak, biographer of Moh., whose work can be reconstructed from the independent quotations given by Hisham and Tabari. AD 741.

(ii) Solon

The earliest Greek statesman of whom we have anything like reliable information is said by Meyer (183, p. 600) to be Solon, one of the archons of Athens at the beginning of the sixth century BC, at a time, that is, when Greek art and literature had hardly begun. Consequently, we cannot expect to find contemporary mention of him. The first appearance of his name in extant Greek literature is found in a fragment of two lines from a comedy of Cratinus (quoted by Diogenes Laertius, I, 62) and in Herodotus' history. Both were written about the middle of the fifth century, that is, more than a hundred years after Solon's prime. Aristophanes and Plato, a little later, mention him a number of times, but Thucydides, writing about the same time as Herodotus, does not, and since I have relied a good deal on arguments from silence, it will be necessary to show that his silence is compatible with Solon's historicity. Thucydides is concerned almost exclusively with the Peloponnesian war, of which he was a contemporary. The only sections of his work which do not deal with it are the

opening paragraphs of Bk. I, where he outlines the development
of Greece prior to the war, in the most broad and general terms;
and also sections 89 to 118 of Bk. I, where he traces the growth
of the Athenian Empire from the year when the Persians left
Greece (478) to the beginning of the war in 432. Thus he is not
concerned with sixth-century Athens at all, and his failure to
mention Solon is therefore not decisive.

Herodotus mentions Solon only by the way, and this is because
he, too, is concerned not with sixth-century Athens, but with the
struggle between Greeks and Persians. What he says about him is
admitted by modern scholars (207) to be unreliable. If no further
evidence, in addition to these fifth-century references, were
forthcoming, we could not be sure that Solon was a historical
personage. Decisive evidence is, however, available from his own
poems, many of which are extant. They outline his political
aspirations and his replies to his critics. That such material was
expressed in verse need not surprise us, for at that time 'the art
of reading and writing was practised for only very limited purposes: a political pamphlet, in order to be effective, had to be
conceived in poetic form; in this way it could be easily memor-
ized and transmitted' (98, p. 72 n.).

Critias the oligarch, who is a speaker in Plato's Timaeus, tells
that when he was a lad it was common for boys who took part in
competitive recitations to recite Solon's poems. This evidence
shows that there was a well-recognized collection of them in the
first half of the fifth century. And according to Linforth, there is
'abundant evidence for the existence of the collection in Herodotus, Plato, Demosthenes and Aristotle'. Some of the quotations
in the later writers could have been drawn from the works of their
predecessors, but some 'are of a kind which can hardly have been
made except from the collection itself' (174, p. 11). Linforth goes
on to remark that 'the greater part of the extant verse can be recognized as the authentic work of Solon with the utmost confidence,
because it is concerned with the public events in which he
played a principal part' (p. 12). From the poems we can follow
'a marked change in his political opinions: before he put his
reforms into effect, he was disposed to lay the blame for the
fortunes of Athens on the greed of the rich; later he was equally
convinced of the folly and incapacity of the lower classes' (p. 9).
Thus, one thing which stamps the poems as genuine is that they
are not written in the interests of any party. Aristotle says that

Solon 'set himself against both parties' of his day, and is able to quote from the poems to prove this.

Aristotle's work, the *Constitution of Athens*, written shortly before his death in 322, illustrates the importance of these poems as historical material. Modern editors have remarked that his account of the Solonian reforms is much more satisfactory than his portrait not only of the preceding but also of the succeeding period. The reason is that these two periods furnished him with no first-rate materials, whereas Solon's poems were available for the time between them. Nevertheless, these poems gave him information only about the 'economic, social, political and, to some extent, psychological factors which led to the Solonian reform', and about 'Solon's desperate struggle with the extreme parties on both sides'. They did not tell him anything about the new constitutional order (as distinct from the new laws) introduced. Consequently, his treatment of this topic is noticeably sketchy. In fact, what exactly Solon's constitutional reforms were can only be conjectured, while his laws have come down to us in detail. They were inscribed on wooden pillars set up in the portico of the archon King where, until the end of the fifth century at least, everybody could inspect them at any time. Fragments of a copy from the fifth century are extant (Meyer, 183, p. 600 n.), and they are, of course, frequently quoted by the Athenian orators long before Aristotle's time. For instance, Lysias, who flourished about 420, quotes obsolete words from them. The obsolete, sixth-century phraseology of Solon's laws is apparent in a number of quotations. And the Athenian orators sometimes refer by number to the wooden pillars on which they were carved.

Solon's work can be dated fairly accurately from the fact that he was an archon and therefore figured in the official lists. Fritz and Kapp tell us 'there can be hardly any doubt that from the first decade of the sixth century regular records had been kept of the names of the chief archons of every year, and by the end of the fifth century the list of the archons from Solon downward had apparently become a well-known and generally accepted means of dating the events of Athenian and, to a large extent, even of non-Athenian history' (98, pp. 20–1). Later, the lists of the victors in the Olympic games came to be used for this purpose, and 'a short time after the death of Aristotle . . . the "Olympiades", which could be simply numbered and did not, like the archon lists, require the constant counting of innumerable names in order to determine the chronological distance of one historical event from another, began to be used as a general chronological framework for Greek history dating from 776BC, the supposed date of the first Olympic contest'. Thus Sosicrates of Rhodes, who flourished some time between 200 and 128 BC, states that Solon 'flourished about the 46th Olympiad, in the third year of which he was archon at Athens' (quoted by Diogenes Laertius, I, 62). This gives the date of 594 BC for Solon's archonship, which is confirmed by statements in Aristotle's *Constitution of Athens* (Chapter 14), where we are told that Pisistratus became tyrant in the archonship of Comeas, thirty-two years after the legislation of Solon. We know from the Parian chronicle—the marble tablet which outlines Greek history down to the archonship of Diognetus at Athens (264/3 BC)—that Comeas was archon 297 years before Diognetus, viz. in 561/560 (174, p. 165). This fixes Solon's archonship at 593/592, and the difference of two years between this and Sosicrates' date of 594 can be accounted for by the fact that after Solon, there were two years of anarchy, when there were no archons. If these two years are not counted, the date of 594 is obtained for Solon's archonship (48, p. 258 n.).

Although Solon's poems and laws establish the main fact in his life, a good deal of legend has grown round him. As early as the fifth century Herodotus tells of his meeting with Croesus—a story which cannot be harmonized with the known chronology, and also follows an obvious tendency—that of stressing his wisdom. As the law-giver of Athens, he had to figure as a man of infinite wisdom. The authorities of the fourth century were only continuing this same tendency when they included him among the seven wise men. With Isocrates (*c.* 380) he appears as the founder of Athenian democracy. And Plutarch makes him a statesman who was educated according to the precepts of philosophy, and who lived his life in pursuance of them.

(iii) Peter as bishop of Rome

While Catholics believe that Peter was bishop of Rome, many Protestant scholars deny that he was ever there at all. Let us review the evidence.

(1) Galatians makes his activities centre in Jerusalem (i, 18; ii, 1–10). A visit to Antioch is mentioned where he angers Paul by

refusing to mix with gentile Christians and even persuading Paul's companion Barnabas not to do so (ii, 11–21).

(2) Romans addresses Christians at Rome who are gentiles (ἔθνη i, 7) with reference to whom Paul has received his apostleship. They are obviously Christians of the Pauline type, for they are justified by faith (v, 1) and are no longer under the Jewish law but under grace (vi, 15; vii, 6). Peter's name is not so much as mentioned.

(3) One of the main objects of Acts is to draw a parallel between Peter and Paul; instead of the conflict between them that we find in Galatians, there is unanimity, Paul following where Peter leads. Since the work closes with Paul preaching in Rome, we should certainly expect the author to mention that Peter preceded or accompanied him there if such a tradition were known. But nothing of the sort is said. We are told that after his second miraculous release from prison Peter 'departed and went to another place'. The phrase indicates that the author does not propose to follow his fortunes further—not that he went to Rome; for in the one passage where he is again mentioned (xv, 16–20) he is at Jerusalem, urging the elders not to require Paul's gentile converts to keep the Jewish law. In this section of the narrative his presence in Jerusalem as a resident is taken for granted.

(4) The epistle which professes to be written by the Church of Rome to the Church of Corinth (I Clement) speaks of Peter's glorious past (Chapter V), but says nothing of his having been in Rome. He is said to have 'endured many labours, and, having thus borne his testimony, went to his due place of glory'. This may imply martyrdom. The writer adds that Paul came 'to the limit of the west' and died there. The phrase could mean 'the westward limit of Paul's activities', i.e. Rome. As the purpose of the whole passage is to draw a parallel between the two men, we can only infer that no tradition of Peter's death in Rome was known to him.

(5) In later documents there are allusions to Peter's martyrdom (e.g. Jn. xxi, 18–19) with no indication of where it takes place.[1]

---

[1] Lietzmann (171, pp. 235–6) argues that both Clement and Jn. must have had some place in mind (a 'genuine tradition of martyrdom' with no indication of place being 'unthinkable'), and this must have been Rome, otherwise the 'real place' would have promulgated its claim, or alternatively several would have competed for the honour. Bauer (22, p. 119) has noted that Antioch did claim Peter as the first of its monarchical bishops, if not as its martyr. And it is characteristic of the mythological process that originally

(6) Ignatius tells the Romans: 'I do not enjoin you, as Peter and Paul did' (iv, 3). This has been taken to suggest that the two had been influential teachers in Rome. However, Justin Martyr, writing there about AD 150, has nothing to say about Peter's having been there. He says much of Simon Magus' activities in the city, but nothing of Peter's polemic against him, which is the subject of many later traditions (see above, p. 189n).

(7) The first witness to Peter's sojourn in Rome who can be accurately dated is Dionysius, bishop of Corinth. He wrote to the Church of Rome in the time of the bishopric of Soter (AD 166–74), thanking the Romans for financial help. A passage from the letter has been preserved by Eusebius (89, III, 25, 8), and in it Dionysius says it is appropriate that the Churches of Rome and Corinth should co-operate, since they were both founded by the joint work of Peter and Paul. No earlier writer knows anything of Peter's having been at Corinth. In Acts it is Paul alone who is represented as labouring there, and in I Cor. iv, 15 he claims the Corinthian Christians as his and his alone. There was of course a Cephas party at Corinth, as we learn from the same source, just as there was a Christ party and an Apollos one (i, 12). Presumably disciples of Peter came there and their followers called themselves 'of Cephas'. We are no more entitled to infer that Peter was at Corinth to found this sect than that Jesus was there to found the Christ party. Nevertheless, what Paul says about the Cephas party seems to have inspired Dionysius' remarks. Schmiedel observes that in the interests of his theory about the co-operation of Peter and Paul he has clearly 'grievously distorted the whole history of his own Church in a point as to which he of all men must be presumed to have been accurately informed. How, then, are we to repose confidence on such a "witness" when he tells us about Rome?' (240, § 25).

The allegation that Peter and Paul founded the Roman Church jointly is in conflict with both Romans and Acts. The author of Romans says he has never met the Christians of Rome (i, 13), who, therefore, could not have owed their conversion to him. When Paul arrives in Rome at the end of Acts he is met by Christians of

---

vague stories are later given an exact setting in time and place. Gibbon notes sardonically that 'in the time of Tertullian . . . the glory of martyrdom was confined to St Peter, St Paul and St James. It was gradually bestowed on the rest of the apostles by the more recent Greeks, who prudently selected for the theatre of their preaching and sufferings some remote country beyond the limits of the Roman empire' (104, II, p. 13 n.).

the city (xxviii, 15), who again must have been converted independently of him. Dionysius takes the myth a stage further. While according to Acts Paul preached in Rome, Clement suggests that he died there, and now Dionysius holds that he was one of the founders of its Christian community. Similarly, the statement that Peter founded the Church there goes beyond all that has been said by Ignatius and Justin.

(8) A little later, Irenaeus speaks of the Church of Rome as having been 'founded and constituted by the two very glorious apostles Peter and Paul' (146, III, 3, 1).

(9) Still later writers assign to Peter a sojourn of twenty-five years in Rome, and make him not merely the joint founder but the sole founder of its Church, so that Paul, whom Irenaeus still places at his side, is gradually eliminated. Eliminating either Peter or Paul from the Roman scene was an inevitable consequence once the supposition arose that monarchical episcopacy already existed in the early Church. Of the two apostles, Peter was naturally preferred to Paul, since, as a close companion of Jesus, he would have received the true faith, and could thus strengthen the authority of Rome in its struggle against heresy (22, pp. 117–18).

In all this we can see a good example of the mythological process. Whether we accept the oldest traditions or not, the later ones are clearly at variance with them. In the earliest documents Peter and Paul are in conflict, and this is resolved (and that only temporarily) by the agreement that Paul should preach to the gentiles and Peter to the Jews (Gal. ii, 9). The next stage (represented by Acts) is to allege that there was no conflict, and that the activities of the two ran on parallel lines—the motive of such stories being to paint the early history of the Church in rosy colours. Next we find allegations of active co-operation between them; they are said to have jointly founded the Churches of Corinth and Rome. In the eighteenth century Herder had noted how strong was the effort on the part of the individual Churches to claim an apostle as their founder. Once such a tradition was circulating it would be eagerly retained and elaborated (280, p. 109). And the final elaboration came when Peter was made not only the founder of the Roman Church but also its first bishop. We saw above that episcopacy is something that developed much later than the dates assigned to Peter.

(iv) Conclusion

The examples treated show the importance of contemporary evidence; where this is not forthcoming, we cannot be sure that the person under discussion existed. Where the earliest documents specify circumstances in which he was (according to later documents) concerned without mentioning him, we can be sure that he did not do what is alleged of him, if he existed at all. In such cases, our suspicions will be confirmed if we find that the later stories duplicate traditions told of other heroes and if we can discern obvious motives for the concoction of the stories. Elsewhere (281) I have tried to show that as a result of the application of all these criteria, William Tell is not now regarded as a historical personage, while Faust can be proved by extant letters of contemporaries, who saw him and commented independently on his behaviour, to have been an itinerant braggart of the early sixteenth century who claimed magical powers. In the case of Faust the facts rapidly became overlaid by a mass of fables which manipulated or invented incidents in the interests of the writer's thesis. Faust was, for instance, made a representative of the interest in the classical world which the Reformation tried to bring into disrepute. A very early tradition represents him as lecturing on Homer at the University of Erfurt (the great seat of German humanism) and as calling up the shades of Homeric heroes to illustrate his lecture. But for the contemporary evidence we could not assume that the Faust stories had any kernel of historical truth at all. I need hardly repeat that in the case of Jesus, contemporary evidence of this kind, or indeed of any kind, is wanting. The gospels are tendency writing in exactly the same sense as the anonymous Faust-book of 1587 is one. In the interests of a certain thesis the Faust-book gives a fantastic biography of a man within fifty years of his known existence. The gospels are separated from the alleged death of their hero by eighty to a hundred years; they arose in an environment where wholesale invention was certainly not more difficult, and are just as clearly written to illustrate a thesis.

Later Faust books pursue different tendencies. In a well-known one his story is adapted to discredit Catholicism. Instead of a philosopher who 'takes eagles' wings' in his pursuit of knowledge, we find here a promising youth led into bad ways through contact with the magic of the Catholic Church. As with the gospels, later writers pursue their different tendencies and, in order to do so, suppress some details and change others—a process which theologians call 'editing'. (cf. above, p. 41.)

The parallel between Tell and Jesus is also striking. In both cases (1) the deeds alleged had been told of previous heroes; (2) there are discernible motives for the circulation of the stories; (3) the silence of contemporary documents is remedied by interpolations and forgeries; (4) although the contemporary testimony is nil, references which assume the existence of the hero become legion within two hundred years of his supposed existence; (5) the later documents give more precise details (e.g. exact dates and names) than the earlier. Tell's struggle against cruel Austrian bailiffs is, for instance, entirely absent from the earliest documents, mentioned in general terms by later ones, and supplied with exact dates only by Tschudi, who composed his chronicle nearly 300 years after these alleged events. Tschudi's dates may be compared with Lk.'s references to Augustus and Quirinius, and the exact setting with which he opens his third chapter: 'Now in the fifteenth year of the reign of Tiberius Caesar, Pontius Pilate being governor of Judaea, and Herod being tetrarch of Galilee, and his brother Philip tetrarch of Ituraea and Lysanias tetrarch of Abilene, in the high-priesthood of Annas and Caiaphas, the word of God came unto John the son of Zacharias in the wilderness'; while the corresponding passages in Mt. and Mk. simply read 'in those days'. And finally (6) in both cases the evidence of scholars has been fiercely resisted by parties committed to the traditional view. These parallels are sometimes dismissed by claiming that, while Tell is first mentioned only two hundred years after his alleged life-time, the earliest references to Jesus are in the writings of men who were contemporary with his friends and acquaintances. But, as I have repeatedly observed, these early Christian writings do not in any way suggest that he lived on earth in the recent past. It is easy to quote, from the Pauline and other early Christian documents, references to Christ or to Christ Jesus, but none of these offer evidence that the author had any knowledge of a historical character.[1] The early Christian writers are silent about the historical personage depicted in the gospels, just as the Swiss chronicles of the fourteenth century

---

[1] This is the answer to J. Peter's objection (209, p. 25) that to deny the historicity of Jesus involves 'discounting' the evidence of the whole of early Christian literature.

H

are silent about the Tell who first appears in a document of 1470.

Earlier documents are not invariably more reliable than later ones. Concerning Solon, Aristotle is regarded as a more reliable source than Herodotus, even though he wrote a century later. But then Aristotle is reliable because he was able to found extensively on material earlier even than Herodotus' history, namely Solon's own poems. Contemporary evidence, then, does not always mean contemporary documents. Quotations from ancient documents by later inquirers are valuable if there is reason for believing that the later writer was able to consult the earlier documents, and that these latter were either contemporary with the events described, or later copies of contemporary documents. This is always a matter of inference. Thus, although none of the extant manuscripts of Solon's poems are of any great age, we saw reason to believe that Aristotle and earlier writers quoted from collections of the poems which had been current since the first half of the fifth century, and which can fairly be held to have been compiled from earlier documents. Similarly, although the extant manuscripts of Josephus are late, we can prove that much earlier ones existed because we find criticism of and quotations from his works in writers who lived long before the time of the extant manuscripts. In this way it is possible to infer how close in time Josephus was to the events he relates. We saw in an earlier chapter that the dating of the gospels depends on the same kind of inference, and that their authors can be shown in this way not to have been contemporary with the events they describe.

One of the objections to accepting the gospels is the silence of the concerted testimony of the first century—pagan, Jewish and Christian. Newman (202, p. 115) tries to answer this by saying that the silence of pagan and Jewish writers is simply an example of what does occasionally and inexplicably occur. As examples he mentions not only the failure of Seneca, Pliny the elder, Plutarch and the Mishnah to mention Christianity, but also the following cases which he regards as equally striking:

(1) 'Lucian, for whatever reason, hardly notices Roman authors or affairs.'

(2) 'Maximus Tyrius, who wrote several of his works at Rome, nevertheless makes no reference to Roman history.'

(3) 'Paterculus, the historian, is mentioned by no ancient writer except Priscian.'

Let us examine these examples.

(1) Lucian, a Greek writer who lived from AD 125–90, was born in Syria and travelled widely as a rhetorician. Many of his works are satires on religion. For instance, his *Alexander, or the false prophet*, is an indictment of the Paphlagonian religious impostor of that name. In this work he refers (section 48) to θεὸς Μᾶρκος (i.e. divus Marcus). This implies that Marcus Aurelius was dead at the time of writing, and so enables us to date the work. It also constitutes a clear reference to 'Roman affairs'. He appears to have visited Rome in his travels, for he says that he met the Platonist Nigrinus there. According to Smith (254) the main purpose of his dialogue which bears the title Nigrinus is 'to satirise the Romans, whose pomp, vain-glory and luxury are unfavourably contrasted with the simple habits of the Athenians'. When Newman says that Lucian 'hardly notices' Roman affairs, he may mean merely that he does not discuss Roman history or Roman literature. The answer is that he did not have occasion to do so.

(2) Maximus Tyrius was a Greek rhetorician and Platonic philosopher who flourished in the latter part of the second century. He spent most of his life in Greece, but travelled and may have visited Rome. Newman's statement that he wrote at Rome goes beyond what can be proved. Forty-one of his lectures or dissertations are extant, and not one is on a historical subject. They are all religious, ethical or philosophical in character, treating of Greek philosophers (Socrates, Plato), or of general questions, like the origin of evil. Furthermore, they are designed for Greek audiences (Zeller, 296, p. 219 n.) and the historical references they contain are such as Greek audiences would appreciate, namely references to early Greece, the Persian wars, and Alexander's conquests. The absence of allusions to Roman history is noteworthy; but since Maximus is dealing with history only by the way, in order to illustrate his precepts, it is not inexplicable. A man who lectured in Greek to Greek audiences on non-historical subjects is not a crucial witness concerning Roman History.

(3) Paterculus' work is a history of the world up to AD 30. Newman's statement that only Priscian refers to it is not true.

Pauly-Wissowa (207) shows that three grammarians quote it, namely Servius in his commentary on Virgil, the author of the scholia to Lucan's *Civil War*, and Priscian. The work appears to be of little merit, both in content and style. It is not quoted by the historians, but at least one of them, namely Sulpicius Severus, may have used it, for 'the phrases he uses to connect his narratives are so strikingly similar to those of Paterculus that one is prompted to explain this as due to direct influence' (207). This feature, unlike others common to the two writers, cannot be explained by their both having drawn on Sallust as a common source.

Newman's examples are, in sum, either not true or not to the point. They do not illustrate the failure of a writer to deal with a topic that falls within his chosen field. The silence of a writer may or may not be significant according to the subject he is discussing. The silence of the earlier chronicles of Switzerland about Tell is decisive only because they set out to deal with the circumstances in which he was (according to the later traditions) active. The same is true of the silence of Josephus, who specifies the religious sects in first century Palestine without mentioning Christians, and records the career of Pilate without referring to his treatment of Jesus. Similarly decisive is the silence of Christian writers like Paul or Clement, who fail to refer to the actions or doctrines of Jesus when (as is often the case) these are relevant to their arguments. I have also noted the failure of Seneca and the elder Pliny to mention the preternatural darkness at the crucifixion in works expressly devoted to such topics as eclipses and earthquakes. These examples cannot be equated with Lucian's silence about Roman affairs, which he has no occasion to mention.

PART TWO

CHRISTIAN ORIGINS

CHAPTER NINE

The Dying God

(i) The suffering Messiah

Did the Jews regard their Messiah as suffering or even dying, or was this a new idea introduced by the Christians? To answer this we must look at Isa. liii.

Isaiah's prophecies did not refer to the remote future but to the problems of his day and age. Thus we saw him (above, p. 28) giving practical forecasts to King Ahaz, who reigned from 735–715 BC, when the two Jewish kingdoms (Israel in the north and Judah in the south) were both pawns between the great empires of Egypt and Assyria. The Assyrians overran the northern kingdom in 722 and Judah in 701. Isaiah, seeing that such catastrophes were imminent, represented them as a terrible judgement which only a remnant of the nation would survive. But these redeemed and blessed ones would turn again to God (x, 21) and would live happily, ruled by the King Messiah of Davidic lineage (ix, 6).

The later chapters of the book are of much later date. The Assyrian Empire collapsed and was replaced by the Babylonian in 623, and in 587 the Jewish kingdom came to an end with the capture of Jerusalem and the exile of its population at Babylon until the rise of the Persian Empire and the capture of Babylon by Cyrus in 538. The author of chapters xl–lv, the so-called Deutero- or Second Isaiah, belongs to a period late in this exile, when the Persian power had become considerable, and he comforts the exiles by holding out the expectation that Cyrus, whom he even designates 'the Lord's anointed' (xlv, 1), will free them.

Deutero-Isaiah also includes four fragments of an older work, the so-called servant poems,[1] written at a time of utter despair for the exiles before the rise of Cyrus. Both in the poems and in Deutero-Isaiah proper we are expressly told that this 'servant of Yahweh' whose sufferings and death are depicted, is Israel. Klausner has noted that ancient Jewish interpreters were divided as to whether the servant is a personification of the whole people Israel or whether he symbolizes only the prophet. He thinks that the reference is in fact to both. Just as the prophet is persecuted by his own people, whom he is seeking to benefit, and thus takes upon himself the iniquities of others, so the nation suffers far more than it really deserves because it is atoning for the misdeeds of all mankind (161, pp. 161-2). It is certainly true that the sufferings and death of the servant are represented as an atonement for the guilt of the gentile races as well as for that of the Jews (xlix, 5-6).

The best-known portrayal of his afflictions is given in the following passage:

> He was despised and rejected of men; a man of sorrows, and acquainted with grief: and as one from whom men hide their face he was despised, and we esteemed him not. Surely he hath borne our griefs, and carried our sorrows: yet did we esteem him stricken, smitten of God and afflicted. But he was wounded for our transgressions, he was bruised for our iniquities; the chastisement of our peace was upon him; and with his stripes we are healed. All we like sheep have gone astray; we have turned every one to his own way; and the Lord hath laid on him the iniquity of us all. He was oppressed, yet he humbled himself and opened not his mouth; as a lamb that is led to the slaughter, and as a sheep that before her shearers is dumb; yea, he opened not his mouth. By oppression and judgement he was taken away; and as for his generation, who among them considered that he was cut off out of the land of the living? For the transgression of my people was he stricken. And they made his grave with the wicked, and with the rich in his death; although he had done no violence, neither was any deceit in his mouth (liii, 3-9).

That this servant is a prophetic portrayal of Jesus Christ, who died for the world's sins, is a Christian interpretation given as early as

---

[1] They are not universally agreed to be older; for a discussion of the many theories concerning them, see Rowley, 230b, p. 5 ff.

the NT (e.g. Acts viii, 31-5). But the official Jewish standpoint never conceded that the servant is the Messiah, and Origen tells that when he cited this passage to the Rabbis in proof of the claims of Jesus, 'the reply was made "that this prophecy referred to the entire Jewish people, represented as an individual, which had been involved in the Dispersion and afflicted"' (287, ii, 192). This attitude is already discernible in Jonathon ben Uzziel of the first century AD who begins his Targum with: 'Behold my servant, the Messiah, shall prosper: he shall be high and increase, and be exceedingly strong.' To reconcile this with Isa. liii he makes all the references to exaltation and glory in the chapter apply to the Messiah, but those to tribulation and sufferings to Israel (20, pp. 143-6).

However, the idea of the suffering Messiah was not rejected by all Jewish writers. For instance, in the Talmud (Sanhedrim 93b) it is inferred from Isa. xi, 3 that God will load him with commands and sufferings like millstones. In Sanhedrim fol. 98b he is called 'the leprous one . . . the sick one, as it is said "surely he hath borne our sickness"' (Quot. 20, p. 12). And according to the book *Sifre*, Rabbi Joses says: 'King Messiah has been humbled and made contemptible on account of the rebellious, as it is said, He was wounded for our transgressions, etc.' (Quot. 244, II, II, 184). As Schürer says, this passage suffices to show that, in the second century AD, Isa. liii, 5 was, in many Jewish circles, explained as referring to the Messiah. This is confirmed by the saying of the Jew in Justin's *Dialogue* (157, Chapter 90): 'He that was to suffer and be led as a sheep we know very well' but not 'he that was to be crucified and die that shameful and ignominious death which is cursed in the law'.

Klausner demurs. He regards the passage from *Sifre* as an interpolation, and emphatically declares that in the whole Jewish Messianic literature up to AD 200 there is no trace of the suffering Messiah, that all the references belong to the later period 'when Christian influences cannot be wholly discounted' (161, p. 405). It is however striking that he does not enter into discussion of the passages Schürer cites from Justin's *Dialogue*, a work which elsewhere in Klausner's book is accepted as providing valuable evidence of current Jewish Messianic ideas. My impression is that Klausner, writing from a Jewish standpoint, is anxious to distinguish as sharply as possible between Jewish and Christian views of the Messiah. (This seems to be why he denies (p. 24) that the

Jews ever regarded their Messiah as divine.) It is, however, clear from his own book how natural it was for the Jews, apart from Christian influences, to conceive their Messiah as suffering for the iniquities of others. We have seen that he regards the servant of Yahweh as both the prophet who suffers to redeem Israel, and as the people Israel whose suffering redeems the gentiles. 'Thus the whole people Israel, in the form of the elect of the nation, gradually becomes the Messiah of the world, the redeemer of mankind. This Messiah must suffer as the prophet suffers' (161, p. 163).

Strack has made the interesting suggestion that the Rabbis, far from taking the idea of the suffering Messiah from the Christians, deleted it from the Talmud in order to set their own religion apart; and that this is why the Talmud only once links Isa. liii with the suffering Messiah (259, p. 68 and note). We saw (p. 199) that the Jews made alterations in the Talmud from fear of the Christian authorities. The desire to distinguish themselves from the Christians (still discernible in Klausner) is a more intelligible motive than receptiveness to Christian ideas; so that they had greater reason to abandon the idea of the suffering Messiah than to accept it from their hated rivals.

Schürer gives much the same explanation as Klausner of the origin of the idea that the Messiah should suffer. It was, he says, a current thought in Rabbinic Judaism that the perfectly righteous man not only fulfils all the commandments but also atones, by sufferings, for the sins which others may have committed, and that his excess suffering is of service to others. All that was necessary was that this idea should be applied to the Messiah. This application was natural enough, since the Messiah was believed to be a powerful and virtuous being, and the idea that suffering gives power and is associated with virtue is almost universal. The Indian Brahmins, for instance, practised self-inflicted suffering in the hope of attaining supernatural power, and many virtuous men or saints are reported to have endured great suffering. The idea may have arisen from the supposed connection between sin and punishment. Suffering is held to atone for wickedness, and excess of suffering is therefore like the opening of a credit account.

Schürer nevertheless adds that 'however much the idea of a suffering Messiah is from these premises conceivable on the soil of Judaism, just as little did it become the prevailing view'. None of the numerous apocalyptic works contains the slightest allusion to an atoning suffering of the Messiah, and 'that the

Jews were far from entertaining such an idea is abundantly proved by the conduct of both the disciples and opponents of Jesus' (on this see above, p. 105).

Another OT passage which is of interest in connection with the suffering Messiah is Zechariah xii, 10, which mentions lamentations over a martyr 'whom they have pierced' after all heathendom gathered together at Jerusalem and perished there—the kind of eschatology that had been introduced by Ezekiel (see above, p. 78). Rowley comments: 'That a suffering deliverer was expected in pre-Christian days may be established from Isa. liii, and that the piercing of a sufferer should herald the dawn of the expected age may be established from Zech. xii, 10.' He adds, however, that there is no evidence that 'Jewish thought had been concentrated on these passages in relation to the Messianic hope in the way it had been concentrated on the Davidic Messiah', nor that 'there had been any serious integration of these passages along with the others in a single whole' (230b, p. 75). He concedes, however, that the passages in Isaiah and in Zechariah are 'eschatological in their reference, in that they deal with the bringing in of the age when God's will should prevail within Israel and beyond'. He also notes that 'some of the predicates of the Davidic Messiah and of the Suffering Servant are common to both figures', which are thus 'related conceptions' with 'many points of connection' (pp. 90-2). Rowley supposes that Jesus was the first to bring them together. The importance of his argument to my purpose is that he considers that they lent themselves readily to this fusion.

A fair summary of evidence is that, in the second century (perhaps earlier), it was possible for orthodox Jews to think of their Messiah as suffering to atone for the sins of the world, but not as dying as an atoning sacrifice. We must next inquire whether the early Christians derived the idea that their god died from Jews who were not orthodox or even from pagans. If so, it would be perfectly feasible for this idea to become superimposed on the Jewish one that the Messiah suffered; and the result would be the idea of a Messiah who died as an atoning sacrifice. In other words, suppose that for some reason the early Christians believed in a god who died, but who was otherwise a supernatural figure with no biography; then, since the fifty-third chapter of Isaiah was admitted to refer to the Messiah, they could hardly avoid connecting it with their slain saviour and seeing in it a striking proof from prophecy of his divinity. This would then explain why it is that the earliest NT references to Jesus not only lack biographical details, but sometimes, as in I Peter, even portray his death almost exclusively by drawing on Isaiah, or on Ezekiel, as does the Book of Revelation (see below, p. 281).

(ii) The dying god

Volney (277) held that deities were originally personifications of the sun, moon, stars, winds and other natural forces.[1] Primitive man personified them because he could explain their spontaneous movement only on the supposition that it sprang from will-power similar to that which dictated his own action. In other words, primitive man used his notion of himself as a model to explain other phenomena. This is undoubtedly true, and had repeatedly been urged from Vico onwards. Only very gradually did men come to explain even the movements of inanimate bodies without reference to their supposed personality. Anaxagoras was obliged to flee the country when he said the sun was a mere lump of matter, and Plato prescribed the death penalty for anyone persistently denying the divine personality of the sun and moon. Now Volney argues that since primitive man regarded the sun animistically, he naturally explained its annual course as a series of adventures of a personality, conceived anthropomorphically. Thus he referred to the winter solstice—the turning-point in the year from which the sun gains in power as the length of daylight increases—as the 'birth' of the sun. And the sun's importance made it divine. It was essential to understand this personage on whose action the annual cycle of vegetation visibly depended.

Volney shows that the stories framed to explain the behaviour of the sun involved frequent references to the zodiacal signs through which it appears to pass in its annual journey. For instance, we have seen (above, p. 33) that the pagans of Syria and Egypt represented the birth of the sun-god at the winter solstice by displaying the image of an infant and declaring: 'behold the virgin has brought forth'. It is at the winter solstice that the constellation of the virgin, the sixth sign of the zodiac, rises above the horizon. Volney holds that the story that the god was born of a virgin on the day of the solstice must originally have been an

[1] For a fuller account of Volney's views, see 282, from which some of the following discussion derives.

attempt to explain the behaviour of the sun. But the sun's behaviour follows a regular pattern which is repeated every year, whereas this explanation of its behaviour is in the form of the life-history of an individual god who lived but once. How could stories about an individual person come into being as explanations of phenomena which are repetitive? Volney answers that, when the sun was born under the sign of the virgin at the solstice, it was natural to speak of this—or to represent it in picture form—as a virgin giving birth to a child. A statement such as 'the virgin has brought forth' would, in the given situation, be understood and not taken literally. When later a calendar was invented and it was no longer so important to observe the stars, the picture or story survived, but lost its solar significance, and people repeated the tale of a virgin producing a son as if this were an event that had happened on earth—although both characters in the story retained the divine attributes which they had possessed when they had been regarded as solar phenomena.

Again, when the constellation of the dragon (pytho) appeared above the horizon, and followed in the trail of the virgin, men naturally spoke of the dragon pursuing her and her son. When the solar significance of this story disappeared, men spoke of an earthly dragon, and hence the myth of the persecution of Apollo by the dragon. When the sun passes through the water signs of the zodiac (pisces) soon after the winter solstice, it was natural to think of the young god-child as being immersed. This later gave rise to stories of gods or heroes such as Dionysus, Sargon and Moses being, at one point in their career, immersed. Again, at the vernal equinox, the sun, which has been below the equator, suddenly appears to rise above it, and so, usually upon dates calculated by the pagan astronomers, its death was mourned (sometimes for a period of three days) and its resurrection celebrated. Hence all the ancient stories of dying and resurrected gods.[1] Furthermore, pictures were common in early times because writing was pictographic. With the invention of alphabetic writing there was opportunity enough for misunderstanding the old pictographs that were no longer used. On this basis, says Volney, it is possible to understand how figures such as Hercules,

---

[1] The resurrection of Osiris and Attis on the third day suggests that they were lunar deities, the new moon being invisible for three days (167, pp. 77-8; 169, 201-2). Osiris lived twenty-eight years on earth—the length in days of the lunar month (39, p. 8).

originally solar divinities, came to be regarded as historical personages who went about doing good.

In recent times Frazer has shown that worship of a saviour-god who died and rose from the dead is of immemorial antiquity. His name may be Tammuz, Attis, Adonis or Osiris, according to the locality where he is worshipped. Details of the ritual vary, but the god is always young and beautiful and loved by a great goddess. He is always mourned as the victim of an untimely death, but is resurrected for the salvation of the mourning world. Frazer considers these deities to be not sun- but vegetation-gods, whose death and resurrection is a personification of the yearly decay and revival of life, particularly of vegetable life (95, p. 325). However, since the vegetation depends on the sun, it is not necessary to hold that myths are either solar or vegetational; they may be composite; and so Frazer's theory will not necessarily contradict Volney's.

The god did not die of his own accord but was killed by his worshippers every spring in order to promote the annual revival of vegetable life. They regarded the winter as an enfeeblement of the spirit of vegetation, which, they thought, could be renewed by being slain and brought to life in a younger and fresher form. Thus 'the killing of the god, that is, of his human incarnation, is merely a necessary step in his revival or resurrection in a better form' (95, p. 300). Frazer relates how this idea—that the god thus slain in the person of his representative comes to life again immediately—was graphically represented in a Mexican ritual by skinning the slain man-god, and clothing in his skin a living man, who thus became the new representative of the godhead.

The annual killing of the god thus involved the actual killing of some person as his human representative. Such ritual may seem to us a fantastic method of procuring good crops. Gilbert Murray has remarked that

> the extraordinary security of our modern life in times of peace makes it hard for us to realize, except by a definite effort of the imagination, the constant precariousness, the frightful proximity of death, that was usual in these weak ancient communities . . . they were helpless against floods, helpless against pestilences. Their food depended on the crops of one tiny plot of ground; and if the Saviour was not reborn with the spring, they slowly

and miserably died. And all the while they knew almost nothing of the real causes that made crops succeed or fail . . . It is
this state of things that explains the cruelty of early agricultural
doings, the human sacrifices, the scapegoats . . . Like most
cruelty it has its roots in terror (196, pp. 34-35).

It was often the king of the tribe who was regarded as the god's
representative, and Frazer shows that the custom of killing these
divine kings, either at the end of a fixed period—one year or a
number of years—or when their strength began to fail, was very
widespread. At a later stage they 'died by deputy' (95, p. 278).
An obvious deputy was the king's son, who might be supposed
to share the divine afflatus of his father (p. 289). An example is
Cronus who 'having an only-begotten son called Jeoud (for in
the Phoenician tongue Jeoud signifies "only-begotten"), dressed
him in royal robes and sacrificed him upon an altar' (p. 293).
Sometimes the deputy was a condemned criminal, as at the Babylonian festival of the Sacaea, when 'a prisoner condemned to
death was dressed in the king's robes, seated on the king's
throne, allowed to issue whatever commands he pleased, to eat,
drink and enjoy himself and to lie with the king's concubines.
But at the end of the five days he was stripped of his royal robes,
scourged and hanged or impaled.' Criminals would be used to
represent the dying god when the original barbaric rite offended
the current morality (94, pp. 69-70). Sometimes the victim's arms
and legs would be broken to make him seem unresisting, or he
might be stupefied with narcotics. Alternatively an animal might
be substituted and treated as if it were a human being. Thus when
a new-born calf was sacrificed to Dionysus it was 'shod in bus-
kins and the mother tended like a woman in childbed'. Frazer
describes such rites as 'a pious and merciful fraud which palmed
off on the deity less precious victims than living men and women'
(95, p. 392). But today anthropologists prefer to assume that these
people were sincere in their beliefs. Dressing in royal robes does
not produce a false substitute, a stupid fraud which anybody could
see through, but actually makes the criminal share the essential
being of the king (just as wearing the skin gives the wearer the
identity of the skin's original owner). Kingship transcends the
person in whom it is, so why kill it in that person when it can
equally genuinely be killed in another or in an animal? Another
method of toning down the original barbaric rite was to make it

into a mock-killing, and this would entail a dramatic ritual in which a man would play the part of the god and pretend to suffer, die and be reborn.

The original purpose of the whole ceremony might at some stage be lost from sight, and then a new explanation of its significance would be sought. The obvious one that would suggest itself would be that the ritual was an annual commemoration of the death of the god, which had occurred only once. Frazer and Robertson Smith (223) both give examples of how in this way what was originally an annual killing of the god came to be regarded eventually as a memorial ritual to his death on a specific historical occasion. It is in fact one of the fundamental principles of modern anthropology that the ritual explains the myth, not vice versa. A ritual tends to persist long after its original cause and significance have been lost from sight, and among the worshippers myths then arise which purport to explain it, although in fact it explains them. In this way we can see how all the attributes of the sun- or vegetation-gods who died annually came in time to be ascribed to an individual who was held to die only once.

As slavery developed and as urban life advanced in the pagan world, the worshippers of Osiris, Attis and other such gods lost touch with the processes of agriculture, and so ceased to connect the death and resurrection of the god with the revival of vegetation. But they had come to believe in their own immortality, and the resurrection of the god was believed to ensure that of his devotees.[1] Thus

> rites which at their outset had been meant only to secure the fertility of the fields . . . came to be understood as bearing on

[1] In quite another connection, Miss Weston has explained (286) how a ritual, originally merely a magical process for procuring good crops and other worldly goods, could later become, in a different environment, a method of influencing the divine powers in one's own favour, with special emphasis on the life hereafter. The form of the ritual would be traditional, but its meaning lost. A new explanation of a quasi-historical character would be devised, and the dramatic ritual would be interpreted as a memorial service. When a new religion supplanted this one, the latter would become isolated in secluded places and finally die out, leaving only a number of tales about the characters. Thus the sequence is: (1) Magical method for improving crops, etc.; (2) Same method reinterpreted, perhaps in urban communities where there was no immediate concern for agricultural affairs; (3) Dramatic ritual explained as memorial service; (4) Disappearance of surviving cult and coming into existence of romances. Miss Weston explains how this happened in one particular instance, but the process she describes is really a general one, and other cases can be made out.

the life of man after death. It was easy to establish the connection, since, if the rites had originally set forth such a victory of life over death as might be seen in the annual renewal of the vegetable world, the men who associated themselves with the death and resurrection of the god might well believe that by such association they too won a new life after bodily death' (29, pp. 97–98).

The spring festival of Cybele and Attis at Rome is an example. Frazer describes how on the 22nd March a pine tree was cut in the woods and brought into the sanctuary of Cybele. The effigy of a young man, doubtless Attis himself, was tied to the middle of the stem, mourned over and buried in a sepulchre. But when night had fallen a light shone in the darkness, the tomb was opened, the god had risen from the dead, and this was hailed by his disciples as a promise that they too would issue triumphant from the corruption of the grave (93, pp. 222–7). Apart from such public rites, these cults which purported to ensure their initiates a happy immortality also had secret or mystic ceremonies: and here too one of the most marked features was the dramatic representation of the central episodes in the stories of the suffering and dying gods, and the belief that the salvation of the initiates depends on the deliverance of the god. Thus Herodotus tells that on the artificial circular lake at Sais the Egyptians were wont to give by night—presumably once a year—representations, called mysteries of the sufferings of a certain one whom he will not name (Osiris). And the Christian writer Firmicius Maternus, who was himself an initiate of the mysteries of Attis or Adonis, has left an account of the ritual which makes it clear that the deliverance of the god brings immortality to the initiates.

Christianity originated in an environment where public and private ceremonies of this kind were common.[1] Hatch remarks that at that time the popular reaction against the vices of the great centres of population took the form of large multiplication of religious guilds, in which purity of life was a condition of membership (136, p. 141). He stresses that both the early Christian habit of forming guilds or communities, and also what they did and the Puritan ideal they taught, is traceable to these pre-Christian ones. Each of the Christian bodies was:

[1] The literature concerning such pagan influences on Christianity is summarized by Cumont (74, pp. 205–6). The latest work I have seen on the subject is Leipoldt's (169).

a community of Saints; 'passing their days upon earth, they were in reality citizens of heaven' (Ep. ad diogn. 5). The earthly community reflected in all but its glory and its everlastingness the life of the 'new Jerusalem'. Its bishop was the visible representative of Jesus Christ himself sitting on the throne of heaven, with the white-robed elders round him: its members the 'elect', the 'holy ones', the 'saved'. 'Without were the dogs, and the sorcerers, and the murderers, and the idolaters, and every one that loveth and maketh a lie': within were 'they which were written in the Lamb's book of life'. To be a member of the community was to be in reality, and not merely in conception, a child of God and heir of everlasting salvation: to be excluded from the community was to pass again into the outer darkness, the realm of Satan and eternal death (136, p. 63).

It was not, he adds, until the end of the second century that ethical ideals were subordinated to doctrinal niceties, and interests became completely absorbed with the struggles for soundness of doctrine.

He describes the mysteries celebrated at Eleusis, near Athens. They included an initiation ceremony to purify the candidate so that he became fit to approach God. He confessed his sins and there followed a regenerating baptism in the waters of the sea, the manner of bathing and number of immersions varying with the degree of guilt he had confessed. Each candidate then sacrificed a pig, and two days later he processed with a lighted torch and sang paeans in honour of the god. There followed three days and nights in which the initiated shared in the mourning of Demeter for her daughter. They broke their fast only by drinking the mystic κυκεών—a drink of flour and water and pounded mint—and by eating the sacred cakes. At night there were dramatic performances enacting the story of Demeter and Persephone, the loss of the daughter, the wanderings of the mother, the joyful reunion. Frazer remarks that this Greek legend is substantially the same as the Syrian one of Aphrodite and Adonis, the Phrygian one of Cybele and Attis, and the Egyptian one of Isis and Osiris; for in the Greek fable, as in the others, a goddess mourns the loss of a loved one, who personifies the vegetation, more especially the corn, which dies in winter to revive in spring (95, p. 393). 'The meaning of the legend' is that 'Persephone who is carried off to the lower world, is the seed-corn, which remains concealed in the ground part of the year; Persephone who returns to her mother is the corn which rises from the ground and nourishes men and animals' (253). But by the time this legend came to be enacted as a sacred drama in the mysteries of Eleusis, it was, for the audience, an assurance of their own immortality (Persephone's return from the underworld showed death giving place to life) and of their purification: those who had been baptized and initiated were lifted into a new life. Death had no terrors for them (136, p. 289).

Different forms of mysteries became blended. Hatch mentions 'a remarkable syncretist painting in a non-Christian catacomb at Rome, in which the elements of the Greek mysteries of Demeter are blended with those of Sabazius and Mithra, in a way which shows that the worship was blended also' (136, p. 290). Prominent in all the various combinations are initiation, including baptism, the sacrifice, and the common meal following it and representing 'an effort after real fellowship, a sense of communion with one another in a communion with God' (p. 291). He goes on to argue that many details in the Christian sacraments of baptism and the Eucharist derive from these pagan practices. Of course he believes that these Christian sacraments originated in the manner specified in the NT, independently of pagan tradition, and argues only that the influence of pagan usages transformed them out of all recognition. But is it not possible that Christian baptism and the Eucharist were copied from these pagan ceremonies, without any such independent origin as that alleged in the gospels?

Belief in a suffering and dying god and the rite of the Lord's Supper are the two most salient features of early Christianity. Paul wrote of a Jesus of whom no traditions were current save that he was the Messiah descended from David, was crucified, and that his resurrection promised his worshippers immortality. Nothing was known of his doctrines or of when he lived. Thus there is nothing in the earliest Christian documents which would have appeared unacceptable to a citizen of the Middle East at the time, when the idea of the dying Saviour was very widespread. I have earlier (p. 33) recorded Justin Martyr's statement that Jesus' virgin birth, passion and ascension constituted nothing new, as compared with what was alleged of the sons of Zeus. And Murray has observed that 'the parts of Christian doctrine which a Levantine pagan of the first century would deny are chiefly the historical statements. Like Paul before his conversion, he would be ready enough to discuss the doctrine of a Hebrew Messiah or a Hellenistic "Saviour", but would refuse to believe that this supernatural being had just arrived on earth in the person of a certain Jew or Nazarene' (198, p. 76). Since it is the historical statements that are lacking in the earliest Christian traditions, it really looks as if Christianity began without them, as one of the many dying-god sects of the time which grew in popularity because of the extent to which it was able to assimilate other myths and rituals.[1] The marked similarities between Christian and earlier ideas were subjects of repeated controversy. Frazer refers to an anonymous Christian writer of the fourth century who tells that the pagans contended that the resurrection of Christ was a spurious imitation of the resurrection of Attis; and that 'the Christians . . . admitted that, in point of time, Christ was the junior deity; but they triumphantly demonstrated his real seniority by falling back on the subtlety of Satan, who on so important an occasion had surpassed himself by inverting the usual order of nature' (95, p. 361). Justin and Tertullian both supposed that the devil used to take a delight in causing the still future mysteries and ceremonies of Christianity to be travestied (see above, p. 33, and below, p. 261). Modern apologists have tended (with Cardinal Newman) to see the parallels as divinely rather than diabolically motivated, and to suppose that Providence decreed that the pagans should do by anticipation, and in a spirit of prophecy, what the Christians were later to do.

The dates of many Christian festivals are also instructive. Their coincidences with pagan ones are too close and numerous to be accidental (see e.g. 95, p. 360). Frazer suggests that the Christian festival of Easter may have been adapted to a similar celebration of the Phrygian Attis at the vernal equinox. The derivation of the crucifixion from myth is certainly suggested by the way in which its date is made to vary from year to year—even though it is supposed to be the commemoration of an event which occurred on a certain day. According to purely solar considerations, the

---

[1] That the Christian Easter festival has assimilated pagan practices is admitted by Weiss, who mentions 'characteristic traits of the Adonis cult' in this connection. He also notes that there is evidence that some Jews practised the religion of Adonis before the Babylonian exile, and also at the time of Jerome, who mentions a shrine of Adonis initiated by Hadrian at Bethlehem (278, pp. 24, 29: cf. 218a, 75–6). But evidence of worship of Adonis in Judaea at the time of the origin of Christianity is not forthcoming. On Osiris worship in Judaea, see Rendel Harris' suggestions (217, p. 23).

god should die or pass into the underworld at the autumnal equinox and 'rise again' at the vernal equinox. In the Christian cult this pair of solar dates is combined by making him die and rise again at the vernal equinox, after the manner of Attis, Adonis and the other gods of vegetation. But while pagan precedents directly influenced the date of Christmas (see above, p. 32), the Easter festival evolved from the Jewish passover,[1] and was dated according to the stipulation (Ezekiel xlv, 21) that the passover should fall on the fourteenth day of the first lunar month, with (eventually) Sunday, the traditional day of the resurrection (see above, p. 176 n.) as the principal feast day.[2] Huber argues (144, pp. 1–12) that the early Christians kept the passover, but considered it unnecessary to kill and eat a lamb, as Christ had already shed his blood for them as a paschal sacrifice (I Cor. v, 7). Jn. also represents Jesus as the paschal sacrifice, and strikingly contradicts the synoptics in order to do so. Mt. says that on the first day of unleavened bread the disciples 'made ready the passover', and that same evening Jesus takes the paschal meal with them, foretells the treachery of Judas, and blesses the bread and wine, reciting the 'take, eat, this is my body' formula (Mt. xxvi, 17–28). He dies on the cross the same day—the Jewish day being reckoned from evening to evening. The fourth gospel, however, makes him merely sup informally with his disciples on the day *before* the passover (Jn. xiii, 1–4); in this gospel there is no use of bread and wine, no 'take, eat' formula. And his death occurs at the very

---

[1] It is perhaps of interest in the present context that some anthropologists have argued that the Jewish passover itself derives from an original rite of human sacrifice. Frazer, for instance, asks:

> Why . . . should the Israelites kill the firstlings of their cattle for ever because God once killed those of the Egyptians? And why should every Hebrew father have to pay God a ransom for his firstborn child because God once slew all the firstborn children of the Egyptians? In this form the tradition offers no intelligible explanation of the custom. But it at once becomes clear and intelligible when we assume that in the original version of the story it was the Hebrew firstborn that were slain; that in fact the slaughter of the firstborn children was formerly what the slaughter of the firstborn cattle always continued to be, not an isolated butchery but a regular custom, which with the growth of more humane sentiments was afterwards softened into the vicarious sacrifice of a lamb and the payment of a ransom for each child (92, pp. 176–7).

[2] See 144, pp. 62, 157. Huber here notes that Christians began to calculate the XIV lunae independently of the Jews only in the third century, probably because the Jews then began to reckon 14th Nisan without reference to the vernal equinox. cf. Schwarz, 246, pp. 13–14.

hour of the preparation for the paschal meal. The idea is clearly that the old sacrifice of a lamb has been superseded.

Huber also shows that the Jews expected the coming of the Messiah on the night of the passover; their final deliverance was to come on the night that had brought them deliverance from Egypt. The Christians, he argues, will at first have celebrated the passover with the same expectations, but when the Messiah repeatedly failed to come, the feast, instead of looking forward to his future triumph, became a commemoration of the victory he had already won at his resurrection. Thus did the Christian Easter evolve from the Jewish passover, and we shall see (p. 297) that this transfer of interest from the future to the past is important for Christian evolution generally.

Since Christianity took much from paganism, we might reason-ably expect it to imitate the pagan dramatic mysteries. These would be imitated because found by experience to be religiously attractive. And if it adapted the drama of the burial and resur-rection of the sun or vegetation god, as we know it to have been regularly enacted in the popular cults of Mithra, Osiris, Attis and Adonis, this would, in time lead to a circumstantial myth of the biography of the god, of whose death the drama would be re-garded as a commemoration, as in the pagan cults mentioned. It has been argued that:

'such narratives as those of the rock-burial and resurrection of the Saviour-God in the gospels are . . . simple developments of those mourning rituals . . . in use in so many ancient systems . . . The lost Attis and Adonis were sought for with lamentation, followed by rejoicing when they were ceremonially found; the body of the slain Osiris was searched for with lamentation, and the prepared image, when found, seems to have been further mourned over and then rejoiced over. Whatever may have been the order of the ceremony, it is certain that the burying of an image of the slain God was a regular part of it. And in the cult of Mithra . . . the stone image of the God . . . was laid on a bier, was mourned for, was placed in his rock tomb in the sacred cave, was withdrawn from that tomb and liturgically rejoiced over (220, p. 381).

That the crucifixion was represented in dramatic form is suggested by Paul's question: 'O foolish Galatians, who did bewitch you,

before whose eyes Jesus Christ was openly set forth crucified?'
(Gal. iii, 1). Frazer thought that the crown of thorns, the scourging
and the kingly title in the gospel stories of the crucifixion derive
from a dramatic ritual or masquerade; but his theory (94, pp.
355 ff.) is both complicated and speculative, and not sufficiently
cogent to warrant restatement here. More convincing is the
suggestion of J. M. Robertson (222) that the gospel passion
narratives, in their least sophisticated form in Mk. and Mt., were
not composed as narratives, but represent the transcript of a
drama. His argument impressed so hostile a critic as Weiss, who
conceded (278, p. 51) that it is certainly remarkable that these
narratives lack all description of persons and events, that they
make the scene change abruptly and without explanation, and
show a preponderance of words or dialogue over narrative—all
features which are perfectly intelligible in a play or the transcript
of a play. Wood contested Robertson's account, but he had difficulty in rebutting the following points: (1) Robertson notes that
the evangelists thrice record prayers which Jesus spoke while his
audience (Peter, James and John) was asleep (Mk. xiv, 32–42).
'There is thus no one present or awake to record his words—
an incongruity which could not well have entered into a narrative
originally composed for writing, . . . but which on the stage
would not be a difficulty at all, since there the prayer would be
heard and accepted by the audience.' Wood replies (292, pp. 42–3)
that 'one or other of the disciples heard what was said before
sleep overtook them', or that, alternatively, Mk.'s informant was
the 'young man who fled naked' (Mk. xiv, 51)—a character
peculiar to Mk., who is not represented as among Jesus' audience
in Gethsemane (cf. above, p. 93): (2) In two successive sentences,
with no pause between, Jesus tells the sleeping three to sleep on
and to arise (Mk. xiv, 41–2). Robertson supposes that 'what has
happened is either a slight disarrangement of the dialogue, or the
omission of an exit and an entrance'. Wood replies (p. 38) that
perhaps Mk.'s first clause is to be taken ironically, or, alternatively,
that 'there is a rapid change of emotion'.

There may, then, have been a play or mystery drama among the
earliest Christians in which the death and resurrection of the god
was enacted, but the evidence cannot be held to have established
that there was one. More important to my purpose is whether the
motivation of the god's death by a legal trial—whether in a drama
or a narrative—can be considered established as a historical

fact. The earliest references, both Christian and pagan, which place the death of Jesus in a historical context, specify his execution under Pilate, and the gospels represent him as crucified as a rebel against Roman government in Judaea. Both A. Robertson and Brandon insist that such a tradition cannot be a myth:

> No Christian who valued a quiet life would invent a story that the founder of his sect had been crucified by a Roman governor as a political offender, if no such stigma really attached to the cult (218a, p. 101: cf. 38a, p. 1).

Judaea was seething with rebellion against Rome between AD 6 and 70, and there were in fact many who preferred to suffer for their convictions than to live a 'quiet life'. Crucifixion was, for instance, the fate of the rebel Judas of Galilee, and later of his two sons, and, as Josephus shows, of hundreds of Jewish patriots during this period (see Brandon, 38a, p. 344). That resistance did not cease after the crushing defeat of AD 70 is evidenced by the revolt of Bar Cochba, AD 132–5. I have shown that the Pauline letters do not envisage any time or place for Jesus' execution, that later I Peter supposes that it took place 'at the end of the times' i.e. the relatively recent past, that the author of the epistle to the Hebrews claims to have met—not Jesus himself, but people who had known him; and that traditions placing his death in the period when Pilate was procurator (AD 26–36) were certainly circulating early in the second century. A Christian writer of that time would naturally have supposed that, if Jesus had come as the Messiah, he would (like other Messianic claimants) have been executed by the Romans (cf. above, p. 100). Furthermore, such a fate could well have seemed, to Jews and Jewish Christians, an honourable death. 'To perish at the hands of the hated Romans, who oppressed Israel, was to die as a martyr and join that venerated company of heroes who had sacrificed their lives for their ancestral faith' (38a, p. 177; cf. p. 218). Pilate would have struck a writer of the early second century as a likely person to have ordered the execution, for, according to both Philo and Josephus, he was particularly detested by the Jews. Philo describes him as 'naturally inflexible and stubbornly relentless', and accuses him of 'acts of corruption, insults, rapine, outrages on the people, arrogance, repeated murders of innocent victims, and constant and most galling savagery'.[1] It also appears from this testimony that he was quite capable of murdering the innocent, so that the supposition that Jesus was his victim would not necessarily imply that Jesus was a rebel against Rome. Furthermore, a Christian writer who stamped Pilate as Jesus' murderer would not need to fear that such allegation would incur Roman displeasure. Both Philo and Josephus criticize Pilate harshly, yet were perfectly loyal to Rome, where Pilate does not seem to have been highly esteemed.[2] There is a further reason why Jesus' death during the procurator-ship of Pilate would have seemed plausible to a writer early in the second century. By then it was firmly believed that Jesus had been on earth in the recent past. But if his earthly sojourn had occurred very recently; if, for instance, he had died in the Jewish war of AD 66–70, then in AD 100 or 110 many who had known him would still be alive; and Christians of the early second century were doubtless struck by the fact that those who could offer plausible reminiscences of him were few and far between. (That claims to have known him were nevertheless made is, of course, evidenced by the epistle to the Hebrews.) Therefore it was inferred that he must have come at an earlier date. I would stress that I am not imputing fraud to these second century Christians. Those who lack understanding of the mythological process are apt to argue that, either a tradition is true, or else it must have been maliciously invented by cynics who knew the facts to be otherwise. The train of reasoning that I am envisaging may be compared with that posited by Schmiedel (see above, p. 44) to explain the origin of certain details in the resurrection narratives, and can be sum-marized as follows. If Jesus is the god of the 'last times' who is soon to bring the world to an end, then his first coming, as well as his second, is surely to be allocated to the 'last times', i.e. is of recent occurrence. But if it had occurred very recently, there would be hundreds who could report in detail on it. As this does not seem to be the case, the occurrence cannot be quite so recent, and therefore probably occurred during Pilate's administration; for he was just the type of person to have murdered Jesus, and

[1] Quoted by Brandon, 38a, p. 68. Even in the gospels, the severity of Pilate emerges from Lk.'s statement (xiii, 1) about the slaughter of certain Galileans 'whose blood Pilate had mingled with their sacrifices'.

[2] He was recalled by Tiberius in AD 36, who, however, died before Pilate arrived in Rome to justify himself, and 'Pilate thus passes out of history' (38a, p. 80).

was also active sufficiently recently for a few contemporaries still to be (or to have recently been) alive.

That a tradition which blamed Pilate for Jesus' death should have been modified, even by the earliest of our evangelists, is also intelligible. If this death was a divine act of salvation, then surely it resulted from the hatred of the Jews, who would not accept his divinity. This, as Brandon says (38a, p. 8), 'might be deemed more spiritually fitting for one regarded as the Son of God'. It would have the added advantage of demonstrating to the Romans that second-century Christians were not Jews, and shared none of the Jews' rebellious aspirations. And so Mk. represents Pilate as doing his best to have Jesus acquitted, but as nevertheless forced into ordering his execution by the malice of the Jewish leaders; while Mt. goes even further, in that he represents the whole Jewish people as responsible for the murder (cf. above, p. 101, and Brandon, 38a, pp. 303–4). I have discussed (above, pp. 98–101) some of the implausibilities which this modification of the tradition introduced into the narratives, but have as yet made no mention of the Barabbas incident, and have reserved it for the present context because it has been adduced as evidence of affinity between the Christian and the pagan dying god.

Mk., having made Jesus fail to deny Pilate's suggestion that he is king of the Jews, represents the procurator, not as condemning him for sedition, but as 'marvelling' at his silence (xv, 5).[1] The evangelist then introduces a new and unexpected incident (I quote the NEB):

> At the festival season the Governor used to release one prisoner at the people's request. As it happened, the man known as Barabbas was then in custody with the rebels who had committed murder in the rising. When the crowd appeared asking for the usual favour, Pilate replied, 'Do you wish me to release for you the king of the Jews?' For he knew that it was out of spite that they had brought Jesus before him. But the chief priests incited the crowd to ask him to release Barabbas rather than Jesus . . . So Pilate, in his desire to satisfy the mob, released Barabbas to them.

[1] Strauss attributed Jesus' failure to defend himself (at both his Jewish and his Roman trial) to the evangelists' desire to represent him as 'the Lamb who was led to the slaughter and opened not his mouth', i.e. as 'the Messiah of whom Isaiah had prophesied (liii, 7)' (262, II, 344).

Brandon has noted that there is no evidence outside the gospels that it was the custom for the Roman governor to release a prisoner at a festival on demand; that Josephus, who was 'specially intent on recording all the privileges which the Roman government at various times had accorded to the Jews', says nothing of such a notable privilege; and that 'such a custom would so dangerously hamper effective government in a country seething with revolt as was Judaea that it is inconceivable that the Romans would ever have tolerated it' (38a, pp. 258–9). Brandon adds, as an illustration, that 'if the Markan story is true, it would mean that on this particular occasion Pilate had to release a desperate patriotic leader', who had just been involved in a 'rising' (Mk. xv, 7) against the Roman rule. Mk., then, would have us believe that 'here was a Roman governor, supported by an efficient military force', who, convinced of Jesus' innocence, 'resorted to an otherwise unknown custom in order to do what he knew was right, i.e. release him'. To achieve Jesus' release, he also behaves as 'a fool beyond belief'. For, in offering the crowd the choice between Jesus and Barabbas, he naïvely expects them to accept Jesus instead of the patriot Barabbas who had struck at their Roman oppressors (pp. 4, 262). Brandon justly observes that this is not history, but a narrative designed to convince 'simple-minded readers', 'humble and poorly educated people', who were 'unlikely to have the knowledge or inclination to check the story', that the Jewish leaders, not Pilate, were responsible for the crucifixion.

The name of Barabbas is generally agreed to mean 'son of the father' (Bar Abba), and in Mt.'s version of the incident, the name appears in some ancient MSS. as 'Jesus Barabbas'. This was the reading of Mt. xxvii, 16 long current in the early Church, and attested by Origen in the third century. He distrusted its correctness because he knew of no sinful man who had ever been named 'Jesus'. With these words he 'not only forgets the high priest' Ἰάσων = Ἰησοῦς, 'that ungodly man' (II Macc. iv, 13), and other bearers of the name whom Josephus mentioned in his writings, but he provides us with an explanation of the cause why later copyists discarded Ἰησοῦν before βαραββᾶν . . . While it can be understood why the name might have been omitted, it is impossible to account for its appearance by arbitrary insertion in certain manuscripts' (Winter, 291, p. 96). Winter thus insists that 'Jesus Barabbas' (Jesus the son of the father) is the original reading.

J. M. Robertson explains (222) this reading from his premise that there was an ancient cult of a god Jesus, or Joshua (on the identity of the names, see above, p. 5 n.). A. Robertson has given (218a, p. 47) the following lucid summary of the theory. In many ancient rites of human sacrifice, the son of the chief or king was killed in place of his father. If there was an ancient cult of a god Jesus or Joshua, then

in accordance with the primitive convention which identifies the victim with the god, 'Joshua son of the Father' would become the style and title of the god himself, and would remain so when the sacrifice was discontinued. When the story of the crucifixion of Jesus was first circulated, the Jews would point out that it was merely a rehash of the ancient and, in Jewish eyes, disreputable myth of Joshua son of the Father—Jesus Barabbas. To meet this objection the Christians inserted in the gospels a story showing that their Jesus and Jesus Barabbas were two different people, and that in fact it was the Jews themselves who had saved Barabbas and sent the Messiah to his death.

J. M. Robertson's theory clearly depends on the premise that there was an ancient Palestinian rite in which the annual victim was 'Jesus the son of the Father'. A. Robertson agrees that there is strong evidence that the Joshua of the OT was originally a divinity, and that the name was thus originally a divine name, but he finds 'no ground for regarding Joshua as originally a saviour-god of the Tammuz type, or as the centre of a secret cult which continued down the centuries until the Christian era' (p. 96 cf. Wood, 292, p. 131).

Let us now see where the evidence of this chapter has led. The idea of the dying god was common in the religions surrounding Christianity and some Jews were prepared to admit that their Messiah must suffer. In consequence it was perfectly feasible for these two quite separate strands to become tied together, for a new Jewish sect to emerge which combined the pagan dying god with the Jewish suffering Messiah. This synthesis may have been effected by Christian borrowing of the pagan dramatic ritual of the dying god. Whether there was a Christian mystery drama or not, the two ideas—the dying god and the suffering Messiah—could well have become linked, and this linkage would have been quite possible without any further historical basis. It would, however, have been facilitated if some teacher of Messianic pretensions had actually been put to death, after which his followers carried on his teaching in the hope that he would come again. In this connection we may recall the Talmudic Jesus ben Pandira, who was stoned to death and hanged on a tree for heresy on the eve of a passover in the reign of Alexander Jannaeus (103–76 BC). We saw above that Löw long ago conjectured that this Jesus was the founder of the Essene of Jessean sect, whose resemblances to the early Christians have long been regarded as striking. Recently, evidence has come to light which has been held to prove that the Essenes had a Messiah who was killed a little time before 63 BC. I refer to the Dead Sea Scrolls, to which we now turn.

(iii) The Dead Sea Scrolls

Between 1947 and 1955 manuscripts were found in a number of caves at Khirbet Qumran by the western shore of the Dead Sea. Some of the manuscripts are copies of OT books and the rest 'form a vast collection of Jewish religious books showing such homogeneity of doctrine that they can come only from the same mystical environment, from one sect' (84, pp. 3–4). About a thousand yards from the site of the cave first discovered the remains of a monastery were subsequently excavated. From coins it could be ascertained that the building was constructed 'in or fairly soon after the reign of John Hyrcanus (135–104 BC)' (12, p. 85). It is natural to assume that the manuscripts form the library of the sect which occupied the monastery, and that the sectarians hid them in the caves when they abandoned it. This occurred when the Romans destroyed the building by fire during the 'great Jewish War, or more exactly . . . in June AD 68. So this is when the scrolls were concealed; which obviously fixes a *terminus ad quem* for the copying of the manuscripts and, *a fortiori*, for the redaction of the works' (84, p. 340). This Jewish community was thus present in Judaea at the time of the birth of Christianity. Harrison (132) agrees that ceramic, palaeographical and numismatic evidence supports this conclusion.

There is wide, though not complete, agreement that the Qumran sect can be identified with the Essenes mentioned by Josephus and Philo[1] who describe them as a religious community with

---

[1] This identification is accepted by Dupont-Sommer, and said by Allegro (12, p. 86) and Burrows (46, p. 274) to be 'probable'. Harrison concedes a

common ownership of property and other characteristics, many of which are in fact emphasized in the scrolls (Dupont-Sommer devotes a chapter to listing the remarkable parallels). The Qumran sectarians repudiated personal wealth in favour of community of goods because they believed in the approach of the day of judgement (12, p. 164). Both Philo and Josephus report that the Essenes lived in villages as well as in many-membered communities, and estimate their numbers at about 4,000. Pliny the Elder mentions one particular Essene establishment near the western shore of the Dead Sea, and this correlates well with the site of the monastery at Qumran. Although aware that the question is not closed, I propose to assume that the Qumran sectarians may be called Essenes.

The Essenes flourished in the two centuries prior to the destruction of Jerusalem by Titus in AD 70, after which they lost ground to the Pharisees, and Dupont-Sommer supposes that they settled at Qumran 'during the reign of Alexander Jannaeus (103–76 BC), who, as Josephus informs us, persecuted the Pharisees. Very likely this repression constituted a serious threat to the Essenes themselves, for they can scarcely have been less hostile towards him than the Pharisees.' Thus the sect was forced to 'settle in Qumran in the desert, far from a Jerusalem given over to wickedness, and to organize itself apart from the official Synagogue in order to establish and perpetuate there the true Israel until the Day of Judgement' (84, p. 91 n.). In the so-called scroll of the *Rule*, the text 'prepare ye in the wilderness the way of the Lord' (Isa. xl, 3), which the gospel writers apply to the preaching of the Baptist, is taken to mean the sect's retreat from Jerusalem into the desert (84, p. 92 and notes).

Among the scrolls discovered in the first cave was a commentary of Habakkuk which interprets the prophecies in the light of what were then contemporary events. The author's method is

---

'general relationship of the Qumran sect to the Essenes' (132, p. 101). Both Burrows and Harrison discuss other views at some length and make it clear that no other Jewish sect contemporary with the Qumran monastery has such striking affinities with the doctrines of the scrolls. The building is clearly pre-Christian, so that the sectarians could not have been either Christians or Jewish Zealots, who formed a prominent party only after the death of Herod. Black (31a, p. 4) accepts the identification of the sectarians with the Essenes, with the qualification that 'the Essene group who held the fort at Qumran at the outbreak of the First Revolt (and thus the last custodians of the Scrolls) had ceased . . . to be the pacific ascetics idealized by Josephus and Philo; they had by then thrown in their lot with Zealot and Pharisaic groups'.

to quote a section of the biblical text and then immediately introduce his commentary with the words 'The explanation of this is'.
The interpretation exhibits the usual arbitrariness of sectarian
exegesis. The words of the prophet, describing the invasion of the
Chaldeans who captured Jerusalem in 586 BC, are violently transposed to the historical and theological circumstances in which the
commentator wrote. As in Daniel, Enoch and other apocalyptic
works, the style is essentially sibylline; the persons and events
are indicated by allusions without giving proper names, save
very rarely. But these allusions were of course intended to be
understood (84, p. 257). Allegro remarks that 'there are some very
good examples in the Habakkuk commentary of the writer deliberately altering his text to fit his interpretation' (12, p. 137).
We have seen the same thing in the gospels.

The commentary identifies the tyranny to which reference is
made in Habakkuk as that of a 'Wicked Priest' or 'Man of Lies'
who is described as having persecuted the elect of God—the sect
to which the commentator belonged and whose leader is referred
to as 'The Teacher of Righteousness'. We are told that he was a
priest, that he demanded from his disciples the exact observation
of the Jewish law, and that God made known to him all the
secrets of divine revelation. The commentator also regards the
end of the world as imminent and thinks that only those who
believe in the Teacher will be saved (84, pp. 262–4, 364).

It seems to be generally agreed that the Wicked Priest was the
high priest of Jerusalem, and that he and his tribunal condemned
the Teacher of Righteousness to some sort of punishment. There
is also wide agreement that this punishment was death—although
Daniélou has recently disputed this, and said that, if true, it
would impair 'the originality of Christianity in its very essence'
(76, pp. 53, 58). Now the Habakkuk commentary expressly says
that the Priest 'swallowed up the Teacher of Righteousness in
the anger of his fury', and Dupont-Sommer points out that the
usual meaning of 'swallow up' in Hebrew is 'to do away with, to
kill' (84, p. 266). Again, the commentator quotes the biblical
text 'O traitors, why do you look on and keep silence when the
wicked swallows up the man more righteous than he?' Then he
comments: 'The explanation of this concerns the . . . [men] who
were silent at the time of the chastisement of the Teacher of
Righteousness and gave him no help against the Man of Lies who
despised the Law in the midst of their coun[cil]' (Quot. 84, p. 261).

The nature of the punishment to which the Teacher was condemned is not indicated here, but the biblical text which forms the
basis of this comment uses this same word 'swallowed up', and
this seems to suggest that he was condemned to death. The evidence is not decisive, but Dupont-Sommer is justified in saying
that the Teacher was 'very probably' put to death (84, p. 360).

The commentator also explains that the Teacher has been
avenged by a catastrophe which befell his persecutors on the Day
of Atonement. The allusion seems to be to some great historical
event, and since the persecutors of the Teacher are the official
priesthood of the country, Dupont-Sommer interprets it as a
reference to the capture of Jerusalem by Pompey in 63 BC,
which in Josephus' description was accomplished with great
slaughter on the Day of Atonement. After telling of the persecution of the Teacher, the commentator adds: 'But at the time of
the feast of rest of the Day of Atonement he appeared before
them to swallow them up and cause them to stumble on the Day
of Fasting, their Sabbath of rest' (Quot. 84, p. 266). 'Cause them
to stumble' means 'destroy them'. This can be proved from the
use of this phrase in another context (84, p. 312 and note). The
whole passage may refer to a supernatural appearance of the
Teacher, who returned from the dead to confound his enemies—
although Dupont-Sommer notes that the Hebrew verb used may
also be translated 'he revealed himself unto them', with no supernatural implication.[1]

Dupont-Sommer then gives other evidence to show that the
Habakkuk Commentary must have been composed in the time of
the Roman domination and not in the preceding Seleucid period
(198–63 BC). He discusses the passages where the author comments
on the sections of the biblical text in which are found descriptions
of the Chaldean invaders. By virtue of his allegorical exegesis
the author applies the biblical sentences to new invaders whom he

---

[1] Some authorities have supposed that the 'he' forming the subject of this
verb is the Wicked Priest. On this interpretation the passage states that he
disturbed the sectaries on the Day of Atonement. Dupont-Sommer denies
that this construction is admissible and says that the subject of the verb can
only be the Teacher of Righteousness. He is able further to support his
argument that the victims of this apparition (or revelation) were the un-
faithful Jews and not the sectaries by showing that, in another of the scrolls,
the same verse from Habakkuk as is here the subject of commentary is applied
to the Jews who allowed themselves to be led astray by evil guides, particularly
in connection with the celebration of the feasts, and to their eventual punishment (84, p. 266 n.).

calls the Kittim. In Daniel (xi, 30) this word is used to designate the Romans (see above, p. 79), and this seems to be its meaning in the Habakkuk commentary, for the commentator tells that 'the Kittim sacrifice to their standards, and . . . their weapons of war are the object of their religion' (Quot. 84, p. 343). The cult of the military standards in the Roman legions is well attested, while there is no evidence that the Seleucid armies behaved in this way.

The commentator also refers to the passage from Habakkuk which reads '(they come) from afar, they fly like the eagle swift to devour'. He applies it to the Kittim and says: 'They come from afar, *from the islands of the sea*, to devour the peoples like eagles, without satisfaction' (Quot. 84, p. 344). The words he has interpolated show that he thinks of the Kittim as coming from distant islands, peninsulas or sea-coasts—for in Hebrew the word for 'islands' is often used in these other senses. This allusion makes sense if interpreted as referring to Italy, a peninsula 1,250 miles from Palestine, but no sense at all if applied to Syria, the home of the Seleucid sovereigns, which is an inland empire near to Palestine. Harrison agrees (132, p. 68) that the Kittim of the commentary are probably the forces of Imperial Rome, and that the commentary was therefore written after 63 BC. Burrows also concedes that the Kittim means the Romans (46, pp. 194–203).

Who the Teacher was and whether he lived shortly before 63 BC or in the previous century of the sect's existence is still disputed. Dupont-Sommer has given what seems cogent evidence that the Wicked Priest who persecuted him can be identified with Hyrcanus II, the son of Alexander Jannaeus. But as far as the present study is concerned these issues are of no account. All that matters to the question of Christian origins is that the sect which believed in the Teacher is definitely pre-Christian and flourished in the two centuries up to AD 68.

For more information about the Teacher we turn to the so-called *Damascus Document*, discovered in a Cairo synagogue in 1896. It was written by a member of a sect which is called the 'New Covenant in the Land of Damascus'. Several fragments of the work have been found in the Qumran caves, and Dupont-Sommer affirms that 'there is no longer any doubt that the sect of the *Damascus Document* is identical with the sect of the scrolls from the desert of Judah' (84, p. 40). The scroll of the *Rule* of the Qumran community repeatedly refers to the sect as 'the Covenant',

I

and in the Habakkuk commentary the sect is referred to as the 'New'—there follows a lacuna which Dupont-Sommer fills with the word 'covenant' (84, p. 259 and note). The significance of the name 'New Covenant' is obvious enough. The idea was that 'these Jews were in their own eyes, and to the exclusion of all other Jews, representatives of the only Covenant agreeable to God, the eternal and final Covenant. The old Covenant concluded under the leadership of Moses had been broken because of Israel's infidelity. The new community was the "little Remnant" foretold by the Prophets, i.e. the true Israel' (84, p. 42).

Even the cautious Professor Harrison agrees that the Covenanters of Damascus have 'striking affinities with the Qumran community' (132, p. 87). These Covenanters, he adds, were 'a group of Priests in Jerusalem who were apparently ousted during a reform movement. They styled themselves "Sons of Zadok" and under the leadership of one known as the "Star" (in fulfilment of Num. xxiv, 17) they migrated to Damascus, where they organized the party of the New Covenant. This sect assumed the nature of a monastic order in Judaism, and flourished under the inspiration of a prominent leader spoken of as the "Righteous Teacher".' This Teacher may well have been the same person, as the Star, even though the text says that the sect had existed for twenty years before the coming of the Teacher (84, p. 122). As in the Qumran Habakkuk commentary, there are references to the persecution of the sectarians by 'the Man of Lies', and to what Dupont-Sommer calls 'a great event still fresh in their memories, an unforgettable catastrophe that had recently struck the wicked congregation. The instrument of this vengeance was a person whom the author describes as "chief of the Kings of Yawan", i.e. Greece, the Hellenized Orient' (84, p. 120). In Dupont-Sommer's opinion this is again a reference to Pompey and his capture of Jerusalem. Burrows brings out the force of this argument when he notes that the expression 'chief of the kings'

does not imply that the person so designated was himself a king, but that all the rulers of the Hellenistic kingdoms were subject to him. The eulogy of the Romans in I Maccabees viii, 1–16 stresses the fact that the Romans, none of whom 'ever put on a diadem' (verse 14) have conquered the kings. The *imperium* conferred upon Pompey by the Senate made him master of the East. The Roman authors glorify his personal dominion over all the conquered kings. None could more fitly be called 'the chief of the kings of Yawan' (46, p. 223).

The *Damascus Document* envisages the Day of Judgement, involving the destruction of the Man of Lies or the Wicked Priest and his adherents, some forty years after the death of the Teacher of Righteousness (132, p. 92; 84, p. 140). Dupont-Sommer argues that, immediately following this event, the Teacher was expected to rise from the dead and usher in the Messianic era. He bases this view on the passage which designates the present time as 'the time of wickedness' which will persist 'until the coming of the Teacher of Righteousness at the end of days' (Quot. 84, p. 131). He thinks too that this naturally suggests that the dead teacher was regarded as the Messiah—something that one could not have inferred from the Habakkuk commentary alone.[1] However, another passage says that 'none of all those men who have entered the New Covenant . . . but have turned back and betrayed it . . . shall be counted in the Assembly of the people or inscribed in their register from the day when the Unique Teacher was taken till the coming of the Anointed'. Daniélou (76, p. 65) takes this text as decisive proof that the Teacher and the Anointed or expected Messiah were regarded as different persons. But Dupont-Sommer's opinion is that it is quite intelligible that the sectarians should call their leader the Teacher of Righteousness when referring to his earthly career but the Messiah when they think of his coming at the end of time. He points out that according to Acts ii, 36 it was likewise only after his death that Jesus became 'Lord and Messiah' (84, p. 139 and note).

There is no doubt that the Damascus Covenanters and the Qumran sectarians had the same Messianic expectations. The coming of 'the Anointed of Aaron and Israel' is mentioned in the *Rule* of the Qumran community (Quot. 84, p. 94) as well as in the *Damascus Document*. There is wide agreement that this phrase 'the Anointed of Aaron and Israel' means two Anointeds—a priestly Messiah of the line of Aaron and a lay one from the line of David,

---

[1] Black does not agree that the Teacher was the Messiah who was to return. He holds that the term 'Rightful Teacher' designates an office which could be held by different individuals, and was not the name for any single historical person. The 'coming of the Teacher at the end of the days' he interprets to mean: the coming forth, from the midst of the sect in God's good time, of a High Priest who would rule in Jerusalem, and not in exile in the desert (31a, pp. 7, 10).

the latter being a war leader who will defeat the enemies of the Jews. Both in the scrolls and in the *Damascus Document* this lay Messiah is also referred to as the 'Prince of the Congregation' who will devastate the earth with his sceptre and slay the ungodly with the breath of his lips (Quot. 84, pp. 112–13 and notes)—as Jesus was expected to do (II Thess. ii, 8). This idea of two Messiahs is common in Jewish thought, and Allegro notes that the Jesus of the epistle to the Hebrews combines both their functions, for in this epistle Jesus is said to be the Davidic Messiah but nevertheless a high priest as well (12, p. 154).

The Qumran sectarians and the Covenanters, then, believed in two Messiahs, and the question at issue is whether the priestly Messiah was regarded as the resurrected priestly Teacher, or whether they were thought of as two different persons. Professor Harrison rightly says that in no document is the Righteous Teacher expressly identified with either of the two Messianic figures (132, p. 70). But he concedes that he was 'a personage of Messianic proportions', and we have seen that, according to Dupont-Sommer's interpretation of the *Damascus Document*, he was expected to be resurrected and appear at the end of days. The same idea appears in one of the scrolls where it is said that 'the Branch of David will arise with the Seeker of the Law and . . . will sit on the throne of Zion at the end of days' (Quot. 84, p. 313). The Seeker of the Law seems to be another name for the Teacher of Righteousness—a name which is also used to designate him in the *Damascus Document*. So in the scroll quoted, it is not only said that the Teacher will return at the end of time, but he is also associated with the Davidic Messiah. The inference is that he is thought of as the other, priestly, Messiah. The evidence does seem to suggest that, even if he was not originally regarded as the same as this Messiah of Aaron, he could easily have become confused with this personage in the course of the two centuries in which the sect flourished.

One of the scrolls, called the *Hymn Scroll*, consists of Psalms in the first person, and one of them makes it clear that faith in the Psalmist is necessary to salvation. He is represented as saying to God: 'At the time of Judgement Thou wilt declare all of them guilty that attack me, distinguishing through me between the just and the guilty.' The words 'through me' show that he makes himself into a sort of touchstone: depending on how men have reacted towards him, with faith or incredulity, so they will be recognized at the time of judgement as the elect or the outcast (84, p. 223 and note). This, we recall, was the doctrine of the commentary on Habakkuk concerning the Teacher of Righteousness. From this and other parallels Dupont-Sommer infers that the Psalmist is identical with the Teacher of Righteousness. It does not, of course, follow that the Psalms were written by him—only that they represent what his disciples were prepared to put into his mouth.

The *Hymn Scroll* also represents the Psalmist as the head and founder of the Church, which is likened to a building constructed on rock and impregnable. This Church is further said to serve the elect as an impregnable refuge during the war against the forces of evil at the end of time (84, p. 220 and notes). Dupont-Sommer reminds us of the parallel in Mt. 'and on this rock will I build my Church and the gates of hell shall not prevail against it'. Another scroll, a commentary on Psalm xxxvii, also represents the sect founded by the Teacher as an edifice. It explains two verses of the Psalm as referring to 'the Priest, the Teacher of (Righteousness whom) . . . (God) established to build for Himself the Congregation . . .' (84, pp. 272, 366). This, incidentally, is one of the passages which prove that the Teacher was a priest.

Another characteristic of the hymns of the *Hymn Scroll* is that in them the Psalmist repeatedly applies Isaiah's servant songs to himself, just as Christian writers were to apply them to Jesus a century later (84, p. 361). For instance, both the Psalmist and Jesus declare themselves to be the person whom Isaiah (lxi, 1–2) says was 'sent to bring good tidings to the humble . . . to proclaim the year of the Lord's favour . . . to console the afflicted' (84, pp. 252, 362; Lk. iv, 16–22). In the hymns the Psalmist repeatedly appears as the man of sorrows, overwhelmed by blows and sickness, despised and rejected. Dupont-Sommer comments that 'this common reference to the Servant is highly significant in that it establishes a particular relationship between the two prophets which is quite unique' (84, p. 372).

The evidence does seem to warrant the conclusion that the Essenes had a Messiah, or a Teacher who could easily be confused with the Messiah, who was persecuted, and probably killed, before 63 BC. Some scholars have argued that his death took place by crucifixion, but the evidence for this is very inconclusive.[1] If

[1] The Qumran commentary on Nahum mentions (in an oblique way) Alexander Jannaeus' persecution of the Pharisees, and having stated that

he is in fact identical with the speaker in the *Hymn Scroll*, then his sufferings and death may have been believed to have a redemptive or atoning significance, like those of Isaiah's servant of Yahweh.[1]

Most Christian scholars admit that many sayings ascribed to Jesus in the NT were not uttered by him at all, and the climate of ideas which enabled them to be put into his mouth has become much more intelligible in the light of the scrolls. For instance Mk. iv, 12, where he says he is deliberately unintelligible in order to prevent any but the elect from being saved, is said by Kuhn (164, p. 85) to be 'very much in accord with Essene theology'. Josephus tells that they took an oath 'to conceal nothing from the members of the sect, as also to reveal nothing to any others but them, even though violence unto death be used against them' (84, p. 46). The scrolls confirm this, and stipulate that nothing is to be communicated to outsiders.

Christianity has been held to be indebted not only to Essene theology but also to Essene ritual. One of the most prominent

---

crucifixion was contrary to the customs of Israel, the commentator goes on: 'But he who was hanged alive upon (the wood)'—there then follows an enigmatic phrase which Dupont-Sommer suggests means 'they will call upon him'. He adds: if this is the correct reading 'the phrase refers to someone who suffered punishment on the cross and became an object of invocation. Who can this extraordinary person be? By whom could he have been crucified? There is nothing to lead us to conclude that it was by Jannaeus; his death may have been ordered by a successor of Jannaeus. The phrase may spring from an association of ideas: although crucifixion is a scandal, there is one crucified man who will on the contrary, become for some an object of prayer' (84, p. 269). Dupont-Sommer seems to be suggesting that the victim may have been the Teacher of Righteousness, condemned to crucifixion by the Wicked Priest whom he regards as the son of Jannaeus. Allegro puts this suggestion more emphatically, saying that we must ask ourselves why it was that the commentator should make any mention of Jannaeus' practice of crucifying his political enemies, and why also he should stress that this was never before done in Israel, being essentially a foreign punishment. A possible answer to these questions, he says, is that 'the sectarians had particular cause to recall this activity of Jannaeus, since their master had suffered the same cruel death, the recognized punishment of a rebel' (12, p. 100). Allegro also notes here that, in the Nahum commentary, an enemy of the sect, called 'the Lion of Wrath', is said to have hung men alive. This probably refers to crucifixion, and it is possible to infer that the Lion is the 'Wicked Priest' or 'Man of Lies' who persecuted the Teacher and that the persecution took the form of crucifixion.

[1] Black (31a, p. 15) affirms that the author of some of the Hymns 'does see in his sufferings and death a redemptive or atoning significance'. Black refers also to Père Starcky's claim to have found a text (still unpublished) which depicts the Qumran priestly Messiah as the Servant of the Lord. If substantiated, this claim would prove the existence of 'a Jewish doctrine of a redemptive Messiah in the pre-Christian period' (p. 14).

Essene rites was baptism. Unlike Christian baptism, and that of John the Baptist, the Essene rite was frequently repeated: Josephus tells that they were obliged to take a daily ritual bath. But Essene and Christian baptism are alike in that both serve as a rite of initiation. Admission to the Essene baths was a sign of acceptance in the fellowship. No novice or non-member was allowed to touch the water (12, p. 107) and a long tirade from one of the scrolls warns that baptism alone is insufficient, that humility and obedience to God's ordinances are necessary for cleanliness (Quot. 84, p. 77). This warning against an entirely materialistic and magical interpretation of rites which do not purify the flesh unless the spirit is truly turned to God only make sense if the Qumran community was essentially a baptist sect (84, p. 49). John the Baptist took the same attitude. That he regarded his baptism as a sacrament which mediated salvation is clear from his words to the Pharisees who seek it from him: 'Ye brood of vipers, who has warned you to flee from the wrath to come?' But he also believed that it would save only those who truly repented. Black tells us that the scrolls have proved that the Essene baptismal rites 'were practised in relation to a movement of repentance, of entry into a new Covenant (and a new Covenanted Israel, the sect itself) in preparation for an impending divine judgement . . . Like Johannite "baptism for repentance unto the remission of sins", the entire setting of Qumran repentance and enrolment into the new Israel is eschatological' (31, p. 97), i.e. is a preparation for the end of the world.

Allegro mentions 'one rite peculiar to Qumran which probably became the sacramental focus of their worship, just as basically the same act did for the Christian Church'. This is the banquet which, according to Allegro, the Essenes believed the Messiah would hold for the elect who survived the great purging of the world in the last days—an idea which also appears in the NT (e.g. Mt. viii, 11; Lk. xxii, 30). Allegro thinks that they frequently performed a rite which was supposed to represent what this banquet would be like, and the 'chief actors', as he puts it, were the two Messiahs (the priestly and the lay Davidic one) and an assembly of priests and laymen who sit at the communion table in order of rank (12, p. 115). Burrows, however, does not agree that there is decisive evidence that the community's communal meals were liturgical anticipations of the Messianic banquet, although he notes that the idea of such a banquet is well known in other Jewish sources (46, p. 101). Rowley thinks that the sect's meals were ordinary monastic communal meals in which the Messiah played 'no special part' (230a, p. 145). However, his own summary of one of the relevant passages from the *Rule* scroll hardly supports this view. He says:

This passage describes what is often called the messianic banquet. It says that in the days of the Messiah, he should come with the priests and members of the sect and they should sit down in the order of their dignity. No one should eat until the priest had first blessed the food, and then the priest should eat first, and after him the Messiah of Israel, followed by the rest of the company, each in the order of his dignity. The text continues by saying that *in accordance with this rule the members of the sect should act at every meal, when at least ten are assembled* (italics mine: for the whole passage see 84, pp. 108–9 cf. p. 85 for a further passage where the food blessed by the priest is specified as 'first-fruits of bread and wine').

Ten is the quorum for a Jewish service, and the mention of this minimum points to the cultic character of the meal. Josephus describes this Essene communal meal as 'a sacred repast in which no one participated unless they had bathed and clothed themselves in sacred garments. The place where the brethren ate was "as a holy place", forbidden to the profane, and an august and mysterious silence reigned there. A priest presided over the meal and prayed before and after it, and it was forbidden to eat before the initial prayer.' This meal 'was in fact, a sacrament, the holiest sacrament of the sect' (84, pp. 49, 50).

We have already seen that Dupont-Sommer identifies the priestly Messiah with the Teacher of Righteousness at his second coming. So he infers not only that 'the supper which the members of the New Covenant celebrated each day referred essentially to the Supper which would take place later when the Kingdom of God had come', but also that 'the humble daily supper was therefore a *constant reminder of the revered Teacher*, and the presiding priest was, so to speak, the representative of, or substitute for, the Priest *par excellence*' (84, p. 50. Italics mine). If this view is correct, the parallel with the Christian Lord's Supper, which is also a 'constant reminder of the revered teacher' could hardly be more striking. Rowley, however, denies that there is any reference to the priestly Messiah in this Essene ritual. He takes the reference to 'the priest' to mean, not the priestly Messiah who is to take precedence over the lay Messiah, but 'just the person who happens to be the head of the community at the time' (230a, p. 146). The passages from the *Rule* scroll make it clear that no one may touch the bread or the wine until it has been blessed by 'the priest'. Once he has done this, he distributes it to his priests, and only then may the Davidic Messiah do the same for his company of laymen. If 'the priest' is a mere abbot, and not the priestly Messiah (or someone impersonating him), it is difficult to understand why he should be given precedence over the Davidic Messiah.

The evidence does establish that the Essenes had a ritual meal which began with the blessing of bread and wine by a priest. Whether the ritual was associated with the Teacher of Righteousness is not agreed, but it was certainly the ritual of a sect which venerated this person as a leader of Messianic proportions, and if Christians assimilated or adapted this Essene ritual, they may well have linked it with such a person. We shall see, in the following section, that both Jewish and pagan ideas have been important in the evolution of the Christian sacred meal.

CHAPTER TEN

Christian Origins

(i) The evolution of the Lord's supper

In the Dionysiac eucharist a bull was slain and eaten as the god. According to Murray there was originally no belief in a god, but only worship of the bull or other animal whose flesh was eaten and whose blood was drunk in order to obtain his *mana* or vital power. He mentions an Arab tribe which cut a camel to pieces alive and consumed every fragment before the life had gone out of the flesh and blood. He adds that among the early Greeks it was the *mana* of the bull that was most sought; his enormous strength, his size and his rage were obviously worth assimilating. But whence the idea that there was a god (conceived as having human form) over and above the bull? Murray answers: 'The *mana* of the slain beast is in the hide and head and blood and fur, and the man who wants to be in thorough contact with the divinity gets inside the skin and wraps himself deep in it.' Not all men would have the right to do so, and the strongest claimant is 'the priest, the medicine-man, the divine king'. According to the theory, this man is originally the only kind of 'god' (apart from the animal) that his society knows. The *mana* he wears gives him immense powers over the weather, the spring crops and autumn floods, and the fertility of the tribe. But his predictions and promises are bound to miscarry from time to time, and his most obvious defence against criticism is to say that he himself is only the representative of an all powerful god who is somewhere up in the skies. Murray has thus constructed a path which leads readily from the divine beast to the anthropomorphic god (196, pp. 19–26).

Once the idea of a god had been evolved, the bull was regarded as representing or symbolizing him, and eating it brought the worshipper into communion with him. Dodds tells us that 'the culminating act of the ritual dance to Dionysus was the tearing to pieces and eating raw of an animal body', and that evidence suggests that 'the cult once permitted the rending, even the rending and eating, of God in the shape of man' (81, pp. XVI-XIX). Once the god had been invented and endowed with human form, a man would naturally be thought a better representative of him than an animal.

A common modification of the original rite was to replace the divine victim with an edible figure which brought the worshipper into some sort of mystic communion with the deity. Such rituals existed not only in the Middle East but also among the Aztecs, whose priests consecrated an image of their deity Vitzili-putzli in dough, broke it and distributed it so that all who partook of it received a portion of the divine substance into themselves. Frazer comments that these pre-Christian Mexicans were thus fully acquainted with the doctrine of transubstantiation (95, p. 490). Such ceremonial eating seems to have been common in the east at the time of the rise of Christianity, for Justin, after describing the institution of the Lord's Supper as narrated in the gospels, goes on to say: 'which the wicked devils have imitated in the mysteries of Mithra, commanding the same thing to be done. For bread and a cup of water are placed with certain incantation in the mystic rites of one who is being initiated' (Quot. 222, p. 307. The Christian cultic meal sometimes consisted of bread and water; see below, p. 264). The nature of Justin's reproach makes it clear that the Mithraic rite is the older. He does not accuse the Mithraists of simple copying, but says that evil spirits have betrayed Christian truths. That the Lord's Supper existed before Christianity is shown even more clearly by I Cor. x, 21, where Paul tells the Corinthian flock that they 'cannot drink the cup of the Lord and the cup of devils', nor 'partake of the table of the Lord and of the table of devils'. Either this means that the pagan cults of Mithra, Dionysus, etc., had their ritual of Holy Communion prior to and independently of Christianity, or else we must assume that in the very beginnings of the Church at Corinth they had already copied an institution originated by a poor and despised sect of Jews (220, pp. 356-7).

The original purpose of the ritual (to assimilate the unrestrained

potency which man envies in the beasts) had been lost from sight
long before our era. In the Dionysiac ritual the tearing and eating
came to be regarded not only as a means of assimilating the god
and his power, but also as a commemoration of the day when the
infant Dionysus was himself torn to pieces and devoured (81, pp.
XVII, XX). Here we have once again a myth which was devised
to explain a ritual (whose real origin had been lost) and which was
of great importance for the subsequent evolution. It stressed the
idea of the dying god, and once it became current it would be
easy to connect the ideas associated with eating the god with
those associated with his death and resurrection. Just as witnessing
the dramatic portrayal of the god's death and resurrection enabled
the onlooker himself to conquer death and be assured of immortality, so eating the god and acquiring his power (including
his power over death) had a like effect. We have in fact already
seen that both rituals were included among the important
ceremonies of the mystery religions at the beginning of our era.
In some cases, the devotees believed they were eating magic food,
conferring immortality, from the sacred vessels of their cult.
Weston compares this with the Christian sacred meal at which
the worshipper becomes one with his god, receiving thereby the
assurance of eternal life. She quotes from the liturgy: 'The Body
of Our Lord Jesus Christ preserve thy body and soul unto
everlasting life' (286, pp. 146-7). And Murray tells how 'the
mystic congregations . . . in their most holy gatherings, solemnly
partook of the blood of a bull, which was, by a mystery, the blood
of Dionysus-Zagreus himself, the "Bull of God", slain in sacrifice
for the purification of man'. Thus already in the Orphic mysteries
eating the god was closely linked with 'belief in the sacrifice of
Dionysus himself and the purification of man by his blood'
(200, pp. 82-83). In sum, the pre-Christian mystery religions
show how easy it was for eating the god to become closely linked
with the purification of mankind by his death and resurrection,
and how the god's rebirth could be connected with the rebirth
of those who ate him, exactly as is the case in the Christian cult.

To understand the specifically Christian evolution we must
start with the common meal, love-feast or Agape. Paul's reference
to it specifies a regularly repeated communal meal at which food is
blessed and eaten. He calls it 'the Lord's Supper', but the term
that became prevalent is 'Eucharist' or 'giving of thanks'. The
reference was originally to the prayers spoken at the meal, and

only later came to designate the whole sacramental celebration (42, p. 144). The meal mentioned by Paul and by the *Didache* (on this work, see note on p. 277 below) is not a token one, but enough of a feast to be capable of degenerating into gormandizing (I, Cor. xi, 20–1). But Paul's command that believers, in order not to endanger its sacredness, are to satisfy their hunger at home (verses 22, 34) points to future developments, where the actual meal becomes the semblance of one.

The meal included a rite (which might precede or follow the full repast) of breaking and eating a loaf consecrated by prayer. Lietzmann notes that this rite is identical with that performed at Jewish religious meals which could be celebrated by any gathering of friends (170, pp. 202, 210). And as in the contemporary pagan cults, one purpose of the meal was to bring believers into true fellowship. 'We are . . . one body, for we all partake of the one bread' (I Cor. x, 17). Schweitzer comments that this 'does not mean that they all eat one loaf, but only that they all share bread which has been consecrated by the same blessing' (248, p. 271). Paul severely rebukes the Corinthians for scrambling over the meal so that it fails in its purpose of promoting fellowship.

The meal of course also aimed at promoting fellowship with God, and Schweitzer argues that what was envisaged was a kind of table-fellowship with Christ. It was thought that those who take part in it will be united with him at the Messianic feast, which he is to give to the elect when he comes in his glory to end the world. We have seen that according to Burrows (46, p. 101), this idea that the Messiah would hold a banquet is well known in Jewish literature, and that some have argued that the regularly repeated communal meal of bread and wine of the Essenes was a rite which enacted what they thought it would be like. If Schweitzer's interpretation of the meal-celebration of the primitive Church is correct, then the early Christians were performing a rite already familiar to the environment in which their faith originated.

As evidence that the early Christian communal meal aimed at establishing table-fellowship with the future Christ, Schweitzer points to the *Didache*, from which we learn that the liturgy of the rite was accompanied by a fervent prayer for the second coming. Paul, too (or his interpolator), says: 'As often as ye eat this bread and drink the cup, ye proclaim the Lord's death till he come' (I Cor. xi, 26), showing that the celebration is a remembering of

the death of Jesus which looks forward to his coming again—
which is what some scholars have held the Essene meal to have
been. The idea is stated even more clearly in the gospels. Mt.
xxvi, 29 represents Jesus as concluding the celebration of the Last
Supper by saying: 'I will not drink henceforth of this fruit of the
vine until that day when I drink it new with you in my Father's
kingdom.' This, says Schweitzer, can only mean that the disciples
will shortly be gathered with him at the Messianic feast. We saw
already (above, p. 257) that the idea that there will be such a feast
is stated in a number of gospel passages.

If we can believe Acts ii, 42, 46, the first Christians ate together
daily, as did the Essenes. The rite is called a 'breaking of bread'.
And when we are told that it was celebrated 'with rejoicing' we
may connect such expression of joy with eschatological emotions,
viz. the expectation that the second coming would speedily
occur (170, pp. 216–17).

The passages in Acts make no mention of wine, and Cullmann
observes that a number of early Christian texts show 'that there
was in existence a cultic meal of which the essential element was
bread, with no mention whatsoever of wine. This is the case in
the Acts of John (Chapters 106–110) and in the Acts of Thomas
(Chapters 27, 49–50, 133). Sometimes another element is added to
the bread, but this is not necessarily wine, and also not always a
drink. Until the third century, in certain districts, blessed bread
was taken with water instead of wine.' He concludes that 'the
Eucharistic meal of the first Christians was, in origin, an ordinary
meal. The formula "to break bread" usually meant "to take a
meal". With the bread one ate and drank whatever one wanted,
because the nature of the food had not as yet any particular
importance.' It had not at that stage become identified with the
body and blood of Christ (73, p. 510).

At some stage this Christian meal came to be regarded as
sacrificial, and this can be explained as a natural development
(already represented in the Pauline letters), influenced by kindred
pagan and Jewish ceremonies. Paul was familiar with meals at
which food was sacrificed to 'demons', i.e pagan deities, and then
eaten. He says that such meals bring about communion with
demons, just as the Christian meal effects communion with God
(see above, p. 144). In both cases the idea was that the spirit or
power or πνεῦμα of the deity enters into the food sacrificed or
consecrated to him, and thus passes into the bodies of those who

eat it, conferring immortality on them (170, pp. 249–51).[1] Paul was also familiar with Jewish sacrificial meals which effect communion with 'the altar', i.e. Yahweh.[2]

In the pagan sacramental meals of the time, another dominant idea was 'communion with a once dead and risen deity, in whose fate the partaker receives a share through the sacramental meal, as we know from the mysteries of Attis and Mithra' (42, p. 148). I Cor. similarly alleges that the Christian meal effects communion with the dying and resurrected god, in that the bread represents his body and the wine his blood. Paul's letters thus contain the ideas that the meal (1) conferred fellowship among believers, and (2) ensured participation in the coming Messianic banquet; also that (3) the food contained the $\pi\nu\epsilon\hat{\upsilon}\mu\alpha$ and (4) brought about mystic communion with the dying and resurrected god. Lietzmann has given evidence that in the Christian cult the first two of these ideas were rapidly supplemented by the third, but both he and Cullmann have shown that the fourth, although present in Paul, long remained foreign to Christian sacred repasts. For instance, the *Didache* represents the Lord's supper as a meal which mediates salvation, without, however, making it a mystery which represents Jesus' redeeming death. It will be worth our while to study details of the *Didache*'s account of the celebration.

The text specifies a 'Eucharist', a formula of thanksgiving, to be pronounced before the holy meal began, and first of all over the wine cup. The words are:

> We give thee thanks, Our Father,
> for the holy vine of thy servant David,
> which thou hast made known to us by thy servant Jesus.
> To thee be glory for ever and ever.

Loisy regards this as an adaptation of the 'grace' said by Jews at their meals, which runs: 'blessed be God who created the fruit

---

[1] That the flesh and blood of Jesus confer immortality is stated in Jn. vi, 54. Ignatius also designates the Lord's Supper as a means of attaining immortality (Eph. xx, 2), and, according to Leipoldt, says this by means of an expression deriving from the cult of Isis (169, p. 85). In an earlier work (168, pp. 49–50) Leipoldt stresses dionysian influence on Ignatius, and points out that Dionysus was the most extensively worshipped of all the pagan gods who died a violent death and rose again.

[2] The Jews who eat the sacrifices, are, says Paul (I Cor. x, 18), 'sharers in the altar'. The Greek has κοινωνοὶ τοῦ θυσιαστηρίου, which means 'fellows or comrades of God', for θυσιαστηρίον has been shown to be a substitute for the divine name.

of the vine'. From this Jewish thanksgiving formula for ordinary drink, the Christian formula has become a thanksgiving for 'the holy vine of David'. This, says Loisy, is 'clearly the vine in Psalm lxxx, here taken mystically for the spiritual Church, the vine of salvation' (177, p. 231 f.). The *Didache* then gives the formula to be spoken over the broken bread:

> We give thee thanks, O our Father,
> for life and knowledge [gnosis],
> which thou hast made known to us by thy servant Jesus.
> To thee be glory for ever and ever.
> As this bread was scattered on the mountains,
> then, gathered in, became one,
> Thus may thy Church be gathered in
> from the ends of the earth in thy kingdom.
> For thine are glory and power,
> by Jesus Christ, for ever and ever (ix, 3–4).

Here, again, the situation is that in which the traditional Jewish thanksgiving for ordinary food would be appropriate (It runs: 'blessed be He who caused the earth to bring forth bread'), but instead, thanks are given for the gifts of 'life and knowledge'. By 'life' eternal life or salvation seems to be meant. And, as we learn from verse 5, the supper has now become a meal restricted to the baptized, and is 'the holy thing which the Lord commanded not to be given to dogs'. Thus at this stage mystical power seems to be ascribed to the elements of bread and wine—they confer salvation on the partakers. There is no suggestion that they are the body and blood of Christ, and neither 'body' nor 'flesh' nor 'blood' is mentioned throughout the whole of this liturgy. The meal is a full one, for chapter x stipulates:

> When you have eaten enough, this shall be your thanksgiving:
> We thank thee, Holy Father,
> for thy Holy name,
> which thou hast caused to dwell in our hearts,
> And for knowledge, faith and immortality
> Which thou hast made known to us by thy servant Jesus.
> To thee be glory forever and ever!
> Thou, Master almighty,
> Thou hast created all things to the honour of thy name.

Food and drink hast thou given for the making glad of man
for which they render thee thanks;
But thou hast also gladdened us with food and drink of the
    spirit and of eternal life
by Jesus thy servant
To thee glory for ever and ever! . . . (x, 1–5).

Robinson (225, § 4) agrees with Loisy in regarding all three of these blessings as Christian adaptations of Jewish graces. In concluding the meal, the president of the company prays for the second coming, saying: 'Come thou Gracious One and let the world pass away' (x, 6). Thus at this stage the meal was still closely connected with eschatological expectations.

We can, then, distinguish two independent strands in the development of the Lord's Supper: the bread and wine sometimes stand for the food of the Messianic banquet and the πνεῦμα of the Lord, and sometimes for the flesh and blood of Jesus. In some writers the two strands are tied together, in others not. The latter of the two ideas is stressed in the epistles of Ignatius, where the writer complains that certain heretics 'abstain from Eucharist and prayer, because they allow not that the Eucharist is the flesh of our Saviour Jesus Christ, that flesh which suffered for our sins, which the Father raised up' (Smyrn. VII). Evidently this interpretation of the meal met with some resistance. But as Schweitzer points out, it would be bound to drive out the other as the eschatological expectation on which the other was based failed to come true. And once the idea that the meal anticipated the Messianic banquet had gone, it would be cut down from a full repast to a distribution of the elements of salvation, namely bread and wine which had been blessed, and which enabled the consumer to partake of the body and blood of Christ (248, p. 272). This stage has been reached by Justin Martyr (I Apol., Chapters 65–7).

The transition to this conception resulted from associating the meal with sacrifice. Already in the *Didache*, the meal figures as a sacrifice, for this work instructs the faithful: 'On the Lord's own day, gather together and break bread and give thanks, after confessing your transgressions, so that your sacrifice will be pure. Let no one who has a quarrel with his comrade meet you until they are reconciled, so that your sacrifice may not be defiled' (Chapter XIV). Lietzmann argues that once Paul had, on the basis of pagan and Jewish analogies, come to regard the meal as a sacrifice, the door was opened to all sorts of new ideas, in that it could become associated with any of the manifold conceptions linked with sacrifice, such as atoning power or forgiveness of sins (170, p. 251). It seems to have been as a result of such a link that the elements of the meal came to be viewed as symbols of the sacrificial victim, the broken bread being his bruised body, and wine his blood poured in sacrifice. This idea is indicated by Paul when he says 'Christ, our passover, is slain for us'.

Lietzmann traces ancient liturgies of the mass to two primitive forms: the Roman liturgy of Hippolytus and the Egyptian liturgy preserved in Serapion (170, p. 174). The former begins with the deacons bringing the bishop the bread and wine offered by the faithful. He blesses this food and drink, and speaks prayers of thanks for the salvation that Jesus has brought us. He says that Jesus suffered in order to overcome death and the devil, and, in connection with this suffering, founded the Lord's Supper and instructed the faithful to repeat it in memory of him. The celebrant recites the words of the institution of the Supper, which he takes partly from Mt. and partly from I Cor., and declares that all present are thinking of Jesus' death and resurrection. He goes on to say that they offer up the bread and wine as a sacrifice. Before the food is consumed by those present, they pray that God's spirit may enter into it.

Lietzmann notes that 'there is no real connection between the sacrifice of the community and the account of the institution of the Supper' (p. 177). Such a connection would be there if, for instance, it were stated that the community was eating and drinking in such a way as to fulfil the instructions of the Lord. But his instructions, as recorded in this liturgy, are that the participants are to be mindful of his death as they eat and drink the bread and wine. They, however, go on to say that they are offering it as a sacrifice, and Lietzmann's point (cf, 170, p. 134) is that this sacrifice has an entirely different purpose, namely to assimilate the divine spirit or $\pi\nu\epsilon\hat{\upsilon}\mu\alpha$ that has come to reside in the food. In later liturgies the final section is linked with the earlier ones by a prayer that God should convert the bread and wine into the body and blood of Christ, so that the community can eat the promised Christ-food. Another way of establishing the connection would be to say that the Lord in his passion has performed a sacrifice, and that the community was now about to perform an analogous sacrifice.

But none of these things in fact is said in this liturgy. A prayer is simply offered that the holy spirit may enter into the elements of the meal and thus into those who eat the meal. 'There is no conception of a transformation here: rather is this a typical example of ancient sacrifice and the meal accompanying it. The power of the deity dwells in the meat of the offering and hence enters into the man who eats it' (p. 178). Lietzmann is here stressing the analogy with pagan sacrificial meals. 'The meal is a sacrifice, and in the sacrifice dwells a divine substance—the holy spirit—which the participants assimilate, thereby becoming strengthened in the true faith' (p. 181)

He turns next to the ancient Egyptian liturgy, and argues (pp. 196, 239) that this, in its original form, is like that of the *Didache*: the prayers refer only to the return of the Lord and to the fellowship of those assembled for the meal. The words of the institution of the Supper are not given, nor is there any reference to the death of Jesus. Thus these references are (1) absent in the original Egyptian liturgy and (2) tied so loosely with the sacrificial meal in the Hippolytan liturgy as to suggest that they were originally independent. Lietzmann supposes that the words of institution were actually spoken by Jesus at the Last Supper. But is it not possible to argue from the state of the evidence that these words were imposed on an early rite in order to give it a basis in a divine command?

The earliest reference to the institution of the meal by the Lord is in I Cor. xi, in a context where Paul is rebuking the Corinthians for scrambling over their food. He says (NEB):

> When you meet as a congregation it is impossible for you to eat the Lord's Supper, because each of you is in such a hurry to eat his own, and while one goes hungry another has too much to drink. Have you no homes of your own to eat and drink in? Or are you so contemptuous of the church of God that you shame its poorer members? What am I to say? Can I commend you? On this point, certainly not!

This takes us to the end of verse 22. The natural continuation of the sense comes with verse 33.

> Therefore, my brothers, when you meet for a meal, wait for one another. If you are hungry, eat at home, so that in meeting together you may not fall under judgement.

But the connection between these two passages is broken by verses 23–32 which give Paul's only account of the divine institution of the meal.

For the tradition which I handed on to you came to me from the Lord himself; that the Lord Jesus, on the night of his arrest, took bread, and, after giving thanks to God, broke it and said: 'This is my body, which is for you; do this as a memorial of me.' In the same way, he took the cup after supper and said: 'This cup is the new covenant sealed by my blood. Whenever you drink it, do this as a memorial of me.' For every time you eat this bread and drink the cup, you proclaim the death of the Lord, until he comes. It follows that anyone who eats the bread or drinks the cup of the Lord unworthily will be guilty of desecrating the body and blood of the Lord. A man must test himself before eating his share of the bread and drinking from the cup. For he who eats and drinks eats and drinks judgement on himself if he does not discern the Body. That is why many of you are feeble and sick, and a number have died. But if we examined ourselves, we should not thus fall under judgement. When, however, we do fall under the Lord's judgement, he is disciplining us, to save us from being condemned with the rest of the world.

In verses 22 and 33 Paul is urging the faithful to share the food in a decent and civilized way: while from verses 23 to 32 he is talking not of this ethical problem, but of the mystical properties of the Lord's body. Some have therefore regarded verses 23–32 as an interpolation, and Weiss, who resists this suggestion, nevertheless admits (279, p. 509–10) that it is not easy to see how Paul's appeal to the words of the Lord, and his explanation of the sacred rite, will help to check the abuse in Corinth of which, before and after this passage, he is complaining. The passage has certainly been tampered with. The AV renders verse 24a as: 'Take, eat: this is my body which has been broken for you.' The RV has dropped the words 'take', 'eat' and 'broken'. The two former are lacking in all the most ancient authorities and were clearly taken from Mt. xxvi, 26 and interpolated into the epistle. Jeremias has stressed that the language of the whole passage is 'unpauline' (148, p. 98), although he argues that it represents not an interpolation but an assimilation by Paul of an ancient liturgical formula into his letter. It is also striking that Paul's other references to a mystical 'new covenant' that has abrogated the old (II Cor. iii, 6, 14: Gal. iv, 24) do not link it with the blood of Jesus. On the other hand, the principal ideas in the passage are not unpauline. He has written in the previous chapter (x, 16–22) of the communion of the body and blood, and his implication there (that it is an opportunity to imbibe the πνεῦμα) is in line with his exhortation here that the Corinthians should 'discern the body'. His point is that those who eat it without due respect for its power offend it, and it then makes its power felt by killing or enfeebling them (verse 30). This exhortation to 'discern the body' is also obviously appropriate in the context of what precedes and follows (his complaint about scrambling over the food). The passage is apt to look like an interpolation because in it Paul is referring to the ritual part of the meal. We saw that these early Christian meals included a religious rite of breaking of bread which might precede or follow the repast.

In sum, the evidence that the passage is interpolated is inconclusive. But its account of the institution of the Supper by the Lord does not, to my mind, constitute an allusion to the historical occasion of the Last Supper, as portrayed in the synoptics. The passage shows no more acquaintance with the biography of a historical Jesus than does the rest of Paul's writings. For, first, Paul here claims to be passing on information received in a vision, a divine revelation, not historical reminiscences. In the RV the passage begins, 'for I received of the Lord that which also I delivered unto you'. We are reminded of Gal. i, 12 where Paul claims that his gospel came to him through supernatural revelation.[1] Second, the English translation misleads us into thinking that the writer of the original knew what we know about Jesus' life. In verse 23 Paul says (according to the RV), 'the Lord Jesus in the night in which he was betrayed took bread . . .'. The Greek has 'delivered', and the translator obviously had Judas in mind. The mistake is corrected by the NEB which runs, 'the Lord Jesus, on the night of his arrest'. But even this interprets 'delivered' with reference to gospel material. We have seen how much the passion narratives have drawn on Isaiah, and in the Septuagint the

---

[1] His express statement here that he did not receive his gospel from any human agency surely refutes Jeremias' theory (148, p. 95) that, by 'received of the Lord', Paul in I Cor. means no more than that the information reached him by an unbroken chain of tradition which reached back to words of a historical Jesus.

suffering servant of Yahweh is more than once said to be 'delivered'. Thus Isa. liii, 6 reads 'and the Lord *gave him up* for our sins'. And verses 12–13: 'he was delivered to death . . . he bore the sin of the many and was delivered because of their iniquities'. The idea is that he was delivered up by the Father as a sacrifice for sinners, and this is what Paul or the interpolator seems to have in mind when he talks about Jesus being 'delivered'.[1] No allusion to definite historical situation is necessarily implied here. Bornkamm (34, p. 149) takes Paul's reference to 'the night in which he was delivered' as proof that the Lord's Supper is 'anchored in a particular historical situation', and is not a 'cultic celebration after the manner of the mysteries, based on a timeless myth'. But to say that an occurrence took place at night hardly places it in a definite historical context. In this connection we may note that Reitzenstein has disputed the usual belief that the injunction 'do this as a memorial of me' (verse 24) is a command to keep a historical occasion in mind. It must, he says, be understood rather in a mystical sense, and he compares it with the pagan text of the same age in which Osiris gives Isis and Horus his blood in a beaker of wine, so that they do not forget him after his death but continue searching until they are reunited with him in his resurrection (214, p. 51). Furthermore, as Gardner has noted, Paul's supernatural revelation

> appears to have taken place at Corinth, during his eighteen months' residence there. Within sight of Corinth and almost within walking distance was Eleusis, the seat of the venerable Mysteries of Demeter . . . The great doctrine taught at Eleusis appears to have been the resurrection of the dead, as presaged and symbolized by the return of Persephone from the world of the dead to the upper air. And the central point of the ceremonial at Eleusis appears to have been a sacred repast, of which the initiated partook, and by means of which they had communion with the gods. It is precisely in the manner of St Paul that he should long to turn a pagan ceremony to Christian use (100, p. 18).

Anrich objected that the evidence we have does not establish that the meal at Eleusis had the effect of bringing the mystae into

---

[1] Jeremias (148, p. 106) detects here an 'unmistakable echo' of Isa. liii. Since the depiction of the passion in terms of Isaiah is unpauline (see above, p. 154), this echo is evidence either of interpolation, or for the theory of Jeremias.

communion with the gods (16, p. 111 n.). But there is no doubt that the sacred meal in the mystery religions did commonly serve this function, as Paul himself admits (see above, p. 144). So Paul's supernatural revelation may simply have recommended to him an established pagan practice.

Lietzmann (170, p. 255) and Cullmann (73, pp. 517–18) claim that Paul obviously knew of the Last Supper from historical tradition, and that he learned by revelation only that this meal was to be the model for the ritual meal of the Christian community. But Paul's words state quite clearly that it was revelation that informed him both of the Lord's institution of the meal, and of the necessity to repeat it regularly. Both these scholars also claim that the words 'this is my body' (which occur both in Paul's reference to the institution of the meal, and in the synoptic accounts of the Last Supper) are inexplicable as a liturgical development from a meal which originally merely gave participants the Lord's πνεῦμα, and that they must therefore have been spoken by Jesus at the Last Supper (170, p. 252). One could just as well argue, from the pagan text to which I have referred, that Osiris must have shed his blood on a historical occasion. Loisy has based a very different inference from that of Lietzmann on the words 'this is my body', given in Mk.' s account of the Last Supper with no elucidation (while in I Cor. the only elucidation is provided by the added words 'which is for you') Loisy argues that these words would be unintelligible to a reader unacquainted with the Christian Eucharist. 'Such mystic sayings have no natural sense except as referring to an established Christian Sacrament, and as explaining it' (177, p. 249). It thus looks as though we have here another example of the principle that the myth arises from and is subsequent to the ritual which it purports to explain.

It remains to study the synoptic narratives of the institution. Mt.'s account is so close to Mk.'s that it need not be regarded as an independent source. Mk.'s narrative runs (xiv, 22–5):

And as they were eating he took bread, and when he had blessed, he brake it, and gave to them, and said, Take ye: this is my body. And he took a cup, and when he had given thanks, he gave to them: and they all drank of it. And he said unto them, This is my blood of the covenant, which is shed for many. Verily I say unto you, I will no more drink of the fruit of the vine until that day when I drink it new in the kingdom of God.

We observe that, as in I Cor. xi, the bread is interpreted simply as the body of Christ with no further explanation, but the cup is directly explained as the 'covenant' made by Christ's death. The blood of a covenant was not life-blood flowing in the veins of the living, but life-blood shed in sacrificial death. So the meaning is: 'My blood is being shed to unite you in a covenant with God.' The symbolism of eating and drinking is combined with the symbolism of a covenant made by sacrificial blood-shedding. 'Thus are brought into combination two characteristics of the Messianic idea: the feast of the Messianic kingdom, and the sacrificial death of the Messiah himself' (225, § 4, 5).

Lk. has supplemented Jesus' statement that he will drink no more wine, until the day of the Messianic banquet, so as to make him say in addition that the passover is about to 'find its fulfilment in the kingdom of God'. Schwartz (246, p. 31) has argued that Lk.'s purpose in making Jesus thus declare the passover obsolete was to provide Christians with a basis for breaking with Jewish passover customs. I quote Lk. xxii, 13–19, NEB.

> They prepared for the Passover. When the time came he took his place at table, and the apostles with him: and he said to them, 'How I have longed to eat this Passover with you be-fore my death. For I tell you, never again shall I eat it until the time when it finds its fulfilment in the kingdom of God'. Then he took a cup, and after giving thanks he said, 'Take this and share it among yourselves; for I tell you, from this moment I shall drink from the fruit of the vine no more until the time when the kingdom of God comes.' And he took bread, gave thanks, and broke it; and he gave it to them with the words: 'This is my body.'

Some manuscripts add: 'Which is given on your behalf: do this unto my remembrance. Also the cup likewise after supper, saying: This cup is the new covenant in my blood, which on your behalf is shed.' These words have been interpolated into a number, but not all, of the ancient MSS., and are not given as part of the body of the text in the NEB. They include an injunction from Jesus to repeat the meal ('do this unto my remembrance'). There is no trace of such a command in Mk. or Mt. Only the interpolated words equate the wine with Jesus' blood. If they are deleted, Lk. depicts a supper of eschatological expectations in which bread is the main constituent. Lietzmann observes (p. 216) that this entirely accords with other passages in Lk.–Acts. The Lord only breaks bread for the disciples at Emmaus (Lk. xxiv, 30, 35), and does not give them a cup of wine. And in Acts ii, 46, the rite is called 'breaking of bread'.

Lietzmann originally regarded Lk.'s phrase 'this is my body' as an interpolation (p. 216 n.), but he withdrew this suggestion because the phrase exists in all extant manuscripts. As, however, these are all late, interpolation is not excluded, and if the phrase is an interpolation, then Lk. (who must have known both I Cor. and Mk.) is resisting their interpretation that the food represents the body of the Lord, and is trying to re-establish the older view that the Christian sacred meal is simply a supper of eschatological expectation. That resistance to the newer view did occur, is, we saw, testified by Ignatius. Lietzmann gives evidence enough that Lk. has 'edited' the passage in Mk.

One difficulty which arises from attempts to interpret the synoptic passages as records of a genuine historical occasion is that the synoptics represent this occasion as a passover meal, but fail to provide it with the essential characteristics of such a meal. They make the supper take place at the correct time—on the evening of Thursday, i.e. the beginning of Nisan 15th (the Jewish day being then reckoned from evening to evening). But as Lietzmann himself notes (p. 213), at a passover meal

(1) A lamb (slaughtered in the temple in the afternoon), is eaten.

(2) The Midrash about the Exodus and sojourn in the desert is pronounced.

(3) Unleavened bread is eaten.

(4) Four beakers are drunk.

Furthermore, as we saw (above, p. 239), the synoptics are contradicted by Jn., according to whom Jesus was crucified in the afternoon of Nisan 14th, when the paschal lambs were being slaughtered in the temple, and was dead by the time of the evening meal. The idea of the writer is clearly to represent him as the true paschal sacrifice.

Jeremias has recently argued that the Last Supper as depicted by the synoptics is, in spite of the difficulties, a genuine passover meal. He says that the words of institution given in Mk. are 'a cultic formula, not purporting to give a description of the Last Supper, but recording the constituent elements of the celebrations of the primitive Church. Since this celebration was not a repetition of the Last Supper with all its historical accompaniments, but the daily assembly of the disciples of Jesus in the table-fellowship of the Messiah, it is but natural that only the rites which continued to be performed by the Church should be mentioned in the liturgical formula' (148, p. 61). Now the words in Mk. do not profess to be a 'cultic formula', but a description of a single historical occasion, including Jesus' words on this occasion. Jeremias' argument seems to be that (1) the Last Supper was a full passover meal, and included the eating of a lamb and the recital by Jesus of the usual passover liturgy; (2) the early Christians had a daily banquet (which was, of course, not a passover meal), at which certain words were spoken as a liturgy (to explain the ritual); (3) it is these words which have become inserted into the synoptic accounts of Jesus' last meal. The theory is of interest here because it shows that an eminent defender of the historicity of the Last Supper admits that the narratives reporting the details derive from a daily repeated rite. Of course, Jeremias insists that the words spoken in this daily rite themselves derive from what Jesus said at the Last Supper. But he admits that the gospels have taken the daily rite and not the historical occasion on which it is allegedly based as the source of their reports of what Jesus said.[1]

It is part of the argument of my preceding chapters that the biographical details of Jesus were built up by the imagination of the early Christians. One of the challenges such a theory has to meet is: whence the community of early Christians if there had been no Jesus? In this and the previous chapters I have outlined a possible answer; namely that the community held pre-Christian

---

[1] Jeremias also argues that, since the paschal setting of the synoptic Last Supper obviously cannot derive from a daily liturgy, it can only constitute a true historical reminiscence (148, p. 56). But he later declares that the nature of Jesus' last meal with his disciples is no triviality, for if it was a passover meal, then 'the link between the old and the new covenant is strongly illuminated' (p. 82). Quite so. Might not the authors of the synoptics have had the same idea, and modelled their account of the meal on it? This is what Huber has recently suggested (144, p. 111). And both Paul (I Cor. v, 7) and the author of the Apocalypse seem to have appreciated this significance of the passover (see below, p. 282).

ideas of the Messiah and copied a pre-Christian Eucharist. The Christian rite was originally a sort of anticipation of the Messianic banquet, and a rite of this character could well have been derived from the Jews, perhaps from the Essenes. Very soon, if not from the first, it acquired features to be found in the pagan sacrificial meals of the day, and this association with sacrifice led in time to connecting it with the sacrifice of the divine victim. The story of the institution of the rite by the Messiah can be regarded as a later fiction to explain the ritual.

Note on the Didache

The *Didache* (or The *Teaching of the Twelve Apostles*) was recovered in 1875 and published in 1883, and its first part seems to consist of the teaching carried to the dispersed Jews by the apostles (i.e. messengers) of the high priest or patriarch. Milman said that such apostles probably existed before the fall of Jerusalem in AD 70 (185, p. 119). Mosheim thought that Paul alludes to them when he terms himself an apostle, not of men, nor by men, but of God himself and his Son Jesus Christ. This presupposes that the Jews to whom Galatians is principally addressed were familiar with 'apostles commissioned by men, namely those sent by the Jewish high priest and magistrates to the different cities of the Roman Empire'. Mosheim also conjectured—long before the discovery of the *Didache*—that these apostles were twelve in number, 'corresponding with that of the Jewish tribes', and that this would 'account for our Saviour's fixing the number of his apostles at twelve' (194, pp. 120–3).

The *Didache* begins with ethical precepts outlining a 'way of life', which is contrasted with the 'way of death', and implies love of one's neighbour and reciprocity. Further exhortations follow; in fact we seem to have here one of those Jewish compilations where ethical maxims from more ancient Jewish literature are strung together for didactic purposes. In the sixth paragraph the 'way of death' is specified as including 'murders, adulteries, lustful desires, fornications, thefts, idolatries . . .' In the next paragraph baptism is enjoined 'in the name of the Father and of the Son and of the Holy Spirit' without explanation of this formula (which is in fact later than most of the matter in the synoptic gospels, see above, p. 135). Next come rules for fasting and daily prayer, then an order for the household Eucharist mentioning neither the Last Supper nor Christ's death. Jewish scholarship (151) describes the work as 'a manual of instruction for proselytes, adapted from the Synagogue by early Christianity and transformed by alteration and amplification into a Church manual'. The first part of the work (the teaching concerning the 'two ways') was thus originally a purely Jewish manual of instruction, and was later supplemented by the Christian rules concerning baptism, etc. This was the theory proposed by Taylor in 1886 (264) and conceded by Harnack (129, pp. 28 ff.). And Ryle admits (231, p. 31) that the work 'appears to be a Christian adaptation, made early in the second century, of a Jewish book of religious instruction'—a view that has recently been re-affirmed by Harder (128). If, however, with a number of Christian writers (e.g. Vokes, 276a, pp. 123 ff.) we regard the document as wholly Christian, then we have to assume that the Christian twelve apostles 'drew up a "Teaching" which proceeded for six paragraphs, nearly half its length, in detailed ethical exhortation without a word about Jesus or the Christ, or a Son of God, and then suddenly plunged into a formula of baptism, naming the Father and the Son and the Holy Ghost, without saying who the Son was'; and we also have to suppose that 'such a document, after being widely circulated, was allowed by the Church to fall into oblivion while believed to be genuine' (220, p. 345). Robertson thinks it much more likely that at least the first six chapters went to form a non-Christian document originally entitled *The Teaching of the Twelve Apostles*, and that Christians adopted this teaching in the first or second century, founded on it a myth that Jesus had twelve apostles and gradually added to it; and that after a time the Church decided to drop the document because its purely Judaic origin and drift were too plain (just as the book of Enoch was dropped after having long been regarded as genuine and respectable). The first six chapters, whether Christian or earlier, are undoubtedly older than the rest, for they inculcate precepts of the Lord without appeal to his 'words' or 'gospel', while the later chapters refer to both. Chapter VIII, for instance, tells us to 'pray as the Lord has commanded in the gospel', and proceeds to quote the Lord's prayer with variants from both Mt. and Lk.

(ii) The Jesus of the Apocalypse

In chapter VI, where I investigated whether the earliest Christian writings suggest that there was a historical Jesus who did what is recorded of him in the gospels, I made no mention of John's Apocalypse, the last book in the NT canon, usually known as the Revelation of St John the Divine. Now that we have studied pagan cults which preceded and accompanied Christianity, it will be possible to give an intelligible account of this book.

Like the Pauline letters, the Apocalypse antedates the gospels. It narrates the visions of John when he was taken up to heaven in a trance. Paul, too, we saw, had this sort of experience, but with the coming of the gospels, this phase of Christianity where prophets tell of their ecstatic experience in heaven is past. Thus Jn. expressly says that no man ever ascended to heaven (iii, 13). The writer of the fourth gospel is, of course, not the same as the author of the Revelation of John. The fourth gospel, we saw, knows nothing of expectations that the world is coming to a speedy and catastrophic end, while this idea dominates the book of Revelation. The latter is furthermore written in what the NBC calls 'extraordinary Greek' which 'differs so widely from the gospel as to make a common authorship of the two books problematic' (p. 1168).

The transition from apocalypses to gospels is the very heart of our problem. The apocalypses included visions of a purely supernatural redeemer. The book of Enoch, for instance, represents the Messiah as a 'transcendental being, pre-existent and exalted above all creatures' (NBC, p. 57), whereas the gospels tell of the sojourn on earth of a man-God. Our problem is to explain how the former idea of the redeemer was gradually replaced by the latter. For the present we must merely note the fact that, in the earliest days of Christianity, apocalypses formed the most important literature. We recall that in one of the NT epistles and in the writings of the earliest Fathers, Enoch is quoted as a sacred book (see above, p. 81). And Enoch's speculations about a heavenly figure who would come down to earth and destroy all but the elect were based on Daniel's. Thus there is evidence that this sort of apocalyptic was practised in Jewish circles for the two centuries prior to the rise of Christianity, and was highly regarded by early Christian writers. By the time a Christian canon was formed in the second half of the second century, Christianity had dropped many of its apocalyptic ideas, and so the adoption of apocalypses into the canon was almost completely blocked. 'To the *Apocalypse of John* was admission alone accorded; but it was placed at the end of the canon, and for a long while it was hard put to even maintain itself in this inferior position' (284, p. 58).

The book of Revelation has been widely admitted to be a redaction of earlier writings (the various suggestions made are discussed by Bousset, 35). Some of the fragments thus welded together may well be of purely Jewish origin, and others are among the oldest Christian literature. Thus xi, 1–2 predicts that the heathen shall tread Jerusalem underfoot, with the exception of the temple which shall be spared. This must have been written before the year 70 when the Romans took Jerusalem after a war of four years and completely destroyed the temple.

In the following account I shall quote the NEB throughout. The Apocalypse begins with the words:

> This is the Revelation given by God to Jesus Christ. It was given to him so that he might show his servants what must shortly happen. He made it known by sending his angel to his servant John, who, in telling all that he saw, has borne witness to the word of God and to the testimony of Jesus Christ.

Jesus here figures as a supernatural being who sends angels on errands, not as a man whose companionship John had known. The text goes on to assure us that the hour of fulfilment of the prophecy of which the revelation consists is at hand.

There follows a message from John to the seven Churches of Asia which mentions Jesus as 'the faithful witness, the first-born from the dead and ruler of the kings of the earth', who loosed us from our sins by his blood. The RV adds that many authorities, some of them ancient, have 'washed' instead of 'loosed'. Next we are told: 'Behold he is coming with the clouds! Every eye shall see him, and among them those who pierced him; and all the peoples of the world shall lament in remorse.' These statements imply that Jesus was killed as an atoning sacrifice. There is no indication when this occurred. The fact that those who pierced him will witness his second coming does not mean that they are still alive and that the piercing must therefore have occurred in the recent past. For it was generally believed that the dead would rise at the second coming. Nor is any indication of the manner of Jesus' death given. 'Piercing' does not necessarily imply crucifixion, and may have been inspired by Zech. xii, 10 (on which see above, p. 229).

John next has a vision of 'one like a son of man', that is, like the heavenly being in human form in Daniel's vision. And 'the hair of his head was white as snow-white wool'—like the ancient of days in Dn. vii, 9–10. His 'feet gleamed like burnished brass refined in a furnace', just as in Ezekiel's vision (i, 7). And 'his voice was like the sound of rushing waters', like the voice of Yahweh in Ezek. xliii, 2. The being described in these terms can only be an aspect of Yahweh, not a mortal. The NBC says (p. 1171) that 'the application to Christ of the attributes of God is a constant phenomenon in this book'. Once again we see that the author of the Apocalypse does not speak of Jesus as a man whose companionship he has known. Jesus is a heavenly figure who, like God himself, can only be seen in a vision.

The next two chapters (ii and iii) give detailed messages to the seven Asian Churches. Chapter iv seems to mark a new beginning. John is caught up by the spirit and taken to heaven. He sees God on his throne, in his hand a scroll sealed with seven seals. Commentators say that seven seals were used for testaments. 'When a testator died the testament was brought forward and, when possible, opened in the presence of the seven witnesses who sealed it, i.e. it was unsealed, read and executed' (NBC, p. 1177). John hears an angel say, 'Who is worthy to open the scroll and to break its seals?' (v, 2). He is then told that 'the Lion from the tribe of Judah, the Root of David' has won this right. In Gen. xlix, 9 the tribe of Judah is compared with the lion, and the Jews believed that the Messiah would come from this tribe. From this it seems that the writer of the Apocalypse has in mind a Messiah who was born on earth. The expression 'root of David' is an allusion to Isa. xi and suggests the same conclusion. Isaiah begins this chapter with the words: 'And there shall come forth a shoot out of the stock of Jesse, and a branch out of his roots shall bear fruit; and the spirit of the Lord shall rest upon him . . . and he shall smite the earth with the rod of his mouth and with the breath of his lips shall he slay the wicked.' In verse 10 Isaiah refers to this person as 'the root of Jesse', and this may be taken as an elliptical way of repeating the words 'a branch or shoot from his roots'. The elliptical form is quoted not only in the Apocalypse but also by Paul: 'There shall be the root of Jesse, the one raised up to govern the gentiles: on him the gentiles shall set their hope' (Rom. xv, 12). It is thus clear that the expression 'the root of David' means the Messiah descended from David.

John next sees this 'Lion from the tribe of Judah' and 'Root of David'. He sees him 'in the very middle of the throne of Yahweh', and not in human form but as 'a Lamb with the marks of slaughter upon him' and with 'seven horns and seven eyes, the eyes which are the seven spirits of God sent out all over the world' (v. 6). The NBC comments (p. 1177): 'A horn in the OT symbolizes power (Ps. lxxv, 4–7) and royal dignity (Zech. i, 18). Jesus has kingly power in a complete measure (the significance of seven) . . . In the OT the seven eyes (signifying omniscience) belong to Jehovah (cf. Zech. iv, 10).'

John learns that this lamb was slain and by his blood purchased for God the elect of all nations (verse 9). We know that the Jews believed in the efficacy of the shedding of blood as a means of placating God. According to Leviticus, 'the blood on the altar makes atonement for sins because it is being given for life that has been forfeited through sin. The blood is valid for atonement only when it is poured out on the altar in death' (180, p. 140, with reference to Lev. xvii, 11). And the idea that the blood of the sacrificed animal conveys new life is found in the worship of Attis, which was extensive at the time when the Apocalypse was written. In this cult, a bull and a ram were sacrificed on a grille under which the initiate stood, and he was reborn as the blood rained down upon him (137, p. 65 ff.). When the Apocalypse pictures Jesus as a slaughtered lamb who redeemed the elect with his blood, a sacrificial death on the altar is indicated. We have already seen that in Chapter One many manuscripts say that the elect are 'washed' from their sins by his blood. This implies the shedding of streams of blood as in sacrifice on the altar. This image of the slaughtered lamb whose blood was poured out would not be a very apposite way of referring figuratively to death by crucifixion, which is relatively bloodless, but could be better applied to someone who had been beheaded or torn to pieces with knives.

Couchoud notes that there are two obvious sources for the idea that the divine redeemer has the form of a lamb. One is Isaiah, whose servant of Yahweh redeems all men when he is slaughtered like a lamb, and the other is the paschal lamb. 'A paschal liturgy underlies the whole book of Revelation. The theme of Exodus is taken up and exalted. Just as the Israelites were preserved from the Destroyer through the blood of the paschal lamb marked on their doors, so will the elect be saved by the blood of the divine lamb' (66, p. 67). Jesus was regarded as the celestial counterpart of the paschal lamb, it being a Jewish idea that earthly things have a perfect counterpart in heaven. And this idea preserved the Easter (paschal) feast among Christians in the general wreck of Jewish rites after the destruction of the temple (see above, p. 240). The *Testament of Joseph* (xix, 8) also pictures the coming redeemer as a lamb. In the vision of the writer, the gentiles appear as beasts who rush upon the lamb but are destroyed by him and trodden under foot. For all these reasons, then, the author of the Apocalypse may have chosen the figure of the slaughtered lamb in order to describe the atoning power of the death of an earthly Messiah, even though this redeemer had been crucified, not beheaded or torn to pieces. What is certain is that the author regards Jesus as a divine figure who spent some time on earth as a descendant of David and died a violent death. Whether he died by crucifixion cannot be inferred with any certainty from the evidence so far given.

In Chapter vi the lamb begins to open the seven seals. As each one is broken, Messianic woes ensue—civil and international war, then famine and death. When the fifth seal is broken John sees the souls of Christian martyrs crying out to God for vengeance. They are told to wait 'a little longer, until the tally should be complete of all their brothers in Christ's service who were to be killed as they had been'. The breaking of the sixth seal brings about an earthquake: the stars fall to earth, the sun turns black and the moon red. The NBC remarks (p. 1179) that 'these signs of the consummation are too regular in eschatological writings for them to be regarded as wholly figurative'. The men on earth are represented as hiding in terror from 'the face of the one who sits on the throne and from the vengeance of the Lamb'. A severe judgement is thus expected from the lamb, and this accords with the representation of him as having seven horns, symbols of power and majesty.

The next section (vii, 1–8) seems to be an interpolation. While the end of chapter vi tells of the terrible earthquake, every mountain and island being moved from its place, the beginning of chapter vii shows angels being instructed to do no damage on earth until those who are to be saved have been marked with a

K

seal on their foreheads. We are told that only 144,000, twelve thousand from each of the twelve tribes of Israel are to be sealed and spared. In the following verses however (vii, 9–10) a vast throng from every nation of the world, which no one could count, is redeemed. Later it is again '144,000 who alone from the whole world have been ransomed'. But now these are not necessarily Jews but 'men who did not defile themselves with women' (xiv, 1–5).

The seventh seal is broken at the beginning of chapter viii. After this John sees that 'the seven angels that stand in the presence of God were given seven trumpets'. They blow them in succession and with each blast further woes ensue. For instance, the fifth trumpet introduces a plague of demoniacal locusts and the sixth a demoniacal army—four angels with squadrons of cavalry which kill a third of mankind.

Between the sounding of the sixth and the seventh trumpets there occurs a passage which describes the scene at Jerusalem during the great day of wrath. For three and a half years the pagans are to have power over the city, except over the temple and the altar, which are to be spared (xi, 1–2). We saw that this passage must have been written before the fall of the temple in AD 70. The continuation says that two witnesses of God are to test the inhabitants of the city with miraculous scourges. Finally, the two are killed and left unburied. 'Their corpses will lie in the street of the great city, whose name in allegory is Sodom, or Egypt, where also their Lord was crucified.' The word 'lie' is italicized in the RV, indicating that the verb is missing in the manuscripts, which read:

> Their dead bodies are . . . in the street of the great city . . . where also their Lord was crucified.

The missing verb may well be 'crucified', for crucifixion was a punishment administered by the Jews after death (Deut. xxi, 22). The verb 'crucified' would seem to be demanded by the parallel 'where *also* their Lord was crucified'. It is here that we have the only mention of the crucifixion in the book, throughout the rest of which the manner of the death of Jesus is indicated by the phrase 'the Lamb that was slain' with shedding of blood. Furthermore, in this parenthesis Jesus is not only said to have been crucified but also to have been crucified in Jerusalem. Such a specific geographical setting goes beyond anything that Paul and other early Christian writers say of him; yet it occurs in that part of the Apocalypse which appears to belong to the oldest Christian tradition, written apparently before AD 70. For these reasons, then, the statement in the parenthesis looks like an editor's gloss. The idea it contains would be far too important to be stated just by the way if it really had belonged to the original conception.

The two witnesses or prophets slain in Jerusalem and left unburied are said to come alive again and ascend to heaven after three and a half days (xi, 11–12). It is thus not Jesus who is said to rise from the dead after three days and ascend to heaven, but the two he sent as witnesses. This again suggests that the story of the witnesses was written by someone who had no acquaintance with the story of the gospel Jesus. Could someone who knew of the gospel story of Jesus' crucifixion in Jerusalem and resurrection on the third day have told the same story of two prophets while saying nothing of Jesus' resurrection on the third day? The statement in the Apocalypse that the 'breath of life from God came into them and they stood upon their feet to the terror of all who saw it' is a quotation from Ezek. xxxvii, 10, which refers to the spiritual quickening of the nation Israel. Hos. vi, 3, also referring to the revival of the nation after a period of dejection, says: 'after two days he will revive us; on the third day he will raise us up' (cp. above, p. 150). These sources account for the origin of the story in the Apocalypse, while it is merely bewildering if we assume it to have been written by one acquainted with the gospel story.

The next incident is the blowing of the seventh trumpet. When this occurs, 'voices were heard in heaven shouting: "The sovereignty of the world has passed to our Lord and his Christ"' and the elders, seated on their thrones before God, say: 'thy day of retribution has come. Now is the time for the dead to be judged' (xi, 18). In order to judge mankind the heavenly lamb takes human form by being born of woman. This event takes place, however, not on earth but between heaven and earth. The woman is no mortal but divine, and has the attributes which the heathen gave to their queen of heaven or Virgo Caelestis, namely, the sun as her robe, the moon at her feet; and she wears a crown of twelve stars or constellations. Among the Babylonians, Damkina the mother of Marduk, is called 'mistress of the heavenly tiara . . . The Egyptians depicted Hathor with the sun on her head. And Leto wears a veil of stars' (112, and 32, Chapter 8). Gunkel says (111, p. 386) that the description of the woman is probably based on a picture. He mentions an engraving in a Berlin museum of a goddess, possibly Ishtar, dressed in the sun, with the moon and seven stars above her. The twelve signs of the zodiac, he adds, form a circle in the heaven, and are for this reason frequently depicted as a crown.

The celestial woman who bears in pain the Son of Man has other children besides Jesus who are said to be the true believers (xii, 17). It seems, then, as if this section of the Apocalypse has taken over the pagan myth of the birth of the sun-god, and adapted it by making the celestial goddess not only mother of the god but also of the elect community. Commentators regard her as also the bride of the lamb mentioned in xix, 7. And the bride is also represented as a town, the New Jerusalem (xxi, 9–10), a symbol of the elect.

While the woman is in labour, a huge dragon waits for the child to be born in order to devour it. Again, we are expressly told that this takes place in the heavens, for while the dragon waits in front of the woman, his tail knocks down a third of the stars so that they fall to earth. But the new-born child is immediately taken up to God and his throne, and Michael and his angels throw the dragon down to earth where, deprived of his prey, he slays and tortures men, even the elect. All these events—from the labour of the woman to the throwing down of the dragon to earth—have no reference to an earthly career of Jesus, and the bearing up of the new-born child to God's throne has nothing to do with the gospel story of the ascension, where the ascent begins on the earth and occurs long after Jesus' birth. The Apocalypse gives us the pagan myth of the persecution of the young sun child by the dragon (see above, p. 231), adapted to Christian purposes, for the dragon is identified with Satan (xii, 9).

This story of the woman in labour both giving birth to the redeemer and also symbolizing the elect community has a remarkable parallel in one of the Dead Sea Scrolls. The Psalmist of the Hymn Scroll compares himself with the woman who is to give birth to the Messiah at the end of time:

And I was confused like the Woman about to bring forth
at the time of her first child-bearing . . .
For the children have reached as far as the billows of Death

And She who is big with the Man is in travail, in her pains.
For she shall give birth to a man-child in the billows of Death,
and in the bonds of Sheol there shall spring from the
crucible (i.e. the womb) of the Pregnant one
a Marvellous Councellor with his might,
and he shall deliver every man from the billows
because of Her who is big with him.

Dupont-Somer draws attention to the last line, where the mother of the Messiah is explicitly associated with his redeeming work, and also to the line which states that the Messiah is the 'firstborn' of his mother. He infers that 'the woman who is to bring him into the world is the congregation of the just, the Church of Saints, victim of the persecution of the wicked' (84, p. 208 and notes).

The following chapters of the Apocalypse (xiii-xviii) express John's hatred for heathen Rome and specify more woes. In chapter xix he sees heaven wide open:

> and before me was a white horse; and its rider's name was Faithful and True, for he is just in judgement and just in war. His eyes flamed like fire, and on his head were many diadems, and he was robed in a garment drenched in blood. He was called the Word of God, and the armies of heaven followed him . . . From his mouth there went a sharp sword with which to smite the nations; for he it is who shall rule them with an iron rod . . . And on his robe and on his leg there was written the name 'King of kings and Lord of lords'.

Commentators agree that this horseman is Jesus. The dead are resurrected to meet their sentence for eternity, the damned being plunged into a lake of fire (chapter xx).

We see that the author of this work is interested almost exclusively in Jesus' second coming, which he thinks is very near. He believes, it is true, that Jesus spent some time on earth as a descendant of David and met a violent death—possibly by crucifixion, although this is not certain. That his death occurred by crucifixion in Jerusalem is a late gloss. The author of the original seems to have only the haziest notions of Jesus' career on earth, and does not give it any historical setting. He certainly never suggests that he has known him while he was on earth. Paul, too, believed in a Jesus who lived at some unspecified period as a descendant of David and was put to death (Paul specifies crucifixion). The problem is to explain what basis these two writers had for supposing that Jesus had already visited the earth and had been put to death there, and why neither of them gives these events any historical setting.

(iii) **Paul's Jesus and the angels**

It seems impossible that the author of the principal Pauline letters had any idea of a human teacher contemporary with himself, of whom he, Peter and the others were disciples in the ordinary sense. There is, however, no doubt that he believed that Jesus the Christ was born and crucified on earth, and 'Christ crucified' is the central dogma of his religious theories. Cheyne (59, § 7) justly notes that 'the crucifixion of Jesus is of slight interest to Paul as a mere historical event: it becomes all-important through the apostle's mystical connection with Christ'. How is this mystical union to be understood? And how does Paul conceive the Christ crucified with whom he is mystically united? To answer these questions we must first understand what Paul has to say about Jesus' relationship to other celestial beings.

In the Jewish literature of the period we find a highly developed angelology. The writer of the book of Daniel (c. 165 BC) was the first by whom angels were individualized and endowed with names and titles, and later apocalyptic literature assumed a heavenly hierarchy of stupendous proportions (see 150). In Enoch seven classes of angels are distinguished—the cherubim, seraphim, ofanim, the angels of power, the principalities, the Elect One (the Messiah) and the elementary powers of the earth. Josephus tells us, concerning the Essene oath, that the sectary undertook to preserve, without alteration, 'the names of the angels', and the Qumran scrolls refer to them at every turn, calling them also 'holy ones', 'spirits', 'gods' (elim), 'honourable ones', 'sons of Heaven'. The members of the Covenant lived in the company of the celestial spirits all the time, and believed that angels, both good and evil, would join in the final eschatological war between themselves and all the heathen nations (84, p. 165).

These angels of Jewish imagination are often represented as occupying different levels in the universe. In the Slavonic Enoch the universe consists of a number of tiers; the abyss, then the prison of the dead, then the earth, then the firmament peopled by

Satan and cruel invisible princes, then seven heavens. In the centre of each heaven is a 'throne' around which throng principalities, dominions and powers. Above them all is God, surrounded by the celestial beings called his powers, his throne, his spirit, his wisdom, his glory, his name. Enoch is taken up by two angels into the various heavens, and in the seventh he sees:

> a very great light, and all the fiery hosts of great archangels and incorporeal powers, and lordships and principalities and dominions, cherubim and seraphim, thrones, and the watchfulness of many eyes [ofanim].

The terms 'thrones', 'principalities', 'powers' and 'dominions' are used to designate celestial beings in the *Testaments of the Patriarchs* (e.g. *Test. Levi* III) and also, as Christian commentators admit (e.g. NBC p. 1046) in the following passages from the NT epistles:

(1) 'In him [the Son] were all things created, in the heavens and upon the earth, things visible and things invisible, whether thrones or dominions, or principalities or powers' (Coloss. i, 16).

(2) Christ sits 'far above all rule and authority, and power, and dominion' (Ephes. i, 21).

(3) 'Neither death, nor life, nor angels, nor principalities, nor things present, nor things to come, nor powers, nor height, nor depth, nor any other creature, shall be able to separate us from the love of God which is in Christ Jesus our Lord' (Rom. viii, 38).

(4) 'Jesus Christ who is on the right hand of God, having gone into heaven; angels and authorities and powers being made subject unto him' (I Pet. iii, 22).

It is clear that Paul not only believes in these angels, but also in the multi-layered universe which, according to Enoch and *The Testament of Levi*, they inhabit. For he tells of a Christian who was 'caught up into the third heaven' and also 'into paradise and heard words so secret that human lips may not repeat them' (II Cor. xii, 2–3, NEB. The continuation shows that this man was Paul himself).

It seems that certain Jews (not orthodox ones, but so-called

Gnostics) not only owned the existence of angels but also worshipped them as divine beings. According to the NBC (p. 1044) the basis of Gnosticism is the doctrine that matter is evil, so that in creation, God cannot come into direct contact with it. 'It is necessary, therefore, to posit a number of emanations of deity, a number of spiritual beings germinating, as it were, the first from God, the second from the first and so on until they sink lower and lower and make contact with matter possible. Only thus could God have created the universe and at the same time maintained His holiness inviolate. It follows, then, that these graded beings are in control of the material universe in which man has to live. He must enlist their support.' The sum total of emanations of the godhead is denoted by the Greek word *pleroma*, and these Jewish Gnostics worshipped the pleroma.

This is the intellectual background against which the Pauline letters were written, and Colossians (ii, 8, 18) seems specifically to combat this doctrine that angelic agencies are necessary to salvation. Paul shows what their true place is, and asserts that one single privileged being, called Jesus the Messiah, absorbs the pleroma in himself, that he is the first after God, or with God, among all the celestial beings. Christ is:

> the image of the invisible God, the firstborn of all creation; for in him were all things created, in the heavens and upon the earth, things visible and things invisible, whether thrones or dominions or principalities or powers: all things have been created through him and unto him and he is before all things, and in him all things consist. And he is the head of the body, the church; who is the beginning, the firstborn from the dead; that in all things he might have the pre-eminence. For it was the good pleasure of the Father that in him should all the fulness [pleroma] dwell, and through him to reconcile all things unto himself, having made peace through the blood of his cross; through him, I say, whether things upon the earth, or things in the heavens (i, 15–20).

The angel worship combated in this epistle must have been fairly common in Paul's day, for we find that John's Apocalypse also tries to discredit it. In his visions John twice falls down and worships an angel who rebukes him for so doing, saying, 'I am but a fellow servant with you and your brothers who bear their

testimony to Jesus' (Rev. xix, 10; xxii, 8). Similarly, the epistle
to the Hebrews (i, 3–4) stresses Jesus' superiority to mere
angels.

Couchoud remarks that in the passage from Colossians we have
the most primitive idea of Jesus—that of a being who absorbed
the pleroma in himself. He also notes that clearly, in Paul's view,
the death of Jesus redeemed creatures in the heavens as well as
on earth. Paul does not explain why this was necessary but it
looks as though he is presupposing that the angels have revolted
after the manner of the story given in Enoch, where we learn that
not only man but also pure heavenly beings, fell from grace, that
fallen angels became progenitors of hosts of evil spirits and were
finally subjugated by the power of heaven and punished. Paul even
teaches that Christians will eventually judge angels. When he tells
the Corinthians to go to court (if at all) with 'saints' i.e. Christians,
and not heathens as judges, he supports this plea by saying that
Christians are eventually to judge both the world and the angels,
and are therefore certainly qualified to judge the trivialities discussed in human law courts (I Cor. vi, 1–3). This passage also
makes it clear that the final reconciliation between God and all
things in heaven and earth has not yet taken place. The great
judgement is still to come. Thus the statement in Colossians that
it was God's pleasure to reconcile all beings to himself by means of
the shedding of Jesus' blood on the cross cannot mean that the
reconciliation has been completely effected by Jesus' redemptory
act, but rather that his death marks the first stage in our redemption. To attain salvation we must continue steadfast in our faith
and the continuation of the passage expressly makes this proviso.

Let us now examine more closely what (according to Paul)
Jesus has done to initiate our reconciliation with God. From Phil.
ii, 5–11 we learn that Jesus is a divine figure who came down into
the material world to suffer an ignominious death. Then he
reascended and received a mystic name as powerful as the name of
God. Couchoud regards this story of the descent and re-ascension
of the divine being as the key to Paul's conception of Jesus and he
remarks (68, p. 122) that we are fortunate enough to possess an
ancient Jewish apocalypse which gives the story in greater detail,
and so fills out the picture which is merely sketched by Paul. He
is referring to so-called *Ascension of Isaiah*, to which we next
turn.

It consists of three originally distinct parts, one of which is

Jewish and the others of Christian origin. Box (37) thinks that they existed independently of each other in the first century, and were combined in their present form by a Christian editor some time in the second. The final part, with which we are concerned, is a Christian writing. It tells how Isaiah had a trance in the presence of King Hezekiah and his court, and thought he was taken by an angel through the seven heavens. When he arrived in the seventh, he saw the departed righteous and finally the divine being—'the Great Glory' himself, together with a second glorious one like him, and a third who is the angel of the Holy Spirit. Then the Most High is heard commissioning 'the Son' or 'the Beloved' to descend through the heavens and the firmament to the world, and even to hell. The title 'the Beloved' which here designates the Messiah, is used in the OT to denote the nation Israel. We are reminded of the way in which 'Servant' and 'Elect' originally referred to the nation, but were later transferred to the Messiah (37, p. xix).

In the seventh heaven Isaiah is not only told that the Lord Christ will descend on earth, but also that 'the god of that world will stretch forth his hand against the Son, and they will crucify him on a tree, and will slay him, not knowing who he is', for he will be there in the form of a man (chapter ix). By 'the god of that world' Satan is meant; for a later passage tells us that the crucifying was done by 'the adversary'.

Isaiah then sees Jesus descend. First he passes into the sixth heaven, where he is praised by the angels there. But in each of the lower heavens he assumes the form of the angels at that level so as to pass through their territory and reach earth unrecognized. Thus 'when he descended into the fifth heaven . . . he made himself like unto the form of the angels there, and they did not praise him nor worship him, for his form was like theirs'. The same happens as he goes through the fourth and third heavens. In the latter he also has to give the angels the password before he can go through the gate unrecognized (x, 24). Again, when he arrives in the second and first heavens he both changes his form and gives the password. Then he 'descended into the firmament where dwelleth the ruler of this world [i.e. Satan], and he gave the password to those on the left, and his form was like theirs, and they did not praise him there; but they were envying one another and fighting; for here there is a power of evil and envying about trifles'. The angels at the level below this are so busy fighting each other that they do not even ask him for the password. We observe that the lower the heaven, the less god-like are the angels inhabiting it. The reason why Jesus does not disguise himself on passing through the sixth heaven is presumably that the creatures there are so god-like that they will not try to frustrate his designs.

There follows an account of his arrival on earth, born of the virgin Mary, etc., which is absent in some of the MSS., and which several scholars regard as an interpolation (37, p. xxiv). It is stressed that on earth he 'was hidden from all the heavens and all the princes and gods of this world' (xi, 16). He 'sucked the breast' in Nazareth as a babe and as is customary in order that he might not be recognized. 'And when he had grown up he worked great signs and wonders in the land of Israel and of Jerusalem. After this the adversary envied him and roused the children of Israel against him, not knowing who he was, and they delivered him to the king and crucified him, and he descended to the angel (of Sheol)' (xi, 19). This probably interpolated section closes with the statements that he rose on the third day, sent out the twelve apostles and ascended (verse 22). Verse 23 begins to describe the re-ascent:

> And I saw him and he was in the firmament, but he had not changed himself into their form, and all the angels of the firmament and the Satans saw him and they worshipped. And there was much sorrow there, while they said: 'How did our Lord descend in our midst, and we perceived not his glory' . . . And he ascended into the second heaven and he did not transform himself, but all the angels who were on the right and on the left and the throne in the midst both worshipped him and praised him and said: 'How did our Lord escape us whilst descending and we perceived not . . .'

According to a statement in the section which is presumably an interpolation, he does not begin this re-ascent immediately after his crucifixion, but stays on earth for some time in his resurrected form. Dibelius remarks that this is probably a distortion of the original effected by some writer acquainted with the gospel traditions. For the surprise which the angels show when he re-ascends is really only intelligible if his re-ascent follows his resurrection directly (78, p. 236). What Dibelius has in mind is that, according to the author of the main body of the text (not the passage he is regarding as an interpolation), Jesus had repeatedly to resort to disguise in order to avoid detection. The implication is that if he had appeared on earth in supernatural form, he would have been detected by the angels at once, and so if he stayed on or near earth in supernatural form after his resurrection, they would have found him out. Therefore the original writer's idea must have been an immediate ascension.

In the third, fourth and fifth heavens, Jesus is greeted with as much consternation as in the second. He then passes through the sixth and finally, 'I saw how he ascended into the seventh heaven, and all the righteous and all the angels praised him. And I saw him sit down on the right hand of the Great Glory' (xi, 32).

According to Dibelius (78, p. 94) the motive of the author of this whole story is to explain to those who believed in a celestial redeemer, called Christ, how it could happen that this figure was able to reach the earth without opposition; why it was that the angels of the various heavens let their worst enemy redeem man without resisting his passage.

What relevance has all this to Paul's idea of Jesus? Couchoud, and Dibelius some years before him (78, pp. 92, 96), answer that Paul seems to have had a revelation very similar to that here ascribed to Isaiah. In I Cor. ii, 9, he tells that God has revealed marvellous things to him—things, he adds, which pertain to our salvation, to God's gift to us (verse 12). We have already seen that he also tells how he was once caught up as far as the third heaven (where he locates paradise, a detail which is in agreement with the Slavonic Enoch), and there heard secret words. These seem to have told him a story (similar to that communicated to Isaiah) of a being who, existing as a god, took human form to suffer death and then re-ascended to the highest heaven to receive the name 'all-powerful' (Phil. ii, 5–11). The purpose of this descent and re-ascent is given in the passage from Colossians (above p. 290). By the blood of his cross he laid the basis for reconciling all things in heaven and earth to the Father; by his death and resurrection he broke the power of those angels who opposed God, and also put an end to man's dependence on angels, good or bad. Man can now commune with God via Jesus, without other intermediaries. Thus Paul declares that we need no longer be slaves to the elemental spirits ($\sigma\tauo\iota\chi\epsilon\hat{\iota}\alpha$) of the universe (Gal. iv, 3–5); that no spirits need now separate us from the love of God (Rom. viii, 38–9); and that the 'rulers of this world' are declining to their end (I Cor. ii, 6). The reference is to Satan and his angels,[1] and in this passage from Corinthians Paul is thus saying that it is these wicked creatures who crucified 'the Lord of glory', not knowing who he was. Couchoud compares this with the *Ascension of Isaiah*, ix, 14: 'And the god of that world will stretch forth his hand against the Son, and they will crucify him on a tree, and will slay him, not knowing who he is.' They do not know his identity because at every stage in his journey down he was transformed into the likeness of the creatures at that level. Just as this work goes on to tell how he rose from the dead and punished them by confronting them in his true form, so too Paul describes (Coloss. ii, 15) how they were tricked and vanquished: 'Having put off from himself the principalities and the powers, he made a show of them openly, triumphing over them in it'. The NEB says he 'made a spectacle of the cosmic powers and authorities, and led them as captives in his triumphal procession'. Dibelius gives evidence that the fundamental theme of the *Ascension of Isaiah*—the failure of forces hostile to Christ to recognize him in his disguise—appears in a number of other ancient works, and so may be accepted as an idea current in Paul's world (78, pp. 97–9). It is hardly necessary to note that if Jesus' activity on earth was such that the angels did not know who he was, he could not have gone about being generally recognized, as he is in Jn. In Mk., too, it is precisely the demons who recognize him as the Christ, and Lk. xxii, 3 has it that Satan engineers his betrayal. Paul's idea of Jesus on earth implies an obscure individual, not the personage of the gospels. Werner notes that for this reason the gospel story of the Temptation, where Jesus is recognized by Satan as the Son of God, cannot be historical.

Paul's statement that 'the rulers of this world are coming to nought' indicates his belief that the world will shortly be brought to an end by the second coming (I Cor. ii, 6; vii, 29–31). He holds that Satan as the god of this age or world[2] is destined to speedy destruction with it. Jesus has yet to destroy the angelic spirits.

---

[1] See above, p. 132. In II Cor. iv, 4 Paul complains that unbelievers are 'blinded by the god of this world', i.e. Satan, for elsewhere in this epistle (e.g. ii, 11) he regards Satan as his adversary. And he tells the Ephesians that before their conversion they 'followed the evil ways of this present age . . . and obeyed the commander of the spiritual powers of the air' (ii, 2 NEB.) The *Ascension of Isaiah* also lets Satan have his residence in the firmament.

[2] Paul uses the expressions 'this world' (ὁ κόσμς οὗτος) and 'this age' (ὁ αἰὼν οὗτος) interchangeably. The two are equated, for instance, in I Cor. i, 20 and iii, 18–19.

His visit to earth has merely broken their power, and now he sits at the right hand of God (Coloss. iii, 1; Rom. viii, 34) and will return to judge mankind and destroy all wicked powers. Paul distinguishes as stages in the winding-up of the universe: first Christ's resurrection, then the resurrection of the dead at his second coming, and finally his destruction of the angels; he will 'abolish every kind of dominion, authority and power'. Then he will abdicate or 'deliver up the kingdom to God the Father', and the celestial harmony will be complete (I Cor. xv, 18–28). Paul expects this final judgement to occur before all the present generation has died (I Thess. iv, 13–18; I Cor. xv, 51 f.).

The later development of Christianity can be understood as an attempt to explain the repeated failure of the final judgement to materialize. Paul's thinking is directed as much forwards to it as backwards to the death of Jesus which has so much improved our chances of surviving it. But when the second coming of Jesus to judge men and the angels failed to occur as quickly as was hoped, Christians would begin to think less about his victory over the angels at his second coming, and more about the victory already gained over them at the crucifixion. Thus, as Dibelius puts it, 'the centre of gravity of Christian expectation shifted from the future into the . . . past' (78, p. 201). Already in II Thess. ii, 2 we find protests against the use of Paul's epistles to support the claim that the second coming was imminent. And as attention became more concentrated on Jesus' sojourn on earth, biographical details would begin to be invented, and traditions initiated which eventually became fixed in the gospels. Apocalypses and apocalyptic visions would be ousted by biographies.

This process would be greatly facilitated by the fact that the Jewish Messianic expectations were far from uniform, and envisaged both a human Davidic leader as well as a supernatural redeemer as described in *Enoch*. In this work, the Messiah or 'Chosen One' is expressly reckoned among the angels (chapter lxi, 10). As expectations of the speedy appearance on earth of such a supernatural figure receded, the Jews would fall back on the old idea of a human Messiah, and what this man was expected to do would give a framework or nucleus for the construction of Jesus' biography. The extent of this framework has struck us already (above, pp. 109–111). Further biographic details could be furnished by interpreting some of the prophecies which referred to a supernatural redeemer in such a way as to make them apply to a human Messiah. Thus Justin and others applied the 'Son of man' prophecy of Dan. vii, 13 to the appearance of the Messiah in humility on earth, because as Werner notes, 'they no longer rightly understood the apocalyptic expression "Son of man", and erroneously applied it to the incarnated being of the Logos-Son' (284, p. 60).

It was, then, disappointment in Jesus' failure to come in his glory to judge and end the world that led believers to concentrate their attention on what had already been achieved by his first coming, and in this way to invent traditions about the details of his stay on earth. This theory of the origin of the gospel narratives can be supported by the demonstration that, once they existed, they were amplified by details which can be shown to have their origin in a similar desire to prove that the phenomena associated with the second coming (which had failed to occur) had been to some extent realized in the first. The reader may recall that Mt. tells how, at the death of Jesus, an earthquake occurred, rocks and graves were split open, and the saints occupying them were resurrected. Since only Mt. records these details, they may be regarded either as his additions to an existing set of traditions about the crucifixion, or as material unknown to, or rejected by, the other evangelists. In either case, we seek a motive which could have led to the formation of such a story. The answer is at hand when we realize (with the help of Werner, see above, p. 103) that catastrophes such as Mt. depicts were what the Jews expected when the world ended, and therefore what the Christians thought would occur at the second coming. Mt.'s story was, then, invented in order to show that Christians need not be disappointed at the failure of the second coming to occur, since the phenomena associated with it had, at any rate in part, been manifested at the first coming. Disappointment is being rectified in that the frustrated hopes of a future dénouement are replaced by faith and belief in one that had already occurred in a definite historical situation. If such motives could lead in this way to the amplification of existing traditions about Jesus' life on earth, they could well have been responsible for the whole historical setting given to it in the gospels.

(iv) Paul's Jesus and the Jewish law

Paul not only believes that Jesus' descent to earth and ignominious death were effected in order to deal with the wicked angels and end their revolt. He also regards Jesus' death as freeing us from the Jewish law. His missionary work in the Greek cities of Asia Minor would have been very much hampered had he required converts to keep these complicated stipulations. The argument he gives to show that this is unnecessary is that a crucified Jesus contradicts the law of Deut. xxi, 23 that a man whose dead body is hanged upon a tree is accursed of God. Paul quotes this passage and comments: 'Christ brought us freedom from the curse of the law by becoming for our sake an accursed thing' (Gal. iii, 13). The argument is: the law says that the man crucified is accursed. Jesus was crucified but could not be accursed. Therefore a case has occurred for which the law is not valid. But as it must be either valid absolutely or invalid absolutely, it is by this one case rendered wholly invalid (248, p. 72).

Paul's rejection of the law in favour of a personal relation to a divine being is, as Gilbert Murray has shown, in line with the whole trend of Greek thought. Aeschylus shows that the law that sin must bring punishment only leads to more and more sin. Aegisthus acted correctly in killing Agamemnon (to avenge Thyestes), and Orestes in killing him. 'Similarly, when Clytemnestra killed Agamemnon the eternal law compelled Orestes to avenge him.' The only escape from this endless chain is by an appeal to a wise and forgiving deity, who can forgive an action which transgresses the law because he understands the motives which led to it, while the law itself is blind, impersonal and 'neither understands nor forgives' but 'just operates' (197, pp. 20–5). Murray then shows that with Plato and Aristotle too, 'the ultimate justice is to be found in an appeal from a law to a person'. But, he adds:

Paul made one great concession to primitive thought which Aeschylus had entirely rejected. When Orestes is pardoned by the will of Zeus, the Furies yield; the Law is deemed to be satisfied; there is no talk of its demanding to be paid off with another victim. But in Paul, when man is to be forgiven, the sin still claims its punishment, the blood will still have blood; and the only way to appease it is for the Divine King, himself or his son, to 'die for the people'. Thus the pollution is cleansed and sin duly paid with blood, though it happens to be the blood of the innocent. Aeschylus, as a poet, was familiar with that conception. He knew how Codrus died, and Menoikus and Macaria, how Agamemnon and Erechtheus and other kings had given their children to die. But for him such practices belonged to that primitive and barbaric world which Hellenic Zeus had swept away, so he hoped, for ever' (p. 28).

Our next question is, what relation does Paul envisage between these two effects of Jesus' death, between the defeat of the angels and the freedom from the law? Paul's answer is that the Mosaic law is itself the work of angels, that it was given to Moses on Sinai not by God but by angels. 'The law,' he says, 'was promulgated through angels, and there was an intermediary (Moses)' (Gal. iii, 19, NEB). This idea is quite alien to the Pentateuch, where Yahweh is represented as dealing directly with Moses, but is common in later Jewish writings, since it was thought that the transcendence of Yahweh would be compromised by a direct appearance (78, p. 187). There is also evidence that the belief that the Messiah would put an end to the validity of the law was common in Jewish circles in pre-Christian times (283, p. 188 n. The English translation (284) abbreviates the original and omits this). Paul combines these two ideas. Christians, he says, are to have contact with God through Jesus; thus they are not to submit themselves to the law which reached mankind only through two intermediaries—the angels gave it to Moses and he passed it on to mankind. Paul sums up by saying that God has bidden him promulgate a new covenant—'a covenant expressed not in a written document, but in a spiritual bond; for the written law condemns to death, but the Spirit gives life' (II Cor. iii, 5-6, NEB). Subservience to the law entails bearing the yoke of angels from whom Christ has freed us:

> During our minority we were slaves to the elemental spirits of the universe, but when the term was completed, God sent his own Son, born of a woman, born under the law, to purchase freedom for the subjects of the law, in order that we might attain the status of sons (Gal. iv, 3-5, NEB).

Christ, then, has freed us from this 'yoke of slavery' (Gal. v, 1), and if we put ourselves under it we return to the power of the 'mean and beggarly spirits of the elements' (Gal. iv, 9). Paul asks the Galatians who are inclined to accept the law: 'Why do you propose to enter their service all over again?' Christ 'ends the law' (Rom. x, 4). At times it almost looks as though Paul is saying that the law was imposed on man by wicked angels, for he says it was given 'because of transgressions' (Gal. iii, 19), and this has been taken to mean that wicked angels imposed these complicated stipulations on man in order to make him sin frequently by breaking them. This interpretation is further supported when we find Paul saying that 'Law intruded into this process to multiply law-breaking' (Rom. v, 20. NEB). Paul gives an example. 'I should never have known what it was to covet, if the law had not said "Thou shalt not covet". Through that commandment sin found its opportunity, and produced in me all kinds of wrong desires' (Rom. vii, 7–9, NEB). However, he immediately goes on to say that 'the law is in itself holy, and the commandment is holy and just and good' (verse 12), and he surely could not have said this if he thought that it was the work of wicked angels. The key to what he has in mind is furnished by his phrase 'through that commandment sin found its opportunity'. It is not the law but sin that is wicked. In Rom. vi-viii sin is frequently personified as a spirit which resides in man—more precisely in his 'flesh'—and tyrannizes him, making him do wrong even when he wills to do right. As soon as man knows the law, and thus knows that certain actions are wrong, sin takes advantage of the situation and creates strong desires to do these wrong things. Thus he says: 'Are we to say then that this good thing (the law) was the death of me? By no means. It was sin that killed me, and thereby sin exposed its true character; it used a good thing to bring about my death.' He goes on to complain of the way this demon sin tyrannizes him.

> It is no longer I who perform the action, but sin that lodges in me. For I know that nothing good lodges in me—in my unspiritual nature I mean—for though the will to do good is there, the deed is not . . . If what I do is against my will, clearly it is no longer I who am the agent, but sin that has its lodging in me (Rom. vii, 18–20 NEB).

Paul's whole argument leads up to the conclusion that Jesus' death on the cross has broken the power of this demon that lodges in the flesh.

What the law could never do, because our lower nature robbed it of all potency, God has done: by sending his own Son in a form like that of our own sinful nature, and as a sacrifice for sin, [OR, to deal with sin], he has passed judgement against sin within that very nature (Rom. viii, 3).

Dibelius (78, p. 123) interprets this as follows: Jesus, in becoming flesh, has been able to tackle sin on its own ground, and in dying as flesh he has 'dealt with' sin, killed it in those mystically united with him. In Gal. vi, 14 the same idea is again stated. 'God forbid that I should boast of anything but the cross of our Lord Jesus Christ, through which the world is crucified to me and I to the world'. The carnal side of the believer has thus died and only his spirit remains. He has thereby become fit for immortal life:

Our old man was crucified with him [Christ] that the body of sin might be done away, so that we should no longer be in bondage to sin; . . . But if we died with Christ, we believe that we shall also live with him; knowing that Christ being raised from the dead dieth no more; death no more hath dominion over him (Rom. vi, 6–9).

A few verses earlier (and also in Gal. iii, 27) Paul had argued that the mystic union of the believer with Jesus is effected by baptism. The NBC explains (p. 950) that there are three actions in a baptism of total immersion, and that Paul regards them all as symbolic. 'Into the water—death; under the water—burial; out of the water—resurrection.' Thus he argued that baptism kills our carnal nature, just as Jesus' flesh was killed on the cross; and that it sets free our spiritual nature, just as Jesus as spirit and not as flesh, rose from the dead (Rom. vi, 4).

In the upshot, then, we find that the death and resurrection of the god, and the sacrament of baptism, serve the same function for Paul as they did in the pagan mysteries; they assure the believer of his own salvation and immortality (cp. above, pp. 235–7).[1] Reitzenstein observes that, in many pagan documents, σωτηρία, i.e. salvation in this life and the next, is linked with baptism in holy water. He adds that the soaking of the initiate in

[1] The most recent Catholic scholarship (233, p. 86) admits that Paul's view of baptism, and even of the Lord's Supper, is 'perhaps' indebted to pagan mystery cults which celebrated the dying and resurrected god.

the blood of a bull in the Phrygian mysteries (see above, p. 282) is similar to the Egyptian baptism which confers rebirth (214, pp. 28, 31). Schweitzer notes that 'the effect of baptism is thought of so objectively that some in Corinth caused themselves to be baptized for the dead, in order that through this baptism, by proxy, they might share in the benefits of the sacraments. Far from combating such a view as superstitious, Paul uses it as an argument against those who cast doubt on the resurrection (I Cor. xv, 29)' (248, p. 19).

Of course, Paul also believed that the death of Jesus was an atonement for the sins of Christians—at any rate for the sins they committed before their conversion. He expressly makes this restriction:

> God designed him [Christ] to be the means of expiating sin by his sacrificial death, effective through faith. God meant by this to demonstrate his justice, because in his forbearance he had overlooked the sins of the past—to demonstrate his justice now in the present, showing that he is both himself just and justifies any man who puts his faith in Jesus (Rom. iii, 25).

Paul's restriction of the atoning efficacy of Jesus' death to past sins is intelligible enough. For in so far as he believed in the speedy end of the world, he thought there was only a past and present to provide for, not a future. He also believed that baptized Christians had died to sin in mystic union with Jesus, so that the problem of sin did not arise for the true believer after baptism. In I Cor. v, 5 he instructs the Corinthians to hand over to Satan 'for the destruction of the flesh' a man guilty of sexual immorality. The idea seems to be that since, for some reason, baptism had failed to kill this man's carnal nature, he must be consigned to that evil being who has the power to destroy the body. And once the body is destroyed, whether it be by baptism or by Satan, the spirit will be liberated, 'his spirit will be saved on the day of the Lord'.

The idea that Jesus died as an atoning sacrifice is in the Apocalypse, and is in any case something that would be perfectly intelligible to the Jews. Paul's originality lies not in this idea of atonement, but in his theories that (1) Jesus died to deprive sin of its power, to negate sin itself; (2) the annihilation of sin in the true believers makes it unnecessary for them to follow the law, so that (3) they are no longer in any way dependent on the angels (through whom the law came to man) but can commune with God through Jesus. Finally (4) Jesus' death on the cross is a clear abrogation of the law (which reserves crucifixion for the accursed), and a means whereby he tricked wicked angels. We see that all these arguments concern man's relation to demons and angels. At every turn we find that Paul's views hinge on the relationships he envisages between man and spirits. Jesus is of interest to him because he has radically changed the relation in which we stand to such creatures.

(v) The origin of Paul's idea of Jesus and the transition to the idea of a historical Jesus

Now that we have seen what Paul's doctrine of Christ crucified implies, we have next to inquire into the origin of the idea. In an earlier section I showed that (1) the idea that the god died to redeem us was common in the pagan world at the beginning of the Christian era: (2) there is evidence that some Jews (though not the majority) believed that when the Messiah came he would suffer (although even they did not believe that he would die as an atoning sacrifice): (3) these two ideas—the pagan dying god and the Jewish suffering Messiah—could have become linked to give the new idea of the crucified Messiah without any further historical basis. There is certainly nothing in Paul's doctrine of mystical union with Christ crucified to suggest that the reference is to a contemporary who had been crucified.

Furthermore, Paul describes an early Christian sacred meal which is indebted to both pagan and Jewish ideas, and which, some scholars have argued, shows some similarities to the ritual of the Essene daily meal. We saw that there is strong evidence that the Essene Teacher of Righteousness (who may also have been one of the sect's two Messiahs) was put to death by his enemies, and that there is some evidence that someone—possibly this Teacher—had been crucified but had nevertheless become the object of an invocation about the time of Alexander Jannaeus. The writings referring to the Teacher tell us a good deal about him. It would certainly not be true to say of him that nothing was known about him except that he was put to death. But the early Christians could easily have taken over ritual from the Essenes without adopting the historical details of the career of the Teacher. What matters in religion is ritual, and we have had examples enough of the way an ancient ritual can survive while becoming associated with new ideas. We saw too that the Essenes were scattered and even persecuted after AD 70, and that as an esoteric sect they did not noise their doctrines abroad. The Essene writers also refer to their Teacher in such a veiled manner that it is very difficult even for modern historians to decipher the references. Hence if the early Christians were not Essenes but had merely taken over some Essene ritual, they are unlikely to have had any accurate detailed knowledge of the Teacher's career. They could well have learned nothing more than that the ritual was associated with a Messianic figure who had been put to death. When this had occurred would not have been clear and would not have interested them. Faith in the redeemer was what mattered. It is obvious enough that these early Christians were concerned more for their own salvation than for any kind of historical facts: and Paul expressly argues that faith is the key to salvation (see above, p. 291). Furthermore, Paul and other early Christians were obsessed with the idea that the Jesus of their faith was very soon to return and bring the world to a catastrophic end. This again meant that they had no motive for attending to historical details of the past. Their overriding interest in the second coming precluded them from caring much about the details of the first. Jesus' career on earth would only begin to be of interest either when his earthly existence began to be disputed or when his second coming was no longer expected to follow immediately.[1]

Even if Paul's belief in Christ crucified can be thus connected with a vague reminiscence of a man with some sort of Messianic pretensions who had been put to death—and Paul's letters contain

---

[1] Christian scholars invoke these very facts as an explanation of the failure of the earliest Christians to record in writing anything about their slain Messiah for years after his alleged death. But other sects, who also expected a prompt end to the world, did not refrain from committing their views to writing. Goodspeed concedes (107, p. 1) that the Christian 'delay in creating literary materials is hard to explain in the light of the literature produced by other Jewish groups, notably the community at Qumran . . . but also by those other groups out of which various apocalyptic predictions emerged'. If there was a historical crucifixion in AD 30, it is remarkable that the earliest Christian literature, the Pauline letters, did not follow until thirty years later (quite apart from the fact that these letters give no indication of the time or place of the crucifixion). If, however, there was no historical crucifixion, and the Pauline letters represent the beginnings of Christianity, then there is no delay to explain.

nothing that would justify the supposition that the *historical* basis
of his belief was anything more concrete than this—we nevertheless cannot suppose that this was its sole basis. It was a very
powerful belief, the centre of his religious teaching, and he must
have had some much more potent reason for believing it than
could have been provided by a vague reminiscence. Let us see
whether we can find some other basis.

The Essenes typify the religious developments which we saw
had occurred in the last centuries of the pre-Christian era. The old
gods were developing into saviours, their worship was becoming
personal and secret and carried on in special brotherhoods,
membership of which depended on certain conditions, in particular on a certain standard of conduct. At secret meetings rites
were performed which had magical virtue. The initiates received
knowledge which assured them of resurrection in another kind of
life. They were forbidden to divulge this knowledge or to speak
to the uninitiated of the rites performed in secret. These new
secret rites are all derived from ideas associated with the older
gods, Dionysus, Osiris, etc., and did not start as entirely new
revelations or inventions. They included dramatic representations
of long familiar myths (see above, p. 235). The Essene brotherhood differed from the Greek mysteries by being based on Jewish
rather than on Greek or Egyptian theology.

The connection between Paul's religious views and these
mysteries of the Greek-speaking world has often been noted.
Jülicher (156, § 4) remarks that when in I Cor. xv, 51 Paul

introduces a piece of his characteristic gnosis concerning the
last day with the words, 'behold, I tell you a mystery,' one feels
that here he is a mystagogue speaking to a circle of mystae; and
in the many passages where he introduces the idea of a 'mystery'
in connection with the gospel he proclaims, the derivation of
his language from the mysteries so eagerly resorted to by the
heathen who were seeking salvation can hardly be mistaken.
He who in the spirit speaks with tongues (I Cor. xiv, 2) utters
mysteries; in I Cor. xiii, 2 'all mysteries and all knowledge'
(gnosis) sum up the highest conceivable attainment of human
learning—it is precisely what is hidden from others that is
known to the true gnostic; and in I Cor. iv, 1 Paul claims to be
recognized by all, not only as a servant of Christ, but also as
a steward of the mysteries of God.

A prominent feature of the pagan mysteries of the time is the claim of the mystae to receive private revelations when in ecstatic union with their god, and the devotees who had experienced such revelations are apt to be scornful of the claims of others, even of other initiates (214, p. 18). Here again the parallel with Paul is striking. *Gnosis* is the word used to designate knowledge of the divine secrets won from such direct intercourse with the deity (Ibid., p. 41).

Paul is by no means the only early Christian writer who shows affinities with the pagan mysteries. Hippolytus of Rome wrote a *Refutation of all Heresies* early in the third century, and the first group of heretics he deals with are Christian mystics, whose teaching, he says, is identical with that of the pagan mysteries. He is able to quote in full a secret document belonging to one of these sects, whom he calls the Naassenes (now known as the Ophites). Mead, who has edited this document (182, pp. 141–98), remarks that 'it is especially valuable as pointing out the identity of the inner teachings of Gnostic Christianity with the tenets of the Mysteries—Phrygian, Eleusinian, Dionysian, Samothracian, Egyptian, Assyrian, etc.' (181, pp. 198–9). We saw above that these mysteries involved belief in a god who died and rose. Can we not infer that the god of the early Christians was another of these, not a historical personage, and that the background of the pagan mysteries suffices to explain Paul's references to Christ crucified?

Gilbert Murray writes that the gnostic sects, which were scattered over the Hellenistic world before Christianity as well as after, believed in a Saviour modelled partly on the Jewish Messiah and partly on the suffering god of the mysteries. This redeemer, he says, has various names, which the name of Jesus or 'Christos', 'The Anointed', tends gradually to supersede.

> The method in which he performs his mystery of Redemption varies. It is haunted by the memory of the old Suffering and Dying God . . . It is vividly affected by the ideal 'Righteous Man' of Plato, who 'shall be scourged, tortured, bound, his eyes burnt out, and at last, after suffering every evil, shall be impaled or crucified' (*Republic*, 362A). But in the main he descends, of his own free will or by the eternal purpose of the Father, from Heaven through the spheres of all the Archontes or Kosmokratores, the planets, to save mankind (196, pp. 162–4).

It might be asked why Paul should specify crucifixion. Thus although his pagan environment could have given him the idea of a suffering, dying and resurrected God, a crucified god—it might be held—suggests a particular historical reminiscence, an actual crucifixion. The answer is that crucifixion has not always been as particularized an idea as it now is. The Latin *crux* and the Greek *stauros* did not originally mean what we now mean by a cross. *Crux* means primarily a gallows, frame or tree on which criminals were impaled or hanged. It can also mean a cross, and also torture or misery. The verb *cruciare* means 'to put to the rack, torture, torment', and came at different times to denote the particular torture which happened to be popular. The Greek σταυρός means an upright pale, stake or pole. The word is connected with the verb ἴστημι, to make to stand. The verb σταυρόω was applied to modes of execution common among the Persians, and it is probable that impalement as well as crucifixion was thus denoted. Paul would, of course, be familiar with what we call crucifixion, as practised by the Romans. When he spoke of Christ crucified, he may have been thinking primarily of torture and execution, not necessarily implying what we understand by crucifixion. Such torture and suffering would not necessarily be different from that undergone by pagan deities. But since the same word denoted the practice of crucifixion he saw around him, he could easily have come to suppose that Christ had been crucified in this sense. That his ideas on the exact manner of Jesus' death are not altogether precise is suggested by the fact that, as we have seen, he makes use of Deut. xxi, 22 to refer to it, saying: 'Christ redeemed us from the curse of the law, having become a curse for us: for it is written, Cursed is every one that hangeth on a tree' (Gal. iii, 13). The passage he here quotes from Deuteronomy refers to the custom of hanging a criminal on a tree *after* execution.

And if a man have committed a sin worthy of death, and he be put to death, and thou hang him on a tree; his body shall not remain all night upon the tree, but thou shalt surely bury him the same day; for he that is hanged is accursed of God.

That execution preceded the 'hanging' is clear from Josh. x, 26, from which we learn that Joshua smote five kings of the Amorites, 'slew them and hanged them upon the trees until the evening'.

This is quite a different thing from crucifixion as we understand the term.

To return to the pagan ideas and the striking affinities between them and those of the early Christians, it is of interest to note that Hippolytus, in the introduction to his *Refutation of all Heresies*, claims to divulge the secrets of the Egyptian and Chaldean mysteries. But not only are the parts of his work where he does this missing, but also the summary of their contents is missing from the Epitome, which is otherwise fully preserved. This looks like a deliberate attempt by some copyist to suppress the information. It is natural to suspect that a Christian copyist might have feared that Christian readers would find the parallels between the pagan mysteries and their own beliefs all too striking.

Religious clubs, then, with special conditions of membership, formed a prominent feature of religious life, Christian and pagan, and Jewish, at the beginning of our era. That early Christians formed societies is beyond doubt. The writer of Heb. x, 25 urges Christians to meet and come together, on the ground that 'the day' (of judgement) is approaching. And the epistles of Barnabas and of Ignatius exhort them not to withdraw themselves and live lives apart, but to consult about common interests. 'In later documents these exhortations cease. The tendency to association had become a fixed habit' (134, p. 30). One can imagine how at such gatherings of illiterate and semi-literate men who believed the end of the world to be nigh some would prophesy the exact circumstances of the end. It may be that misunderstanding played a large part in the evolution: when some more mystic members of the club spoke of the purely supernatural figures of their faith, the others might have supposed some reference to a historical figure to have been intended, and then this idea would have been clothed in flesh by the addition of biographical details.

The way in which doctrines and ideas could have been evolved at these meetings is indicated in I Cor. xiv, 26 ff. (NEB):

> To sum up, my friends: when you meet for worship, each of you contributes a hymn, some instruction, a revelation, an ecstatic utterance, or the interpretation of such an utterance.

Some, then, made ecstatic utterances, not understanding what they were saying, while others supplied an interpretation, 'If it is a matter of ecstatic utterance, only two should speak, or at most three, one at a time, and someone must interpret' (verse 27). The interpretation of unintelligible utterances would lead to the establishment of all sorts of doctrines. And at these meetings, anyone could stand up and promulgate a 'revelation' he had received: 'Of the prohets, two or three may speak, while the rest exercise their judgement on what is said. If someone else, sitting in his place, receives a revelation, let the first speaker stop. You can all prophesy, one at a time, so that the whole congregation may receive instruction and encouragement' (verses 29–32). Only at a later period did prophecy become the prerogative of a small élite, who led, and even claimed maintenance from, the community. This is the stage of development referred to in the *Didache*, where we are told that 'every genuine prophet who is willing to settle among you is entitled to his support. Likewise every genuine teacher is, like a labourer, entitled to his support. Therefore take all the first fruits of vintage and harvest, of cattle and sheep and give these first fruits to the prophets; for they are your high priests' (Chapter 13). Under such conditions rival prophets and rival teachers would inevitably compete, and this would lead to the sort of doctrinal strife we have repeatedly found early Christian writers complaining of. The suggestion has been made above (p. 164) that it was in response to such dissensions that the Asian Churches centralized their authority, leading to the rise of monarchical episcopacy. By then many doctrines had become fixed and settled, and the problem was not to enrich them with others by consulting inspired seers, but to provide a quasi-historical basis for what was already believed.

Couchoud makes the interesting suggestion that liturgical needs may well have led to the composition of written gospels. 'The Christians no longer observed the Mosaic law. They could hardly have continued the ritual readings from the Pentateuch. And we know that in the days of Justin (I Apol. lxvii, 3) readings from the gospels replaced readings from the law and preceded the recitation of passages from the prophets. This indicates for what purpose the gospels were composed.'[1] Couchoud adds that they

---

[1] An intermediate stage between a spoken prophecy and a written gospel would be represented by a pseudonymous epistle, which, as Aland has recently argued (9, pp. 7–8), would be read by its author to his own congregation in the service of worship. The congregation knew the author as their priest, but accepted his epistle as the work of the apostle James or John or Peter because he spoke with the apostle's voice. When at such a service a prophet got up and preached the word of the Lord, everyone knew the

'were composed at the time when prudent bishops were trying to wrest the leadership of the flock from the seers and prophets. The gospels gave them straightforward reading-matter . . . calculated to limit the free inventions of the spirit' (68, p. 162).

We saw that the pagan mysteries included dramatic performances, particularly of the death and resurrection of various gods. Witnessing a drama enacting the way the god had vanquished death assured the believer of his own immortality. The catechumen did not seem to ask when or where the god died. Nor is there any reason why he should have done so. He was seeking ecstasy and an assurance of salvation rather than enlightenment. But the organizers of any particular sect had to defend its tenets and procedure from the counter-attractions of rivals, and here argument was called for. In the case of the early Christians, their ideas were based in part on Jewish theology, and so one method of defending them would be to search the scriptures for proof that they were in accordance with divine revelation. This method is adopted by the author of I Peter, who says that the prophets foretold the sufferings of Jesus and constructs details of Jesus' biography by drawing on Isaiah. Another technique would be for writers to authenticate their views by claiming to have received special revelations, as Paul does. Another method of arguing the case for the death and resurrection of a particular god would be to place his death in a historical setting where it would seem plausible. The first sign of this technique in Christian literature occurs in Ignatius and in one of the Pastoral epistles, where we learn that Jesus 'witnessed the good confession before Pontius Pilate'. I have already argued (above, p. 242) that the choice of Pilate as the culprit is not surprising. If he had behaved in the AD 30's after the fashion reported by Josephus and Philo, he must have been remembered early in the second century—when the Pastorals were written (see above, p. 151)—as a notorious shedder of Jewish blood. Already in I Peter we find the earthly career of

---

prophet and his human affairs. 'But when he spoke with inspired utterance it was not he that was heard but the Lord or the apostles or the Holy Spirit himself . . . What happened in pseudonymous literature of the early period was nothing but a shift of the message from the spoken to the written word . . . When the pseudonymous writings of the NT claimed the authorship of the most prominent apostles only, this was not a skilful trick of the so-called fakers, in order to guarantee the highest possible reputation and the widest possible circulation for their work, but the logical conclusion of the presupposition that the Spirit himself was the author.'

Jesus placed in the 'last days'. This is not hard to understand. Since Jesus was essentially the God of the last days who would bring the world to a terrible end, his first appearance on earth could be regarded as marking the beginning of the world's final epoch. From this position it was but a step to understand the term 'last days' to mean the recent past, so that his sojourn on earth could be held to have been sufficiently recent for him to have been one of the victims of the notorious Pilate.

There was no doubt rival literature with other theories and justifications, but this was later destroyed by the triumphant party. It is however clear even from the surviving orthodox writings that other ideas than were acceptable to them were current. Paul warns the Corinthians against those who preach 'another Jesus' (II Cor. xi, 4). The epistle of Jude complains of 'mockers, walking after their own ungodly lusts. These are they who make separations, sensual, having not the spirit' (verse 19). And II Pet. ii similarly vilifies other sects. In I Tim. vi, 20 Timothy is urged to 'turn away from the profane babblings and oppositions of the knowledge [i.e. gnosis] which is falsely so called; which some professing have erred concerning the faith'. It is evident that each of the rival sects supposed that it alone held the key to salvation.

In sum, certain sectarian ideas about the God Jesus were defended by claiming special insight, by finding his fortunes prefigured in the scriptures, and by outlining historical circumstances in which he was active. Once he had in this way been endowed with a detailed biography, the original idea that he was a supernatural being wearing a temporary disguise was lost sight of, and some began to think that he started his career as a man and was only later raised to supernatural status. As every reader of Church history knows, such squabbles went on for centuries. Was the carpenter's son divine from the first, or did God only elevate him at some stage in his career, e.g. at his baptism or death? Did he possess a complete human nature with all human infirmities? Was there ever any conflict between the human and the divine parts of his being? Werner points out that indications that the relation between his human and his divine nature constituted a problem are already present in some synoptic passages. Thus in Mt. xxii, 41-5, and its parallels, Jesus is made to repudiate the Davidic descent that the genealogies claim for him. He says that the Christ or Messiah cannot be a descendant of David, because

David, in an inspired psalm, gives to the future Messiah a title —namely Lord—which no man would give to one of his own descendants. As Werner puts it: 'If the Christ was David's "Lord", then he belonged to a higher order, which raised the question of how could he then at the same time be David's son, i.e. a man' (284, p. 126).

The solution to the problem offered by some synoptic passages is that Jesus was a man until his death, but that 'by suffering, death and rising on the third day he attained to his (Messianic) lordship'. Werner adds that the same theory appears in Acts, which announces 'several times, as the doctrine of the original Jerusalem community, the view that the "Nazarean Jesus", was "a man approved of God" . . . and was, through suffering, death and resurrection made *kyrios* and Christ'.

Finally I would stress the significance of a point mentioned earlier, namely that the saviour gods honoured in the mysteries were not new. The old gods had come to be regarded in a new light, as mediators of salvation. Jesus too is a mediator God. Schweitzer makes the interesting observation that Paul talks repeatedly of mystic union with Christ, but never with God. He explains this by saying that, in Paul's view, 'so long as the natural world endures, even down into the Messianic period, angelic powers stand between man and God and render direct relations between the two impossible' (248, p. 10). He refers to Rom. viii, where Paul rejoices that the angels cannot separate the elect from God. The idea is not that the elect have direct access to him, but that they are one with Christ, who 'stands at God's right hand to plead their cause'. Thus the love of God comes to them only indirectly. Paul says he is 'convinced that there is nothing . . . in the realm of spirits or superhuman powers . . . that can separate us from the love of God in Christ Jesus our Lord' (verses 34, 39, NEB). In the Pastorals, Jesus is actually called 'the mediator between God and men' (I Tim. ii, 5).

We can perhaps better appreciate the success of this idea of a supernatural being who came to earth to suffer, and die, and reconcile us with the supreme God, if we understand that the invention of such mediators has repeatedly occurred in the evolution of religions, and for the obvious reason that, as the old god becomes a more distant and august figure, the worshipper feels the need for a deity who is less remote and therefore more likely to hear and answer prayers. Robertson has shown how general this tendency is: that many savages recognize a supreme God or creator to whom they do not sacrifice or pray. His evidence suggests that these gods were originally worshipped more actively, but have become so ineffable that the worshipper despairs of eliciting their assistance and directs his prayers and attention to nearer deities, who often figure as the sons or daughters of the supreme one. The Jewish God, he shows, has also become much more remote than he was in the earliest documents. For the Jews prior to the exile, 'Yahweh was a tribal God, like Moloch . . . fighting for his people (when they deserved it) like other tribal Gods; a magnified man who talked familiarly with Abraham and Sarah, and wrestled with Jacob'. But gradually he became more august, with the result that, at the beginning of our era, 'among the common cravings of the age was the need for a *near* God, one ostensibly more in touch with human sorrows and sufferings'. Given this psychic need, it is not hard to understand how Paul and others could find a hearing for their belief in a mediator God who loved men enough to come and suffer and die for them. Just as Apollo, Athene, Attis, Heracles and Dionysus (all widely worshipped), figure as children of the remote Zeus, so this Judaeo-Greek Logos had to become the son of Yahweh. Later, Jesus in his turn became a relatively remote figure, and among Catholics, Mary or the saints are made to play the part of mediator, prayers being addressed to them rather than directly to him (220, pp. 52–7; 222, pp. 95–8; 221, p. 76). Of course, this tendency to invent new mediators is to a certain extent checked by the fixation of beliefs in sacred books and dogmas.

(vi) Conclusion

Christian origins can be accounted for, with reasonable plausibility, without recourse to a historical Jesus. The evidence needed for a *probable* reconstruction is not available, and my suggested reconstruction is simply one of several possible alternatives. It can be summarized as follows:

(1) By the first century BC 'Messiah' had come to mean a redeemer whose advent was imminent. As the political position of the Jews under the Roman yoke seemed hopeless, it was thought that he would have to be more than a mere mortal, that only a

supernatural personage would be powerful enough to put things right. And so some Jews began to expect a supernatural figure who would descend from the skies, annihilate the world and judge mankind.

(2) The thought that judgement would be effected by a supernatural personage naturally led to reflection on the relationship between him and the angels of Jewish belief. Paul's view was that Jesus the Messiah absorbs all the 'pleroma' in himself; he combats the Jewish Gnostics who worshipped angels, and thinks that only Jesus is properly an object of adoration.

(3) As the moral judge of mankind, the Messiah was naturally conceived as not only a powerful but also a pre-eminently moral figure. Consequently, he was in some circles expected to suffer excessively, it being believed that suffering (a) confers supernatural powers and (b) indicates great virtue. Once the idea that he should suffer became current, it was possible to link him with any of the pagan gods who suffered and died, and to transfer to him some of the beliefs held about them.

(4) This idea of the dying god was common in the Middle East at the beginning of our era. Pagan mystery plays enacted his death, burial and resurrection which were believed to have occurred in the distant past.

The Jewish idea of the Messiah, however, concerned a personage who would come in the future. So the pagan idea of the god who died to redeem us could only be combined with the Jewish belief in the coming of the Messiah if it were supposed that the Messiah had come in the past to suffer and die, and would come again in the future to triumph. The synthesis of the two ideas—the Jewish future Messiah and the pagan dying god—would surely have been greatly facilitated by the teaching of the Qumran Essenes. They had had a priestly Teacher who had been persecuted, had died and was—some scholars think—to return soon, at the end of time. He may have been identical with the priestly Messiah the sect was expecting at the end of time—or if the two were not originally identical they could well have become regarded as so in the course of the sect's history, or in the minds of those who adapted Essene ideas. This Teacher may well have been a historical personage, for, if Dupont-Sommer's dating is correct, documents mention him within a few years of his death, and also sketch his earthly career in non-supernatural terms. The Essenes either themselves made current the idea of a Messiah who was put to death, or else this idea could readily have arisen from their teaching, thus facilitating the link between the Jewish Messiah and the pagan dying god.

(5) Both the Essenes and the pagans had ritual meals. The Essene meal was probably an anticipation of the Messianic banquet; it was believed that those partaking of the food would be admitted to table-fellowship with the Messiah when he came. The pagan meals were sacrificial; meat was offered to deities and then eaten. The sacred meal of the early Christians seems to have blended these two ideas of table-fellowship and sacrifice. It was, of course, possible for the early Christians to take over the ritual of the Essene meal, and the accompanying idea of table-fellowship with the Messiah, without also adopting the historical details about the career of the Teacher of Righteousness on earth. An ancient ritual frequently survives while becoming associated with quite new ideas.

(6) The association of the Christian meal with sacrifice led in time to linking many Jewish ideas of sacrifice with it. Thus atoning power was ascribed to the sacrifice and people participated in it for the forgiveness of sins. Furthermore, in the pagan sacrificial meals, the dominant idea was communion with a once dead and risen deity, in whose fate the partaker received a share through the meal. This idea that the meal gives mystic communion with the god became more and more prominent in the Christian meal as the older idea that it was a Messianic banquet receded due to the repeated failure of the end of the world to occur and the resulting dampening of eschatological excitement.

(7) Once the idea that the meal effected mystic communion became dominant, it would be cut down from a full repast to a distribution of the elements of salvation. It was again by association with the idea of sacrifice that these came to be connected with the sacrifice of the divine victim, the god who gave his life for us; so that the bread and wine eventually became symbols of the body and blood of the sacrificed god.

(8) At first the death of the god was conceived as a mystic sacrifice which had redeemed the elect and would ensure their survival in the coming judgement. Nothing was known of the circumstances in which it occurred, and such details were without interest to men who daily expected the terrors of the second coming. In the Apocalypse there is not even a clear indication of his manner of death, although nothing in this work contradicts the idea that he died by crucifixion. This is certainly how all the

L

other early Christian writings represent his manner of death—
e.g. the *Ascension of Isaiah*, the Pauline letters.

(9) Paul, obsessed with fears about the powers of the angels in
the firmament, found consolation in his visions, which informed
him that the redeemer had come down to earth in order to trick
and put to shame these beings; and that he had tricked them by
suffering an ignominious death at their hands. This idea that the
redeemer had been crucified was later strengthened by musing on
Psalm xxii. In Paul's day the idea caught on partly because it was
of such great use in freeing the gentile devotees of the new religion
from the Jewish law. Thus he was able to argue that the crucifixion
abrogated the law and broke the power of the angels who had
imposed it on man.

(10) The Messiah's final reckoning with the angels was expected
shortly at the great judgement. But as the second coming failed to
occur, Christians began to think less about his coming victory
over these angels, and more about the victory he had already
gained over them at the crucifixion. As attention came, in this
way, to be concentrated more and more on Jesus' sojourn on
earth, biographical details would begin to be invented. This
tendency to endow him with a detailed biography was greatly
assisted by the polemical need to combat rival theorists who
doubted or denied that he had visited the earth at all. It may have
been partly in order to controvert these rivals that Christian
writers began to allege that they had seen him while he was on
earth, thus transferring his earthly career from the distant to the
recent past. In any case, Jesus was the god of the 'last days', the
god who would soon bring the world to a catastrophic end. Hence
the appearance he had already made on earth was held (e.g. by I
Peter) to mark the beginning of the final era of world history. In
this sense he was said to have visited earth in the last days. This
could easily be misunderstood to mean that his visit was very
recent, and once this idea was firmly established, the choice of
Pilate, a notorious shedder of Jewish blood, as the man responsible for his death, is not surprising.

(11) The emphasis of the early Christian societies on purity of
living would lead the devotees to ascribe to their god—now
become a man–god—all manner of ethical teachings. All these
strands—The Messianic redeemer, the saviour of the world with
his blood and the teaching god—became fused in a composite
biography.

The extent to which orthodox writers admit many of the premises on which my arguments are based is something that deserves greater publicity. Hoskyns and Davey not only concede that some of the earliest references to Jesus' passion are adapted from Isaiah and that the gospel accounts of the crucifixion draw extensively on Ps. xxii; they even stress the following considerations which are of prime importance to my account of Christian origins:

(1) If, when St Paul was writing, stories about Jesus were being carefully treasured and passed on from mouth to mouth, it seems strange that only in one or two places does he definitely quote them (141, p. 147).

(2) The Pauline and Johannine writings . . . imply that the historical figure of Jesus, the life which he lived in the flesh, is of little importance in comparison with the experience of the 'Christ-Spirit' possessed by primitive Christians (p. 151). And—

(3) This conception of the relation of history to spiritual experience is exactly that of the contemporary religions of the Greco-Roman world. These, the mystery religions, although highly diverse in details, agree in attaching themselves to some story of a hero god or gods. They make no pretence to show the validity of the story as history. They were not for a moment concerned to do so. But they held out the prospect of salvation which could be attained by means of certain rites and dramatizations of the story of their god (p. 152).

If, then, the early Christians conceived Jesus 'exactly' as these pagans conceived their saviour gods (whom no one now believes to have existed), what right have we to reject the suggestion that Jesus may well be no more historical than they?

EPILOGUE: SOME RECENT STUDIES OF JESUS

(i) Bornkamm

In spite of their concessions, which I have just quoted, Hoskyns and Davey remain confident that Christianity began with a historical Jesus, not with a 'Christ-myth which was subsequently clothed with flesh and blood' (141, p. 81 n.). This latter possibility, they say, 'cannot be considered in an historical study since on this assumption the Jesus of history would become a proper subject for historical investigation only at the Last Judgement'. The meaning appears to be that a historical study cannot be concerned with a non-historical character. Yet when we approach the question of the origin of any religion, we naturally ask whether the persons associated by tradition with that origin had a historical existence or were merely mythical. To exclude such considerations from a historical study is arbitrary.

The politeness with which Hoskyns and Davey refer to the view that Jesus was mythical is today unusual. Bornkamm (33, p. 25) calls this view 'an unrestrained tendencious species of modern criticism which it is not worth our while to investigate'. Morison (191, p. 10) calls it an 'absurd cult' which has 'ceased to carry any weight'. That neither of these two writers gives a fair statement of the evidence on the matter is obvious from their references to Josephus, whom they both designate as a 'ferocious opponent' of Christianity (33, p. 25), as 'a writer notoriously contemptuous of the whole Christian movement' (191, p. 12). Josephus in fact makes no mention of Christianity.

Bornkamm does not inspire confidence when he takes NT

statements which he admits to be 'spurious' as proof of the reality of the resurrection because they proceed from the feeling of the writer that the risen Christ is with him (33, p. 18). Since he regards Jesus' baptism as 'among the best attested data of his life' (p. 49) it is of interest to study his account of the evidence for it. He believes, as did Strauss, that it is historically true that John baptized Jesus, but Christian legend is that in doing so he anointed him as the Messiah. In Mt. iii, 14 John is represented as recognizing Jesus as 'the mightier one' who is to come after him, and as at first refusing him baptism on this ground. His recognition of Jesus as the Messiah is then confirmed by a supernatural revelation. The heavens open, the Holy Spirit hovers over Jesus in the shape of a dove, and a voice from heaven is heard to say 'this is my beloved son in whom I am well pleased'. However, the synoptic gospels later represent John as sending his own disciples to Jesus to inquire whether he is 'he that cometh' or whether they are to 'look for another' (Mt. xi, 2–4). Strauss inferred that what actually happened was that John baptized Jesus, without recognizing him as the Messiah, and with no supernatural revelation; that later he made the inquiry as to who Jesus was; that after all this had been recorded, the story was amplified to include the episodes in which Jesus appeared as the Messiah. In support Strauss was able to show that the words 'my beloved Son,' spoken by the voice from heaven, look like one of the many phrases concocted in order to agree with prophecy; for in Isaiah, Yahweh says of his servant: 'Behold . . . my beloved in whom my soul is well pleased', and Mt. himself (xii, 17) interprets this as applying to the Messiah. Moreover, Justin betrays that it was the Jewish notion that the Messiah would be unknown as such to himself and others until Elijah as his fore-runner should anoint him, and Jesus himself designates the baptist as Elijah. All this is plausible enough, except for the insistence that there was a historical event, a baptism to serve as a nucleus for the narratives. The Jewish expectation that the Messiah would be anointed by his fore-runner may well have inspired the whole of the present narrative.

I have commented earlier (p. 88) on the character which Bornkamm assigns to Jesus. He talks much of Jesus' 'immediacy', saying that he does not, like the Rabbis, derive his authority from sacred texts (cf. above, p. 201). So because documents written, according to Bornkamm himself, by Christian enthusiasts present a Jesus who claims the highest authority, we are to believe in a historical figure who possessed this quality of 'immediacy'. Bornkamm also believes Jesus to have been extremely perspicacious. 'Again and again one finds in his encounters the trait that he knows people and sees through to their thoughts; this trait is quite frequently developed by the evangelists into something miraculous' (p. 53). Such miracle narratives are, for Bornkamm, unhistorical; nevertheless, 'the essential thing is that in all of them this same trait reappears, by means of which the historical Jesus can be recognized' (p. 54). Bornkamm's technique can be summarized by saying that he claims to discern some kernel of historical truth in admitted myths. There is no justification for the claim.

(ii) Morison

To what extent Morison's views carry weight can be estimated from his claims (191, pp. 13, 113) that: (1) 'the real Jesus of history' can be seen in Jn.'s story of the woman taken in adultery (widely admitted on the strongest evidence to be an interpolation, see above, p. 15) and (2) we know Jesus' twelve apostles 'better than any other single group of persons in antiquity' (when in fact no NT lists of the twelve contain identical names, see above, p. 135, and most of the twelve are hardly mentioned at all except in these lists). Morison naïvely accepts certain gospel stories as true because they read 'like a transcript from real life', and because he can see no motive for their invention. One of his examples is 'the pathetic little story of Peter's fall and repentance' (p. 100). But we know from Galatians that some early Christians were bitterly hostile to Judaizing apostles, and this readily accounts for stories discrediting them in later literature.[1] Morison thinks that Jesus' historicity is assured by the testimony of Mk., the oldest gospel and the one which 'stands in a special relationship to the teaching of Peter'. That this is so 'has been a tradition of the Church from the very dawn of Christendom and will be disputed by few' (191, pp. 123–4). The reader is not to know that the reference is to the tradition about the origin of Mk. which Papias inaugurated towards the middle of the second century (see above, p. 177–9). Morison's phrase 'from the very dawn of Christendom' implies a date about a century earlier, since he supposes that Christianity

---

[1] cf. Winter's account (above p. 97) of Peter's denial as a tendency story.

had spread over the Eastern Mediterranean coast 'within twenty years of the resurrection' (p. 114).

Morison is concerned principally with Jesus' trial, death and resurrection. He regards it as certain that he was charged with threatening to destroy the temple and rebuild it in three days—a charge recorded only by Mk. xiv, 58 and by Mt., who, as Morison admits (p. 19), may here be dependent on Mk. Morison asks what Jesus said that formed the basis of this charge, and finds the answer in Jn. ii, 19–21, where Jesus says to 'the Jews': 'Destroy this temple and in three days I will raise it up.' The evangelist comments. 'But he spake of the temple of his body.' We may note the following facts:

(1) Jn. records this utterance in the chapter which begins with the miracle at Cana, witnessed by Jesus' mother and disciples, yet unknown to the synoptics, and said to be the first of the signs by which he revealed his glory and led his disciples to believe in him, whereas in the synoptics he had refused to give such a sign (cf. above, p. 128). The feast at Cana is followed by the cleansing of the temple (placed by the synoptics at the end, and not, as in Jn., at the beginning of Jesus' public career), and it is after this that he talks about the destruction of the temple, meaning his own body. This utterance is, of course, unknown to the synoptics.

(2) According to all three synoptics Jesus, before his arrest, predicts the destruction of the temple of Jerusalem (e.g. Mt. xxiv, 1–2), which is to occur at the end of the world, and of course says nothing of any rebuilding. All such discourses are absent from Jn., who makes the second coming mean not the supernatural appearance of Jesus to end the world, but the coming of the Holy Spirit into the hearts of believers.

Jn.'s interpretation of the second coming is clearly an attempt to eliminate the eschatology present in the synoptic statements about it. His statement that Jesus taught of the destruction and resurrection of the temple, meaning his own body, also looks like an attempt to adapt to his own use the synoptic statements about the destruction of the temple of Jerusalem. These are bound up with the eschatological expectations which Jn. rejected, and so, if he used them at all, he had to give them a totally new meaning. We may further note that the passage in the fourth gospel is the first of many where Jesus says something ambiguous, which he means to be taken in a sense which is far from obvious, so that his audience, not unnaturally, misunderstand him. The context makes this clear:

> The Jews therefore answered and said unto him, What sign showest thou unto us, seeing that thou doest these things? Jesus answered and said unto them, Destroy this temple and in three days I will raise it up. The Jews, therefore, said, forty and six years was this temple in building, and wilt thou raise it up in three days? But he spake of the temple of his body.

Other examples are:

(1) He tells a Pharisee 'except a man be born anew, he cannot see the kingdom of God' (iii, 3), and is asked: 'Can a man enter a second time into his mother's womb?' Whereupon he explains that he means being 'born of water and the Spirit'.

(2) He asks a woman at a well for a drink. When she remonstrates, he says that if she knew him, she would ask him for water. She replies that he is in no position to give anyone a drink, for he has nothing with which to draw water. He explains that the water he has to offer is drawn from the well of eternal life (iv, 10–14).

(3) When the disciples urge him to eat, he declares: 'I have meat to eat that ye know not.' They inquire whence he obtained these provisions, but he tells them: 'My meat is to do the will of him that sent me' (iv, 31–4).

It is difficult to believe that Jesus spoke in this manner to his audiences when it is unknown to the synoptics. In sum, then, the statement in Jn. about the temple meaning Jesus' body is one of a whole series absent both in form and substance from the other three gospels.

Jn.'s statement is important to Morison's argument, for he supposes that the priests learned from these words of Jesus at his trial that he threatened to rise again three days after his death. This, so Morison argues, led the priests to ask Pilate for permission to put a guard on the sepulchre to prevent his resurrection—a request known only to Mt. (xxvii, 62–4) who alone represents the sepulchre as guarded. Morison supposes that the guards were Jews from the temple, not Romans. He next rejects Mt.'s statement that the sepulchre stone was rolled away by an angel as the women were approaching, and accepts instead Mk.'s version that they found it already rolled away on their arrival. He argues that only the guards could have removed the stone: they alone were on the spot, and sufficiently numerous to move it (p. 158). The theory is that they fell asleep while on duty, but were disturbed, possibly by some supernatural appearances of the risen Jesus (p. 192). They were sufficiently alarmed by 'something' to roll away the stone and see whether he was still in the tomb, but found it empty and fled in alarm to report the matter to the priests (p. 165). The commotion they caused on their way may well have 'drawn more than one sleeper from his bed', and, according to Morison, one of these people thus disturbed was a young man who had overheard Jesus' statement on his way to Gethsemane— that 'after I am raised up, I will go before you into Galilee' (Mk. xiv, 28). There is no indication in Mk. that these words were heard by any but the disciples, and a little later 'a great multitude with swords and staves' arrives to arrest him, and all his supporters flee. The text continues:

And a certain young man followed with him, having a linen cloth cast about his naked body; and they laid hold on him; but he left the linen cloth and fled naked (verses 51-2).

Morison's theory is that this youth was with Jesus when he entered Gethsemane, and did not arrive only later, with the multitude; that he overheard Jesus' words to the disciples about being 'raised up' and 'going before them into Galilee'; that on the Sunday morning, he was awakened by the excited guards bursting into Jerusalem, declaring that something was wrong with the tomb; that, recalling Jesus' words, he 'lost no time in going personally to the grave, arriving there apparently a few minutes before the women' (p. 164). This explains Mk.'s statement that they found it already occupied by a young man in a white robe who

saith unto them, Be not amazed: ye seek Jesus, the Nazarene, which hath been crucified: he is risen: he is not here: behold the place where they laid him! But go, tell his disciples and Peter, He goeth before you into Galilee; there shall ye see him, *as he said unto you.* And they went out, and fled from the tomb; for trembling and astonishment had come upon them; and they said nothing to any one; for they were afraid . . .

The words I have italicized indicate, in Morison's view, that the speaker had overheard what Jesus said on the way to Gethsemane. The speaker is not a supernatural being, but 'just a young man wearing a white garment' (p. 158). Only later gospels (Mt. and Lk.) make him into an angel.

Mt. records that the guard was instructed by the priests to say that they had fallen asleep while guarding the tomb, and that while they slept, the disciples stole the body. At the same time Mary Magdalene (according only, we may note, to Jn.) was telling the disciples, not that Jesus had risen, but that 'for some unexplained reason the body had been removed' (pp. 178-9). Morison argues that these facts explain why the women's experience at the tomb was not used as evidence by Christians in their controversy with Jews. To mention the visit of the women would have been to make it very difficult to rebut the charge of having abducted the body. In sum, then, the emptiness of the tomb was accepted by both sides in the dispute. This theory is, however, open to the serious objection that, if the Christians really had to meet the charge of abducting the body, it is most remarkable that they did nothing to expose its hollowness. They would surely be expected to have said to the priests: you allege that all the men in your guard fell asleep; that meanwhile we arrived and moved the stone (so large that, in Morison's view, the combined strength of a number of men was necessary to move it); that the commotion thus caused and the subsequent removal of the body failed to awaken the guards. Since, however, the documents represent the Christians as saying nothing of the sort, this suggests that the whole story of the guard and of the priestly charge of abducting the body is legendary. Morison admits that there is an intelligible motive for the Christians to have invented the guard, namely to make it appear that the body could not have been stolen, and that Jesus, if he disappeared from his tomb, must have done so by supernatural means. But, he says, if the guard story were a Christian legend, the men would not have slept. 'A guard which slept was of no use to the Christians, and was futile and dangerous as an apologetic.' This appears to overlook the fact that, according to the only canonical evangelist who mentions the guard at all, it did not sleep, but was merely, after the event, instructed by the priests to pretend that it had done so. It is essential to Morison's case that the story of the guard and the priestly instructions to it to lie were, as he puts it, 'widely circulated in apostolic times' (p. 88). But this ill accords with the fact that only Mt. mentions it, and his reference itself clearly indicates a writer well removed in time from the events he describes; for he tells that the saying that the disciples stole the body 'was spread among the Jews and continueth until this day' (xxviii, 15).

(iii) **Schonfield**

Schonfield (243) has followed Morison's method of constructing a biography by drawing freely on all four gospels, accepting what suits the needs of his thesis, and rejecting as legendary what does not. Schonfield believes that Jesus somehow got into his mind that he was the Messiah, and therefore arranged his life as closely as he could in conformity to prophecy. If we find, therefore, that incidents in his recorded life appear to have been accurately foretold by the Hebrew prophets, this is not necessarily because the evangelists have reported inaccurately (although he does admit, p. 155, that some gospel incidents have been invented to accord with prophecy) but because Jesus managed to arrange things so that they agreed with the predictions of the prophets. Schonfield notes (pp. 44–5) that Hoskyns and Davey suggest much the same theory, although as Christians, they do not state it so unambiguously as he.

According to him, the Jews were not expecting the Messiah to be a supernatural personage, nor a militant war leader, but a gentle righteous man. In order to exclude the first of these alternatives he takes the Messianic title 'Son of man' to mean a mortal man (p. 82). But this, we saw (above, p. 82), is precisely what it does not mean in the book of Enoch. In order to exclude the second alternative, Schonfield quotes (p. 35) from the seventeenth of the *Psalms of the Pharisees*, but does not include verses 23–6 which show so clearly that the Messianic king was expected to be a war leader, who would free the Jews from Pompey's army which had recently (63 BC) captured Jerusalem:

Behold O Lord, and raise up to them their king, the Son of David, according to the time which thou seest, O God: and let Him reign over Israel thy servant, and strengthen him with power that he may humble the sinful rulers; and may purify Jerusalem from the Gentiles who trample her down to destruction, so as to destroy the wicked from thy inheritance; and to break their pride like the potter's vessel: to break with a rod of iron all their firmness (216, pp. 430-1).

The Dead Sea Scrolls also give evidence that a war leader was included in the complex and not entirely consistent Messianic expectations of the times (see above, p. 253). Philo too gives a Messianic interpretation to Num. xxiv, 17: 'there shall come forth a star out of Jacob, and a sceptre shall rise out of Israel, and shall smite through the corners of Moab, and break down all the sons of tumult.' Philo comments that the one who shall come forth will 'lead his host to war', and 'will subdue great and populous nations' (210, § xvi, p. 371).

It suits Schonfield's theory that the Jews should be expecting a meek Messiah, for his theory is that Jesus, believing himself to be the Messiah, deliberately had himself arrested in order to die on the cross as an atoning sacrifice (243, p. 87). He rode an ass into Jerusalem in deliberate fulfilment of the prophecy of Zechariah (see above, p. 101-2). 'We may believe' that he 'no doubt' instructed Lazarus to supply the animal for this purpose (pp. 119, 134), although there is nothing to this effect in the gospels, not even in the fourth, without which 'we might never have heard of Lazarus' (p. 100). When Jesus rode into Jerusalem, the bystanders recognized the fulfilment of prophecy and therefore hailed him as their Messianic king. In this way he made himself guilty of treason against Caesar thus forcing the sanhedrim to arrest him, if they were not to be accused of aiding and abetting (pp. 119-23). But before his arrest he wished to keep the passover with his disciples in Jerusalem, and could only do so at a house where the sanhedrim would not suspect his presence. This house was supplied by 'John the priest', his 'beloved disciple' (p. 138). That this personage owned a house in Jerusalem is 'confirmed' (p. 141) by the fact that Jesus on the cross entrusted his mother to John, who 'from that hour took her into his own home' (Jn. xix, 27). (The conflict with the synoptics, who make Jesus speak different words from the cross, and who do not suggest that Mary was present, is not so much as mentioned.) Jesus then facilitated the task of the sanhedrim by engineering his own betrayal by a 'familiar friend' in order to fulfil the prophecy of Psalm xli, 9 (p. 134). This he effected by persuading a woman to waste costly oil in anointing his feet—for burial, as he said—thus infuriating Judas (Jn. xii, 1–8) and giving him the idea that money was to be made by betraying his master. 'The conjunction of the idea of wealth and anointing for burial registered' in Judas' mind (p. 135). One can only comment that if Jesus' betrayal was an important element in his plan, he was fortunate to achieve it by this improbable sequence of events! This detail in Schonfield's argument again illustrates his heavy dependence on the fourth gospel. He repeatedly designates it as unreliable, but yet supposes that its author 'had access to some genuine unpublished reminiscences of the unnamed Beloved Disciple' (pp. 99–100). Schonfield's reconstruction of the trial before Pilate is taken almost exclusively from Jn. (pp. 151, 153), for the obvious reason that only in this late work is the incident handled with any show of plausibility (see above, p. 100).

'Prophecy' also assured Jesus that he would be resurrected (cf. above p. 105) and he did not leave this matter entirely to God, but arranged to be crucified on the eve of the Sabbath, knowing that he would not be left on the cross, but would be taken down well before sunset when the sabbath commenced (p. 161). He also made sure that someone would drug him on the cross, and that Joseph of Arimathea would then seek permission from Pilate to have the apparently dead body taken down. He did not confide his plan to his disciples, but to this Joseph who 'is one of the great mysteries of the gospels' in that he 'enters the story unheralded, and after his task is fulfilled . . . disappears completely from the NT records' (p. 163). Jesus 'could have got to know him through Nicodemus' (p. 165) who is another of the characters of whom we would 'never have heard' but for the fourth gospel. The drug was administered to him on the cross by someone sent for the purpose by Joseph (p. 167). These few accomplices later took him from his tomb 'at the first possible opportunity for the entirely legitimate purpose of reviving him' (p. 172). Before dying he did regain consciousness for long enough to urge them to take a message to his disciples that he would rise and meet them in Galilee (p. 173). When he expired it was 'too risky' to take the body back to the tomb, which the women and the disciples therefore discovered to be empty. And when Jesus' messenger approached them, they took him, in their fright and confusion, for Jesus himself (p. 179). That they should make such a mistake is particularly likely in the case of Mary Magdalene, whom we know to have been 'unbalanced, since Jesus had to cast out of her seven demons' (p. 176). This seems to Schonfield to be the best explanation of the gospel resurrection narratives, which, he declares, do establish that 'various disciples did see somebody, a real living person' (p. 173).

The second part of Schonfield's book is concerned with the history of early Christian writings. He concedes that all four canonical gospels were written later than AD 70, but supposes that they are based on a lost book which set down the prophecies believed to have been fulfilled by Jesus, and which also contained some account of his teaching and activities. There were thus 'written accounts of Jesus within about fifteen years of his death' (p. 236), so that 'we can be convinced that Jesus really lived' (p. 240). The crucial question would be whether there is any reason to suppose that this alleged document of AD 50 referred to a *historical* Jesus. To judge from the way Jesus is represented in the earliest extant Christian literature, this is unlikely. But it is a question that Schonfield does not even raise. He simply takes for granted that references to Jesus in AD 50, as in the later gospels, will necessarily be to a historical personage.

(iv) Schweitzer

Schweitzer's reconstruction of Jesus' life (247) is no longer a recent work, but is likewise based on the premise that he deliberately adapted his behaviour to fulfil Messianic prophecies. It is considerably less naïve than Schonfield's argument, and merits attention. While Schonfield insists that the Jewish Messiah was expected to be a man, Schweitzer bases his theory on the very opposite premise that he was to be a supernatural personage. His theory, which he calls 'consistent eschatology', is that Jesus believed that he would be transformed into the 'Son of man' who was to come down from the clouds, bring the world to a catastrophic end, and inaugurate the 'kingdom of God' with a universal judgement of the living and dead. Jesus thought that the movement of repentence initiated by the Baptist was forcing the advent of the kingdom (Mt. xi, 12), and he was even convinced, when he sent his disciples out to preach its coming, that it would overtake them on their tour (Mt. x, 23, cf. above, p. 90). But they returned to him without mishap, and his disappointment that the kingdom had not come caused him to seek solitude and shun the crowds he had formerly sought.[1]

Schweitzer holds that Jesus kept secret his conviction that he was the Messiah. When he asked his disciples at Caesarea-Philippi 'who do men say that I am?' (Mk. viii, 27), Peter knew the truth and replied that he was the Messiah. This Schweitzer explains by supposing that the Transfiguration in the presence of Peter, James and John took place earlier, even though Mt. and Mk. place it later and tell how the three saw their master talking with Moses and Elijah, and heard a heavenly voice calling 'This is my beloved Son in whom I am well pleased; hear ye him' (Mt. xvii, 5)—a vision which Schweitzer explains as a psychological illusion due to the intense eschatological expectations of the times (247, p. 382 f.). The three meet this revelation that Jesus is the Messiah with the objection that Elijah had not yet come, and Jesus counters by saying that the Baptist was Elijah. Schweitzer asks: if the Transfiguration really occurred after the incident at Caesarea-Philippi, why did the three not make their objection there? If Jesus could not be the Messiah because Elijah had not been, why did Peter say he was at Caesarea-Philippi and the other disciples fail to demur? And why should Peter (again assuming that the texts give the correct order of events) labour against the declaration he had made at Caesarea-Philippi? Schweitzer reconstructs the true sequence as follows: the secret was revealed to the three at the Transfiguration and Jesus immediately told them to tell no one of it. But when he asked his question at Caesarea-Philippi, Peter betrayed the secret to all the twelve. This explains why in Mk. (although not in Mt.) Jesus 'does not seem either surprised or particularly pleased at the knowledge of his disciple' (p. 382).

Jesus, then, does not reveal his Messianic secret to the twelve; it is betrayed to them. What he does reveal is his decision to suffer and die, which Schweitzer motivates as follows. When he sent out the disciples, Jesus regarded the πειρασμός, which must precede the coming of the kingdom, as a universal tribulation to be undergone by all in the last days: hence his prophecies of

---

[1] This alleged change in Jesus' behaviour is in fact not borne out by Mk. He had earlier sought solitude (iii, 9; iv, 35–6), and, then as later, his motive was to rest (vi, 31). He later continued to teach the people as before (vi, 34), fed five thousand and toured 'villages and cities' (vi, 56). He later (vii, 14) 'called to him the multitude again' . . .

sufferings and persecutions they were to expect. But when they returned to him and nothing of the sort had occurred, he reflected in solitude (hence his flight from the people) and decided on the basis of Isaiah liii (see above, p. 226) that God would mercifully spare mankind from the πειρασμός: that he alone needed to suffer and die that the kingdom might come (p. 385).

It will be obvious that such a Jesus was a deluded visionary, who is not, as Schweitzer concedes (p. 399), a proper object of worship. He was convinced that the world would come to a speedy end and that he himself would then appear as the Messiah. Against all the evidence, purely on the basis of his consciousness of his own importance, he was convinced that John the Baptist was Elijah. When his expectations that the tribulation of the last days was at hand were disappointed he arbitrarily—and Schweitzer stresses the arbitrariness—decided that God had singled him out to suffer this tribulation alone. Again, his supposition was not realized. His death was not followed by the end of the world and his appearance on clouds. Schweitzer supposes that this conception of Jesus solves the inconsistencies and incredibilities of the gospels, at any rate of those sections of Mk. and Mt. which narrate his 'public ministry', from his baptism to his crucifixion—minus, of course, the allegations of miracle. How Schweitzer explains these away can be illustrated from his comment on the feeding of the 5,000:

> The whole is historical except the closing remark that they were all filled. Jesus distributed the provisions which he and his disciples had with them among the multitude, so that each received a very little, after he had first offered thanks. The significance lies in the giving of thanks and in the fact that they had received from him consecrated food. Because he is the future Messiah, this meal becomes without their knowledge the Messianic feast. With the piece of bread which he distributes to them through the disciples, he dedicates them as participants in the coming Messianic meal and gives them the guarantee that they who were his fellows at table in his lowliness will break bread with him in his splendour (p. 373).

Apart from the fact that this interpretation requires us to envisage five loaves being distributed among 5,000 people, there is the added difficulty that the Jesus who was, according to Schweitzer's comment (p. 351) on Mk. iv, 10–12 (cf. above, pp. 62–3) deliberately unintelligible to the people in order not to 'thwart the plans of God' by giving any but the elect a chance to be saved, nevertheless indiscriminately determines that the whole multitude shall be admitted to the kingdom.

His whole theory that Jesus' Messianic consciousness was a secret is not easy to reconcile with the texts. Mt.'s account of his baptism implies that all who heard the voice from heaven were informed that he was the Messiah. In Mk. 'unclean spirits' repeatedly name him, in the presence of the disciples, as 'the Holy one of God', 'the Son of God' (i, 24; iii, 11). Schweitzer supposes that the disciples do not understand the greeting, since no one was expecting a mere mortal to be the Messiah (p. 369). But Jewish Messianic expectations were far from uniform (see above, pp. 76–8, 253). Because of this premise that a mere miracle-working mortal was unacceptable as Messiah, he takes the Baptist's question 'Art thou he that cometh?' (Mt. xi, 3) as meaning, not 'are you the Messiah?' but 'are you Elijah?' The mention of 'Christ' in this context is rejected as the work of the evangelist (p. 371).

Schweitzer gives little indication of how much gospel material has to be discounted in the interests of his theory. For instance, he stresses the importance of Mt. x and xi, where Jesus sends out the disciples and prophesies universal tribulation to usher in the kingdom. Yet at the end of chapter XI he is represented as saying: 'Come unto me all ye that labour and are heavy laden, and I will give you rest. Take my yoke upon you and learn of me: for I am meek and lowly in heart; and ye shall find rest unto your souls. For my yoke is easy and my burden light.' Are we to believe that the man who had just told his disciples that they 'shall be hated of all men for my name's sake' (x, 22), who had just proclaimed that he was 'come to set a man at variance against his father, and the daughter against her mother,' etc., (x, 35) could have gone on to give these quite contradictory assurances? And if both sets of utterances cannot be historical, what basis have we for accepting the 'eschatological' and rejecting the other? Schweitzer has no right to claim that his theory makes complete sense of the texts. He has to pick and choose his passages like anyone else who tries to extract an intelligible historical personality from them.

All the writers I have discussed in this epilogue simply take for granted that the gospels can supply some reliable information

M

about a historical Jesus. It is time this assumption was challenged. Even with its aid, much speculation is needed to supplement the records. Those who deny the historicity of Jesus have so often been accused of basing their case on wild speculation, of constructing, in Loisy's phrase, 'air-drawn fabrics' (177, p. 11). But it should now be obvious to the candid reader that an intelligible Jesus can be extracted from the gospels only by the kind of speculative inferences that have been held to discredit the mythicist case.

NUMBERED LIST OF REFERENCES, WITH BRIEF
NOTES ON THE AUTHORITIES CITED

The first four references are referred to in the text by the abbreviations shown here

1. *Biblica, Encyclopaedia Biblica,* ed. Cheyne and Black, London, 1903. The editors state in their preface that they 'identify the cause of religion with that of historic truth', and this principle of telling the truth, however much this appears to conflict with cherished dogmas, makes their work invaluable.

2. CB, *The Century Bible*; a vol. of text and commentary for each Biblical book. General editor W. F. Adeney (lecturer in history of doctrine at Manchester, d. 1920), 1901, etc.

3. NEB, *The New English Bible, New Testament,* Oxford, 1961

4. NBC, *The New Bible Commentary,* ed. Professor F. Davidson (and others), 2nd edn., London, 1961

5. Abbott, E. A. (Headmaster of City of London School, d. 1926), art. Gospels, § 1–107 in *Biblica*

6. Adam, Professor Karl (Catholic, Professor at Munich, retired 1949), *Das Wesen des Katholizismus,* 7th edn., Düsseldorf, 1934. (This book has appeared in many languages.)

7. Adeney, W. F. (cf. 2 above) edn. of Lk. in CB.

8. Adeney, W. F. (cf. 2 above) edn. of Thess. in CB.

8a. Aglio, A., *Antiquities of Mexico,* vol. VI, London, 1830

9. Aland, K. (and others), *The Authorship and Integrity of the NT,* London, 1965

10. Albright, W. F. (Professor Emeritus of Semitic languages, John Hopkins University), *The Archaeology of Palestine,* London, 1956

11. Alfaric, P., *Origines sociales du christianisme* (a posthumous work), Paris, 1959

12. Allegro, J. M. (orientalist of Manchester University, member of international team working on the Scrolls), *The Dead Sea Scrolls*, Penguin Books, 1957

13. Altaner, B. (Professor of Patrology, Würzburg), *Patrology*, Eng. trans. by H. C. Graef, Freiburg, 1958 (the German original first appeared in 1938)

14. Althaus, P. (Professor at Erlangen), *Der gegenwärtige Stand der Frage nach dem historischen Jesus*, Munich, 1960

15. Angus, S. (Professor of Theology, Sydney), *The Mystery Religions and Christianity*, London, 1925

16. Anrich, G. (Professor of Church History, Tübingen), *Das antike Mysterienwesen in seinem Einfluss auf das Christentum*, Göttingen 1894

17. Aufhauser, J. B. (Professor at Munich), *Antike Jesus-Zeugnisse*, Bonn, 1925

18. Baring-Gould, Rev. S. (d. 1924), *The Lost and Hostile Gospels*, London, 1874

19. Barnard, L. W., *Studies in the Apostolic Fathers*, Oxford, 1966

20. Baron, D., *The Servant of Jehovah*, London, 1921

21. Bauer, Bruno, *Kritik der Paulinischen Briefe*, Tl. II, Berlin, 1851. Bauer's radical criticism led the Prussian authorities to terminate his appointment at the University of Berlin in 1842.

22. Bauer, W. (Professor at Göttingen), *Rechtgläubigkeit und Ketzerei im ältesten Christentum*, Tübingen, 1934

23. Baur, F. C. (d. 1860, Founder of the Tübingen school of critical theology), *The Church History of the First Three Centuries*, Eng. trans. by A. Menzies, London, 1878

24. Beasley-Murray, G. R., art. Apocalypse, in NBC.

25. Bell, H. I. and Skeat, T. C., *Fragments of an Unknown Gospel*, London, 1935

26. Bellinger, A. R., *The Excavations at Dura-Europos, Final Report*, vol. VI, London, 1949

27. Bennett, W. H., edn. of I and II Peter in CB.

28. Bettenson, Rev. H. (of Charterhouse), *The Early Christian Fathers*, Oxford, 1956

29. Bevan, E. R., art. Mystery Religions in *The History of Christianity in the Light of Modern Knowledge* (a collective work), London, 1929

30. Bieder, W. (Professor at Basle), art. Apostelgeschichte in *Biblisch-Historisches Handwörterbuch*, ed. Reicke and Rost, Göttingen, 1962–4

31. Black, M. (Professor of Divinity, St. Andrews), *The Scrolls and Christian Origins*, London, 1961

31a. Black, M., *The Dead Sea Scrolls and Christian Doctrine*, London, 1966

32. Boll, F., *Aus der Offenbarung Johannis*, Leipzig, 1914

33. Bornkamm, G. (Professor of Theology, Heidelberg), *Jesus von Nazareth*, 3rd edn., Stuttgart, 1959

34. Bornkamm, G., 'Herrenmahl und Kirche bei Paulus', *Studien zu Antike und Urchristentum*, 2nd edn., Munich, 1963

35. Bousset, W. (Professor of NT Exegesis, Göttingen, d. 1920), art. Apocalypse in *Biblica*

36. Bousset, W., *Kurios Christos*, 3rd edn., Göttingen, 1926

37. Box, Rev. G. H. (Professor of OT Studies, London, d. 1933), edn. of *The Ascension of Isaiah*, London, 1917

38. Brandon, Professor S. G. F., *The Fall of Jerusalem and the Christian Church*, London, 1951

38a. Brandon, Professor S. G. F., *Jesus and the Zealots*, MUP, 1967

39. Brückner, M., *Der sterbende und auferstehende Gottheiland in den orientalischen Religionen und ihr Verhältnis zum Christentum*, Tübingen, 1908

40. Budge, Sir E. A. W. (Orientalist of the British Museum, d. 1934), *Gods of the Egyptians*, 2 vols., London, 1904

41. Budge, Sir E. A. W., *Egyptian Ideas of the Future Life*, 3rd. edn., London, 1908

42. Bultmann, R. (Professor of Theology, Marburg, retired 1951), *Theology of the NT*, Eng. trans. by K. Grobel, vol. I, London, 1952

43. Bultmann, R., *Kerygma and Myth*, ed. H. W. Bartsch, London, 1953

44. Bultmann, R., *Jesus Christ and Mythology*, London, 1960

45. Burkitt, F. C. (Professor of Divinity, Cambridge, d. 1935), *Jewish and Christian Apocalypses*, London, 1914

46. Burrows, Professor Millar, *More Light on the Dead Sea Scrolls*, London, 1958

47. Bury, J. B. (Regius Professor of Modern History, Cambridge, d. 1920), edn. of Gibbon's *Decline and Fall*, vol. V, London, 1898

48. Busolt, G. (Professor of History, Göttingen, d. 1920), *Griechische Geschichte*, 2nd edn., vol. II, Gotha, 1895

49. Canney, M. A., art. Cross (§ 1–4) in *Biblica*

50. *Catholic Encyclopaedia*, art. Demoniacs

51. *Catholic Encyclopaedia*, art. Genealogy

52. *Catholic Encyclopaedia*, art. Witchcraft

53. Cerfaux, L., 'Le titre kyrios', *Revue des sciences philos.* XII (1923)

54. Charles, Archdeacon R.H. (d. 1931), edn. of *The Book of the Secrets of Enoch*, Oxford, 1896

55. Charles, Archdeacon R.H., art. Eschatology in *Biblica*

56. Charles, Archdeacon R.H., edn. of *The Book of Enoch*, Oxford, 1912

57. Charles, Archdeacon R.H., *Religious Development between the Old and New Testaments*, London, 1914

58. Cheyne, T. K. (Professor of Holy Scripture, Oxford, d. 1915), art. Messiah in *Biblica*

59. Cheyne, T. K., art. Cross § 5–7 in *Biblica*

59a. Cheyne, T. K., art. Nazareth in *Biblica*

60. Committee of scholars of the Oxford society of historical theology, *The NT in the Apostolic Fathers*, Oxford, 1905

61. Conder, Colonel C. R. (d. 1918), *The City of Jerusalem*, London, 1909

62. Cone, O., art. James (epistle) in *Biblica*

63. Cone, O., art. Peter (epistles) in *Biblica*

64. Conzelmann, H. (Professor at Zürich), art. Jesus Christus in *Die Religion in Geschichte und Gegenwart*, 3rd revised edn. in 6 vols., ed. K. Galling, Tübingen, 1957–65

65. Conzelmann, H., *Der erste Brief an die Korinther*, Göttingen, 1969

66. Couchoud, P. L. (doctor who resigned his practice to undertake historical and archaeological research, d. 1959), *The Book of Revelation*, Eng. trans. C. Bonner-Bradlaugh, London, 1912

67. Couchoud, P. L., *The Enigma of Jesus*, Eng. trans., London, 1924 (with a preface by Sir J. G. Frazer on the character and qualifications of the author)

68. Couchoud, P. L., *Le mystère de Jésus*, Paris, 1926

69. Cross, F. L. (and others) (Professor of Divinity, Oxford), *Studies in Ephesians*, London, 1956

70. Cross, F. L., *The Early Christian Fathers*, London, 1960

71. Cullmann, O. (Professor of Theology, Basle), 'Die neuen Arbeiten zur Geschichte der Evangelientradition' (1925), in *Vorträge und Aufsätze*, 1925-1962, hrsg. K. Fröhlich, Tübingen and Zürich, 1966

72. Cullmann, O., 'Unzeitgemässe Bemerkungen zum- "historischen Jesus" der Bultmannschule' (1960), in *Vorträge*, as cited under 71 above

73. Cullmann, O., 'Die Bedeutung des Abendmahls im Urchristentum' (1936), in *Vorträge*, as cited under 71 above

74. Cumont, F. (Belgian orientalist, d. 1947), *Die orientalischen Religionen im römischen Heidentum* (German trans. from the 4th French edn.), Darmstadt, 1959

75. Cutner, H., *Jesus: God, man or myth?* New York, 1950

76. Daniélou, Fr Jean, *The Dead Sea Scrolls and Primitive Christianity*, New York, 1962

77. Dessau, H., *Geschichte der römischen Kaiserzeit*, Berlin, 1930

78. Dibelius, M. (Professor of Theology, Heidelberg, d. 1947), *Die Geisterwelt im Glauben des Paulus*, Göttingen, 1909

79. Dibelius, M., *Die Formgeschichte, des Evangeliums*, Tübingen, 1933

80. Dibelius, M., *From Tradition to Gospel* (Eng. trans. of 79 above, by B. L. Woolf), London, 1934

81. Dodds, Professor E. R., *Euripides' Bacchae*, Oxford, 1960

82. Drews, A. (Professor of Philosophy, Karlsruhe, d. 1935), *Die Christusmythe*, Tl. I Jena, 1910: Tl. II, Jena 1911

83. Driver, G. R. (Professor of Semitic Philology, Oxford), art. in *Times Literary Supplement*, May 19, 1961

83a. Dunkerley, R., *Beyond the Gospels*, Harmondsworth, 1957

84. Dupont-Sommer, Professor A., *The Essene Writings from Qumran*, Eng. trans. by G. Vermes, Oxford, 1961

85. *Encyclopaedia Britannica*, art. Gnosticism

86. *Encyclopaedia of Islam*, art. Muhammad

87. Epiphanius (Saint, Bishop of Constantia, d. 403), *Panarion haer.* (treatise on heresies) in J. F. Migne, *Patr. Gr.*, vol. XLI, Paris, 1863

88. Epiphanius, *Panarion haer*, in Migne, as above, vol. XLII

89. Eusebius (Bishop of Caesarea, d. 337), *Ecclesiastical History*, with an Eng. trans. by Lake (Loeb Classical Library) vol. I, London, 1959, and vol. II, London, 1957

90. Fabia, P., *Les sources de Tacite*, Paris, 1893

91. Farrer, J. A., *Paganism and Christianity*, London, 1891

92. Frazer, Sir J. G. (d. 1941), *The Golden Bough*, 3rd edn., Pt. III, *The Dying God*, London, 1911

93. Frazer, Sir J. G., *The Golden Bough*, 3rd edn., Pt. IV, *Adonis, Attis Osiris*, London, 1907

94. Frazer, Sir J. G., *The Golden Bough*, 3rd edn. Pt. VI, *The Scapegoat*, London, 1913

95. Frazer, Sir J. G., *The Golden Bough*, abridged edn., in 1 vol., London, 1922

96. Frend, W. H. C. (fellow of Caius College, Cambridge), 'The archaeologist and Church History', *Antiquity*, XXXIV, 1960

97. Frend, W. H. C., 'Fresh light on the NT', *The Listener*, May 11, 1961

98. Fritz and Kapp, edn. of Aristotle's *Constitution of Athens*, New York, 1950

99. Gardthausen, V., *Augustus und seine Zeit*, vol. I, Leipzig, 1891

100. Gardner, Percy, *The Origin of the Lord's Supper*, London, 1893

101. Gaster, T. H., *Passover. Its History and Traditions*, London, 1958

102. Gaster, T. H., *Thespis. Ritual, Myth and Drama in the ancient Near East*, New York, 1950

103. Ghillany, F. W. von (clergyman in Nürnberg who resigned his living, d. 1876), *Die Menschenopfer der alten Hebräer*, Nürnberg, 1842

104. Gibbon, E., *The Decline and Fall of the Roman Empire*, Everyman edn. in 6 vols., London, 1960, with notes by O. Smeaton

105. Goguel, M. (Professor of Theology, Paris, d. 1955), *Jesus the Nazarene. Myth or History?* Eng. trans. F. Stephens, London, 1926

106. Goguel, M., *The Birth of Christianity*, Eng. trans. H. C. Snape, London, 1953

107. Goodspeed, E. J., *A History of Early Christian Literature*, revised edn. by R. M. Grant, Chicago, 1966

108. Graetz, Professor H. (orthodox Jewish historian, d. 1891), *History of the Jews*, Eng. trans. vol. II, Philadelphia, 1893

109. Grant, F. C., *The Gospels, their origin and growth*, London, 1957

110. Gresham Machen, J. (Protestant fundamentalist, Pro-

fessor at Philadelphia, d. 1937), *The Virgin Birth of Christ*, London, 1930

111. Gunkel, H. (Professor of Theology, Halle, d. 1932), *Schöpfung und Chaos* Göttingen, 1895

112. Gunkel, H., *Zum religionsgeschichtlichen Verständnis des NT*, Göttingen, 1903

113. Haag, H. (Catholic Professor of OT Exegesis, Tübingen), *Bibellexikon*, Zürich, 1956, art. Comma Joanneum

114. Haag, H., art. Dreifaltigkeit

115. Haag, H., art. Evangelien

116. Haag, H., art. Jesus Christus

117. Haag, H., art. Kindheitsgeschichte Jesu

118. Haag, H., art. Leben Jesu Forschung (Barth und Brunner)

119. Haag, H., art. Maria

120. Haag, H., art. Stammbaum Jesu

121. Haag, H., art. Volkszählung

122. Haag, H., art. Wunder

123. Haenchen, E. (Professor at Münster), art. Apostelgeschichte, in *Die Religion in Geschichte und Gegenwart* (as under 64 above)

124. Haenchen, E., *Die Apostelgeschichte*, 5th revised edn., Göttingen, 1965

125. Hall, P. H., *Papias*, New York, 1899

126. Halliday, Sir W. R. (Professor of Ancient History, Liverpool), *The Pagan Background of Early Christianity*, London and Liverpool, 1925

127. Hanson, Professor A. T., *Studies in the Pastoral Epistles*, London, 1968

128. Harder, G. (Professor at Berlin), art. Lehre der 12 Apostel in *Biblisches-Historisches Handwörterbuch* (as under 30 above)

129. Harnack, A. (Professor of Church History, Berlin, d. 1930), *Die Apostellehre und die jüdischen beiden Wege*, Leipzig, 1896

130. Harrison, P. N., *The Problem of the Pastoral Epistles*, Oxford, 1921

131. Harrison, P. N., *Polycarp's Two Epistles*, Cambridge, 1936

132. Harrison, Professor R. K., *The Dead Sea Scrolls*, London, 1961

133. Hastings, *Encyclopaedia of Religion and Ethics*, art. Virgin Birth

134. Hatch, Rev. E. (Reader in Ecclesiastical History,

Oxford, d. 1889), *The Organisation of the Early Christian Churches*, London, 1881

135. Hatch, Rev. E., *Essays in Biblical Greek*, Oxford, 1889

136. Hatch, Rev. E., *The Influence of Greek ideas and usages upon the Christian Church*, London, 1890

137. Hepding, H., *Attis, seine Mythen und sein Kult*, Giessen, 1903

138. Herklots, Canon H. G., *How the Bible Came to Us*, Penguin Books, 1959

139. Hochart, P., *Etudes au sujet de la pérsecution des Chrétiens sous Néron*, Paris, 1885

140. Hornton, R. F., edn. of Titus (epistle) in CB.

141. Hoskyns, Sir E., and Davey, Rev. F. N., *The Riddle of the NT*, London, 1957

142. Howie, C. G., *Ezekiel, Daniel*, London, 1961

143. Howell Smith, A. D., *Jesus Not a Myth*, London, 1942

144. Huber, W., *Passa und Ostern*, Berlin, 1969

145. Huxley, T. H. (biologist, d. 1895), *Science and Christian Tradition*, London, 1904

146. Irenaeus, Bishop (d. 200), *Against Heresies*, in *Early Christian Fathers*, translated and edited by C. C. Richardson, London, 1953

147. James, M. R., editor (Provost of Eton, d. 1936), *The Apocryphal NT*, Oxford, 1953

148. Jeremias, Professor J., *Die Abendmahlsworte Jesu*, 3rd edn., Göttingen, 1960

149. Jeremias, Professor J., *Das Problem des historischen Jesus*, 2nd edn., Stuttgart, 1960

150. *Jewish Encyclopaedia*, art. Angelology

151. *Jewish Encyclopaedia*, art. Didache

152. Johnson, S. E., 'The Dead Sea Manual of Discipline and the Jerusalem Church of Acts', in *The Scrolls and the NT*, ed. Stendahl, London, 1958

153. Jolley, A. J., *The Synoptic Problem for English Readers*, London, 1893

154. Josephus, Flavius, *Antiquities of the Jews*, Eng. trans. by H. Thackeray, Loeb Classical Library, 6 vols., London, 1930–65

155. Josephus, Flavius, *The Jewish War*, Eng. trans. by H. Thackeray, Loeb Classical Library, 2 vols., London, 1927–8

156. Jülicher, Professor G. A., art. Mystery in *Biblica*

157. Justin (martyred *c.* 165), *Dialogue with Trypho the Jew*, ed. Williams, London, 1930

158. Justin, *The First Apology* in *Ante Nicene Christian Library*, ed. Roberts and Donaldson, vol. II, Edinburgh, 1868

159. Käsemann, E., 'Das Problem des historischen Jesus', *Zeitschrift für Theologie und Kirche*, LI (1954)

160. Keller, Dr W., *Die Bibel hat doch recht*, Eng. trans. by W. Neil, *The Bible as History*, London, 1956

161. Klausner, J. (Emeritus Professor of Hebrew literature in the University of Jerusalem), *The Messianic Idea in Israel*, Eng. trans. Stinespring, London, 1957

162. Kleist, J. A. (Catholic, Professor of Classical languages, St. Louis), edn. of his own translation of *The Epistles of St. Clement of Rome and St. Ignatius of Antioch*, Westminster (Maryland) 1946 (*Ancient Christian Writers*, vol. I)

163. Kleist, J. A., edn. of his own translation of *The Didache, The Epistle of Barnabas, The Epistles and the Martyrdom of St. Polycarp, The Fragments of Papias, The Epistle to Diognetus*, Cork, 1948 (*Ancient Christian Writers*, vol. VI)

164. Kuhn, K. G., 'The Lord's supper and the communal meal at Qumran', in *The Scrolls and the NT*, ed. Stendahl

165. Laible, H., *Jesus Christus im Talmud*, Berlin, 1891

166. Lecky, W. (d. 1903), *History of the Rise and Influence of the Spirit of Rationalism in Europe*, vol. I, London, 1897

167. Leipoldt, J. (Professor at Leipzig), *Sterbende und auferstende Götter*, Leipzig, 1923

168. Leipoldt, J., *Dionysos*, Leipzig, 1931

169. Leipoldt, J., *Von den Mysterien zur Kirche*, Hamburg, 1962

170. Lietzmann, H. (Professor of Theology, Berlin, d. 1942), *Messe und Herrenmahl*, 3rd edn., Berlin, 1955

171. Lietzmann, H., *Petrus und Paulus in Rom*, 2nd edn., Leipzig, 1927

172. Lightfoot, Bishop, J. B. (d. 1889) (quoted by Harrison, P.N.)

173. Linck, K., *De antiquissimis veterum quae ad Iesum Nazarenum spectant testimoniis*, Giessen, 1913

174. Linforth, *Solon the Athenian*, in *Univ. of California Publications in Classical Philology*, VI, Berkeley, 1919

175. Lohfink, N. (Catholic Professor at the papal Bible institute in Rome), *Die Bibelwissenschaft historisch kritisch*, Cologne, 1966

176. Lohfink, N., Altes Testament. *Historische christliche Auslegung*, Cologne, 1967

177. Loisy, A. (Catholic priest who left the Church, d. 1940), *The Birth of the Christian Religion*, Eng. trans. Jacks, London, 1948

178. Löw, Rabbi Dr Leopold, *Ben Chananja*, vol. I, Szegedin, 1858

179. Manen, Professor W. C. van, art. Old Christian Literature in *Biblica*

180. Manley, Rev. G. T., *The New Bible Handbook*, London, 1960

181. Mead, G. R. S., *Fragments of a Faith Forgotten*, London 1900

182. Mead, G. R. S., *Thrice-greatest Hermes*, vol. I, London, 1906

183. Meyer, Eduard (Professor of Ancient History, Berlin, d. 1930), *Geschichte des Altertums*, vol. III, 2nd edn., Stuttgart, 1937

184. Michel, O. (Professor at Tübingen), *Der Brief an die Römer*, 12th revised edn., Göttingen, 1963

185. Milman, Dean H. H. (Ecclesiastical historian, d. 1868), *History of the Jews*, vol. III, New York, 1832

186. Mitteis, L. and Wilcken, *Grundzüge und Chrestomathie der Papysruskunde*, vol. I (i), Berlin, 1912

187. Moffatt, Rev. J., art. Timothy and Titus (epistles) in *Biblica*

188. Mommsen, T. (Professor of Ancient History, Berlin, d. 1903), *Res gestae divi Augusti*, Berlin, 1883

189. Mommsen, T., *The Provinces of the Roman Empire*, vol. II, Eng. trans., London, 1909

190. Moore, Rev. G. F., art. Molech in *Biblica*

191. Morison, F., *Who Moved the Stone?* 2nd edn., London, 1953

192. Morton, Rev. A. Q., art. in *The Observer*, November 3, 1963

193. Morton, Rev. A. Q., and J. McLeman, *Paul*, London, 1966

194. Mosheim, J. L. von, *Commentaries on the Affairs of the Christians before Constantine*, Eng. trans. Vidal, vol. I, London, 1813

195. Muir, Sir W., *The Life of Mohammed from Original Sources*, Edinburgh, 1923

196. Murray, G., *Five Stages of Greek Religion*, London, 1935 (3rd impression 1946)

197. Murray, G., edn. of Aeschylus' *Oresteia*, London, 1946

198. Murray, G., *Stoic, Christian and Humanist*, London, 1950

199. Murray, G., edn. of Euripides' *Ion*, London, 1954

200. Murray, G., *Euripides' Bacchae*, London, 1957

201. Newman, Cardinal J. H. (Anglican priest, received into Catholic Church in 1845, d. 1890), 'Milman's view of Christianity', in *Essays Critical and Historical*, 7th edn. vol. II, London, 1887

202. Newman, Cardinal J. H., *Development of the Christian Doctrine*, London, 1890

203. Norden, E. (Philologist at Berlin), 'Josephus und Tacitus über Jesus', *Neue Jahrbücher für das klassische Altertum*, etc., XXXI, (1913)

204. Orchard, B. (editor), *A Catholic Commentary on Holy Scripture*, London, 1953

205. Origen (d. 254), *Contra Celsum*, Eng. trans. with introduction and notes by H. Chadwick, Cambridge, 1953

206. Origen, *De principiis*, Eng. trans., with introduction and notes by G. W. Butterworth, London, 1936

207. Pauly-Wissowa, *Real-encyclopädie der klassischen Altertumswissenschaft*, Stuttgart, 1894, etc., arts. Solon, Velleius Paterculus

208. Pauly-Wissowa, *Real-encyclopädie*, arts. Kypros (histor. Übersicht), Achaia.

209. Peter, J., *Finding the Historical Jesus*, London, 1965

210. Philo, *De praemiis et poenis*, in Loeb edn. of his *Works*, London, 1954, vol. VIII

211. Ramsay, Sir W. M. (archaeologist, d. 1939), *St. Paul the Traveller*, London, 1895

212. Ramsay, Sir W. M., *The Bearing of Recent Discovery on the Trustworthiness of the NT*, 1915

213. Ramsey, Archbishop Dr M., *The Resurrection of Christ*, 2nd edn., London, 1956

214. Reitzenstein, R., *Die Hellenistischen Mysterienreligionen*, Leipzig, 1910

215. Rendel Harris, J., *The Apology of Aristides*, Cambridge, 1891

216. Rendel Harris, J., *The Odes and Psalms of Solomon*, vol. II, Manchester 1920

217. Rendel Harris, J., *Jesus and Osiris* (Woodbrooke Essays, No. 5), Cambridge, 1927

218. Robertson, A., *The Bible and its Background*, London, 1942

218a. Robertson, A., *Jesus: Myth or History*, London, 1949 (a useful survey of both positions)

219. Robertson, A., *Origins of Christianity*, London, 1953

220. Robertson, J. M. (Liberal MP, known today mainly from his writings on Elizabethan literature), *Christianity and Mythology*, 2nd edn., London, 1910

221. Robertson, J. M., *The Jesus Problem*, London, 1911

222. Robertson, J. M., *Pagan Christs*, 2nd edn., London, 1911

223. Robertson Smith, Professor W., *The Religion of the Semites*, London, 1894

224. Robinson, Very Rev. J. A. (d. 1933), art. Canon in *Biblica*

225. Robinson, Very Rev. J. A. (d. 1933), art. Eucharist in *Biblica*

226. Robinson, J. A. T., *Honest to God*, London, 1963

227. Robinson, J. M. (Professor of Theology, S. California), *Kerygma und historischer Jesus*, 2nd revised edn., Zürich and Stuttgart, 1967. This is not a German translation of the author's *A New Quest of the Historical Jesus*, 1959, but a revised edition, which he has written in German (with the help of the translator of his earlier work) as a result of his stay in Göttingen as visiting Professor of Theology, in 1959. The footnotes of the introduction give a very valuable bibliography of recent discussion concerning the historical Jesus

228. Rodwell, J. M., edn. of *Koran*, London, 1876

229. Rordorf, W., *Der Sonntag . . . im ältesten Christentum*, Zürich, 1962

230. Rossington, H. J., *Did Jesus Really Live?* London, 1911

230a. Rowley, H. H., *The Qumran Sect and Christian Origins*, Manchester, 1961

230b. Rowley, H. H., *The Servant of the Lord*, 2nd revised edn., Oxford, 1965

231. Ryle, Rt Rev. H. E., ch. II in *A Companion to Biblical Studies*, ed. W. E. Barnes, Cambridge, 1916

232. Sanday, W. (Professor of Divinity, Oxford, d. 1920), *The Gospels in the Second Century*, London, 1876

233. Schlier, H., *Besinnung auf das NT Exegetische Aufsätze*, II, Freiburg, 1964

234. Schmiedel, P. W. (Professor of NT Exegesis, Zürich, d. 1935), art. Acts in *Biblica*

235. Schmiedel, P. W., art. Gospels, § 108–57 in *Biblica*

236. Schmiedel, P. W., art. John, Son of Zebedee in *Biblica*

237. Schmiedel, P. W., art. Mary in *Biblica*

238. Schmiedel, P. W., art. Ministry in *Biblica*

239. Schmiedel, P. W., art. Resurrection and Ascension Narratives in *Biblica*

240. Schmiedel, P. W., art. Simon Peter in *Biblica*

241. Schmithals, W., *Die Gnosis in Korinth*, Göttingen, 1956

242. Schoeps, Professor H., *Theologie und Geschichte des Judenchristentums*, Tübingen, 1949

243. Schonfield, H. J., *The Passover Plot*, London, 1965

244. Schürer, E. (Professor of NT Exegesis, Göttingen, d. 1910), *History of the Jewish People in the Time of Christ*, Eng. trans. by J. Macpherson and others, Edinburgh, 1898 (refs. to this work give first the Division, then the vol. number, both in Roman)

245. Schürer, E., Theologische Literaturzeitung, Leipzig, 1906, Nr. 9

246. Schwartz, E., 'Osterbetrachtungen' (1906), in *Gesammelte Schriften*, Bd. V, Berlin, 1963

247. Schweitzer, A., *Geschichte der Leben-Jesu Forschung*, Tübingen, 1906

248. Schweitzer, A., *The Mysticism of Paul the Apostle*, Eng. trans. by W. Montgomery, London, 1931

249. Sidebottom, E. M., *James, Jude and 2 Peter*, London, 1967

250. Slater, W. F., edn. of Mt. in CB.

251. Smalley, Beryl, *The Study of the Bible in the Middle Ages*, Oxford, 1952

252. Smith, W. B. (Professor of Mathematics, Tulare, d. 1934), *Ecce Deus*, London, 1912.

253. Smith, W., *A Classical Dictionary*, 15th edn., London, 1877, art. Demeter

254. Smith, W., *A Classical Dictionary*, 15th edn., London, 1877, art. Lucianus

255. Soden, H. von, art. Chronology in *Biblica*

256. Sperber, J., 'Die Schreiben Muhammads an die Stämme Arabiens', *Mitteilungen des Seminars für orientalische Sprachen*, ed. E. Sachan, Berlin, vol. XIX, 1916

257. Stauffer, Professor E., *Jesus, Gestalt und Geschichte*, Berne, 1957

258. Steinmann, Abbé J., *La critique devant la Bible*, Eng. trans. as *Biblical Criticism*, London, 1959

259. Strack, H. (Professor at Berlin, the foremost Protestant

authority in Germany on Rabbinical literature, d. 1922), *Einleitung in den Talmud*, Leipzig, 1894

260. Strack, H., *Jesus, die Häretiker und die Christen nach den ältesten jüdischen Angaben*, Leipzig, 1910

261. Strack, H. and Billerbeck, P., *Kommentar zum NT aus Talmud und Midrash*, Munich, 1922, vol. I

262. Strauss, D. F. (biographer of Jesus whose work, first published in 1835, was translated into English by George Eliot. My references are to his second biography of Jesus, written for the laity), *New Life of Jesus*, Authorized Eng. trans., 2nd ed., London, 1879, (2 vols.)

263. Streeter, Rev. B. H. (d. 1937), *The Four Gospels*, London, 1936

264. Taylor, C., *The Teaching of the Twelve Apostles, with illustrations from the Talmud*, Cambridge, 1886

265. Taylor, Rev. V., *The Gospel According to St. Mark*, London, 1952

266. Taylor, Rev. V., *Life and Ministry of Jesus*, London, 1955

267. Tertullian (fl. *c.* 200), *Tertulliani quae supersunt omnia*, ed. F. Oehler, 3 vols., Leipzig, 1853: *Apologeticum* in vol. I, pp. 111–305; *Adversus Marcionem*, in vol. II, pp. 45–336

268. Theophanes, *Chronographia*, ed. C. de Boor, Leipzig, 1883, vol. I

269. Thirlwall, Bishop C. (historian of Greece), *Letters, literary and theological*, ed. Perowne and Stokes, London, 1881

270. Travers, Herford, R., *Christianity in Talmud and Midrash*, London, 1903

271. Travers, Herford, R., *Pharisaism*, London, 1912

272. Travers, Herford, R., *Judaism in the NT period*, London, 1928

273. Tylor, Sir E. B. (anthropologist d. 1917), *Primitive Culture*, London, 1891

274. Usener, H. (Professor of Classical Philology, Bonn, d. 1905), art. Nativity in *Biblica*

275. Usener, H., *Das Weihnachtsfest*, 2nd edn., Bonn, 1911

276. Vidler, Rev. A., essay in *Objections to Christian Belief*, London, 1963

276a. Vokes, F. E., *The Riddle of the Didache*, London, 1938

277. Volney, C. F. (d. 1820), *Les Ruines, ou Méditation sur les Révolutions des Empires*, Paris, 1791

278. Weiss, J. (Professor of Theology at Heidelberg, d. 1914), *Jesus von Nazareth, Mythos oder Geschichte*, Tübingen, 1910

279. Weiss, J., *Das Urchristentum* Tl. II, Göttingen, 1917

280. Wells, G. A., *Herder and After*, The Hague, 1959

281. Wells, G. A., 'Criteria of Historicity', *German Life and Letters, New Series*, vol. XXII, No. 4 (October, 1968)

282. Wells, G. A., 'Stages of NT criticism', *Journal of the History of Ideas*, vol. XXX, No. 2 (April, 1969). I am grateful to the editors of this Journal for permission to use part of this article in the present work. (cf. p. 40 above)

283. Werner, Professor M. (Professor of Theology, Bern, until 1958), *Die Entstehung des christlichen Dogmas*, Berne, 1941

284. Werner, Professor M., *The Formation of Christian Dogma*, Eng. trans. S. G. F. Brandon, London, 1957

285. Westcott, Bishop B. F. and Hort, F. J. A., *NT* (in the original Greek), London, 1881

286. Weston, Jessie L., *From Ritual to Romance*, New York, 1957 (first published in 1920)

287. Whitehouse, Rev. Professor O. C., edn. of Isaiah in CB.

288. Whittaker, J., *The Origins of Christianity*, London, 1909

289. Williams, C. S. C., *A commentary on the Acts of the Apostles*, London, 1957

290. Windisch, H., 'Das Problem der Geschichtlichkeit Jesu', *Theologische Rundschau, Neue Folge*, I (1929)

291. Winter, P., *On the Trial of Jesus*, Berlin, 1961

291a. Winter, P., 'Josephus on Jesus', *Journal of Historical Studies*, I (1968)

292. Wood, H. G., *Did Christ Really Live?* London, 1938

293. Wrede, W., *Das Messiasgeheimnis in den Evangelien*, Göttingen, 1901

294. Wright, G. E., *The Westminster Historical Atlas to the Bible*, London, 1946

295. Wright, G. E., *Biblical Archaeology*, London, 1957

296. Zeller, E. (Professor of Theology and later of Philosophy, d. 1908), *Die Philosophie der Griechen*, vol. III, (2) 5th edn., Leipzig, 1923

INDEX OF BIBLICAL REFERENCES

GENERAL INDEX